Shakespeare's Dramatic States

THE McDONALD
CENTER FOR
AMERICA'S FOUNDING
PRINCIPLES

MERCER
UNIVERSITY

THE A. V. ELLIOTT CONFERENCE SERIES

Guided by James Madison's maxim that "a well-instructed people alone can be permanently a free people," the McDonald Center exists to promote the study of the great texts and ideas that have shaped our regime and fostered liberal learning.

WILL R. JORDAN and CHARLOTTE C. S. THOMAS, Directors

No Greater Monster nor Miracle than Myself: The Political Philosophy of Michel de Montaigne, ed. Charlotte C. S. Thomas (2014)

Of Sympathy and Selfishness: The Moral and Political Philosophy of Adam Smith, ed. Charlotte C. S. Thomas (2015)

The Most Sacred Freedom: Religious Liberty in the History of Philosophy and America's Founding, ed. Will Jordan and Charlotte C. S. Thomas (2016)

Promise and Peril: Republics and Republicanism in the History of Political Philosophy, ed. Will R. Jordan (2017)

When in the Course of Human Events: 1776 at Home, Abroad, and in American Memory, ed. Will R. Jordan (2018)

Power and the People: Thucydides' History and the American Founding, ed. Charlotte C. S. Thomas (2019)

From Reflection and Choice: The Political Philosophy of the Federalist Papers and the Ratification Debate, ed. Will R. Jordan (2020)

Liberty, Democracy, and the Temptations to Tyranny in the Dialogues of Plato, ed. Charlotte C. S. Thomas (2021)

The Beginning of Liberalism: Rexamining the Political Philosophy of John Locke, ed. Will R. Jordan (2022)

The Founding: Essential Documents, ed., Will R. Jordan (2023)

Governing Oneself and Others: On Xenophon of Athens, ed. Charlotte C. S. Thomas (2024)

Natural Man, Citizen, Philosopher: The Political Philosophy of Jean-Jacques Rousseau, ed. Will R. Jordan (2025)

Shakespeare's Dramatic States

Ambition, Interpretation, and the Public Good

Edited by Charlotte C. S. Thomas

MERCER UNIVERSITY PRESS
Macon, Georgia

Endowed by
TOM WATSON BROWN
and
THE WATSON-BROWN FOUNDATION, INC.

MUP/ P741

© 2025 by Mercer University Press
Published by Mercer University Press
1501 Mercer University Drive
Macon, Georgia 31207

All rights reserved. This book may not be reproduced in whole or in part, including illustrations, in any form (beyond that copying permitted by Sections 107 and 108 of the U.S. Copyright Law and except by reviewers for the public press), without written permission from the publisher.

30 29 28 27 26   5 4 3 2 1

Books published by Mercer University Press are printed on acid-free paper that meets the requirements of the American National Standard for Information Sciences—Permanence of Paper for Printed Library Materials.

Printed and bound in the United States.
This book is set in Adobe Caslon.
Cover/jacket design by Burt&Burt.

ISBN   979-8-89736-023-9

Library of Congress Cataloging-in-Publication Data

*For Tom and Ramona McDonald,
with deep gratitude for their generosity and friendship*

CONTENTS

Contributors — ix

Acknowledgments — xi

Introduction, Charlotte C. S. Thomas, Mercer University — 1

1. 'A King of Shreds and Patches': A Fragmentology of Shakespeare and the Public Good
   Deneen M. Senasi, Mercer University — 7

2. Questions, Questions, Questions: Shakespeare's Ambiguous *Winter's Tale*
   Stuart Warner, Roosevelt University — 36

3. Pursuing Happiness in Shakespeare
   Sujata Iyengar, University of Georgia — 51

4. Transcendent Ambition: Machiavelli and Shakespeare on Coriolanus and Julius Caesar
   Vickie Sullivan, Tufts University — 67

5. *Virtù, Fortuna,* and Nation: Ruler and Citizen in Machiavelli's *The Life of Castruccio Castracani of Lucca* and Shakespeare's Bastard in *King John*
   Khalil Habib, Hillsdale College — 94

6. The Theology of *Coriolanus*
   Kevin M. Cherry, University of Richmond — 129

7. The Power of the Particular: Liberal Education and Cosmopolitanism in *Titus Andronicus*
   Bernard Dobski, Assumption University — 155

8. "Law and Form and Due Proportion": *Richard II*, Sir Thomas More, and the Challenge of Constitutional Reform
   L. Joseph Hebert, St. Ambrose University — 183

9. Macbeth and "the milk of human kindness": Nature, Natality, Sex, and Politics in the Scottish Play
    Clinton Allen Brand, University of St. Thomas, Houston   213

10. Banning Shylock
    Carol McNamara, Great Hearts Institute for Classical Education   239

11. A Place in the Story: Autobiographical Shakespeare
    Sheila T. Cavanagh, Emory University,   260

12. Shakespeare and Political History: Bastards, Nepo-babies, Oligarchs
    Gary Taylor, Florida State University   281

Index   303

CONTRIBUTORS

CLINTON ALLEN BRAND, Associate Professor and Chair of English, University of St. Thomas, Houston

SHEILA T. CAVANAGH, Professor of English and Director of the World Shakespeare Project and the Emory Women's Writers Resource Project, Emory University

KEVIN M. CHERRY, Associate Professor of Political Science, University of Richmond

BERNARD J. DOBSKI, Professor of Political Science, Assumption University

KHALIL HABIB, Associate Professor of Politics, Hillsdale College

L. JOSEPH HEBERT, Professor and Chair of Political Science, St. Ambrose University

SUJATA IYENGAR, Professor of English, University of Georgia

CAROL MCNAMARA, Director, Great Hearts Institute for Classical Education

DENEEN M. SENASI, Professor of English and Director of the Writing Program, Mercer University

VICKIE B. SULLIVAN, Cornelia M. Jackson Professor of Political Science, Tufts University

GARY TAYLOR, Robert O. Lawton Distinguished Professor of English, Florida State University

CHARLOTTE C. S. THOMAS, Executive Director of the Association for Core Texts and Courses; and Professor of Philosophy, Co-Director of the

McDonald Center for America's Founding Principles, and Director of the Great Books Program at Mercer University.

STUART D. WARNER, Professor of Philosophy and Director of the Montesquieu Forum, Roosevelt University

ACKNOWLEDGMENTS

Shakespeare's Dramatic States: Ambition, Interpretation and the Public Good is collection of essays is based on the 2024 A. V. Elliott conference for Great Books and Ideas, the 16th annual conference sponsored by the McDonald Center for America's Founding Principles, entitled "Shakespeare's Politics."

The McDonald Center for America's Founding Principles began as a small conference in the Spring of 2008. It secured initial funding that summer through Mercer University's Academic Initiatives Monetary (AIM) fund, and has grown substantially each subsequent year. Neither this volume, nor the conference it is based upon, nor any of the other important work now done by the McDonald Center would have been possible without the foresight of then Mercer President, William D. Underwood, the confidence of the AIM committee, the support of then College of Liberal Arts Dean Lake Lambert, and the entrepreneurial spirit of the Center's founders. Anita Gustafson and Tom Scott have continued in this tradition and showed the McDonald Center consistent support and encouragement during their time as Dean of the College of Liberal Arts and Sciences.

In the Spring of 2013, the McDonald Center received a generous endowment gift from Mr. A. V. Elliott, for whom our annual conference is now named. Also in 2013, Thomas and Ramona McDonald made an endowment gift to support all of the Center's work, and with it they gave us their name. We are, and always will be, in deep debt to the Elliotts and McDonalds for their support.

Our "Shakespeare's Politics" conference was both a gathering of Shakespeare scholars and also the culmination of a yearlong reading group made up of Mercer faculty and students. I would like to thank all of the participants in that group by name. Each of them contributed significantly to the excellent conversation that animated our conference and this volume of essays, which it inspired. So, thank you to my colleagues: Will Jordan, Kevin Honeycutt, Patrick Jolley,

Chris Grant, Amy Nichols-Belo, Deneen Senasi, Rachel Guo, Benjamin Hoyt, Gordon Johnston, David Swigart, and Marc Jolley. And thank you to our students: Latoya Bartley, Eduardo Brand, Coy Eberhardt, Joshua Daniels, Kate Grant, Riley Hall, Ian L'Abate, Cameron Nixon, Brandon Scoggins, Carolina Stover, Harumi Kano Torres, Harris Wallace, Papa Guerrero, Gabrielle Gurrola, Joshua Jung, Charles Lovern, Ifeoma Mbanaso, Lucy Roach, Caroline Wood.

A few of our students participated on a student panel at the conference, and made us extremely proud. So, special thanks go out to Gabrielle Gurrola ('27), Riley Hall ('27), Lucy Roach ('25), Carolina Stover ('27), Harris Wallace ('27), and Caroline Wood ('27) for the energy, seriousness, and courage to develop your thoughts about Shakespeare's politics and present them to your teachers, peers, and this auspicious crowd of Shakespeare scholars.

I'm sincerely thankful to Clinton Allen Brand, Sheila T. Cavanagh, Kevin M. Cherry, Bernard J. Dobski, Khalil Habib, L. Joseph Hebert, Sujata Iyengar, Carol McNamara, Deneen M. Senasi, Vickie B. Sullivan, Gary Taylor, and Stuart D. Warner for presenting their scholarly work at the Elliott Conference, for interacting so thoughtfully with each other and our students at the conference, and for submitting their revised essays for publication in this volume. It has been a great honor to learn about Shakespeare from these brilliant, thoughtful people.

Many, many thanks are due to Marc Jolley and to the whole staff at Mercer University Press who, as always, have produced a beautiful book and have been a pleasure to work with.

Finally, it continues to be a great privilege to work as codirector of the McDonald Center with one of its founders, Will Jordan. I am grateful to have the opportunity to work with Will to foster important conversations among good people about great ideas. Without Prof. Jordan's energy, thoughtfulness, and good judgment, there would be no McDonald Center.

Introduction

Charlotte C. S. Thomas

Shakespeare often played fast and loose with historical facts, but his works offer insights into human things that give us entrée to historical understanding and an orientation toward some of the most fundamental questions of politics, morality, and philosophy. This quality of his work and thought seems to be behind claims such as Matthew Arnold's that Shakespeare is "the poet of human nature." Some of the American Founders certainly read Shakespeare in this way. In a 1771 letter to Robert Skipwith, Thomas Jefferson wrote, "a lively and lasting sense of filial duty is more effectually impressed on the mind of a son or daughter by reading *King Lear*, than by all the dry volumes of ethics and divinity that ever were written." It is in this spirit that Mercer's McDonald Center for America's Founding principles chose "Shakespeare's Politics" as the theme for our year-long faculty/student reading group and annual A. V. Elliott Conference on Great Books and Ideas during the 2023–24 academic year. We gathered colleagues and students to read plays together throughout the year, and we invited scholars to campus to present their ideas about Shakespeare's politics. This volume represents the culmination of that work.

In our opening essay "'A King of Shreds and Patches': A Fragmentology of Shakespeare and the Public Good," Deneen M. Senasi turns our attention to the way that lines from Shakespeare's work are fragmented, or "sharded" as she calls it, in knowledge, public access to that knowledge, and recourse to such knowledge in the particular collective experience of mourning the assassination of Abraham Lincoln. These Shakespearean threads and patches have long been intertwined, she argues, with conceptions of the public good. Why Shakespeare has been thought to have a role to play in our understanding of the public good is a question for which, she admits, we haven't world enough or time in this volume, but that readers of Shakespeare have for generations understood him to have such a role is uncontroversial. Not only do we fragment Shakespeare, on Senasi's account, but we have also for centuries stitched those fragments together in new ways and in new contexts. In that poetic activity we bring Shakespeare into our lives and discourse, but we also stitch our communities and our vision of the common good together in the process.

Stuart D. Warner is also concerned with the efforts Shakespeare often requires of his readers and in the implications such effort have for understanding and engaging political life. Warner's focus is not on fragmentation, however, but on ambiguity, particularly in *The Winter's Tale*. In "Questions, Questions, Questions: Shakespeare's Ambiguous *Winter's Tale*," he argues that the play's failure to provide answers to a host of questions that it raises, both explicitly and implicitly—from the identity of Perdita's father to the cause of Mammilius's death to the dramatic date of the play to the roles paganism and Christianity occupy within the play to the return of Hermione in the final scene—all bear on the intractably ambiguous and unsettling character of political life.

Sujata Iyengar looks back to Thomas Jefferson's understanding of Shakespeare as a teacher of morality. In particular, Iyengar describes Jefferson's reliance on Shakespeare for the idea of "the pursuit of happiness" that makes its way into the *Declaration of Independence*, and she argues that *Much Ado About Nothing* epitomizes what Shakespeare understood the "pursuit of happiness" to mean. Iyengar argues that Shakespeare studies (and the humanities in general) offer a means for us to pursue happiness, not just to attempt to understand it. She also points out that to "enshrine 'the pursuit of happiness' as a founding principle for a republic is unreasonable and magnificent." It is also, on her account, what makes us human.

Vickie Sullivan's "Transcendent Ambition: Machiavelli and Shakespeare on Coriolanus and Julius Caesar" is the first of several essays in this volume that make Shakespeare's History Plays the center of attention. Machiavelli serves as a reference point that clarifies some of what is distinctive about Shakespeare's presentation of these two central figures from the political history of Rome. The differences between Coriolanus and Caesar are substantial, but they also address a common problem: the republican need for strong leadership and the threats to republicanism that ambitious leaders pose. Sullivan explores this dynamic with an eye to Shakespeare's references to Christianity throughout the Roman plays. Christian imagery in *Julius Caesar*, in particular, illuminates significant differences between Caesar and Coriolanus both in terms of their ambitions and in how they pursue them. The engagement of Christian themes in the Roman plays also suggests opportunities to bring them into conversation with Shakespeare's plays set in the Christian era.

Like Sullivan, Khalil Habib in "*Virtù, Fortuna*, and Nation: Ruler and Citizen in Machiavelli's *The Life of Castruccio Castracani of Lucca* and Shakespeare's Bastard in *King John*" employs Machiavelli to clarify Shakespeare's presentation of a fundamental political dynamic. In Habib's case, what is at issue is the presentation of characters who do not fit with their regimes. Machiavelli presents Castruccio as one destabilized the political order by pursuing his ambitions to empire. The Bastard in Shakespeare's *King John* offers an alternative approach to politics by one who is not at home in the political order in which he finds himself. The Bastard is animated by patriotism rooted in moral conviction, which fosters his more enduring legacy.

In "The Theology of Coriolanus," Kevin Cherry is also interested in the beliefs that support Roman institutions and the political implications for those whose fundamental beliefs are different than those of the regime. Coriolanus's commitment to virtue implies an understanding of the highest good that he does not share with the Roman people. Disagreement with the people about the good sits beneath Coriolanus's downfall, but it also suggests a problem for republics in general. Successful republican politicians, it seems, must either abandon any understanding of the highest good that is not shared by the people, or he must appear to have abandoned it. Popular support, it seems, and virtue cannot both be attained without dissembling.

Bernard J. Dobski, in "The Power of the Particular: Liberal Education and Cosmopolitanism in Titus Andronicus," also looks to one of Shakespeare's Roman plays to better understand the conditions for the possibility of a functional republic and the consequences of a misunderstanding or disagreement about those conditions. Dobski argues for the importance of a strong sense of national character as a precondition for a successful republican regime. He explores the idea of cosmopolitanism as an alternative and argues for its insufficiency. Extending the benefits of democracy beyond the boundaries of one's political community requires, paradoxically, the preservation of those boundaries. Titus's failure to honor such boundaries contribute, Dobski argues, to the crimes against humanity that play explores.

L. Joseph Hebert continues to explore the structural tensions between popular opinion and strong political leadership, but moves us into Shakespeare's British plays. "Law Form and Due Proportion: Richard II, Sir Thomas More, and the Challenge of Constitutional Reform" begins by directing our attention to the restaging of *Richard II* just before the Essex rebellion in 1601 and the subsequent conviction and life imprisonment of Shakespeare's patron, Southampton. Elizabeth's allies, it seems, saw too much of the Queen in Richard. From there, Hebert develops a case for the apparently irresistible temptation for monarchs to grasp power and the turmoil such ambition creates, even for the most virtuous leaders. The case of Thomas More illuminates the way that freedom of speech and the rule of law challenge monarchical ambition. More also shows that the path to stable kingly power is "the regular and regulated exercise of that power in support of 'law and form and due proportion,'" an arrangement far more easily described than achieved.

Clinton Brand's approaches Macbeth's ambition from a very different perspective. In "Macbeth and the 'milk of human kindness': Nature, Natality, Sex, and Politics in the Scottish Play," Brand takes up the strange mystery of Lady Macbeth's child (or children) to whom she refers in dialogue, but who are apparently no longer living.

Introduction

He traces allusions to natality through the play, the way that they are interwoven with images of nature, and the role they play in the Macbeth's attempts to realize their ambitions to rule. The absent child is a privation that speaks to the necessity of contingency in human, and thus political, life. In the context of hereditary monarchy, the absent child also conditions the power the Macbeth's seek as, ultimately, a totalitarian dead end, a Heideggerian "being towards death."

Carol McNamara emphasizes the role of interpretation within Shakespearean drama and incumbent upon us as readers of Shakespeare in "Banning Shylock." She begins her account as Harold Bloom begins his account of the *Merchant of Venice* with an acknowledgment of the obvious and undeniable antisemitism of the play. She pushes more deeply into the play to argue that it is not simply antisemitic, however. The play explores the limits of Antonio's Christianity as well as Shylock's Judaism, and the uncomfortable fit both have with Venetian culture. McNamara also points us toward a consideration of the mechanics of the comic conclusion of the play to illuminate the qualities of character that Shakespeare presents as capable of transforming these apparently insoluble differences into differences that can be contained within a functional political order. Portia, she argues, exemplifies the essential role of interpretation in the preservation of the rule of law, and the power of well-interpreted law to create the conditions for peace, if not happiness.

Continuing the theme of interpretation, Sheila T. Cavanagh provides a wonderful survey of a very specific form of contemporary Shakespearean adaptation: one-person plays that intertwine Shakespearean texts with autobiography. In "A Place in the Story: Autobiographical Shakespeare," Cavanagh highlights seven playwright/performers who find poetic resonance with Shakespeare, but who also push back on the outdated perspectives he espouses as well as contentious aspects of his influence on literature and culture. Collectively, these contemporary works reinforce for Cavanagh "the notion that Shakespeare will not be tarnished or otherwise harmed by continual study, performance, and interrogation."

Our volume closes with a cautionary tale. In "Shakespeare and

Political History: Bastards, Nepobabies, Oligarchs," Gary Taylor presents a bit of his own autobiography to highlight some of the challenges to Shakespearean interpretation created by time, distance, and contingency. Taylor also argues for the limited value of certain approaches to seeking understanding of history and politics from Shakespearean texts created by Shakespeare's own limited perspectives. He extends his caution to include the suggestion that all poetic texts are subject to such limits and that we must appeal to the "documentary authority" of non-poetic texts to supplement the "charismatic authority" of Shakespeare (or any poet) in order to explore his understanding of politics.

'A King of Shreds and Patches':
A Fragmentology of Shakespeare and the Public Good

Deneen M. Senasi

There's something rotten in the state of Denmark, something that makes the ghost of a dead king walk the battlements, his countenance, "more in sorrow than in anger"; something, as we learn, "touching the lord Hamlet" intimately, something unnatural, "as in the best it is," that overshadows the kingdom and its less exalted subjects as well; something that casts a pall over what we might call the "public good." Thus, the perceptive Marcellus, a martial everyman keeping the night's watch, diagnoses the danger to the realm in a line of surpassing clarity and concision: "Something is rotten" he says, "in the state of Denmark."[1] At the heart of this "rotten state" Hamlet identifies his uncle, Claudius, as "a king of shreds and patches." An indictment of a rule not cut from whole cloth—fully integrated with the fabric of the kingdom as his father's was—but something stitched rather than woven together, marred by seams and made from scraps, themselves cast off or "cut purse" pieces of a garment not made for him and for which he is not made. Mingling imprecations against Claudius as both husband and king in the closet scene between Hamlet and his mother, Shakespeare reminds us that this filial tragedy—as the prince puts it "to kill a king and marry with his brother"[2] is one that necessarily touches, and indeed tears at the state itself, and with it the interwoven tapestry of identities and interests from which a sense of something like the public good might emerge.

This is the original context of the line from which I take my title, but with all due respect to the Danish prince, I mean to read

---

[1] All references to Shakespeare are from *The Norton Shakespeare*, General Editor, Stephen Greenblatt, (New York: Norton, 1997), *Hamlet*, 1.5.67.

[2] Ibid., 3.4.28.

this phrase—like Ophelia's advice on the wearing of rue—with a difference, taking it as a kind of controlling metaphor for these reflections on Shakespeare and the public good. As you may have noticed, the opening sentence of this talk is itself a thing of "shreds and patches," a self-conscious lifting of fragments of lines stitched together with words of my own as a means of articulating an idea. Those of you familiar with the play no doubt heard those shards of Shakespeare ring out as the sentence unfolded, recognizing something already known in the midst of that opening gambit to an as yet unfamiliar argument. That sense of *something known* interwoven with the *unknown* or even the *unknowable* will be central to the dynamic I hope to trace, following fragments of Shakespeare flung like the silken strands of Whitman's "noiseless patient spider" across the "vacant vast surrounding"[3] of public discourse and its senses of the public good. Like the work of Whitman's spider (or any other of its kind), these strands appear and disappear in richly recombinant configurations as they traverse historical periods and cultural contexts; woven to a particular purpose by one or by many within the web of discourse, this "sharding" of Shakespeare appears not as "single spies, / But in battalions,"[4] if I may be permitted another fragment of a line from *Hamlet*. And it is in those fragments and their fungible efficacy that we may eke out a kind of cartography of some (but by no means all) of the attempts to articulate, define, and/or shore up "the public good" by means of such "shreds and patches" of Shakespeare as may be found in the public imagination.

I want to pursue this dynamic of the "sharding" of Shakespeare along three interwoven strands: knowledge, access, and application. Specifically, *knowledge* of Shakespeare (and the educational practices by which some acquired it in nineteenth-century America); broader *public access* to such knowledge (as illustrated in the establishment of the Shakespeare Memorial Library in Birmingham, England in the

---

[3] Walt Whitman, "A Noiseless Patient Spider." https://www.poetryfoundation.org/poems/45473/a-noiseless-patient-spider.

[4] *Hamlet*, 4.5.74–75.

same century), and the *recourse* to such knowledge in the collective experience of tragedy and loss following the assassination of Abraham Lincoln. But first, a word about a keyword in my title: fragmentology. As Lisa Fagin-Davis notes: "The study of medieval manuscript fragments has developed into its own specialization in recent years," emerging as an interdisciplinary field in which scholars work to "interpret the layers of evidence in early manuscript fragments—identifying the original text, understanding its reuse, and tracing its modern history—in order to understand the complete story of a fragment from its origins to today."[5] I am borrowing this term to represent not a fragmentary dispersal of a manuscript's *leaves* but of an entire canon of dramatic *lines*. Making use of this approach to fragments excised from a once complete manuscript, I hope to follow bits of Shakespeare sheared off from their original place in the coherent whole of the play-text as they appear, recontextualized and repurposed within public discourse. While I cannot trace "the complete story" of such fragments in the time we have today, I would like to share a few partial ones, through which we might catch a glimpse of the discursive and institutional threads along which such "shreds and patches" of Shakespeare may intertwine with conceptions of the public good.

That Shakespeare has been perceived as having a role to play in the public good is attested to by an array of writers and thinkers across the centuries. "Had we world enough and time," as Andrew Marvell would say, we might spend more than the time given to this talk on just this question, but since this is only one of the fragments I hope to piece together, I will offer only a few highly compressed examples. In her 1928 novel, *Orlando*, Virginia Woolf argues that "a silly song of Shakespeare's has done more for the poor and the wicked than all the preachers and philanthropists in the world."[6] A testament, no doubt, to her time-traveling, gender-transcending

---

[5] Rare Book School Courses 2022. https://rarebookschool.org/courses/manuscripts/m100v/.

[6] Virginia Woolf, *Orlando,* New York: Harcourt Brace, 1956, 173.

protagonist's centuries-long devotion to the power of the written word, as well as a sweeping claim for Shakespeare's particular influence in grappling with questions of the public good. Woolf's depiction of a mere "silly song" as a fulcrum for such good reminds us of the fragmentary nature of most members of the public's experience of Shakespeare, yet in this small part of a much larger whole, she finds the seed of an even greater good at work. A shard of Shakespeare so small Hamlet might have questioned whether it should be seen as "a prologue to a play or the posey of a ring,"[7] in Woolf's assessment, thus constitutes an instrument of action in service of the public good.

The potential energy of such fragments also resonates in James Baldwin's 1964 essay, "Why I Stopped Hating Shakespeare." Contextualizing this dynamic of parts to wholes in the formative interplay of language and experience, Baldwin describes reencountering Shakespeare whilst living in France: "What I began to see—especially since, as I say, I was living and speaking in French—is that it is experience which shapes a language; and it is language which controls an experience." In that context, Baldwin concludes that Shakespeare fulfills the responsibility of the poet "to bear witness, as long as breath is in him to that mighty, unnamable, transfiguring force which lives in the soul of man, and to do his work so well that when the breath has left him, the people—*all people!*—who search in the rubble for a sign or a witness will be able to find him there."[8] Envisioning a more inclusive testament in the fragmentary "rubble" of human experience, Baldwin's emphasis on Shakespeare bearing witness for "*all people,*" like Woolf's insistence on the benefits of his "silly song" to the wicked and the poor, clearly situates his work within a prospective public good.

While Baldwin and Woolf describe a dynamic predicated on the accrual of individual encounters, Jane Austen considers a sense

---

[7] *Hamlet*, 3.2.136.

[8] James Baldwin, "Why I Stopped Hating Shakespeare," *The Cross of Redemption: Uncollected Writings*, ed. Randall Kenan, New York: Pantheon, 2011, 76–79.

of the public good shaped by a national lexicon of Shakespeare's thought and language. In her 1814 novel, *Mansfield Park*, she pens a scene in which several characters engage in reading Shakespeare's *Henry VIII* aloud. When Edmund Bertrum praises Henry Crawford's reading, the latter confesses he's never actually seen the play, saying: "But Shakespeare one gets acquainted with without knowing how. It is part of an Englishman's constitution. His thoughts and beauties are so spread abroad that one touches them everywhere."[9] Edmund concurs, suggesting: "His celebrated passages are quoted by everybody; they are in half the books we open, and we all talk Shakespeare, use his similes, and describe with his descriptions." Here Austen's observant eye notes the degree to which "we all talk Shakespeare," down to the granular detail of each successive century's borrowing of his similes and descriptions in our everyday discourse. In contrast with Polonius' maxim to "neither a borrower, nor a lender be"[10] she identifies a widespread borrowing in public discourse with Shakespeare as English culture's most fecund and frequent lender. This dispersal in what Edmund calls "bits and scraps" across the discourse community of the English gentry illustrates the "sharding" of Shakespeare as an aspect of public life in Austen's eighteenth century and beyond.

'The play's the thing': Piecing Together the Public Good in the Plays of Shakespeare

The play's the thing
Wherein I'll catch the conscience of the king.

~ Hamlet [11]

If, as these and other writers suggest, something in Shakespeare so bespeaks the public good, evidence should logically appear throughout the canon, and the short answer is, it does. Indeed, I find myself

---

[9] Jane Austen, *Mansfield Park*, New York: Norton, 1998.
[10] *Hamlet*, 1.3.81
[11] Ibid., 2.2.633–634.

tempted to argue that most, if not all, of the plays reveal an interest in conceptions of the public good. So much so that, once one looks for it, these texts read like a veritable commonplace book of the concept, inscribing "shreds and patches" of that aspirational state in such a way that indeed, "one touches them [almost] everywhere," from *As You Like It* and *Hamlet*, to *Henry V*, *Measure for Measure*, *Coriolanus*, and *Julius Caesar* (just to name a few). To get a glimpse of this larger whole, I will offer a few necessarily compressed instances that will stand, I hope, as the Chorus in *Henry V* says of the few actors representing the armies at Agincourt, "as ciphers to this great account."[12] And it is a "great account," one that presents not a single conception of the public good repeated many times over but a more nuanced, often ambiguous rendering, so that the concept itself emerges in Shakespeare's hands like a multifaceted prism held up to the light by means of the plays, where we can see both its beauty and its flaws.

One such facet depicts the public good as a kind of moveable feast defined by the character of the ruler, so that a great deal depends upon *who* and *where* he is. Given early modern conceptions of sovereignty and governance, such an approach is hardly surprising, and is borne out in the many examples of dramatic usurpations and restorations to power found in the plays. Thus, when Duke Senior is forced into exile in the Forest of Arden in *As You Like It*, the public good follows him there. As the Duke himself describes it: "And this our life, exempt from public haunt, / Finds tongues in trees, books in the running brooks, / Sermons in stones, and good in everything."[13] Introducing a tension between the "public *good*" and the "public *haunt*" of the court, Shakespeare transposes the former into the natural order of the forest. He does not, however, leave the Duke and his companions there, choosing instead to return them to those same "public haunts" by the end of the play, presumably carrying with them this expanded sense of the public good as a function of character, rather than pomp or place.

---

[12] *Henry V*, Prologue, line 18.
[13] *As You Like It*, 2.1.15–17.

'A King of Shreds and Patches'

This question of character and the public good, as we have seen, resonates in Hamlet's description of Claudius as a murderous "king of shreds and patches," but such an indictment is not limited to the "killing of a *king*." Instead, Shakespeare entertains the possibility that the killing of a king's *subjects* wantonly and without "good cause" may also tear at the fabric of his rule. We see this more perspectival sense of the public good in *Henry V* the night before the battle of Agincourt, when the king moves among his men in disguise.[14] Here, Shakespeare invites us to consider how the king's interests and responsibilities may *diverge* from those of his subjects, and as in the figure of Marcellus in *Hamlet*, he conveys this tension in the voice of an ordinary soldier. In this debate between Hal, as a king disguised, and Williams, as what the Prologue might call a "crookéd figure [attesting] in little place a million,"[15] the play pauses before the still uncertain glories of Agincourt to give voice to a common man's sense of the public good.

Thus, when Henry, presenting himself as a mere soldier says: "Methinks I could not die anywhere so contented as in the King's company, his cause being just and his quarrel honorable," Williams calls that predicate into question, saying:

> But if the cause be not good, the king himself hath a heavy reckoning to make, when all those legs and arms and heads, chopped off in a battle shall join together at the latter day, and cry all, "We died at such a place," some swearing, some crying for a surgeon, some upon their wives left poor behind them, some upon the debts they owe, some upon their children rawly left. I am afeard there are few die well that die in a battle, for how can they charitably dispose of anything when blood is their argument? Now, if these men do not die well, it will be a black matter for

---

[14] This point emerged from a discussion with two of my Mercer students, Katherine Grant and Iquadine Osbourne in a course on Public Writing and the Future of the Humanities during the Spring 2024 semester. I am grateful for their insightful comments in class discussion, which helped me clarify my own thinking on this point.

[15] *Henry V*, Prologue 15–16.

the king that led them to it, who to disobey were against all proportion of subjugation.[16]

While Shakespeare gives Henry the lion's share of textual space for his riposte, Williams' speech provides a striking image of those dismembered bodies sacrificed in the name of the "public good" vested in the king's cause. Anticipating the frontispiece to Hobbes' 1651 *Leviathan*, Williams' everyman envisions the body politic not in terms of an accretion of whole bodies culminating in the king as head, but as a horrific thing of "shreds and patches" composed, like Frankenstein's Creature, of fragments of once whole men converging in a searing indictment of the king in the matter (and manner) of their deaths.

Williams's damning vision of a ruler's disregard for the public good is taken up again in *Measure for Measure*, this time with an eye towards the very real possibility of corruption and behind-the-scenes machinations. Having failed in his responsibility to protect the public good by enforcing the law, the Duke turns to subterfuge to set things to right in Vienna. Temporarily vesting his power in Angelo, he pretends to journey outside the city. In revealing his plans only to a friar in whose order he will conceal himself, the Duke justifies this deception as a means of restoring a public good eroded by his own laxness: "We have strict statutes and most biting laws, / Which for this fourteen years we have let slip, / Even like an o'ergrown lion in a cave / That goes not out to prey."[17] When the friar points out that it is within the Duke's power in his own person to "unloose this tied-up justice,"[18] he demurs. Arguing that "sith 'twas my fault to give the people scope / 'Twould be my tyranny to strike and gall them," he explains he has instead "on Angelo imposed the office, / Who may in the ambush of my name, strike home."[19] This restoration of a public good by "ambush" displaces the exercise of

---

[16] *Henry V*, 4.1.130–132 and 138–151.
[17] *Measure for Measure*, 1.4.19–31.
[18] Ibid., 1.4.33.
[19] Ibid., 1.4.35–41.

authority as well as the responsibility for it. An unacknowledged break in the otherwise singular prerogatives of rule parceled out to two men: the one led to believe he holds power and the one actually wielding it.

Shakespeare thus shows us another rule of "shreds and patches" in the Duke's plan to reestablish the public good by cobbling together Angelo's power by proxy and his own incognito machinations. That these aspects of power are at odds with one another is illustrated in the darkly comic business of the Duke's attempt to substitute the unrepentant criminal Barnadine's head for that of the relatively blameless Claudio to satisfy Angelo's order of execution. Such tension also sheds light on the public good itself as a thing of "shreds and patches," wrested from acts that seem far from good in themselves as the play struggles to strike a balance between the Duke's former laxness and Angelo's hypocritical severity. *Measure*'s unsettling conclusion—with its strangely performative, unnecessarily cruel restoration of order in the Duke's progress back into the city and its presumptuous absorption of Isabella as his bride despite her avowed intention to take the veil—returns us to *Henry V*'s vision of dismembered soldiers sacrificed not to the public good but a ruler's self-indulgence. Here the dismembering is more figurative (a sword of Damocles that never falls, for example, on Claudio's head), but it is nonetheless real as the Duke intentionally dismembers the body politic in order to reconstruct it in a manner he finds more fitting. Along the way, individual members are seemingly torn from that body only to be patched on later in a different place or a different form. Thus, the public good emerges from an array of failures, contingencies, and machinations whose irregular seams (stitched together, not woven, even in the hands of the "rightful" ruler) are always in danger of being torn asunder again.

'Speak the speech': Shakespeare's Speaking Part in the Discourse of the Public Good

Speak the speech, I pray you, as I pronounced it to you, trippingly on the tongue.

~ *Hamlet* [20]

Part of the "patched" nature of the public good, of course, lies in the concept of the "public" itself: a necessarily heterogeneous, often conflicted group whose perspectives and prerogatives are seemingly always up for debate. Shakespeare's canon dramatizes this discourse of the public good, highlighting the difficulty in articulating the shared interests or values that may bind together so variegated a group. At the same time, indeed often in the same play, he demonstrates how the promise of the public good may be subject to manipulation by those for whom the concept is little more than a means to an end. In this context, while "the people" may have a claim to some good from the state, "the mob" may not, yet, both aspects of the public come into play in Shakespeare's dramatic discursive inquiry. Both *Coriolanus* and *Julius Caesar* explore lines of demarcation between the people and the mob, while also reflecting on what may happen when one gains ascendancy over the other. Both plays open with scenes of crowd and conflict, calling into immediate question whether those so gathered constitute "the people" or a mere "mob," the latter a ragtag assemblage that implicitly threatens the integrity of the state. So much depends, it seems, upon which aspect of the public appears in a given moment and who might be able to define or direct it. Seen in this light, the "public good" emerges not just as a thing of "shreds and patches" in its own right but also as a discursive fulcrum for political power.

Thus, in *Coriolanus*, Caius Martius describes ordinary citizens as "fragments,"[21] implicitly opposing them to the wholeness of Rome he sees himself embodying. This perception is strengthened

---

[20] *Hamlet*, 3.2.1–2.
[21] *Coriolanus* 1.1.245.

when Martius is granted the title "Coriolanus" after singlehandedly defeating an entire enemy town. This "addition" to his identity, a supplement to his apparent plenitude serves only to affirm his sense that the public—whether Roman or Volscian—represents little more than disjointed odds and ends of the body politic awaiting his more comprehensive will to scatter and subdue them. Continuing the logic of parts to wholes, Coriolanus' wounds (which he must publicly display in his bid to become a consul of Rome) are, in their visual rhetoric, opposed to the polyphonic voices of the people vested with the authority to accept or reject him in that role. And in this exchange between Coriolanus and the people, who to him remain a mob of mere "fragments," Shakespeare sows the seeds of conflict and contestation which will escalate into a grave threat to the public good, when the rejected warrior joins forces with Rome's enemies.

Julius Caesar takes *Coriolanus*'s fractious crowds a step further, implicitly positioning the public as a character in its own right, one that *acts* as well as *being acted upon*. From the opening scene's depiction of crowds making a holiday in celebration of Caesar's victory over Pompey, the play fixes our attention on the public as a cry of many voices. Shuttling back and forth between the cacophony of the mob and the articulate will of the people, this dynamic culminates in a pair of speeches made by Brutus and Antony in the aftermath of Caesar's assassination. Both begin with an appeal to shared identity and interests, with Brutus hailing the crowd as "Romans, countrymen, and lovers," while Antony appeals to them as "Friends, Romans, countrymen."[22] Both show themselves to be effective rhetoricians, each in his turn shaping public perspective on the assassination, but it is Antony who most effectively deploys the concept of the public good for his own ends. In the aftermath of Caesar's death, it is worth noting, Antony is a man apart and in danger of losing his own life, while the conspirators are joined in a mutual purpose. Acting upon his listeners by citing (and inciting) their claim to the public good, he avails himself of the people as an ally whose

---

[22] *Julius Caesar*, 3.2.14 and 3.2.82.

numbers far exceed those of the conspirators' party. In doing so, he positions the crowd along a knife's edge, poised somewhere between "countrymen" who mourn and a "mob" that kills, with his words, as Gertrude complains in *Hamlet*, "like daggers,"[23] egging them on towards action.

While Brutus speaks of what *Rome* stands to gain in the death of Caesar, Antony speaks of what *the people* have lost, insistently defining that loss in terms of the public good. Subtly undercutting Brutus' indictment of Caesar as "ambitious," he reminds his audience that the latter "brought many captives to Rome / Whose ransom did the general coffers fill," asking "Did this in Caesar seem ambitious?"[24] He tells them: "When that the poor hath cried, Caesar hath wept;" concluding that "Ambition should be made of sterner stuff."[25] Antony's characterization of Caesar as a benefactor of the people—money for the general coffers, tears for the poor—frames his memory in the collective concept of the public good. At the same time, he calls into question the privileging of individual interest embedded in Brutus' claim that his ambition was a palpable threat to the republic. Antony's performative reluctance to read Caesar's will naming the people as his heirs ultimately reveals the latter has left not only money "To every several man," but a form of property as well. As he explains: "he hath left you all his walks, / His private arbors, and new planted orchards."[26] Replacing Caesar's private privileges with the people's public ones, Antony describes how "He hath left them you / And to your heirs forever" as "common pleasures"[27] to be enjoyed by all. In this way, the question of what the people have gained through Caesar's generosity is made particular and concrete, while what they have lost in the death of such a benefactor is relentlessly underscored.

---

[23] *Hamlet*, 3.4.85
[24] *Julius Caesar*, 3.2.97–99 and 100–101.
[25] Ibid., 3.2.100.
[26] Ibid., 3.2.261–262.
[27] Ibid., 3.2.263–264.

This alignment of the public good with the murdered man presents the death of Caesar as not only a private grief but a public loss. Though they had cheered Brutus' indictment of Caesar moments before, one plebian suggests "If you think rightly of the matter / Caesar has had great wrong."[28] Antony artfully inches the crowd from the "people" who praised Caesar's killers to the "mob" they will soon become, rushing out in search of vengeance and even killing poor Cicero, the Poet, because he bears the same name as one of the conspirators. This fusion between the lost leader and the nascent mob rings out in Antony's description of the moment when "great Caesar fell," as he cries: "O, what a fall was there my countrymen! Then I and you and all of us fell down / Whilst bloody treason flourished over us."[29] This collective fall strikes at the heart of the public good, implicitly authorizing the crowd to avenge that loss, and in doing so, complete their passage from a mournful people to a bloodthirsty mob.

As in *Measure for Measure,* Shakespeare offers a "patched," contingent image of the public good, but with a focus here on collective, rather than individual action. While *Measure* dramatizes an established leader grappling with the public good, elsewhere he envisions a more fragmented *dramatis personae* contending for control of the concept. Though the Duke has failed to ensure the public good in Vienna, as the "rightful" ruler, he has the prerogative to act, and Angelo's authority necessarily proceeds from his. In *Coriolanus* and *Julius Caesar,* we find a sense of the public good more open to intervention by an array of individual actors, while the mercurial public, vacillating between its mirror images of the "people" and the "mob," casts its piebald shadow over the central figures of the play.

Acting on one another by acting on the public, as the latter is shredded and patched together by the turning of a word or phrase—"he was ambitious;" "know you not you are his heirs?"—the public good is less an aspirational goal than a means to an array of conflicting ends. A means, however, with the capacity for action in its own

---

[28] Ibid., 3.2.119–120.
[29] Ibid., 3.2.184–186.

right, even as it remains vulnerable to manipulation. This ambiguous field of influence and action further complicates the plays' overall sense of the public good, which even in these briefly sketched examples, begins to resemble one of Shakespeare's own wily fools, dressed from top to toe in "shreds and patches" of motley thought.

'Read on this book': Shakespeare and the Production of Public Knowledge

Read on this book,
That show of such an exercise may color
Your loneliness.

~ *Hamlet* [30]

In Shakespeare's own lifetime the public's primary point of contact with his works came in the performance of his plays. As a necessary antecedent, of course, the actors in those productions must come to know the lines of the plays in order to present a character on the stage. In this context too, we find the logic of "shreds and patches," since in preparing a production, actors were given copies of only their own parts, accompanied by their cues, rather than a complete copy of the play-text. As Simon Palfrey and Tiffany Stern note in *Shakespeare in Parts*, in the early modern theatre, an actor's 'part' indicated not only the character portrayed but also "the written paper, often made into a roll, on which that part was transcribed."[31] As a result, "that particular fragment of text—the actor's own words and his cues"[32] were the means by which players "conned," or came to know those aspects of Shakespeare's thought they would give voice to on the stage.

In addition to conning their roles from fragments, actors were also expected to deliver particular speeches on demand as a

---

[30] *Hamlet*, 3.1.49–52.

[31] Simon Palfrey and Tiffany Stern, *Shakespeare in Parts*, Oxford: Oxford University Press, 2007, 1.

[32] Ibid., 1.

demonstration of their quality as a performer. Hamlet's request that the First Player deliver the Hecuba speech upon their arrival at Elsinore, as well as his strategic insertion of lines of his own devising into their performance of *The Murder of Gonzago*, illustrates the degree to which dramatic production itself may constitute a thing of "shreds and patches." Moments before the play within the play, Hamlet adjures the actor to "speak the speech, I pray you, as I pronounced it to you, trippingly on the tongue; but if you mouth it, as many of our players do, I had as lief the town-crier spoke my lines."[33] Hamlet's insistence that the player "speak the speech" in a particular way is something more than an author's fit of ego, for in the delivery of those lines lies the success or failure of his strategy to "catch the conscience of the king."[34] Thus, Shakespeare dramatizes the sharding of dramatic speech as a means of producing an otherwise inaccessible knowledge, on stage and in full view of the court. With Horatio bearing witness as a figure for the public at large, such sharding is designed to clarify the rationale for revenge by providing more complete knowledge of whether or not the ghost spoke true. For Hamlet, to "speak the speech" means at one and the same time to conceal and to convey, cloaking his intentions in a patchwork of original text and his own inserted lines that, like Shakespeare's broader discourse on the public good, appear together in motley array.

This sense of Shakespeare's thought appearing in motley array is also found in the plays' passage from the spoken words of performance to the printed modality of the First Folio. While performance was the primary mode in which the public encountered Shakespeare's thought, early editions of the plays, themselves often patched together from fragmentary actors' parts, also began to appear. Underscoring the variable nature of the seventeenth-century reading public, the Folio's frontmatter emphasizes the printed book's accessibility to all those with the means to purchase it. In "To the Great Variety of Readers," Shakespeare's original editors, John Heminges and Henry Condell

---

[33] *Hamlet*, 3.2.1–4.
[34] Ibid., 2.2.633–34.

envision an audience stretching from "him the most able to him that can but spell."[35] Emphasizing the broadly accessible nature of their offering, they describe the construction of the Folio as a corrective on behalf of a public "abused with diverse stolne and surreptitious copies, maimed and deformed by the frauds and stealthes of injurious impostors that expos'd them." Early print editions, often cobbled together from actors' incomplete "parts" were subject to errors and inconsistencies in some printed editions. With the Folio, Heminges and Condell argue, such "deformed" patchwork texts "are now offer'd to your view cur'd, and perfect of their limbes."[36] In this way, the First Folio emerges from fragmentary antecedents in the quartos and octavo editions, both "good" and "bad." The Folio's monumental body of work can thus be seen as a thing of "shreds and patches" ostensibly made whole, offered in a newly "complete" form as an inarguable value for public consumption.

Heminges and Condell's appeal is unabashedly commercial, repeatedly imploring readers to "buy" the First Folio, yet it also centers questions of the public's access to and judgement of the plays. Positing Shakespeare's works as akin to those "common pleasures" Caesar bequeaths to the people, the editors hold out the promise of a new form of explicitly *public* knowledge: "Well! It is now publique, and you will stand for your privileges, wee know: to read, and censure."[37] This "privilege" to judge or "censure" the plays invites the public into a different relationship with Shakespeare by means of his book where, the editors insist, they "will finde enough, both to draw and hold"[38] their attention. In this seemingly irresistible attraction, the First Folio, followed by a dizzying array of printed editions across the centuries, foregrounds several questions concerning how the public may have come to know and "be held" by Shakespeare's

---

[35] John Heminges and Henry Condell, "To the Great Variety of Readers," Front Matter to the 1623 First Folio. https://www.shakespeare.org.uk/explore-shakespeare/shakespedia/shakespeares-works/shakespeares-first-folio/.
[36] Ibid.
[37] Ibid.
[38] Ibid.

thought. Who was reading Shakespeare and how were they reading him? In what contexts, for what purposes, and how might such reading impact the production of public knowledge in service of the public good? As the putative foundation of such knowledge, it is worth noting that, though Heminge and Condell acknowledge its "patched" origins," the frontmatter's insistent claims of "perfect" completeness, present the First Folio's hundreds of pages and hundreds of thousands of words as a kind of comprehensive inheritance, something worth *having* and worth *knowing*.

Heminges and Condell's democratizing call "To the Great Variety of Readers" in seventeenth-century England finds a responsive audience in nineteenth-century America. As Jill Gage notes, in the nineteenth century, Americans began "to adopt [Shakespeare] as one of their own," with James Fenimore Cooper famously suggesting that "Shakespeare is the great author of America."[39] Yet as Joseph Haughey points out, the plays were primarily considered recreational reading, not "something worthy of study at a university."[40] In this context, students most often experienced the plays not in their entirety, but as speeches or monologues included in handbooks on oratory and elocution,[41] such as William Scott's 1803 *Lessons in Elocution*, and what Phillip Christensen describes as a "distinctly *American* Shakespeare" in the widely-used McGuffey Rhetorical Readers.[42] In this context, Charles Frey notes, Shakespeare was primarily considered "a writer of lofty moral tags, many of which were quoted approvingly by American presidents."[43] Quotation by political leaders

---

[39] Jill Gage, Newberry Library, "Shakespeare in the Nineteenth-Century United States." https://dcc.newberry.org/?p=15987.

[40] Josephy Haughey, "The History of Shakespeare in American Schools," *Shakespeare Unlimited* Podcast, January 7, 2020. https://www.folger.edu/podcasts/shakespeare-unlimited/history-of-shakespeare-in-schools/.

[41] Ibid.

[42] Phillip H. Christensen, "McGuffey's Oxford (Ohio) Shakespeare," *Journal of American Studies*, Vol. 43, No. 1[2009]: 101–15.

[43] Charles Frey, "Teaching Shakespeare in America, *Shakespeare Quarterly*, 1984, Vol. 35, No. 5, *Teaching Shakespeare* (1984), pp. 541–59.

clearly gives Shakespeare's thought a place in the public discourse of the period where more extended engagement with the play-text as a whole would have proved cumbersome. Yet before such shards of Shakespeare could be dispersed, before the impulse to do so could develop, the plays themselves must be known, perhaps even recognized as potential epistemes of the public good. In this respect, it was students' reading of the plays for pleasure in their own rooms and in their university literary societies that in the late nineteenth century brought Shakespeare into "the formal curriculum."[44] An erratic, incremental passage from those "lofty moral tags" and "pleasure" reading to a recognized course of study that, along the way, wove a variegated array of encounters with Shakespeare into the fabric of America's public discourse.

Those lucky enough to benefit from such a formal course of study, of course, represent only one part of the larger question of how Shakespeare's thought makes its way into the public imagination. A singular commitment to *this* aspect of the question is found in the life's work of George Dawson, an Englishman who, as it happens, visited the U.S. in 1874 as part of James Redpath's "Star Lecture Course" series. A decade earlier, Dawson, a progressive city leader in Birmingham, England, argued persuasively for the establishment of the first *public* library dedicated to making Shakespeare accessible to all. The result: Birmingham's Shakespeare Memorial Library, officially founded in April, 1864 in honor of the three hundredth anniversary of Shakespeare's birth. Its mission as a "uniquely democratic Shakespeare collection," including a publicly-owned First Folio, continues to this day, as illustrated in the recently completed *Everything to Everyone Project*, which "aims to renew the Birmingham Shakespeare Memorial Library not just for but *with* the diverse population of today's Birmingham."[45]

---

[44] Ibid.

[45] *Everything to Everybody: Birmingham's Shakespeare Memorial Library,* West Midlands History, Foreword by Adrian Lester, pg. 5, Introduction by Tom Epps, pg.6, "The Everything to Everybody Project" by Euwan Fernie, pg. 31.

In April 1876, Dawson delivered his annual address to members of Birmingham's "Our Shakespeare Club," in which he advocated for the study of Shakespeare as an aspect of the public good. He writes: "I rejoice to see the growth of toleration of men towards one another, and amongst the causes that have made that larger spirit of to-day more a temper of men's minds than a principle of their politics, I count the increased study of Shakespeare."[46] He asks his audience to consider "whether Shakespeare has made you less genial, less gracious…less full of power to enjoy this wondrous world and all the good things therein," noting for his own part that "the man has enlarged my horizon, deepened the little good that was in me, ministered never to what was evil."[47] Dawson's emphasis on what he sees as Shakespeare's capacity to "deepen the little good" within us as individuals finds its proliferative public analogue in the institutional framework of the Memorial Library. In that accessible space created to "contain [as far as practicable] every edition and translation of Shakespeare, all the commentators, good, bad, and indifferent,"[48] he shows us one way the public may come to know and make use of Shakespeare's thought, as they leave the library, like so many bees among the flowers, laden with whatever bits and pieces of Shakespeare strike their fancy or meet their present needs. By centering access to Shakespeare's work as a public right, rather than a point of privilege, Dawson facilitates the dispersal of any "shreds and patches" of the public good that may be found there with each patron's visit.

---

[46] George Dawson, "Anniversary Speeches," *Shakespeare and Other Lectures*, George St. Clair, ed. London, Kegan Paul, Trench & Co, 1888. 124–125.
[47] Ibid.
[48] *Everything to Everybody: Birmingham's Shakespeare Memorial Library*, West Midlands History, "The 'Our Shakespeare Club,'" 8.

'Cry Havoc': The Assassination of Abraham Lincoln in a Shakespearean Context

Cry "Havoc!" and let slip the dogs of war...
~ *Julius Caesar*[49]

Once stitched into the social fabric, these "shreds and patches" remain in latent form until occasion ignites them. I want to consider one such occasion in the assassination of Abraham Lincoln on April 14, 1865. Lincoln's abiding admiration of Shakespeare is well documented. Having first encountered him in the "shreds and patches" of oratory handbooks like Scott's 1803 *Lessons in Elocution,* he moved on to a sustained engagement with the plays that would endure throughout his life. Ascending to the presidency at the outset of civil war, he seems by character and by context not unlike a figure in one of the plays themselves. Indeed, Ethan Anderson has described Lincoln as "Shakespeare's Greatest Character."[50] This recent attribution is supported by a more contemporary source in Walt Whitman's memorial lecture, "The Death of Lincoln," first presented in New York in 1879.[51] Recounting his first glimpse of Lincoln in February 1861, Whitman recalls a stop the president-elect made in New York on the way to his inauguration, where he was met by a crowd's "sulky, unbroken silence." Whitman describes the moment when Lincoln

---

[49] *Julius Caesar*, 3.1.299–301.

[50] Ethan Anderson, "Lincoln: Shakespeare's Greatest Character," National Endowment for the Humanities Division of Research Programs, 8 December 2020. https://www.neh.gov/blog/lincoln-shakespeares-greatest-character.

[51] Whitman gave the lecture several times. Flowing the New York lecture on the anniversary of the president's assassination on April 14, 1879, he also presented the talk in both New York and Philadelphia in 1880 and Boston in 1881. He continued to deliver the lecture "in different cities and to different kinds of audiences, usually in April or May, until 1890." See Anne Holmes, "Remembrance: Whitman's 'The Death of Lincoln' and the By the People Whitman Campaign," Library of Congress Blogs, April 14, 2021. https://blogs.loc.gov/catbird/2021/04/remembrance-whitmans-the-death-of-lincoln-and-the-by-the-people-whitman-campaign/.

"look'd with curiosity upon that immense sea of faces, and the sea of faces return'd the look with similar curiosity. In both there was a dash of comedy, almost farce, such as Shakespeare puts in his blackest tragedies."[52] Seen in this light, we might well imagine the sixteenth president as a "Shakespearean" leader grappling with questions of the public good on an order of magnitude that had never before been seen in the United States.

Other details from Lincoln's life in the months and years leading up to the assassination support this framing. These include his habit of carrying copies of the plays with him when he traveled, his ability to recite entire speeches from memory, and his practice of reading segments of the plays aloud to those around him, including, it is said, from his favorite play, *Macbeth*, the night before he was shot. Lincoln also concerned himself with the impact of particular passages, as illustrated in an 1863 letter to the prominent actor, James Hackett, in which he expresses his preference for a soliloquy by Claudius over Hamlet's more oft-cited "To be or not to be" speech. Claudius' soliloquy, "O, my offense is rank," as it happens, is included in Scott's *Lessons in Elocution*, one of those "shreds and patches" through which the president's nascent relationship with Shakespeare is thought to have been formed. Lincoln writes: "Unlike you gentlemen of the profession, I think the soliloquy in *Hamlet* commencing 'O, my offense is rank' surpasses that commencing 'To be or not to be.' But pardon this small attempt at criticism!"[53] For Andersen, this suggests "Lincoln was reading Shakespeare in those executive years with a monopolizing eye toward how they spoke to his own experience as president, using the plays, in part, to give voice to the natural guilt he felt as leader of the bloodiest war effort the nation had ever endured."[54] This sense of the plays being used by the

---

[52] Walt Whitman, "The Death of Lincoln," published by David McKay, Philadelphia, 1892, 2–3.

[53] Letter to James H. Hackett from Abraham Lincoln, August 17, 1863, The Alfred Whital Stern Collection of Lioncolniana, Library of Congress, http://hdl.loc.gov/loc.rbc/lprbscsm.scsm0853.

[54] Andersen, "Lincoln: Shakespeare's Greatest Character."

sitting president to grapple with questions of the public good in the midst of a brutal war illustrates the degree to which Shakespeare was integral to Lincoln's daily life, as well as his understanding of leadership.

This suffusive Shakespearean context extends to the circumstances of his death as well. Lincoln's assassin, John Wilkes Booth, was a member of a well-known family of Shakespearean actors. On November 25, 1864, John Wilkes appeared with his brothers, Edwin and Junius, in a benefit performance of *Julius Caesar* at the Winter Garden Theatre. The sold-out performance, featuring Edwin as Brutus, Junius as Cassius, and John Wilkes as Antony, raised four thousand dollars for a statue of Shakespeare in Central Park, which still stands today. On April 14, 1865, John Wilkes Booth took to the stage again for a very different purpose. Leaping from the president's box at the Ford Theatre moments after shooting Lincoln in the back of the head, he declaimed a Latin tag attributed to Brutus in the killing of Caesar: "sic semper tyrannis." In speaking such words in such a moment, Booth appears to fall back on an actor's instinct for recitation, for speaking in parts, to convey his rationale for an act he hoped would number him, in the words of Shakespeare's Cassius, among those "men that gave their country liberty."[55] Thus, the assassin avails himself of the actor's technique, turning to something *known* – a fragment of speech delivered from the stage – in an attempt to justify an *unknown* of immediate urgency: the murder of a president.

When the president died, the outpouring of grief took many forms, including an array of broadsides printed with songs and poems designed to bind the nation's public performance of mourning together. Most featured original compositions created in response to Lincoln's death, but one took a different approach, invoking passages from *Macbeth* in an offering described as "Shakespeare Applied to Our National Bereavement."

---

[55] *Julius Caesar* 3.1.132.

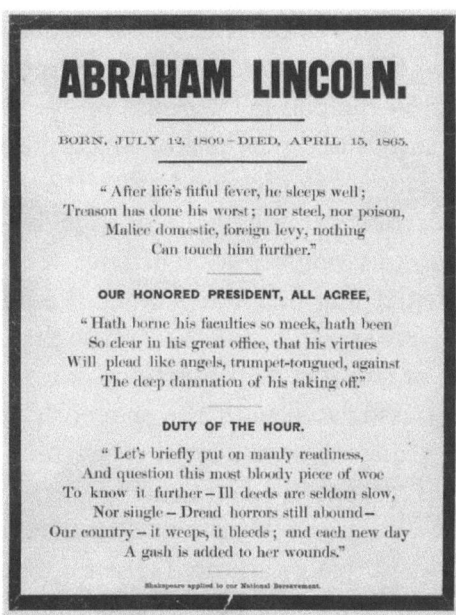

Figure 1. "Shakespeare applied to our National Bereavement" Alfred Whital Stern Collection of Lincolniana, (Library of Congress), Boston: B. B. Russell & Co., Loring, B. J. Remich, 1865.

Intriguingly, the broadside does not identify the play, and the framing concept of the title is printed in a very small font, almost as if the creators expected the audience to recognize the lines and their repurposing with little or no prompting. The passages themselves are woven into the broadside's message, making it too a thing of "shreds and patches." The first two focus on the play's murdered king, Duncan, as a figure for Lincoln, while the third is patched together from different speakers in different parts of the text: the first spoken by Macbeth in Act 2.3 at line 157, the second by Banquo in the same scene, lines 150–151; the third is from William Davenant's 1873 adaptation of Shakespeare's play, and the fourth is spoken by Malcom in Act 4.3, lines 50–51. This extensive sharding bespeaks a thorough knowledge of the play (and Davenant's adaptation), as well as an expectation of success underwritten by mourners' ability to recognize the lines *as* Shakespeare (whether they knew they were from *Macbeth* or not), and by the assumption that these lines carry with them a capacity to work on the public imagination.

In this way, "shreds and patches" of Shakespeare are woven together in a shared language of loss and grief. The broadside's synthesis itself, of course, constitutes a fragment in its own right, one now held by the Library of Congress as an artifact of a larger impulse to cobble together something like a lexicon of the public good in the aftermath of Lincoln's assassination. This sense that a brief quotation may bring a kind of comfort or protection is also reflected in other fragmentary relics associated with the sixteenth president. On the night he was shot, Lincoln wore a great coat with a silk lining bearing an embroidered quotation taken from a speech given on the Senate floor in 1850 by Daniel Webster, who like Shakespeare, was someone the president deeply admired. The quotation, "One Country, One Destiny"[56] resonates with a speech Lincoln had made just days before his death, on 11 April 1865, outlining the task of Reconstruction, which like Webster's speech, emphasized the relationship between the parts and the whole of American democracy.

It is worth noting that Webster's speech is itself marked by the presence of Shakespeare in a line from *Julius Caesar* cited in the speech and taken as its title: "Hear Me For My Cause." Addressing the tensions that would later culminate in secession and civil war, Webster writes:

> I have a part to act, not for my own security or safety, for I am looking out for no fragment upon which to float away from the wreck, if wreck there must be, but for the good of the whole, and

---

[56] Bequeathed by Lincoln's widow to the president's favorite doorman, Alphonse Donn, the coat was held by the Donn family for more than a century, during which time some were allowed to cut small pieces from the lining as souvenirs. It is now held by the Ford's Theatre National Historic Site. Exposure to light has made the lining's condition makes it fragile, so a replica is displayed instead. https://artsandculture.google.com/asset/detail-of-lincoln-s-great-coat/8gHP2R0T-p1iJQ.

the preservation of the whole; and there is that which will keep me to my duty during this struggle, whether the sun and the stars shall appear, or shall not appear, for many days. I speak today for the preservation of the Union. 'Hear me for my cause.'[57]

Anticipating the rending of that unity that had bound the states together, Webster shears off an imminently recognizable line from Shakespeare to be patched onto his present purpose. From Webster's pre-war speech and Lincoln's citation of it in the form of a personal garment to the broadside's synthesis of lines from *Macbeth* in the wake of the president's death, fragments of Shakespeare are stitched onto these moments of history like a patch across a tear, as the nation reaches for a shared language of imminent loss and purposeful remembrance.

'Something rich and strange': Shakespeare's Recombinant Parts and Labor

Full fathom five thy father lies,
  Of his bones are coral made;
Those are pearls that were his eyes;
  Nothing of him that doth fade
But doth suffer a sea-change
Into something rich and strange.
  ~*The Tempest*[58]

Shakespeare thus interweaves private woe with public mourning and public mourning with a shared language that just may be sufficient to that loss. The result is a patchwork piece sewn by many hands, a polyphonic cry raised in many voices fused by the "shreds and

---

[57] Webster's speech was first reported in U.S. Congress, Senate, *Congressional Globe*, 31st Cong., 1st sess, 476–83. The text cited here was taken from a version later revised by Webster printed in the *Congressional Globe*, 31st Cong., 1st sess, Appendix, 269–76. https://www.senate.gov/artandhistory/history/resources/pdf/Webster7th.pdf.

[58] *The Tempest*, 1.2.400–405.

patches" of language through which they speak. Shot through with the differences of individual memory and experience, this shared language of loss and grief reflects Shakespeare's sense that "the web of our life is a mingled yarn, good and ill together."[59] In a similarly variegated vein, Ophelia holds out pansies in her mad scene, saying "That's for thoughts,"[60] as in her own mind, she grapples with the unfathomable idea that Hamlet has killed her father. Turning to something *known*—the cultural meaning attributed to the flower—she wrestles with "out of joint"[61] fragments of language in an attempt to navigate the terrifying *unknown* in which she finds herself. It is a very human impulse, this recourse to something already known in the face of shattering loss or debilitating uncertainty, and in this brief fragmentology, I have tried to trace some of the ways "shreds and patches" of Shakespeare may be used in such moments to shore up the public good.

In his memorial lecture, Whitman decries the lack of such a language more than a decade after Lincoln's death. A shared language he sought but could not find despite presenting this annual address around the anniversary of the assassination beginning in 1879 and continuing through 1890. Noting his desire to memorialize Lincoln's death in fitting terms, he writes:

> Now fifteen years bygone – my heart has entertained the dream, the wish, to give of Abraham Lincoln's death its own special thought and memorial. Yet now the sought-for opportunity offers, I find my notes incompetent (why, for truly profound themes is statement so idle? Why does the right phrase never offer?) and the fit tribute I dream'd of waits as unprepared as ever.[62]

Here, Whitman lays bare what is at stake in the idea of a truly evocative shared language, one that binds a heterogeneous public

---

[59] *All's Well That Ends Well*, 4.3.69–72.
[60] *Hamlet*, 4.5.174.
[61] Ibid., 2.1.189.
[62] Whitman, Lincoln Memorial Lecture, 1.

together as a means of speaking *to* and *for* their collective experience. As Anaïs Nin reminds us: "The role of a writer is not to say what we can all say, but what we are unable to say."[63] That so great a writer as Whitman confesses himself "unable to say" what is needed in a public lecture dedicated to that express purpose underscores the challenges inherent in finding such a language. Asking "Why does the right phrase never offer?" he deprecates his own efforts, while at the same time suggesting something about why those shards of Shakespeare on the 1865 broadside may well have been "applied to our national bereavement." Taken together, Shakespeare's place in public discourse, his status as "the great American author," and his pride of place in Lincoln's life and his presidency perhaps appeared to hold out hope that through those "shreds and patches" cobbled together for the nonce, the "right phrase" might be found.

This deeply human need to find the "right phrase" in such moments is with us still, and Shakespeare's role in that discursive dynamic continues unabated in the twenty-first century. I do not mean to suggest that this dynamic is exclusive to Shakespeare, only that his place in the history of culture makes him a strongly illustrative case.[64] Asked how poems enter her daily life, the critic, Helen Vendler, herself no stranger to Shakespeare, put it this way: "They help me to know what I am feeling. Out of the depths of my heart will come a quotation completely unbidden. And then I will think, Oh, so that's what I'm feeling."[65] Vendler's description of her own

---

[63] Anaïs Nin, *The Diary of Anaïs Nin*, Vol. 1, ed. Gunther Stuhlmann. New York: Mariner Books, 1969.

[64] Though they lie outside the historical framework of the present analysis (and will be taken up in a separate essay), it is worth noting two other examples of this dynamic: The Shakespeare Hut, a performance space that staged fragments of the plays for soldiers in London in World War I and Francis Collmer's *Shakespeare in Time of War*, which compiled quotations to offer "a ringing voice that shall speak" to the collective experience of conflict. See Ailsa Grant Ferguson, *The Shakespeare Hut*, 2019 and Frances Collmer, *Shakespeare in Time of War, 1916*.

[65] Helen Vendler, "The Art of Criticism No. 3" interviewed by Henri Cole, *Paris Review*, Issue 141, Winter 1996.

experience finds an analogue in public discourse in what took place at a campaign stop for Robert Kennedy on April 4, 1968, the night Martin Luther King was assassinated. Speaking at a rally in Indianapolis, Kennedy set aside his prepared remarks, choosing instead to speak of King's death directly, even though authorities had warned him against addressing the deeply distressed crowd.[66] In his unscripted speech, Kennedy quotes Aeschylus' *Agamemnon* from memory, telling the crowd: "My favorite poet was Aeschylus. He wrote: 'In our sleep, pain which cannot forget falls drop by drop upon the heart until, in our own despair, against our will, comes wisdom through the awful grace of God.'"[67] In this centuries-old fragment, alive with the persistent memory through which he had internalized it, Kennedy finds Whitman's elusive "right phrase," interweaving it with words of his own as he reaches for a shared language of loss and grief for the death of Martin Luther King Jr. in real time.

As so often happens, Shakespeare appears to anticipate and enact such moments, this time in his late romance, *The Tempest*, where Ariel extolls the "sea-change" of death itself. The lyric's blazoning of the seemingly drowned king's body details that change, as part by part, its human form is overwritten in "shreds and patches" of coral and pearls. Ariel's song recounts a process of persistent, adaptive value in which an array of heterogeneous parts converge in the creation of hybrid forms. Like the "pearls that were his eyes," Shakespeare's language delights in its own richly recombinant nature, whether within the world of the play or in the world beyond where, as we have seen, it may itself be broken apart and transposed "into something rich and strange." A "sea-change," though which such lines removed from their original context, lead us back to the plays

---

[66] Liam Stack, "When Robert Kennedy Told an Indianapolis Crowd of King's Assassination," *The New York Times*, April 4, 2018.

[67] Senator Robert F. Kennedy Statement on the Assassination of Martin Luther King, Jr., Indianapolis, Indiana, April 4, 1968, The John F. Kennedy Presidential Library. https://www.jfklibrary.org/learn/about-jfk/the-kennedy-family/robert-f-kennedy/robert-f-kennedy-speeches/statement-on-assassination-of-martin-luther-king-jr-indianapolis-indiana-april-4-1968.

themselves. As John Berger argues, "every authentic poem contributes to the labour of poetry. And the task of this unceasing labor is to bring together what life has scattered or violence has torn apart." He adds, "Poetry can repair no loss, but it defies the space which separates. And it does this by its continual labour of reassembling what has been scattered."[68] Berger is speaking, of course, of the inscape of the poem as a site of reassembly and reunion, but we can apply the same reasoning to the scattering of those "shreds and patches" with which this essay has been concerned in their capacity to create a shared language of collective experience.

This then is the richly recombinant "labour" of all those parts, those sheared off shards of Shakespeare in the discourse of the public good. While, as Berger suggests, they may stop short of the complete "repair" of what has been lost, in "reassembling what has been scattered" they may gesture towards a shared language that, however fleetingly, makes of us more a "people" than a "mob." Of course, with any writer whose language and ideas are so entrenched in public discourse, there is always the possibility that those widely dispersed fragments could just as easily be deployed in the service of something other than the public good. As Gary Taylor notes in a piece on *Henry V* and the Iraq war published in *The Guardian* in 2003,[69] there is a danger that, in a given moment, Shakespeare may have "thought for us" instead of our doing the thinking ourselves. Yet there is some comfort in the Chorus' plea that we "piece out [the play's] imperfections with [our] thoughts," for as he continues, "'tis your thoughts that now must deck our kings,"[70] attiring them in scrutiny as well as "wonder" as, upon occasion, we seek out a shared language of the public good by means of those "shreds and patches" of Shakespeare that may yet be found, even now, in the public imagination.

---

[68] John Berger, "The Hour of Poetry," *The Sense of Sight: Writings by John Berger*, New York: Vintage International, 1985, 249.

[69] Gary Taylor, "Cry Havoc," *The Guardian*, 2003. https://www.theguardian.com/stage/2003/apr/05/theatre.classics.

[70] *Henry V*, Prologue 24–30.

Questions, Questions, Questions: Shakespeare's Ambiguous *Winter's Tale*

Stuart D. Warner

> He calls them Minute Philosophers. Right, said Crito, the modern Free-thinkers are the very same with those Cicero called Minute Philosophers, which Name admirably suits them, they being a sort of Sect which diminish all the most valuable Things, the Thoughts, Views, ad Hopes of Men; all Knowledge, Notions, and Theories of the mind they reduce to Sense; Human they contract and degrade to the narrow low standard of Animal Life, and assign us only a small Pittance of Time instead of Immortality.
>
> —George Berkeley, *Alciphron: or, the Minute Philosopher*

Clarity is a scarce resource in Shakespeare's *The Winter's Tale*. No matter how far we go in interrogating the play, questions are hardly ever resolved, resulting in further questions issuing forth, to which answers never fail of falling short, leading us to wonder—why such persistent ambiguity?[1]

Leontes' failure to get Polixenes to extend his stay in Sicilia beyond the "nine stages of the watery star" (I.2.50)[2] that he had been there—and we should be interested in why he wants him to stay any longer—lead him to insist that Hermione not remain silent and to try to persuade him to do so, which she does, and somewhat easily at that. Her immediate success and the conversation that then ensues

---

[1] For conversations about *The Winter's Tale* and allied matters, the author gratefully acknowledges the guidance provided by Vickie Sullivan, Gina Buccola, Ronna Burger, Tom Merrill, Zarko Minkov, Marina Marren, Mary Ann McGrail, the late Paul Cantor, Benjamin Warner, and Charlie Thomas. He was inspired to start teaching the play by the light shed on it by the late Richard Kennington.

[2] All references to *The Winter's Tale* are from the *The Oxford Shakespeare* edition, edited by Stephen Orgel (Oxford: The Clarendon Press, 1996).

between Polixenes and her soon lead Leontes to be overtaken and seized by a jealous rage—perhaps of Hermione, perhaps of Polixenes, perhaps of both—thereby setting much of the rest of the play into motion. Let us begin to turn, with some attention to detail, to that very conversation.

It takes Hermione all of nineteen short lines to convince Polixenes to remain in Sicilia for one more week. However, the brief exchange between them about him continuing his stay there is immediately followed by a longer one in which Hermione playfully peppers Polixenes with questions about his childhood spent together with Leontes in Sicilia. These questions had already been prepared, after a fashion, by the opening scene of the play, a conversation between Archidamus and Camillo, the principal subordinates of the two rulers, in which one of the subjects under discussion was that very childhood, and how Bohemia and Sicilia—that is, the kings themselves—had been apart ever since. That the two of them were "trained together in their childhoods" (I.1.21) raises a host of questions, beginning with how it was that the future ruler of Bohemia had spent his younger days in Sicilia. Maybe he had been sent there for his education; maybe something else. Archidamus mentions the "insufficience" (I.1.14) of Bohemia compared to that of Sicilia, and that might be part of the reason why. The play itself, however, provides no guidance to us at all.

Regardless, Archidamus highlights matters related to youth and character by noting the extraordinary promise of the young Mamillius, a consideration Camillo seconds by suggesting that the elders, even those on crutches, are motivated to continue living so as to be able to witness the boy come of age. In so doing, irrespective of whether both of them are engaged in flattery or whether they are offering honest assessments of Mamillius' many virtues, they are implicitly comparing the boy's present youth with that time in the past when Leontes and Polixenes were young, an issue Leontes himself will raise when he is engaged directly with his son in the second scene. Once we notice this, and couple it with the insertion of Time as the chorus, if not narrator, of the play at the start of Act IV, we are better able to be attentive to the many specific temporal placeholders in the first act—to minutes and hours (I.2.43, 287), to days (I.2.446), weeks (I.2.39), months (I.2.41, 101), and years (I.2.154)[3]—as well as more general notions such as forever (I.2.103, 106) and eternal (I.2.63), to say nothing of the four seasons of the year.

After Hermione convinces Polixenes to remain in Sicilia for but one more week she turns back to the time when Polixenes and Leontes were youths together—two future monarchs. But on how each came to rule, she is silent, for her interest is in the private lives of the two rulers, not their public lives or their coming to age as rulers. At the start of their give and take, innocence dominates the stage, as Polixenes affirms in response to Hermione:

We were as twinned lambs that did frisk i'th' sun,
And bleat the one at th'other; what we changed
Was innocence for innocence—we knew not
The doctrine of ill-doing…(I.2.66–69).

To which Hermione follows up, "By this we gather / You have tripped since" (I.2.73–74). Of course, the meaning of these words would change somewhat if a question mark ended the sentence rather than a period. Nonetheless, Polixenes turns to the "temptations" that have been born to himself and Leontes since, and thus these bring up his unnamed wife and Hermione's own "precious self," which had not yet "crossed the eyes / Of my young playfellow" (I.2.76ff), Leontes. Hermione's reply at this juncture is of greater importance than it seems, yet it will be far from clear at first that that is the case:

Of this make no conclusion, lest you say
Your queen and I are devils. Yet go on;

---

[3] Twenty-three years in particular, which appears three separate times in the play—I.2.154; II.3.198; III.3.58.

Th' offenses we have made you do we'll answer,
If you first sinned with us, and that with us
You did continue fault, and that you slipped not
With any but with us (I.2.80–84).

It is in the very next line that Leontes asks whether Polixenes has been "won yet," which seems to suggest that in Leontes' mind a competition is ongoing between Hermione and himself and, of greater import, which further suggests he has not been listening to the dialogue between Hermione and Polixenes, but rather only standing off to the side and observing it—in which circumstance one wonders exactly what he sees or thinks he sees: that is, do we have here a matter of seeing or hearing or seeing and hearing?

Setting aside those concerns, though, and returning to Hermione's reply to Polixenes, we should record that there she uses pronouns a dozen times, which carries us to the matter of precisely how she is using them. For example, consider her earlier quoted comment that "By this we gather/You have tripped since" (I.2.73–74). "We" is typically a plural pronoun, but here it seems to be used in the singular sense—unless, that is, she is referring to herself and Polixenes' wife. But what about the "you": does this refer to Polixenes alone or to Leontes as well? Earlier she remarks, "Come, I'll question you/Of my lord's tricks and yours when you were boys" (I.2.59–60). "Yours" is incontestably singular, while it is surely the case that "you" in the first instance is singular and in the second is plural, referring to both Polixenes and Leontes. Shortly thereafter she states, "Of this make no conclusion, lest you say/Your queen and I are devils" (I.2.80–81). Here, "you" is certainly singular. Put more generally, Hermione shows she knows how to use "you" in the singular and in the plural, and knows how to use "we" and "us" in the plural and in the singular. Now, in lines 80–84 above, how is she using them? If the "us" is used in the plural to refer to Polixenes' wife and Hermione, the remark can be interpreted as perfectly innocent; if, however, we read it in the singular as making reference to Hermione and to Hermione alone, it is anything but—images of "sluicing," Sir Smile, and fishing in a neighbor's pond close at hand.[4] One of the several cruxes of the play involves the issue of the paternity of the daughter to whom Hermione will give birth in Act II. The threat against Polixenes' life, Hermione's trial, the departure of Camillo, the deaths of Mamillius, Antigonus, and his entire crew all turn on Leontes' burning jealousy and his contention that Polixenes has fathered the child to which Hermione is about to give birth. Polixenes had been in Sicilia for nine months; and in Act IV, Polixenes offers a defense of horticultural bastardry. This might make it appear that Shakespeare has tilted the paternity scale in the direction of Polixenes. That "Hermione" was the name of the daughter of Helen, wife of Menelaus,[5] and that the name "Polixenes" means, perhaps ironically, something like "very hospitable" inclines similarly. Nonetheless, Leontes' jealous fit seems unwarranted on the basis of practically everything leading up to it. Indeed, the scholarship on the play overwhelmingly insists that Leontes is the soon to be newborn's father—this as implied by the unreasonableness of his jealousy.[6] Hermione's pronoun use, which we have tracked, is, however, remarkably ambiguous as regards whether or not she has been involved in hanky-panky with Polixenes. That such a pivotal scene in the work should be crafted in a way that occludes its meaning and significance from view must be telling.

A turn, though, to Mamillius is in order, if only because he establishes the title of the play as well as the tone of its first three acts. Hermione addresses him in the beginning of Act II, asking "What wisdom stirs among you? Come, sir, now, / I am for you again. Pray sit you by us, / And tell's a tale" (II.1.20–22). Mamillius responds "A sad tale's best for winter"—indicating it is winter at that time in Sicilia—and that this tale will be about a man who "Dwelt by a churchyard—I will tell it softly, / Yon crickets shall not hear it"

---

[4] Cf. I.2,191ff.

[5] Cf. Homer, *Odyssey*, IV.1–14.

[6] Cf., for example, Stanley Cavell, "Recounting Gains, Showing Loses: Reading *The Winter's Tale*," in *Disowning Knowledge: In Six Plays of Shakespeare* (Cambridge: Cambridge University Press, 1987), 215; and S.L. Bethell, *The Winter's Tale: A Study* (London: Staples Press Limited, 1947), 87.

(II.1.25; 30–31). The crickets are typically glossed by the various editors of the play as Hermione's ladies-in-waiting. But given Mamillius' obvious familiarity with them, why would he not want them to hear this tale—why is it that Hermione is the only fit one to hear it?

Despite Mamillius' indisputable importance to the play, he has only twenty-two spoken lines (compared to, for example, twenty lines for Emilia, a minor character, and the 128 lines assigned to Perdita). Notably, every one of them is either a direct response to a question another character raises—either Leontes, a lady-in-waiting, or Hermione—or related to a question of his own. No one in the play is associated with questions more than he is. Only in the first two acts does he appear on stage and speak; however, after Leontes separates him from his mother in Act II, he is mute.

In the third scene of the second act we learn that Mamillius is ill, which Leontes takes to be the consequence of him having to bear noble witness to his mother's dishonor; then, in the third act, we will hear tell of Mamillius in the midst of Hermione's trial, a trial which Leontes believes will exonerate *himself* of the charge of "being tyrannous" (III.2.5), presumably the one repeatedly levied against him by Paulina, albeit other than juristically. Cleomenes and Dion have just returned from the Oracle at Delphos, and Leontes orders that the seal of the oracle be broken and that it be read: "'Hermione is chaste, Polixenes blameless, / Camillo a true subject, Leontes a jealous tyrant, / his innocent babe truly begotten, and the king shall / live without an heir if that which is lost be not / found'" (III.2.130–135).

Five lines and a mere twenty-two words later, Leontes dismisses oracle's prophecy as irrelevant to the case at hand: "There is not truth at all i'th' oracle. / The sessions shall proceed; this is mere falsehood" (III.2.137–138). His judgment alone shall reign; his judgement alone is sufficient to convict Hermione (and Polixenes and Camillo *in absentia*). Immediately after this dismissal, a servant enters to announce that Mamillius is "gone," which Leontes questions, "How? Gone?" Upon hearing the servant's deadly answer, Leontes casts blame upon himself: his son's death is Apollo's punishment for him elevating his own judgment above that of the oracle's.

When Leontes at first rejects the truth of the oracle, he could not at that moment have rejected it for being ambiguous: in fact, he takes it to be completely transparent. Indeed, of all of the significant aspects of *The Winter's Tale*, the oracle is one of clearest and most straightforward: this does not mean that every element of the oracle is true, or that any element is, but we know, or will soon know in the instance of Perdita, exactly what is being asserted. Nevertheless, what Leontes should have come to recognize about the oracle, but never did, is that the death of Mamillius is a precondition for the last plank of the oracle being true. What we, on the other hand, should recognize, though, is that the temporal framework in which the aforementioned events take place is simply incoherent. At the very moment that Leontes rejects the veracity of the oracle, Mamillius would already have been dead. That is, the order of events had to have been that Mamillius dies, the servant leaves the location where that took place, Leontes denounces the oracle, and the servant then arrives to inform Leontes of Mamillius' demise. What Leontes takes to be divine punishment is something other. He has replaced the temporal order in which the events actually took place with the temporal order in which certain events presented themselves to him, and to which he has affixed Apollo's vengeance.

Regardless, the announcement of Mamillius' death leads Hermione to faint, which is soon followed by Paulina's announcement of her death, which brings about Leontes' initial repentance. This, however, does nothing to ameliorate the situation for which he feels responsible: Hermione will be gone for sixteen years and Mamillius will be gone forever. His family is, by his lights, no more: "The causes of their death appear, unto / Our shame perpetual" (III.2.235–236).

As mentioned earlier, Leontes, in so revealing a way, conceives of the trial as being about his rule and his judgment—that is, as being about him: it is imperative for him to be right. Nevertheless, despite this conception, indeed perhaps because of it, Hermione faces two charges, adultery and treason, a private and a public wrong. Leontes sees each of these as a threat to his own legitimate rule and a threat to the legitimate rule of his progeny. This brings us back to Mamillius, beginning with his name. The name at first blush is related to the diminutive of the Latin for breast (*mamilla* and *mamma*), and thus points back to his mother. This also connects inversely to the shape of eggs as Leontes invokes them in Act I: "yet they say we are / Almost as like as eggs" (I.2.128–129). I would like to suggest, however, that Shakespeare's coinage might also derive from a Roman law enacted in 109 B.C.—*Lex Mamilia*. which was proposed by Gaius Mamilius. The law concerned, as did the special tribunal he led, corruption and treason which surfaced during the Jugurthine War (112–106 BC).[7] He also was named in laws having to do with boundary disputes—particularly questions having to do with the divide between public and private lands. Leontes' bitterness toward Hermione, his allegations about her infidelity and political treason, fit with the concerns of these Roman laws. This possibility also comports with Leontes' preoccupation with the "infection" or "disease" which he believes has come to plague Sicilia, a concern that dominates act one, scene two of the play.[8] In all of the various references, the infection or disease of the body politic turns out, upon even a rudimentary examination, to be the jealousy that has come to afflict Leontes.

One asks then, from what did the five or six-year old Mamillius die? Truly it is impossible to say. No one would suggest we simply take Leontes' word for it! Yet, it is not beyond the realm of possibility that he is at least partially correct, and Mamillius died from the grief of seeing his mother arrested and about to undergo trial (although he might have attributed the wrongdoing to Leontes); perhaps, for any number of reasons, he took his own life; perhaps his death points to the divisiveness of personal and political jealousies; or perhaps it is just not important to the play that we are able to identify the cause of his death. Connected to this indeterminacy, in the final act of the play we find Leontes penitent for bringing about Hermione's

---

[7] Cf. Sallust, *The Jugurthine War*, ch. 40.
[8] Cf. I.2.143; 204; 259–260; 301–303; 379–381; 393; 412; and 418.

apparent death: he mourns over her unceasingly. About Mamillius' death, however, following Leontes' pledge to visit the chapel where Hermione and Mamillius will lie together in the same grave (III.2.237), the play is entirely silent—or, as one says, crickets.

Mamillius' death, though, brings about the need for another to set the scene, a chorus, Time, who enters the play at the beginning of Act IV in order to depict the passage of time from the end of the third act until the second scene of the fourth. Time's speech consists thirty-two lines, in sixteen rhymed couplets, covering the sixteen years—"I slide / O'er sixteen years" (IV.1.5–6)—that pass from the conclusion of Act III to the start of Act IV.[9] These couplets give a sense of order, precision, and coherence, one of which reinforces the backdrop of these notions: "The same I am ere ancient'st order was, / Or what is now received" (IV.1.10–11). However, Time is also highlighting a divide between an ancient and what we might call a modern order.

Within the context of these orders, Time mentions three individuals—Leontes, Florizel, whose name we hear for the first time, and Perdita, whose name we hear for the second time, the first being in Antigonus's dream—which occurs the evening prior to being chased and eaten by a bear, which is the evening before he leaves the baby upon land—in which the already deceased Hermione, and Antigonus suspects this to be true, speaks to him about "the babe...[who] is counted lost forever, Perdita" (III.3.31–32). That the baby's name comes to him in a dream—Does he write the name down and leave it in the fardel for someone to discover?—is not the strangest thing about it. Much stranger still is that in the dream Hermione urges that "Places remote enough are in Bohemia; / There weep, and leave it crying" (III.3.30–31). But right after recounting the dream from the evening before he lays Perdita down on land, which means he was already upon the supposed coast of Bohemia.

---

[9] Only Autolycus' song later on in Act IV follows suit as a series of rhymed couplets, but that covers a shorter span, twelve lines in all, and lacks the breadth and seriousness of the poetry of Time.

Questions, Questions, Questions

Why go there in the first place? He told Leontes he would follow his order and leave the baby in "some remote and desert place" (II.3.175), but why Bohemia—especially since he had already pledged himself to Hermione's innocence? Antigonus's report of his dream makes it appear that it was Hermione's spirit that led him there; however, he would have had to have been there already! Neither temporally nor spatially do his actions make sense. Moreover, toward the end of his description of the dream he states of the baby that she is the issue of Polixenes—yet how did he arrive at that change of mind?

Act III stretches toward its end with Antigonus's death and the death of his crew in a storm—all in the aftermath, looking back to Sicilia, of Mamillius' death. However, the act ends not with death, but the life of "things newborn" (III.3.110), dressed in a "bearing-cloth" (III.3.111), that is, a baptismal gown. These elements underscore the peculiar *mélange* within the play of pagan elements—signaled by a litany of names of important ancient Greek (and Roman) figures,[10] as well as the role of Apollo in the play—and Christian ones—a churchyard, a chapel, repentance, a baptismal gown, and a nod in the direction of resurrection at the end of the play. Almost the entirety of the confluence of pagan and Christian elements occurs in Sicilia. Surprisingly enough, Christian elements do not figure in Act IV (in Bohemia); instead, the act draws upon literary allusions to Ovid's *Metamorphoses* and *Fasti*—in which instances of rape masquerade as pastoral beauty.[11]

The mixture of pagan and Christian elements in the play is instructive in its own right. But the pagan is pre-Christian, that is, the *time* before Christianity; thus, the religious divide has a temporal correlate to it. It is just this correlate that Time is referring to in the

---

[10] Archidamus, Camillo (the Italianate of the Roman Camillus), Cleomenes, and Dion, as well as Antigonus (which calls to mind Antigone), Leontes (which calls to mind the Leontini, who settled in Sicilia), Polixenes (connected to hospitality), Autolycus (as he appears in Ovid's *Metamorphoses*) and, of course, Mamillius. Paulina, the feminine form of Paul, also comes to mind here.

[11] Cf. IV.4.2; 27ff; and 116

earlier quoted lines about the ancient order—that is, the ancient world—and the one that is now received—that is, the modern world. But why should Shakespeare have incorporated these two dimensions into the same play, such that appeals can intelligibly be made to the agency of Apollo and that of Giulio Romano, a sixteenth-century Italian artist, in the very same act, and the final one at that—particularly in a manner that allows them to exist simultaneously and seemingly to function almost indistinguishably from each other? No wonder it is impossible to specify a dramatic date of the play!

But let us turn to that final act and to Hermione's return to the stage. The beginning of that act anticipates her return insofar as she is the object of conversation among Cleomenes, Dion, Leontes, and Paulina. There, the conversation centers upon whether Leontes should look to remarry, which Paulina firmly opposes. Within that context, Paulina raises the specter of the oracle's prophecy. Not only is no one as worthy as Hermione, whom Leontes freely admits to having wronged, but there also remains the matter of the "lost child" (V.1.40), on whom any succession depends. Paulina's suggestion seems to be that if Leontes remarries, he risks producing another heir, which would contravene what Leontes perceives as Apollo's command: whatever innocence he has recovered would thereby be lost.[12] It becomes clear from this exchange, that for sixteen years Leontes has been following Paulina's counsel. Why, then, is she so unyielding on the question of remarriage—especially since nowhere else in the play, her name notwithstanding, does she exhibit any inclination toward piety?

Of course, such steadfastness would make sense if Hermione were still alive, and if Paulina had, perhaps in concert with her, helped to keep her alive and hidden for sixteen years. But if she did so, why? Immediately after the news of Mamillius' death and following Hermione's collapse, Leontes is deeply sorrowful and repentant for his impiety against Apollo; he pledges to embrace Hermione and Polixenes once more. Given that, why does Paulina return only to

---

[12] Cf. I.2.68; and II.2.39.

announce that Hermione is dead? Does she not trust Leontes? Does she fear he will return to his old ways? Perhaps the death of Mamillius and the impending doom facing the child who was cast away weigh on her.

However, soon after Perdita is recognized through the several artifacts Antigonus had left with her, she learns that Paulina has a gallery of statues, including one of her mother, which has been "many years in doing" (V.2.94), which she desires to see. Leontes, Paulina, Florizel, Perdita, Camillo, and various Lords proceed to the gallery, and there Paulina draws open a curtain and shortly after what appears to be a stone statue begins to come alive, seemingly awakened by the music Paulina has ordered to be played. Once Hermione begins to "stir," Paulina admonishes those present,

> Start not; her actions shall be as holy as
> You hear my spell is lawful. Do not shun her
> Until you see her die again, for then
> You kill her double (V.3.104–107).

And still, as Paulina insists to the others, "It is required / You do awake your faith" (V.2.94–95), if the statue is to speak and move.

In all of this we find more than a fleeting reference directing us toward the idea of Christian resurrection: one who has died has come back to life. This understanding has already been anticipated through the idiom found in the beginning of Act V, where we find a profusion of Christian inflected terms: "a saint-like sorrow"; "redeemed"; "penitence"; "graced"; "holy"; "holier"; and "bless"—all in the span of thirty lines.[13] However, there is a parallel, pagan interpretation of the scene, perhaps even more becoming, found in Ovid's *Metamorphoses*—the tale of Pygmalion, a sculptor living celibately because of how corrupt and vile women are in his estimation. He carves a woman out of ivory, an ideal of sorts, which he then begins to caress and adore. He prays to the gods for help and Venus

---

[13] Cf. V.1.2ff.

responds, animating the statue, turning it into a living woman. She is no longer hard and cold, as was the case, upon Pygmalion's touch, but soft and warm—just like Hermione began to appear to Leontes.[14]

Strangely, Leontes questions nothing of what he has witnessed: his longed-for Hermione is with him again—albeit looking sixteen years older! Having questioned the gods once before, he does not now dare to question what Paulina has revealed behind the curtain. Hermione, however, upon hearing from Paulina at some point—surely prior to the curtain opening—that Perdita has been found, speaks—her only lines in Act V—reflecting on the circumstances before her:

> You gods look down,
> And from your sacred vials pour your graces
> Upon my daughter's head! Tell me, mine own,
> Where has thou been preserved, where lived, how found
> Thy father's court? For thou shalt hear, that I
> Knowing by Paulina that the oracle
> Gave hope thou wast in being, have preserved
> Myself to see the issue (V.3.121ff).

This sounds nothing like the idea of resurrection or the tale of Pygmalion. One might say that just as the elders in the first scene of the play were said by Camillo to be waiting for Mamillius to come of age before perishing from illness or old age, so Hermione "preserved herself" because of what she learned from Paulina—that the oracle "gave hope." A question to ask, though, is, what exactly is that hope? All the oracle had said is that Leontes would be without an heir unless that which is lost is found; indeed, Hermione had heard the prophecy read, to which she had responded "praisèd" (III.2.135). Perhaps, then, there will be no heir to the throne. What seems clear, however, is that, Hermione, by her own admission, has been hidden

---

[14] Cp. Ovid. *Metamorphoses*, X.281 to *The Winter's Tale*, V.3.35 and 66.

away, and Paulina has been implicated in this. Yet who has been directing this undertaking—Hermione or Paulina or both of them? Regardless, framing the matter this way provides an alternative account to Hermione's reappearance than the Christian or pagan one.

With Hermione's return, Leontes now can reclaim his wife; with the arrival of Perdita, Leontes now has an heir; with her arrival, Hermione has a daughter. Leontes announces at the end of the play that Camillo and Paulina shall wed, and that Perdita and Florizel are betrothed. At some point in the future, with the eventual passing of Leontes and Polixenes, it is likely that they will jointly rule both Sicilia and Bohemia. Whatever their ties at the start of the play, they are bound once more. What has been set aside, however, is the question as to who has fathered Perdita. If it was Leontes, all is in order; if it was Polixenes, then it is anything but, as the rulers would be step-brother and step-sister. That would also mean the end of Leontes' line, something from the outset of the play he has been eager, if not desperate, to continue on after his passing. And this gets at a fundamental problem of the play: how does one decide and guarantee political legitimacy in a regime where progeny matters so much?

In Act IV Camillo schemes to return to Sicilia. To do so, he implicates Florizel and Perdita in his plans. At no point prior to that or upon arrival in Sicilia does Florizel exhibit any qualities that would lead one to think that here is a dynamic and prudent political ruler in the making; in fact, he seems to have little interest in political affairs, his attention directed entirely to the affairs of the heart. It is at this juncture in the play that our thoughts go back to Mamillius. Perhaps the elders, Archidamus, and Camillo intuited something in him. To be sure, Hermione thought so. While at the beginning of Act II she finds him past enduring, she still quickly turns to him in pursuit of wisdom. Had he lived, it is likely he would have ruled Sicilia following Leontes; he would not have ruled Bohemia. What sort of ruler would he have been? He is associated with wisdom and the authority of age (or, if you will, antiquity, as implied by the elders embrace of him. Perhaps he represents a form of political wisdom that with his death is now lost to both Sicilia and Bohemia.

In any case, *The Winter's Tale* is a play in which the divine, represented by Apollo, and the cosmic, represented by Time, evince order and regularity. The human realm, on the contrary, including the political realm, is topsy-turvy—it is a cacophony of events, circumstances, and people: there is nothing symphonic about it. As a result, much in the human realm both looks like itself and like something else, making it difficult to judge what the itself is and what the something else is. The human things are a messy *mélange*, and someone who might be able to make sense of things and manage them is not to be found.

De profundis clamavi ad te, Domine

Pursuing Happiness in Shakespeare

Sujata Iyengar

Thomas Jefferson crucially turned to fiction, rather than to the classical tradition or to English sermons, as a source for ethical reflection. He writes, famously, that Shakespeare is more effective as a teacher of morality than moral philosophers in part because fiction combines this ethical reflection—an "exercise" or "practice" of moral reasoning—with the experience of enjoyment:

> The entertainments of fiction are useful as well as pleasant. That they are pleasant when well written, every person feels who reads…every thing is useful which contributes to fix us in the principles and practice of virtue…exercise produces habit; and in the instance of which we speak, the exercise being of the moral feelings, produces a habit of thinking and acting virtuously. We never reflect whether the story we read be truth or fiction. If the painting be lively, and a tolerable picture of nature, we are thrown into a reverie, from which if we awaken it is the fault of the writer.… We are therefore wisely framed to be as warmly interested for a fictitious as for a real personage. The spacious field of imagination is thus laid open to our use, and lessons may be formed to illustrate and carry home to the mind every moral rule of life. Thus a lively and lasting sense of filial duty is more effectually impressed on the mind of a son or daughter by reading King Lear, than by all the dry volumes of ethics and divinity that ever were written.[1]

Jefferson's imagined "son[s] or daughter[s]" find themselves "warmly interested" in an imaginary "practice of virtue," especially if

---

[1] Thomas Jefferson, "From Thomas Jefferson to Robert Skipwith [Shipwith], with a List of Books for a Private Library, 3 August 1771," *Founders Online*, National Archives, accessed February 6, 2025, https://founders.archives.gov/documents/Jefferson/01-01-02-0056.

they can envision themselves in similar situations. Jefferson's required reading thus includes not only those "dry volumes of ethics and divinity" such as "Locke on government" or "Hume's essays," but also racy fiction by contemporary novelists such as Henry Fielding or emotive dramas by Restoration tragedians such as Thomas Otway.[2] Jefferson's moral exemplar is Shakespeare's tragedy *King Lear*.[3]

So moving did eighteenth- and nineteenth-century Shakespeareans consider *King Lear* that the great lexicographer and Shakespearean Samuel Johnson found even reading the play too traumatic, writing in 1765: "I was many years ago so shocked by Cordelia's death, that I know not whether I ever endured to read

---

[2] John Locke (1632–1704), English philosopher, whose *Second Treatise on Government* (1689) proved particularly influential on later political theory; David Hume (1711–1776), Scottish philosopher and prolific author, whose *Essays and Treatises on Several Subjects* (1758) include well-known treatments of aesthetics, political theory, morality, law, and money; Henry Fielding (1707–1754), English novelist, author of the racy parody *Joseph Andrews* (1742) and the picaresque frolic *Tom Jones* (1749), among others; Thomas Otway (1652–1685), English tragedian little performed today but best-known for his *Venice Preserved* (1682).

[3] William Shakespeare, *King Lear* (1608 and 1623). *King Lear* retells the story of the legendary Ancient Briton King Leir. The aging and irascible monarch unreasonably demands of his three daughters to say which one loves him best (a motif familiar from world folklore as the "love-test") to decide which of them should receive the greater part of his kingdom upon his abdication in her favor. (The love-test, or "Love Like Salt," is classified as type 923 in the Aarne-Thompson-Uther folklore index; *King Lear* itself combines the opening of type 923 with the "Cinderella"-type tale, 510. See Hans-Jörg Uther, *The Types of International Folktales: A Classification and Bibliography, Based on the System of Antti Aarne and Stith Thompson* [Helsinki: Suomalainen Tiedeakatemia/Academia Scientiarum Fennica, 2004].) Lear/Leir banishes his youngest and best-loved child, Cordelia, when she refuses to utter the rank flatteries of her sisters, but the two elder women connive against their father, turning him out of doors during a storm and driving him to madness or senility. The all-forgiving Cordelia returns to rescue her father but reaches him too late to save either his life or her own. To underscore the themes of filial ingratitude and misplaced parental partiality, Shakespeare interweaves with Lear's sorrows the parallel plot of courtier Gloucester and his loyal but neglected son Edgar, both tricked by Edmund, Gloucester's charming but ill-intentioned bastard.

again the last scenes of the play till I undertook to revise them as an editor," and the Romantic writer Charles Lamb (who insisted that Shakespeare ought *only* to be read, never performed, the better to extract its moral and aesthetic lessons) claimed in 1811 that "the Lear of Shakespeare cannot be acted."[4] It is therefore unsurprising to see Jefferson assign to reading and "reverie" in particular a high value.

We might dismiss Jefferson's words as mere platitudes—literary critics from Horace to Sir Philip Sidney have, after all, likewise praised literature for hiding its moral content in superficial but pleasant details, as if fiction were a sugar-coated pill.[5] Yet as a reader and book recommender, Jefferson urges his correspondents to pay attention to "Criticism on the Fine Arts," including "Burke on the sublime and beautiful," and "Ld. Kaim's [Henry Home, Lord Kames'] elements of criticism."[6] Jefferson even carefully specifies of which edition of Shakespeare—Edward Capell's—he thinks best for a library.[7] Moral precepts are formed, suggests Jefferson's canon, through reading and reflecting upon the words of the best writers.

---

[4] Samuel Johnson, editor and commentator, *The Plays of William Shakespeare* (London, 1765), 6:159, repr. Michael Stapleton, *Historical Editions of Shakespeare*, https://shakedsetc.org, accessed February 6, 2025; Charles Lamb, "On the Tragedies of Shakespeare," *The Reflector* (1811), repr. *The Complete Works of Charles Lamb*, ed. R. H. Shepherd (London: Chatto & Windus, 1875), 261, repr. Google Books, accessed August 2, 2024.

[5] Quintus Horatius Flaccus, Roman poet, usually known as "Horace" in English letters, lived from 65 BCE-8 BCE; Sir Philip Sidney (1554–1586), Elizabethan statesman and poet, is best known for his sonnet-sequence *Astrophil and Stella* (1591) and his *Defense of Poesie* (1595).

[6] Edmund Burke, Anglo-Irish politician and philosopher (1729–1797) whose *Essay on the Sublime and the Beautiful* (1757) profoundly influenced Immanuel Kant and the later study of aesthetics; Henry Home, Lord Kames (1696–1782), Scottish jurist and philosopher, who published a popular treatise in 1762 called *Elements of Criticism*.

[7] Edward Capell (1713–1781), English Shakespearean, whom some scholars call the first modern Shakespearean editor because of his return to the earliest printed editions available to him for his ten-volume edition of the plays in 1767–68.

Jeffersonian "reverie" then seems to combine the state of mind that a present-day college instructor might call "immersive reading" and the activities such a teacher might call "reflective practice" and "dialogue" into Jefferson's recommendations: we are to lose ourselves in fiction and to apply its lessons to our own lives, morality, and social responsibilities, and to do so through the skilled exercise of the writer's craft and through reading or hearkening to what other writers and thinkers have had to say.[8] The skill of the fiction writer provokes the immersion, introspection, and "reverie" that ethical behavior requires.

Jefferson takes from Shakespeare and from drama, fiction, and the humanities the encouragement to enshrine a revolutionary and unprecedented goal for a new nation: the quality that the Greeks called *eudaimonia*, the Greek word for well-being, happiness, and self-determination, to be achieved through the quest for *arete* (excellence). The term *eudaimonia* is rarely used by the early moderns and never by Shakespeare, but prominent in present-day philosophical discussions of happiness. *Eudaimonia* or "the pursuit of happiness" is created through the active practice of virtue, including upright behavior, the joy of social communion, and a shared process—through dialogue—of coming to and committing to an ethics of society. Yet this distinctly American happiness includes not merely the stern moralism of seventeenth-century Protestant divines (who

---

[8] The adjective "immersive" has been used to describe an "engrossing" aesthetic experience since the 1960s; *Oxford English Dictionary*, s.v. "immersive (adj.), additional sense," *OED Online*, June 2024, accessed 31 July 2024, https://doi.org/10.1093/OED/9377978778, with references to "immersive reading" beginning in the 1980s and growing exponentially since the 2000s. The "hockey-stick" curve takes off in 2009, according to the Google Ngram Viewer, which searches word or phrase frequency within the Google Books archive, accessed 31 July 2024, https://books.google.com/ngrams/graph?content=immersive+reading&year_start=1800&year_end=2022&corpus=en&smoothing=3).
"Reflective practice," "reflection," or "reflective writing" as a pedagogical tool is most commonly associated with the experiential learning models of John Dewey in *How We Think* (Boston: DC Heath & Co, 1910). The dialogue form, of course, has been associated with pedagogy since antiquity.

typically used the phrase "pursuit of happiness" as a synonym for seeking divine salvation and eternal bliss, rather than terrestrial fulfilment), but rather and more expansively as the ethical impulse we find in Shakespeare's plays to seek *eudaimonia* through the knowledge of self and other and through a combination of spiritual joy, bodily pleasure, and excellence or skill.

In this essay, I will argue that one of Shakespeare's most joyful of comedies, *Much Ado About Nothing* (1598), epitomizes this pursuit of happiness.[9] I will begin by briefly contextualizing Jefferson's use of the phrase "the pursuit of happiness" and by summarizing some of the traditions that inform the word *happiness*. Then I argue that *Much Ado About Nothing* shows us how to pursue happiness by pursuing happiness for others, even when it seems as though that pursuit tends towards our own pain rather than our immediate gratification. I will conclude by mentioning briefly how Shakespeare pursued happiness; how Shakespeareans pursue happiness; and the role of the humanities in that pursuit.

Thomas Jefferson adapts in the Declaration of Independence—though there is some debate about this—John Locke's phrase "life, liberty, and estate," from *Two Treatises of Government* (1689).[10] As Gary Wills and others have suggested, Jefferson seems to replace "estate" with another a phrase taken from Locke, but this time from the *Essay Concerning Human Understanding* (also 1689): "the pursuit of happiness."[11] The *Jefferson Encyclopedia* suggests Jefferson may have also had in mind George Mason's Virginia Declaration of

---

[9] William Shakespeare, *Much Ado About Nothing*, ed. Barbara Mowat, Paul Werstine, Michael Poston, Rebecca Niles, *Folger Shakespeare Library Editions*, https://www.folger.edu/explore/shakespeares-works/much-ado-about-nothing/read/, accessed February 26, 2025. Future references to the play come from this text and will be cited parenthetically in-text by act, scene, and line number.

[10] John Locke, *Two Treatises of Government and a Letter Concerning Toleration*, ed. Ian Shapiro (Yale University Press, 2003), 125.

[11] Gary Wills, *Inventing America: Jefferson's Declaration of Independence* [1979] (repr. New York: Knopf, 2018); John Locke, *An Essay Concerning Human Understanding* [1689], ed. Roger Woolhouse (London: Penguin, 1997), 244–45.

Rights (1776), which uses the words "life" and "liberty," but which also separates the action of "acquiring and possessing property" and that of "pursuing and obtaining happiness."[12]

Wills concludes his chapter on the word "pursuit" with the aphorism: "Men in the eighteenth-century felt they could become conscious of their freedom only by discovering how they were bound: when they found what they *must* pursue, they knew they had a *right* to pursue it."[13] This kind of happiness seems to foreshadow what nineteenth- and twentieth-century psychologists called "self-actualization" and what Amartya Sen and Martha Nussbaum have in the twenty-first century called the "capabilities approach" to human development.[14] To quote Ingrid Robeyns's summary, "The capability approach purports that freedom to achieve well-being [we could also say "the pursuit of happiness"] is a matter of what people are able to do and to be, and thus the kind of life they are effectively able to lead."[15]

Wills suggests that Jefferson took both from Locke and from Henry Home, Lord Kames the belief that both individual happiness and life and liberty, when understood fully, mean an "equal pursuit for the happiness of all."[16] The persons included in Home's "all" are

---

[12] *Jefferson Encyclopedia*, https://www.monticello.org/research-education/thomas-jefferson-encyclopedia/pursuit-happiness/, accessed February 6, 2025; George Mason, "The Virginia Declaration of Rights (George Mason's Draft)," *Document Bank of Virginia*, University of Virginia Libraries, https://edu.lva.virginia.gov/dbva/items/show/184, accessed February 6, 2025.

[13] Gary Wills, *Inventing America: Jefferson's Declaration of Independence*, 1979 (repr. New York: Knopf, 2018), 247.

[14] Amartya Sen, *Development as Freedom* (Oxford: Oxford University Press, 2001); Martha Nussbuam, *Creating Capabilities: The Human Development Approach* (Cambridge, Mass.: Harvard University Press, 2011).

[15] Ingrid Robeyns and Morten Fibieger Byskov, "The Capability Approach," *Stanford Encyclopedia of Philosophy* (Summer 2023 Edition), eds. Edward N. Zalta & Uri Nodelman, https://plato.stanford.edu/archives/sum2023/entries/capability-approach/, accessed August 2, 2024.

[16] Henry Home, Lord Kames, "Of the Principles of Action," *Essays on the Principles of Morality and Natural Religion* (Edinburgh, 1751), 76–91, 78, in

worth considering. Notably, despite his belief in the divine scattering of the earth's peoples after the Tower of Babel and in the subsequent creation of distinct human races or species (a kind of polygenesis), Home seems to have imagined such separate races to be on similar tracks towards contented societies and personal fulfilment, "refus[ing] to rank races" and even—unusually for his time—firmly attributing perceived "inferiority" between races as a sign of "condition" (environment) rather than of innate disability or deficit.[17] Home's notion of happiness, then, extends to all peoples of the world, despite his belief in human speciation. Jefferson, in contrast, remained "diffiden[t]" about the question, and in the draft of the Declaration that became canon removed his initial strictures against the slave trade and his hopes that science would find a "common origin" for human beings (monogenesis) that would prove no one group inferior to another.[18]

Today, as our sense of who belongs in America and who is an American is necessarily more inclusive, we can agree with America's founders that such happiness—*eudaimonia*, self-actualization—is necessarily utopian and, moreover, unobtainable for and by a single individual. Thus we have the right to pursue happiness, but not, as in Mason's Virginia declaration, both to pursue and to obtain it. Such a concession can even imply—as I will later contend—that happiness may be found in the pursuit of happiness for others.

The words *happiness, joy, pleasure, felicity, enjoyment,* and so on had a variety of meanings in Shakespeare's England, and the word "happiness" meant predominantly good fortune or good hap, as

---

Eighteenth Century Collections Online, University of Michigan Library Digital Collections, https://name.umdl.umich.edu/004843595.0001.000, accessed August 2, 2024.

[17] Geoffrey Galt Harpham, *Theories of Race, 1750–1900,* https://www.theoriesofrace.com/, accessed August 2, 2024.

[18] Geoffrey Galt Harpham, *Theories of Race, 1750–1900,* https://www.theoriesofrace.com/, accessed August 2, 2024.

Kevin Laam has argued.[19] Such happiness could happen only by *happenstance*, by God's will. "Felicity" connoted divine bliss or redemption, as in the phrase *felix culpa* or happy Fall, used to describe the Fall of Man in Genesis that, under this argument, directly led to the Birth of Christ and the Resurrection. True felicity could only be enjoyed in heaven, but earthly beings could and did experience "joy" on earth, not only through contemplating the heavenly future but also by en*joy*ing the blessings of heaven on earth. *Eudaimonia*—the happiness contemplated by virtue ethicists—lay in what Boethius (brought to English readers via Chaucer and frequently read and translated by able Latinists, including Queen Elizabeth I) called "the consolation of philosophy," a resignation or equanimity towards the haps and happenings in one's life, whether through a pagan (Stoic) devotion to virtue (justice, temperance, bravery, wisdom, and following one's own true nature) or through devotion to Christ and the afterlife.[20]

If you were a low-church Protestant, such as the Danish radical preacher Niels Hemmingsen, you might believe in another way to achieve earthly happiness. Hemmingsen's *The Faith of the Church*

---

[19] Kevin Laam, "Shakespeare and Happiness," Literature Compass, 7: 439–451 (2010), accessed August 2. 2024, https://doi.org/10.1111/j.1741-4113.2010.00711.x. See also Richard Chamberlain, "What's happiness in *Hamlet*?," in *The Renaissance of Emotion*, ed. Richard Meek and Erin Sullivan (Manchester: Manchester University Press, 2015), 153–74; Neema Parvini, "Shakespeare's Moral Compass," in *Shakespeare and Virtue Ethics*, ed. Julia Reinhard Lupton and Donovan Sherman (Cambridge: Cambridge University Press, 2023), 98–109, and Katarzyna Lecky's essay in that collection, op. cit; and *Positive Emotions in Early Modern Literature and Culture*, ed. Cora Fox, Bradley Irish, and Cassie M. Miura (Manchester: Manchester University Press, 2021).

[20] Geoffrey Chaucer, *Chaucer's translation of Boethius's "De consolatione philosphiæ,"* ed. Richard Morris (London: Early English Texts Society, 1868), in *Corpus of Middle English Prose and Verse,* University of Michigan Library Digital Collections, https://name.umdl.umich.edu/ChaucerBo, accessed August 2, 2024; Queen Elizabeth I, "Elizabeth's translation of the Consolation of Philosophy" (1593), SP 12/289 f.48, *The National Archives* (UK), https://www.nationalarchives.gov.uk/education/resources/elizabeth-monarchy/elizabeths-translation-of-the-consolation-of-philosophy/, accessed August 2, 2024.

Militant (1581), translated by Thomas Rogers, appears to be the first appearance of the word *eudaimonia* in English.[21] From Hemmingsen's Calvinist perspective the pursuit of happiness is the commitment to an ethical mode of living or a "right way of life," whether or not one achieves it, mainly because the seeker's ultimate goal is salvation ("in respect of the event"). At the same time he acknowledges that such a "right way" involves more than faith, although for some him faith must form part of it. He first defines "Blessednes, which thing man through the instinct of nature desireth…called of the Philosophers with one consent *eudaimonia*, & of diuines somtime felicitie, and somtime blessedness" as human beings' true purpose, "the true felicitie of man: for which he was both at the first created, and afterward redeemed."[22] Next he redefines this Blessedness as happiness, understood not only as a present good but as setting yourself on a course towards future fortune:

> he rightlie and trulie maie be caled happie, who is not onelie without al sense of trouble, and sorrowe, and dreadeth none euil to come, but also which doth so abounde with store of al good thinges, that he can desire no more, being sure perpetuallie to possesse the good thinges wherewith he doth abounde. This is the definition of absolute and perfecte happinesse: nowe whoso bindeth himselfe with a right course to atteine the same, is called happie, in respecte of the euent.[23]

Hemmingsen subordinates multiple concepts of happiness—peace of mind or freedom from "all sense of trouble," prosperity in a

---

[21] Niels Hemmingsen [Nicholas Hemmingius], *The Faith of the Church Militant*, trans. Thomas Rogers (London, 1581), repr. *Early English Books Online, Proquest*, accessed August 2, 2024.

[22] Ibid, sig. Z7v. In keeping with standard scholarly practice in early British studies, I cite books published before 1700 by signature or folio, which allows researchers to identify the location of a quotation more accurately than page number, since pagination is so frequently incorrect in this era. Scholars using digital resources or text may prefer to look up quotations by "search string" or a sequence of words.

[23] Ibid., sigs. Z7r-v.

"store of good things," pleasure in one's accumulated wealth, and enough satisfaction in one's possessions to "desire no more"—to the pursuit of the "right course," virtue.

So far (although my search has not been exhaustive) I have not found the phrase "the pursuit of happiness" elsewhere in English any earlier than 1657. The bulk of these seventeenth-century texts are sermons that identify "the pursuit of happiness" as the quest for divine salvation. Intriguingly, a now-lost manuscript by the Republican poet George Wither, presumed destroyed during the English Civil War, took the phrase for its title, according to an advertisement from 1660 that describes *The Pursuit of Happiness* as "*a character of the extravagancy of the Authors Affections and Passions in his youth.*"[24] The manuscript is described as a product of "his riper years," which suggests that happiness here connotes the absence of "extravagancy" and passion, taking us closer to Stoic or Boethian equanimity.[25] Playwright Thomas Killigrew has his warrior woman Cicilia lament of her lover Lucius in Act 3, scene 3, line 2 of *The Second Part of Cicilia & Clorinda, Or, Love in Arms* (1664) that "his jealousie has so humbled my heart, so discouraged me in the pursuit of happiness, that my soul is grown desperate."[26] Here Cicilia's happiness is simultaneously good fortune, the satisfaction of her desires, and contentment or peace, all shattered by Lucius's distrust. The poem "The Cure," by Shakespeare's adaptor Nahum Tate (1676), distinguishes between "the pursuit of happiness" through love that befuddles the lovesick shepherd Corydon and the "virtue" prescribed to Corydon by his wise elder Claius.[27]

As we approach the turn of the eighteenth century, Edward Stillingfleet preaches a sermon at Whitehall before Queen Mary in

---

[24] George Wither, *Fides Anglicana* (London, 1660), repr. *Early English Books Online*, *Proquest*, accessed August 2, 2024, *ProQuest*, sig. M3r.

[25] Ibid., sig. M3r.

[26] Thomas Killigrew, *Comedies and Tragedies*, London, 1664, repr. *Early English Books Online*, *Proquest*, accessed August 2, 2024, sig. 3N3r.

[27] Nahum Tate, *Poems* (London, 1677), repr. *Early English Books Online*, *Proquest*, accessed August 2, 2024, sig. I8v.

which he admits that Christian divines could learn from the "ancient philosophers" some principles that he distills.[28] In this he follows the Christianized understanding of happiness that coexisted in the Renaissance with the strong tradition of virtue ethics derived from Aristotle and other non-Christian thinkers. The classical virtues admired by the early moderns and—as Jeffrey Rosen argues—by the Founding Fathers included justice, temperance, bravery, generosity, wisdom, industriousness and self-discipline.[29] We might more accurately then define *eudaimonia* as the experience of living life fully and ethically, "the felt experience of the everyday practice of virtue," in Katarzyna Lecky's helpful phrase.[30]

In imagining the "pursuit of happiness," then, Jefferson drew upon not only Christian tradition but also those "ancient philosophers" and, I suggest, from a Shakespearean world. This Shakespearean world attempts (as Lecky has argued) to reconcile or at least to dramatize the tension between the pursuit of happiness as pleasure and the quest for well-being through a virtuously lived life. *Much Ado About Nothing* exemplifies these tensions among competing pursuits of happiness.

Set in a honeyed interlude after the conclusion of a successful war, during the duration of a wedding party, *Much Ado About Nothing* dramatizes both the frivolous and fun pursuits of an aristocratic, worldly household—dressing up, playing pranks, feasting, masquerading, making music—and the more serious question of what comprises virtue in men and women. The technical main plot concerns the slander of the beautiful heiress Hero, falsely framed by Don John, the disgruntled illegitimate brother of the Prince Don Pedro.

---

[28] Edward Stillingfleet, *A Sermon Preached before the Queen at White-Hall, February 22d, 1688/9 by Edward Stillingfleet* (London, 1689), repr. *Early English Books Online, Proquest*, accessed August 2, 2024, sigs C3v-Cr.

[29] Jeffrey Rosen, *The Pursuit of Happiness* (New York: Simon and Schuster, 2024).

[30] Katarzyna Lecky, "Eudaimonia (Happiness)," in *Shakespeare and Virtue: A Handbook*, ed. Julia Reinhard Lupton and Donovan Sherman (Cambridge: Cambridge University Press, 2023), 44–52, 44.

Thanks to Don John's machinations, Don Pedro, Hero's fiancé Claudio, and her own father, Leonato are convinced that Hero has slept with another man the night before her wedding and humiliate her at the altar. Defended only by her cousin Beatrice, Claudio's friend Benedick, and the Friar who officiates at the abortive ceremony, Hero feigns death until a bungling police constable, Dogberry, and his staff somehow uncover Don John's mischief and clear her name. The more popular sub-plot presents the sparring erstwhile lovers Benedick and Beatrice and their friends' successful scheme to make them fall in love (again?) with each other through a pair of matched eavesdropping scenes that trick Beatrice into believing Benedick is in love with her and Benedick into believing that Beatrice is in love with him. Sub-plot and main plot collide with Beatrice's challenge to Benedick to "Kill Claudio"—to defend the honor of her falsely accused cousin against his friend Claudio—immediately after Beatrice and Benedick have vowed their love for one another.

All the forms of happiness I have discussed appear in the play: fortune, blessedness, joy or delight, pleasure, and the quest for virtue. Often these forms are mingled. We hear characters wish Hero and Claudio joy on their upcoming wedding with the words "God give you"—or "them"—or "me"—"joy," which acknowledges both the role of blessedness or good fortune and the fragility of joy (2.1.290, 327; 3.4.24). Claudio's uncle reportedly weeps for joy at the news of his nephew's valor, upon which Leonato, Hero's father, exclaims, "How much better is it to weep at joy than to joy at weeping!" (1.1.126), a statement that prefigures the hard-won happy ending of the play and the unresolved pleasure that Don John admits taking in others' pain. Don Pedro's response to Leonato's joke about Hero's parentage, "Be happy, lady" (1.1.107) sets up the play's pattern—from this very first scene to the wedding scene to Claudio's jokes to Benedick about cuckoldry in the final denouement—of calumniated women.

Claudio's own expressions of joy are transactional or conditional. Believing mistakenly that Don Pedro has stolen his love for himself, he mouths bitterly, "I wish him joy of her" (2.1.191). Reconciled (at least for the time being), he comments on his own taciturnity: "Silence is the perfectest herald of joy. I were but little happy if I could say how much.—Lady, as you are mine, I am yours. I give away myself for you and dote upon the exchange" (2.1.300–303). Note the transactional language towards the end of the speech: *as you are mine*, I am yours…I dote upon *the exchange*. Hero's father—as we learn in the abortive wedding scene—dotes under similar conditions: "Bring me a father that so loved his child, / Whose joy of her is overwhelmed like mine, /And bid him speak of patience" (5.1.9–11). Find me an equal, he cries, someone against whom to measure myself. Only then, in comparison to a peer, can he grieve—or love.

We can track the changing relationship of Beatrice and Benedick through their understanding of happiness. At the opening of the play Beatrice bitterly comments that it is a "a great happiness to women" (using the word in its sense of "good fortune") that Benedick swears he loves no one, since women are therefore spared "a pernicious suitor" (1.1.126). She adds for good measure that she is as opposed to marriage as is Benedick. Claudio takes Benedick at his word and throws in a joke about cuckoldry to boot: Benedick's marriage could only take place as a stroke of good or ill fortune; it would "*hap*pen," and if it did, he would be "horn-mad" (1.1.263)—frenziedly jealous to be wearing the legendary "cuckold's horns." During the first eavesdropping scene, Don Pedro comments on Benedick's appearance of good fortune, his "outward happiness" (2.3.188). And after the scene we see Benedick offer us a new sense of the word *happy*: "Happy are they that hear their detractions and can put them to mending" (2.3.231–3). Those who can hear their moral failings outlined and begin to ameliorate them are happy in the sense of fortunate but also in the sense of virtuous. Benedick resolves to change, to follow a new course.

Benedick's new course leads him to transfer his unthinking loyalty from the world of men who assume women's fallibility—and to value women accordingly—to the world of Beatrice and the women who demand justice for slander. Benedick ends the play with another tired joke about cuckoldry, but this time the laugh is on the prince: "Prince, thou art sad. Get thee a wife…there is no staff more reverend than one tipped with horn" (5.4.126–8). The demand for an absolute guarantee of fidelity and the assumption that circumstantial evidence can prove either faithfulness or its opposite leads to tragedy in Shakespeare's later treatment of this theme, *Othello*. Benedick realizes that mistrust is the thief of happiness. In the words of a social media hashtag, popularized during the #MeToo movement against sexual violence and harassment: #BelieveWomen.[31] Beatrice must also learn to trust Benedick after his earlier betrayal, which we learn happened some time before the play begins:

> PRINCE: Come, lady, come, you have lost the heart of Signior Benedick.
>
> BEATRICE: Indeed, my lord, he lent it me awhile, and I gave him use for it, a double heart for his single one. Marry, once before he won it of me with false dice. Therefore your Grace may well say I have lost it. (2.1.271–6).

Their learning is mutual, although we may feel that Beatrice's cause for distrust is greater.

The play includes other characters who pursue happiness in multiple senses. Dogberry, the bumbling, malapropism-prone constable, pursues happiness as virtue, doing his duty doggedly. While he's far from achieving excellence or *arete*, he is successful in bringing the culprits to light and exonerating the slandered Hero. In some productions he has a kind of dignity, making us think that his shoddy work is compassionate policing rather than careless ineptitude: "Truly, I would not hang a dog by my will, much more [he means

---

[31] The phrase "Believe Women" with regard to sexual assault victims is most closely associated with the journalists Jessica Valenti and Jaclyn Friedman and their pioneering essay collection *Believe Me: How Trusting Women Can Change the World* (New York: Seal Press, 2020), but it began to appear in conference proceedings and law review articles some years earlier; see Dan Subotnik, "Why not Believe Women?," *Touro Law Review* 34, no. 4 (2018), 995–1024.

"much less"] a man who hath any honesty in him" (3.3.62).

More troublesome in his pursuit of happiness is the dastardly bastard, Don John. Self-actualization for him means actively creating mischief. When asked why he is "out of measure sad" (1.3.1), he responds by defining happiness or at least self-fulfillment as villainy:

> I had rather be a canker in a hedge than a rose in his grace, and it better fits my blood to be disdained of all than to fashion a carriage to rob love from any. In this, though I cannot be said to be a flattering honest man, it must not be denied but I am a plain-dealing villain. I am trusted with a muzzle and enfranchised with a clog; therefore I have decreed not to sing in my cage. If I had my mouth, I would bite; if I had my liberty, I would do my liking. In the meantime, let me be that I am, and seek not to alter me. (1.3.25–35).

It is hard to feel sympathy towards Don John, but it is very Shakespearean to find the pressure points of early modern morality. In Don John and Shakespeare's other bastards—most expressively through Edmund in *King Lear*—Shakespeare exposes the early modern double standard that excuses profligacy in men but excoriates it in women, and he points out the human and material cost to the children of these extra-marital unions. In *Much Ado* and his later plays about male jealousy Shakespeare also introduces the tensions of self-actualization: Don John's self-proclaimed right to flourishing tramples on everyone else's. The demands of Othello, Leontes, and Posthumus (in *Othello*, *The Winter's Tale*, and *Cymbeline* respectively) for security kill or threaten to kill their wives.

But beyond morality or usefulness, Shakespeare—and the humanities writ large—provide a means to both joy and *eudaimonia*. Shakespeare himself sought happiness through the acquisition of property, wealth, and status; through family ties; and through creative expression in both drama written for profit and poetry written (at least at first) privately, like the rhymes that Beatrice and Benedick confess to having secretly written to and about each other. *Much Ado About Nothing* is about trifles and nothing, "paper bullets of the brain" (2.3.243). Such trifles, too, are part of the pursuit of happiness, the part that mellows or humanizes those "dry volumes of ethics and divinity" and that considers test cases, limits, and solutions. There is no *need* for happiness and no guarantee that one will find it. To enshrine "the pursuit of happiness" as a founding principle for a republic is unreasonable and magnificent. Yet in Jefferson's moral exemplar, *King Lear*, Shakespeare identifies this quest for the magnificent, the unnecessary, the beautiful, the more-than-functional, as what makes us distinctively human:

> O, reason not the need! Our basest beggars
> Are in the poorest thing superfluous.
> Allow not nature more than nature needs,
> Man's life is cheap as beast's (2.4.304–307).[32]

According to *The Declaration of Independence*, to pursue happiness is to pursue the unreasonable, magnificent dream of America.

---

[32] William Shakespeare, *King Lear*, edited by Barbara Mowat, Paul Werstine, Michael Poston, Rebecca Niles, Folger Shakespeare Library, accessed 2 Aug. 2024, https://www.folger.edu/explore/shakespeares-works/king-lear/read/.

Transcendent Ambition: Machiavelli and Shakespeare on Coriolanus and Julius Caesar

Vickie Sullivan

William Shakespeare's drama presents a wide variety of the human experience. He stages, for example, events surrounding the Trojan War in Asia Minor—in what was during his time the Ottoman Empire. The dramatist also presents ancient Athens during the lifetime of its first founder, the mythological Theseus; that same Athens centuries later during the time of the Peloponnesian War; ancient Rome, which is both pagan and republican; Egypt just as it, as well as the remainder of Rome's vast conquests, was about to fall under the rule of the Roman emperors; England under kingship before the advent of Christianity; the Christian monarchies of Britain and Scotland during medieval times; and the republics of Northern Italy in which commerce is flourishing. Across the various ages they inhabit, his characters live vastly different lives guided by vastly different moralities and aspirations. The playwright stages a wide swath of the range of human alternatives—social, political, and religious.

In so presenting this range of human options, Shakespeare, himself a subject in a Christian monarchy, shows a particular fascination with pagan Rome—particularly the republic. Our poet penned four Roman works—one poem and three plays—dealing with the founding, the political transformations, and the decline of the Roman republic: *The Rape of Lucrece*, *Coriolanus*, *Julius Caesar*, and *Antony and Cleopatra*. Shakespeare's Roman works, therefore, present the founding, the decline, and fall of the Roman republic.[1]

---

[1] This essay is deeply indebted to more extensive treatments of Shakespeare's Roman works, see Jan H. Blits, *The End of the Ancient Republic: Shakespeare's 'Julius*

Examination of Shakespeare's Roman plays reveals that the playwright engages in a deep analysis of ambition. The plays reveal that ambition fueled Rome's outstanding soldiers to remarkable accomplishments in service to the republic; they also reveal that the great men's ambition brought them into conflict with the republic as they strained for supremacy. Ultimately, the republic succumbed to the transcendent ambition of Julius Caesar. Thus, Shakespeare's Roman plays stage an enduring problem of politics—how ambition threatens a republic internally.

So enduring a political problem is ambition for a republic that a young Abraham Lincoln offered a monitory history to his young nation:

> Many great and good men sufficiently qualified for any task they should undertake, may ever be found, whose ambition would inspire to nothing beyond a seat in Congress, a gubernatorial or a presidential chair; *but such belong not to the family of the lion, or the tribe of the eagle.* What! think you these places would satisfy an Alexander, a Caesar, or a Napoleon?—Never! Towering genius distains a beaten path.... Is it unreasonable then to expect, that some man possessed of the loftiest genius, coupled with ambition sufficient to push it to its utmost stretch, will at some time, spring up among us?[2]

For Lincoln, ambition is a pernicious internal threat—a threat that emanates from the passions of individuals of outstanding talents—that republics must confront and contain if they are to endure. It was, in fact, this internal threat that caused the downfall of the

---

Caesar" (Lanham, Md.: Rowman & Littlefield, 1993); Paul A. Cantor, *Shakespeare's Rome: Republic and Empire* (Ithaca: Cornell University Press, 1976); Paul A Cantor, *Shakespeare's Roman Trilogy: The Twilight of the Ancient World* (Chicago University Press, 2017); and Michael Platt, *Rome and Romans according to Shakespeare* (Lanham, MD: University Press of America, 1983).

[2] Abraham Lincoln, "Address to Young Men's Lyceum of Springfield, Illinois: The Perpetuation of Our Political Institutions," January 27, 1838, in *Lincoln: Speeches and Writings 1831–1858* ed. Roy P. Basler (New York: Library of America, 1989), 34–5.

Roman republic as Julius Caesar ascended to sole rule, whom Lincoln here adduces.

Our poet, however, engages in an even deeper analysis of ambition in his Roman plays—an analysis that marries the political with the religious. His plays reveal an awareness that less than a mere half century after the death of Julius Caesar, Christ would be born in an Eastern province of the Roman Empire—a territory Rome had conquered when it was still a republic. The birth of this new religion in the lands that pagan Rome had conquered would have far-reaching consequences for Europe. It was a monumental transformation. Montesquieu, a thinker of great acuity, wrote in his private notebook that from the perspective of the "things of the world" the ascendency of Christianity had to "be the strangest event of its kind that has ever occurred." What amazes Montesquieu is that the new religion is "received by those philosophers who were abandoning Paganism because of its extravagance."[3] Then, of course, there is the remarkable fact that the Romans, rapacious conquerors, adopted the new religion that lauded meekness and decried war. Rome went from the center of an earthly empire to the seat of a spiritual one. Augustine and Friedrich Nietzsche, of course, are also observers of this transition, although from quite different perspectives.

Shakespeare too observes Rome's role in this monumental transition through his treatment of transcendent ambition in the plays *Coriolanus* and *Julius Caesar*. His play *Coriolanus* follows an extraordinary warrior of the newly founded republic, whose first battle, in fact, is against the followers of the expelled king who wish to bring kingship back to the city. He earns the honorific name Coriolanus after he conquers the enemy city of Corioles. He is remarkable not only for his military prowess but also for his extreme contempt for the people. On Shakespeare's rendering, Coriolanus's ambition is so extreme that he seeks a preeminence that would give him a god-like status. Failing to understand his own desire and how he might satisfy

---

[3] Montesquieu, *My Thoughts*, trans. Henry C. Clark (Indianapolis: Liberty Fund, 2012, *pensée* 969, 273).

it within the constraints of his human nature, Coriolanus is ruined, ultimately repudiated both by his native city and the one to which he defects.

Whereas Shakespeare's Coriolanus cannot satisfy his transcendent ambition, his Julius Caesar does. His play *Julius Caesar* depicts "a man who became a god."[4] The play begins after the titular character has subverted the republic, ruling over his former compatriots by his singular will, and ends with the martyred Caesar adored by the people. His former compatriots, cast from power, believe that they can restore the republic by assassinating Caesar, but their plan fails in the extreme. They kill the body but cannot extinguish the spirit of the martyred Caesar. Historically, Caesar was worshipped in life as well as in death; his successors, the Roman emperors, ruled in his name and some attained his divine status.[5] In Shakespeare's depiction, Julius Caesar bears many Christ-like features. Indeed, Shakespeare endows his play *Julius Caesar* with references redolent of the birth of Christ, the coming of Christianity, and its later liturgical practices.

Thus, Shakespeare reveals himself to be concerned not only with how leaders of overweening ambition threaten republican rule but also with the movement of history in Europe, Northern Africa, and the Near East—that is, in the territory that would later be called Christendom. His Coriolanus and Julius Caesar strive to transcend not only a political regime but also human limits to the extent possible. Shakespeare stages how that ambition came to dominate Rome, and prefigured the ascendancy of Christ's empire in the lands that would ultimately become the former Roman empire and the new empire of Christ, a divine being who ruled after his martyred death and possessed successors who ruled in his name.

---

[4] Allan Bloom, "Morality of the Pagan Hero," in *Shakespeare's Politics* (New York: Basic Books, 1964), 75; cf. Blits, *End of the Ancient Republic*, 65 and n.8.

[5] Aleš Chalupa, "How Did Roman Emperors Become Gods? Various Concepts of Imperial Apotheosis" *Anodos: Studies of the Ancient World* (2006–2007): 201–207.

Shakespeare's staging of this transition from Paganism to Christianity and its invocation of extreme ambition that desires to surpass the ordinary limits of human life is reminiscent of the analysis of Niccolò Machiavelli, a famous—notorious even—political thinker who lived from 1469–1527. In the *Discourses on Livy*, Machiavelli presents a long line of ambitious men in the ancient Roman republic who desired to rule alone—to be preeminent. He shows how, over the course of centuries, they learned that the way to preeminence was through the adoration of the people; he shows how they become ever more clever and more insidious in attaining that adoration. Machiavelli infuses his depiction of some of Rome's ambitious men with terms redolent of the way a man became a god in Roman territory—not just Caesar but also Jesus Christ. Machiavelli suggests that the most extreme form of political ambition is the desire to rule as a god on earth. Machiavelli's treatment of republican Rome illustrates that transcendent ambition ultimately eventuated in the rule of Christianity.

In depicting the overweening ambition of some of Rome's great men, Shakespeare's presentation of Rome shares important similarities with the analysis of Machiavelli in the *Discourses*. They both broach these deep political and religious issues that fundamentally transformed the lands in which Rome conquered.[6] Although we do

---

[6] Bloom touches on Shakespeare's Coriolanus's and Caesar's desires to be god-like (e.g., "Morality of the Pagan Hero," 85 and 87). Blits offers a penetrating analysis of *Julius Caesar* in which he shows "what at first glance appear dull failures in Caesar's attempt to become a king are in fact disguised successes in his attempt to become a god" (*End of Ancient Republic*, 65). Cantor examines the question of how mighty Rome succumbed to the weak Christians at length in *Shakespeare's Roman Trilogy*, pursuing in particular the question of whether Rome itself sowed the seeds of its decline in the assessments of Nietzsche and Shakespeare. Cantor explores Shakespeare's depiction of "the tyrannical desire of the Roman heroes" as a "will to apotheosis" (*Shakespeare's Roman Trilogy* 169, 163–81). Neither Blits nor Cantor links Shakespeare's treatment of Rome's heroes to Machiavelli's treatment of their extreme ambition. As Cantor, however, suggests that Machiavelli may have been a key source for Shakespeare's understanding of the meaning of Christianity

not know if Shakespeare read any of Machiavelli's works, we do know that the playwright knew of his predecessor's existence and of his reputation. Shakespeare names Machiavelli twice in his corpus: once associating him with fraud when, in *The Merry Wives of Windsor*, the Host asks "Am I politic? am I subtle? am I a Machiavel?" (3.1.99–100) and the other with force when the future Richard III boasts that he can "set the murderous Machiavel to school" (*Henry VI*, 3. 2.195). Shakespeare evinces an interest in Machiavelli's thought.

Shakespeare's interest in Machiavelli's thought includes a shared recognition of the importance of the transcendent ambition of Rome's great men in driving the transformation of pagan Rome into Christian Rome. For both the political thinker and the playwright the martyrdom and apotheosis of Caesar and that of Christ share important similarities, and both underscore that the path to apotheosis is through the appeal to the people.

Shakespeare's Depiction of Coriolanus

The Roman republic was a martial regime, and the historical character of Coriolanus stands as the exemplar of its warrior ideal. A young man when Rome expelled King Tarquin and his followers, Coriolanus first serves as a soldier on Rome's behalf against the forces of Tarquin who wish to subdue the new republic in order to return Tarquin to the kingship. As a member of the patrician class, Coriolanus is extremely contemptuous of the plebeians, who do not fight with the vigor he does. Rather than embracing the martial virtues, they care about material things—the plunder of war—more than valor and are in fear of their lives. Indeed, as a fighter, Coriolanus surpasses even those of his own class. He reminds a contemporary reader of Nietzsche's beast of prey—an exemplar of master

---

for pagan Rome (70 and 155), this essay can be said to complement Cantor's outstanding work.

Transcendent Ambition

morality.⁷ What Shakespeare distinctly emphasizes in his depiction of Coriolanus is his character's desire to be singularly preeminent. In Shakespeare's hands, unlike Shakespeare's historical sources, the character seeks a god-like status.

Shakespeare alerts his audience to their entry into a world very different from their Christian milieu when in the first act the mother of Coriolanus dismisses the notion that she might fear for the welfare of her son in battle and instead relishes that very prospect:

> The breasts of Hecuba,
> When she did suckle Hector, looked not lovelier
> Than Hector's forehead when it spit forth blood
> At Grecian sword, contemning.⁸ (*Coriolanus* 1.3.38–41)

Not only does Coriolanus's mother here pay homage to the mythic Trojan origins of the Romans, but she offers a tableau glorifying the gore of war, inverting the serene image of the mother with child so familiar to Christians.

In depicting the battle in which the fighter earns his honorific, Shakespeare highlights his exceptional status. The fact that Coriolanus achieves this feat alone is so important that Shakespeare has several characters proclaim the fact: a soldier warns: "Clapped to their gates; he is himself alone, / To answer all the city" (*Coriolanus* 1.4.51–2); his commanding officer recounts: "Alone he entered / The mortal gate of th' city, which he painted / With shunless destiny" (*Coriolanus* 2.2.108–10); a herald announces: "Know, Rome, that all alone Marcius did fight / Within Corioles gates" (*Coriolanus* 2.1.152–3); and Coriolanus himself declares: "Within these three hours, Tullus, / Alone I fought in your

---

⁷ See Friedrich Nietzsche, *On the Genealogy of Morals*, essay 1 section 11 and Cantor, *Shakespeare's Roman Trilogy*, 73–4

⁸ References to Shakespeare's plays will appear in the text by act, scene, and line number and will be drawn from *The Complete Pelican Shakespeare*, ed. Alfred Harbage (New York: Viking, 1974).

Corioles walls, / And made what work I pleased" (*Coriolanus* 1.8.8–10) and "O, me alone!" (*Coriolanus* 1.6.76).[9] In this manner, Shakespeare makes a highly significant change in Plutarch's account—a change that, in fact, strains credulity. In Plutarch's version, Coriolanus does not capture Corioli by himself, but instead leads a troop of Roman soldiers in the successful attack.[10] In contrast to Plutarch, Shakespeare's Coriolanus is alone in his conquest.

After the preeminent warrior accepts the name of Coriolanus, he seeks the office of consul, the highest magistracy in the city. To assume it, he needs the assent of the plebeians of Rome, but the people deny him this office when he refuses to wear the gown of humility which would show them the bodily wounds he has suffered in battle. In Shakespeare's tragedy, he stands before the people refusing to make a public revelation of his wounds. He complains: "I cannot / Put on the gown, stand naked, and entreat them / For my wounds' sake to give their suffrage." His desire to "o'erleap that custom" defies the example of his predecessors who sought the consular office (*Coriolanus* 2.2.134–36; see also 2.3.157–171). The warrior seeks to depart from tradition because he recoils at the suggestion that he fought for the sake of the people's good regard and their votes. His valor depends not on any recognition from the people, he asserts. When the tribunes hear of his refusal, they endeavor to have Coriolanus's election revoked.

The repugnance of Coriolanus to the practice of a warrior displaying his wounds to the people is entirely Shakespeare's invention. In Plutarch's version, Coriolanus stands for election and reveals his wounds without reserve.[11] It is Coriolanus's perceived arrogance, and

---

[9] Cantor, *Shakespeare's Rome*, 93.

[10] Plutarch, *The Lives of the Noble Grecians and Romans*, trans. Dryden and ed. Arthur Hugh Clough, 2 vol., *Coriolanus*, 1:296.

[11] Plutarch writes: "Marcius, therefore, as the fashion of candidates was, showing the scars and gashes that were still visible on his body, from the many

those of his young compatriots after his election that arouses the ire of the people and tribunes, according to Plutarch.

In both versions, Coriolanus reacts violently to the attempt to keep him from the consul's chair and is exiled as a result. In Plutarch's version, Coriolanus leaves Rome with three or four clients.[12] Shakespeare has him depart Rome "alone," a point the titular character underscores (*Coriolanus* 4.1.29). Again, Shakespeare in contrast to his source, emphasizes this warrior's singular nature.

On Shakespeare's depiction, Coriolanus's singularity goes well beyond his lone heroics and solitary exile, however. What Shakespeare depicts ultimately is Coriolanus's desire to transcend human boundaries altogether and to become a god.[13] In the first scene of the play, a tribune of the people condemns what he sees as the warrior's arrogance: "Being moved, he will not spare to gird the gods" (*Coriolanus* 1.1.251). In other words, the hero's arrogance knows no bounds; he would spar even with the divine beings. Later, another tribune confronts Coriolanus directly with his desire for preeminence, associating it with divine aspirations: "You speak o' th' people / As if you were a god to punish, not / A man of his infirmity" (*Coriolanus* 3.1.81–3). Of course, Sicinius and Brutus, who utter these accusations, intend to discredit their despised enemy with these seemingly hyperbolic comparisons that warn of the dangerous character of his ambition.

Nevertheless, one cannot easily dismiss as mere stratagem all occurrences in the play of a character likening Coriolanus to a

---

conflicts in which he had signalized himself during a service of seventeen years together, they were, so to say, put out of countenance at this display of merit, and told one another that they ought in common modesty to create him consul" (Plutarch, *Coriolanus*, 1:301).

[12] Plutarch, *Coriolanus*, 307. Cantor too notes this change from Plutarch's version of events (*Shakespeare's Rome*, 99 and 217n.1).

[13] Bloom, "Morality of the Pagan Hero," 85; Cantor, *Shakespeare's Rome*, 100 and 102; Platt, *Rome and Romans*, 103.

god. His prowess as a warrior compels not only his enemies but also his friends and supporters to make the same comparison in an effort to furnish the true measure of his accomplishments. For instance, Coriolanus's former military commander, when describing Coriolanus's success in commanding the troops of Rome's enemy after his defection, declares: "He is their god. He leads them like a thing / Made by some other deity than nature, / That shapes man better" (*Coriolanus* 4.6.91–3). One of Coriolanus's friends describes Coriolanus's success commanding the Volscians: "What he bids be done is finished with his bidding. He wants nothing of a god but eternity, and a heaven to throne in" (*Coriolanus* 5.4.22–4).

Even more importantly, Coriolanus gives voice to this desire himself. As he is poised to strike his homeland, his family—his mother, his wife, and his son—confronts him. He steels himself against their entreaties and declares:

> Let the Volsces /
> Plough Rome and harrow Italy! I'll never /
> Be such a gosling to obey instinct, but stand /
> As if a man were author of himself /
> And knew no other kin. (*Coriolanus* 5.3.33–7)

Here Coriolanus proclaims that he is not constrained by the limitations that other human beings know; he declares that he is the creator of himself.[14] Coriolanus's striving to transcend human limitations falters, however, at the very moment he proclaims himself to be a self-generating being,

His mother, the author of his existence, denies the notion that he is the author of himself. Volumnia's fear and grief stir her

---

[14] For Coriolanus as an expression of the desire for autonomy, see Stephen Greenblatt, *Shakespeare's Freedom* (Chicago: University of Chicago Press, 2010), 106–111.

eloquence. She recalls her maternal pride that exalted in his triumphs on behalf of his city and bemoans the pain of "the mother, wife and child" who would witness the "the son, the husband and the father tearing" their "country's bowels out." She invokes the "mother's womb" that "brought" him "to this world" and the horrid image of his treading on that very womb in the act of conquering his homeland. She refers to the ignominy in which he would be held as the destroyer of his native city, noting that his "chronicle" would assure that "'his name'" would be "'abhorred'" to "'th' ensuing age.'" She acknowledges that he had "affected the fine strains of honour" that "imitate the graces of the gods" but notes that his attempt has come to naught (5.3.145–50).

Coriolanus relents at this point on his attack on Rome. His inchoate ambition pushes him to seek ever more autonomy; he strains to transcend his human nature. As a human being, that type of transcendence is simply unavailable to him, of course. He does not comprehend that his ambition for transcendence—the transcendence that is available to a human being—could be fulfilled by cultivating the regard—the love—of the people. Indeed, his revulsion is immediate when confronted by the prospect that his wounded body would testify to his devotion to the people, making him dependent on the people for their regard. But that very dependence is, in fact, the vehicle to political transcendence.[15] Shakespeare's Coriolanus fails to grasp that the type of greatness available to him as a political man would be based on the regard of the people. The people would regard him as their god. His failure in this regard, however, is not at all surprising given that he is "ill

---

[15] It might be said that Coriolanus also misunderstands the divine nature, as even gods have a need to be worshipped. See Aristophanes' speech in Plato's *Symposium* 190C. Cf. Cantor, *Shakespeare's Rome*, 97.

schooled" (*Coriolanus* 3.1.320); the beast of prey is not an interesting animal.[16]

Machiavelli's Depiction of Transcendent Ambition

One of the deepest themes that Machiavelli's *Discourses on Livy* addresses is the very issue that Shakespeare depicts in Coriolanus—that is, the phenomenon of overweening ambition in great individuals. Machiavelli examines in detail a succession over centuries of the most ambitious among Rome's great men and acknowledges that ambitious leaders are necessary for a martial republic like Rome. Their overweening ambition for glory propelled the city's foreign conquests. That same ambition, though, was also an internal danger needed to be channeled, controlled, and confronted, Machiavelli shows. The Roman republic struggled long with this difficulty and ultimately failed. He notes that "the ambition of the nobility" ultimately "corrupted that republic" (3.11, 244).[17] On Machiavelli's depiction, the succession began with the very birth of the republic—with Coriolanus, in fact—and eventuated in the ascension of Julius Caesar. Between the beginning and end of the republic there were several other ambitious figures such as Spurius Cassius, Spurius Maelius, Manlius Capitolinus, and Camillus who failed in various ways in their attainment of preeminent rule and thus the overthrow of the republic (see, for example, *Discourses* 3.1, 8, 23, and 28). Ultimately, Caesar embraced the avenue that repulsed Coriolanus —that is, the thirst for transcendent ambition can be slacked through the worship of the populace.

---

[16] Nietzsche, *Genealogy of Morals*, essay 1, section 6. Cantor, *Shakespeare's Roman Trilogy*, 5 and 125.

[17] References to Niccolò Machiavelli, *Discourses on Livy*, trans. Harvey C. Mansfield and Nathan Tarcov (Chicago: University of Chicago, 1996) will appear in the text and be to book, number, and page number. References to Machiavelli's Italian will be indicated by *Opere* and are drawn from *Tutte le opere*, ed. Mario Martelli (Florence: Sansoni, 1971).

Machiavelli's analysis presents Caesar as having gained the transcendence that his predecessors had vainly pursued; Caesar was worshipped as a god.

Machiavelli confirms that he understands the profundity of the ambition that fueled Rome's great men when he describes it as a desire to transcend political life—to attain a god-like status. For example, in discussing Camillus, a great military leader who led the capture of Veii, a neighboring town in Italy, and then returned from exile to save Rome from capitulating to the Gauls, Machiavelli expatiates on the precise nature of the fear that some in Rome harbored of his ambition. He explains that because Camillus "had his triumphal chariot pulled by four white horses," some Romans "said that because of his pride he wished to be equal to the sun" (*Discourses* 3.23, 269). Thus, Machiavelli confirms the justifiable suspicion that some Roman observers of Camillus had—specifically, that an exceptionally accomplished and ambitious leader in Rome might desire to be worshipped as a god.

Although Camillus may have harbored this extreme ambition, he failed to pursue the correct avenue to its satisfaction, according to Machiavelli's analysis. Camillus was hated—not adored—by the people. The Roman general incurred the people's hatred when he ordered that the plunder from Veii, which had already fallen into the hands of the soldiers, be dedicated to fulfilling his oath to Apollo. In relating this incident, Machiavelli notes that the "principal" way that a leader becomes "hateful to the people" is "to deprive it of something useful" (*Discourses* 3.23, 269). Thus, Machiavelli indicates that, although Camillus very well may have harbored the desire to become divine, the people would not venerate him because they did not regard him as the vessel for their own relief. In his sternness to the people, Camillus can be said to be akin to Coriolanus.

Machiavelli, in fact, treats Coriolanus in an early chapter of the *Discourses*—a chapter in which he broaches that most extreme ambition, what Machiavelli terms in this chapter, a desire "to pass beyond [*transcendere*] a civil way of life" (*Coriolanus* 1.7, 25; *Opere* 88). In this context the desire to pass beyond or to transcend surely indicates the ambition to overturn the republic in order to rule alone, and thus to overturn "a civil way of life." But the verb "to transcend" would also describe the goal of an individual who wanted to become a god—to transcend, in some measure, human life itself. That is precisely the terms in which Shakespeare dramatizes Coriolanus's ambitious striving, as we have seen. Machiavelli indicates in this chapter, however, that he does not regard Coriolanus as posing much danger to Rome's civil way of life. Indeed, he fails even to mention in this context that Coriolanus defected to Rome's enemy and was poised to lead its adversaries against Rome. Machiavelli's disregard here of the external threat that Coriolanus posed to his homeland suggests that he is on the lookout for internal rather than external dangers.[18] Machiavelli's emphasis is confirmed, of course, by history. Machiavelli knows that the Roman republic would succumb not to an external but rather to an internal one—a threat that emanated from one of its own leading men.

In another chapter Machiavelli broaches the possibility that another type of Roman leader—one who is loved rather than hated—might attain a god-like status. It occurs early in the *Discourses* when he is justifying his selection of Rome as the exemplary republic that warrants the sustained attention that he devotes to it in the work. He acknowledges that some critics of Rome have found the republic distasteful because it was always tumultuous and ultimately eventuated in tyranny. He puts in the mouth of Rome's unnamed critics the following observation: Rome's ruin came when the people "later began to adore [*adorare*] any man that they saw could beat down the aristocracy" (*Discourses* 1.5, 18; *Opere* 84). Although Machiavelli will ultimately

---

[18] Machiavelli mentions Coriolanus in passing in *Discourses* 1.29, noting that "Coriolanus and Camillus were made exiles for the injuries that both had done to the plebs" (66).

embrace tumultuous Rome as his exemplary republic, he will not reject this characterization of Rome that he puts in the mouth of a critic of that republic. It turns out, in fact, that his depiction of Rome in the *Discourses* shows that the Roman republic was ultimately overturned by just such a leader—that is, by Julius Caesar—who sided with the people and who was adored as a result.

Machiavelli indicates that Caesar's ultimate success in establishing a tyranny depended on the unsuccessful forays of his ambitious predecessors; the dangerous impulses of a long series of men who sought to be preeminent within the republic ultimately weakened the people's republican resistance to blandishments. He adduces the example of Spurius Maelius who lived in the early republic. Being both ambitious and rich, he purchased grain to distribute gratis to the people during a dearth. He sought to slake his ambition through an appeal to the people, the very avenue that so repulsed Coriolanus. The Senate recognized early, Machiavelli recounts, "the inconvenience that could arise from that liberality" (*Discourses*, 3.28, 276). Clearly, the inconvenience that the Senate recognized was Spurius's desire to wield power in the republic by gaining the people as his adherents. The Senate responded to this exigency by appointing a dictator who put Spurius Maelius to death. The people did not object to this harsh punishment exacted against their benefactor.

Similarly, Capitolanus, a man of "much virtue of spirit and body," who received the honorific name by heroically saving the Capitol of Rome from the onslaught of the Gauls, too sought to make himself preeminent man in the city. Machiavelli comments that he "would have been a rare and memorable man if he had been born in a corrupt city" (*Discourses* 3.8, 239). Machiavelli defines corruption of a republic as the accumulation of "adherents" and "partisans" of a particular leader due to the benefits he bestows on them (*Discourses* 1.34, 74). These partisans are ready to follow their benefactor to the detriment of their fatherland. It is that worshipful following that Machiavelli finds so threatening.

Over the course of generations, however, Rome did become corrupt. Ultimately, military leaders gained the adherence of their soldiers and of the populace more generally. Machiavelli points to the ascendance of Marius as a watershed. Not only was Marius a popular leader of the army, but he also led a party of the people. In befriending the people, Marius actually followed the path of the Gracchi, who sought to win the favor of the people by redistributing the lands that the Romans had conquered and the patricians largely held. In the successive generation, Caesar arose and triumphed, and that triumph transformed Rome. Machiavelli explains that "Caesar had made himself head of Marius's party," and "in coming to grips Caesar was left on top." Julius Caesar succeeded in toppling the republic, in ruling alone, and in becoming a god. After his assassination, Caesar was worshipped as a god. He succeeded where all of his ambitious Roman predecessors had failed—where Coriolanus, Camillus, Capitolanus, Spurius Maelius, the Gracchi brothers, and Marius, among others, had failed. Machiavelli says of Caesar: "He was the first tyrant in Rome such that the city was never again free" (*Discourses* 1.37, 80). Machiavelli's declaration that after Caesar Rome was "never again free" is a remarkable statement that deserves some reflection. It means that since Caesar's time, Rome has not been free. In Machiavelli's estimation, it was not free in his own time. From the time of Caesar, through the rule of the emperors, through the conversion of Rome to Christianity, through the exaltation of Rome as the Holy City of Catholicism, Rome has not been free, Machiavelli declares. Thus, in his view, Rome was fundamentally and permanently transformed by Caesar's ascension.

Machiavelli's Treatment of the Danger of Caesar

Caesar represents the ultimate threat, in Machiavelli's view. He was the Roman who succeeded in attaining what so many before him had sought unsuccessfully. Driven by his overweening ambition, Caesar transformed the Roman republic into a tyranny. Machiavelli offers Caesar as the epitome of the very grave threat of an ambitious man who captures the allegiance of the people. The ascendence of Machiavelli's Julius Caesar anticipates in some respects that of Jesus Christ.

Caesar features prominently in a chapter of the first book of the *Discourses* in which Machiavelli treats the supreme danger of a man who builds a following among the people. There he gives two named examples, Caesar in Rome and Cosimo de Medici in Florence. In discussing these cases, Machiavelli emphasizes that once their following becomes so strong that the danger to the republic is obvious, then it is too dangerous to act against the threat. When Cosimo's opponents finally sought to oppose his ascension, they had him exiled, but he prevailed upon his return. When Caesar's opponents finally acted, they assassinated him, but he was regarded as a martyr for the people. So powerful a figure did Caesar become that after his death others—his successors—ruled under his name. In a sense, then, Julius Caesar ruled after death. Machiavelli warns republics against the dangers of martyrdom in this chapter.

In elaborating on the extreme danger such a circumstance presents, Machiavelli speaks in general and evocative terms: "For if in a republic one sees a noble youth arise who has an extraordinary [*istraordinaria*] virtue in him, all eyes of the citizens begin to turn toward him and agree in honoring him without hesitation, so that if there is a bit of ambition in him, mixed with the favor that nature gives him and with this accident, he comes at once to a place where the citizens, when they become aware of their error, have few remedies to avoid it." This general statement suggests that Caesar and Cosimo are not the only examples he could adduce. There are others, apparently. When such an individual arises in a republic, the threat is acute. He describes the threatening individual in most evocative terms. He is "a noble youth" toward whom "all eyes turn." The noble youth attracts the attention of the "citizens" who "honor" him because of the "extraordinary [*istraordinaria*] virtue in him" (*Discourses* 1.33, 71–72; *Opere*, 115).

It is necessary to consider what Machiavelli means by "extraordinary virtue." Obviously, he means at least a degree beyond the ordinary, but he has also used the adjective "extraordinary" to refer to the miraculous. For example, Machiavelli says of Fra Savonarola, a religious leader in Florence, who led a popular movement in Florence, that the citizens believed his claim that he spoke with God without having ever seen anything "extraordinary [*straordinaria*]" from him (*Discourses* 1.11, 36; *Opere*, 95). In this context, then, Machiavelli uses the word to mean the miraculous. Savonarola's followers believed that he spoke with God even though they had not witnessed anything miraculous from him. Thus, in Machiavelli's lexicon, extraordinary can refer to the miraculous—to the divine. In treating the noble youths of extraordinary virtue, Machiavelli points not merely to those who possess a virtue beyond the ordinary but also to those whose virtue could be described as miraculous.

Of course, there is another example of a "noble youth" who gained adherents precisely because of what was understood as his "extraordinary"—that is, his miraculous—virtue. Less than half a century after Caesar was assassinated, Christ was born in an Eastern province of Rome. What Machiavelli says of the youths who threaten republics, one may say of Christ's ascension: "one [saw] a noble youth arise who [had] an extraordinary virtue in him, all eyes of the citizens [began] to turn toward him and agree in honoring him without hesitation" (*Discourses* 1.37, 72). The results of the martyrdom of Christ far exceed those of Caesar, of course.

After his crucifixion, Christ rules on earth as the heavenly Prince of Peace, claiming a universal and divine kingdom.

As we have seen, Machiavelli emphasizes the youthfulness of the extraordinary individual who overturns a republic. That aspect of his presentation also points to the unspoken example of Christ in this chapter. Machiavelli places this discussion of the danger of martyrdom in the thirty-third chapter of the first book. Christian tradition teaches that Christ was martyred at the age of 33.[19] Machiavelli's treatment of the danger of martyrdom in the *Discourses* links Caesar's ascendance, martyrdom, and rule after his death to Christ's life and legacy.

Shakespeare's Depiction of Julius Caesar

In depicting the Roman Caesar, Shakespeare dramatizes the link between Caesar and Christ—the link that Machiavelli had already drawn in the *Discourses*. The playwright shows how a human ruler overturned the Roman republic and became a god. Shakespeare imbues his depiction of Julius Caesar with Christian imagery that draws a parallel between the martyred Roman and the martyred Christ.

The religious references in the play are unmistakable. For example, in a scene that has no historical source and thus appears to be Shakespeare's own creation, one of the conspirators, Decius, having boasted of his abilities to manipulate through flattery, volunteers to retrieve Caesar from his home and bring him to the Capital where the conspirators plan to carry out the assassination. When Decius encounters Caesar, the dictator expresses hesitation about going to the Senate due to ill omens, and recounts in some detail a dream, which he attributes to his wife:

---

[19] Luke 3:23. Vickie B. Sullivan, "Catherine Zuckert on Machiavelli's New Understanding of Politics," *The Review of Politics* 80 (2018): 279.

> She dreamt to-night she saw my statue,
> Which, like a fountain with an hundred spouts,
> Did run pure blood; and many lusty Romans
> Came smiling and did bathe their hands in it.
> <div align="right">(<i>Julius Caesar</i> 2.2.76–9)</div>

True to his charge and to his claims on his own behalf, Decius flatters Caesar by giving a most favorable interpretation of the dream. Rather than being a sign of a most ominous import, the conspirator tells Caesar that it was a "vision fair and fortunate" and elaborates:

> Your statue spouting blood in many pipes,
> In which so many smiling Romans bathed,
> Signifies that from you great Rome shall suck
> Reviving blood, and that great men shall press
> For tinctures, stains, relics, and cognizance.
> <div align="right">(<i>Julius Caesar</i> 2.2.84–9)</div>

The anachronistic Christian terms, with which Shakespeare imbues Decius's flattery, are striking and unmistakable. Decius draws favorable meaning from the fountain of Caesar's blood from which "great Rome shall suck [r]eviving blood" in a manner that evokes the Christian Communion. In the Christian tradition, Christ's blood, which he shed for humanity's eternal salvation, would become a sacrament, in which the wine Christians drank would be transubstantiated into Christ's blood—a blood that would, they believed, "revive" them, offering them a new life, an eternal life after death. Thus, Decius claims that "great Rome" shall receive "[r]eviving blood" from Caesar, but after Constantine, great Rome itself would draw "[r]eviving blood" from Christ.

Decius's next lines in which he predicts that "great men shall press / For tinctures, stains, relics, and cognizance," also has a general Christian cast as it appears to evoke the Catholic practice of venerating the relics of Christian saints—fragments of bone, locks of hair, bits of cloth, for instance. Upon closer inspection, though, the Christian elements that Decius's premonition evokes have resonance with Christ in particular. The prime relics in the Christian tradition are those that relate to Christ's passion, fragments of the true cross, the Holy Grail—the cup from which Christ drank at the Last Supper—and the shroud which covered his body after crucifixion. The latter, of course, contained "stains" that were revered. Thus, Shakespeare has his pagan conspirator, so confident in his abilities to manipulate, draw an unknowing equivalence between the people's savior and the Christian savior. In addition, Decius's specification that "great men" will seek these mementos of Caesar, foreshadows the ultimate conversion of Rome's elite to the religion that first attracted the disposed to its teachings. Thus, Shakespeare's pagan character unwittingly presages the immensity of the transformation that Christianity would bring to Rome.

Shakespeare also offers dramatic irony earlier in the play. When the conspirators meet in the garden of Brutus just before dawn on the Ides of March, Shakespeare adds the detail of their befuddlement with respect to their location. As Cassius and Brutus speak apart, Decius asks: "Here lies the east; Doth not the day break here?," to which Cinna assents but to which Casca disagrees, declaring:

> You shall confess that you are both deceived.
> Here, as I point my sword, the sun arises,
> Which is a great way growing on the south,
> Weighing the youthful season of the year.
> Some two months hence, up higher toward the north
> He first presents his fire; and the high east
> Stands, as the Capitol, directly here. (*Julius Caesar* 2.1.105–111)

Here Shakespeare's Romans debate the direction of the sunrise, not cognizant that in less than a handful of decades a new Son will rise in the High East that will overshadow their capital.[20]

Antony's speech at Caesar's funeral garners the people's pity for their fallen benefactor and arouses their anger at his slayers. Antony likens Caesar to a sacred object. He says:

> Let but the commons hear this testament,
> Which (pardon me) I do not mean to read,
> And they would go and kiss dead Caesar's wounds
> And dip their napkins in his sacred blood;
> Yea, beg a hair of him for memory,
> And dying, mention it within their wills,
> Bequeathing it as a rich legacy
> Unto their issue. (*Julius Caesar* 3.2.130–7)

The Christian imagery here is unmistakable. Antony invokes Caesar's sacred blood, just as the Christian sacrament will invoke Christ's; Antony refers to the beneficence of a new testament that will bring newfound hope to the people just as will the New Testament of the Christians;

Antony offers the relics of Caesar as things worthy of reverence, just as Christian believers will venerate the relics of Christ's passion as well as of their saints.[21] Again, Shakespeare's Caesar powerfully anticipates Christ.

Shakespeare also displays Caesar bequeathing the people a rich legacy, in a manner that evokes the one that Christ will later bestow. Antony reads Caesar's testament to reveal that, in

---

[20] Cf. Cantor, *Shakespeare's Roman Trilogy*, 40–41.

[21] For the Christian imagery in *Julius Caesar*, see, for example, *End of the Ancient Republic*, 80. See also Roy W. Battenhouse, *Shakespearean Tragedy Its Art and Its Christian Premises* (Bloomington, Ind.: Indiana University Press, 1969), 92–3.

addition to bequeathing the people seventy-five drachmas, Caesar has willed them land:

> Moreover, he hath left you all his walks,
> His private arbors, and new-planted orchards,
> On this side Tiber; he hath left them you,
> And to your heirs for ever—common pleasures,
> To walk abroad and recreate yourselves.
> Here was a Caesar! When comes such another?
> (*Julius Caesar* 3.2.247–52).

The above question, with which Antony ends his havoc-inducing oration, draws a "Never, never!" from his audience (*Julius Caesar* 3.2.253). Spectators of Shakespeare's play who discern the parallels between Caesar and Christ will note the dramatic irony of the Romans' response and know that Antony's question demands a different response. Such spectators know that another benefactor will be born, whose death as a martyr will promise benefits that surpass even those that Caesar offers in his testament; the land that Jesus' death promises far surpasses the land that the Roman people gained as a result of Caesar's. Christians will come to embrace the doctrine that declares that through Jesus's death believers are granted eternal life in another land—a land that transcends their earthly home. The people of Rome will in time come to embrace this doctrine that offers a wholly new understanding of human life. The death of Jesus will offer the people a means by which they can truly "recreate [them]selves" (cf. *Julius Caesar* 3.2.351).

After descending from the pulpit and drawing the crowd around Caesar's mangled corpse, making it the focus of the people's attention, Antony declaims:

> For I have neither wit, nor words, nor worth,
> Action, nor utterance, nor the power of speech
> To stir men's blood. I only speak right on.
> I tell you that which you yourselves do know,
> Show you sweet Caesar's wounds, poor poor dumb mouths,
> And bid them speak for me. But were I Brutus,
> And Brutus Antony, there were an Antony
> Would ruffle up your spirits, and put a tongue
> In every wound of Caesar that should move
> The stones of Rome to rise and mutiny. (*Julius Caesar* 3.2.221–30)

Of course, the mutiny that follows Antony's address belies his false modesty; his oratory does, in fact, move the "stones" of Rome to revolt.[22] Antony is using the wounded body of Caesar to underscore that Caesar lived—and more importantly died—for the people of Rome. Antony makes the wounds of Caesar speak. They give surety for the fact that the aristocrats hated Caesar for befriending the people; the people's benefactor died because he loved the people. Caesar's wounds are to be revered in the same way that Jesus's wounds would come to be revered.

Such Christian imagery in *Julius Caesar* helps to highlight Shakespeare's Coriolanus's deficiency in attempting to gain the transcendence that Caesar won through his martyrdom. For Shakespeare's Coriolanus the revelation of his wounds would suggest that he somehow needs the people's approval, their recognition. The autonomy he seeks rebels at such dependence. But Antony's pitiful rhetoric that exalts Caesar's mortal wounds reveal that such dependence is the path to the type of transcendence available to human beings who wish to be regarded as a god. The notion of fighting for the

---

[22] Cf. the first scene of play in which a tribune chastises the plebeians who are in the streets celebrating Caesar's triumph over Pompey, crying: "You blocks, you stones, you worse than senseless things" (*Julius Caesar* 1.1.35).

people—nay, dying for the people—is a powerful one. A god requires worshippers, after all.[23]

Moreover, the reverence for Caesar's wounds and the connection thereby established to Christ becomes more striking later in the play when Octavius confronts Brutus and Cassius before the battle of Philippi. There, Julius Caesar's successor vows not to sheathe his sword until "Caesar's three-and-thirty wounds / Be well avenged" (*Julius Caesar* 5.1.53–54). Octavius's numbering of Caesar's wounds as 33 is an invention; Plutarch numbers the wounds at 23.[24] Just as Machiavelli draws a likeness between Caesar and Jesus when he speaks of the danger of an appealing young man in the thirty-third chapter of the *Discourses*, so Shakespeare draws the likeness between Caesar and Christ when he numbers Caesar's wounds with that very number that evokes the age of Christ at his crucifixion.

Conclusion

Both Machiavelli and Shakespeare concern themselves with transcendent ambition in ancient Rome and explore how that passion transformed the city. Both depict the first Roman manifestations of that desire as fiercely aristocratic ones that despise the people and their needs, vainly seeking an apotheosis that would be devoid of worshippers. Shakespeare shows a Coriolanus who, by attempting to eschew all dependency, desires to be "author of himself" (*Coriolanus* 5.3.36).

---

[23] "Coriolanus, who would not stoop, did not conquer, while Caesar, who used the people's fear of ambition to conceal and advance his own ambition, became their god" (Blits, *End of the Ancient Republic*, 77).

[24] Plutarch, "Julius Caesar," 2: 242. Blits too notes this discrepancy between Shakespeare and Plutarch on the number of wounds and suggests that Shakespeare made the change to equate Caesar with Jesus. Blits does not, however, note that Machiavelli had already drawn that equation through the same iconography (*End of the Ancient Republic*, 57n30 and 80).

Machiavelli's rendition of the history of the Roman republic reveals that later ambitious men in Rome would seek the adoration and the reverence of the people. For centuries, the republic was able to forestall their efforts until the ascendance of Julius Caesar. At that point, the republic fell; Julius was Rome's first tyrant, and Rome was never again free, according to Machiavelli (*Discourses* 1.37).

Both Machiavelli and Shakespeare show how Julius Caesar attained divine status by embracing the very type of dependence that Coriolanus eschewed. Julius Caesar was elevated because the people regarded him as the vessel of their relief. Shakespeare's Antony displays the wounds that Julius Caesar's body suffered because of his own devotion to the people, whereas Shakespeare's Coriolanus would not disclose his wounds to the people, repudiating the notion that he fought for their good regard.

Shakespeare depicts how Caesar's legacy became that of a benefactor of the people. Antony proclaims that he left a testament that, in addition to silver, gave the people land across the Tibur in which they could "recreate" themselves. The adoration of the people, the martyrdom, the wounds, the spirit that defies physical death, the testament, the sacred objects all prefigure the coming of Christ in the Eastern Empire, His passion and His resurrection.

For both Machiavelli and Shakespeare, then, Rome and the demise of its republican politics prefigures the new religion that repudiated the accomplishments of pagan Rome. Although Shakespeare's *oeuvre* indicates that he is aware of Machiavelli's reputation, it is not clear that the poet derived the connection of Caesar's ascendancy to that of Christ directly from Machiavelli's *Discourses*. Perhaps the Englishman drew it from some other intellectual tradition or derived it independently. Nevertheless, Shakespeare's treatment of transcendent ambition establishes him as be a thinker on politics and religion, one who grapples

Transcendent Ambition

with world-historical events and the transvaluation of values. His portrayal of Caesar's achievement of his ambition to "soar above the view of men" (cf. *Julius Caesar* 1.1.74) shows that the playwright contemplates the transformation that Montesquieu deems "the strangest event of its kind that has ever occurred."

Virtù, *Fortuna*, and Nation: Ruler and Citizen in Machiavelli's *The Life of Castruccio Castracani of Lucca* and Shakespeare's Bastard in *King John*

Khalil M. Habib

Niccolò Machiavelli's *The Life of Castruccio Castracani of Lucca* (*LC*) and William Shakespeare's *King John* (*KJ*) present Castruccio Castracani and Philip the Bastard as dynamic figures whose contrasting approaches to leadership, loyalty, and national identity reflect their authors' distinct visions of political order in turbulent times.[1] Both characters arise from obscure and lowly positions to play pivotal roles in their respective countries. Machiavelli presents Castruccio in both Book 2 of *Florentine Histories* (*FH*), where he appears briefly within the context of the factional conflicts undermining Florence's unity and security, and more extensively as a philosophical ideal in *The Life of Castruccio Castracani of Lucca*, a work written in 1520 and dedicated to his friends, Zanobi Buondelmonti and Luigi Alamanni. The *FH* presents the political problems, namely church/state relations and factionalism and instability, that his other works, such as the *Prince* and the *Discourses on Livy* are intended to solve. Consequently, Machiavelli presents Castruccio in *FH* as a foil to Florence's factionalism and lack of political leadership. In *LC*, he portrays him as a hero who embodies unity and leadership Florence

---

[1] All citations to these works are to these editions: Niccolò Machiavelli, *The Life of Castruccio Castracani of Lucca*, trans. Allan Gilbert (Durham, NC: Duke University Press, 1965), 547; William Shakespeare, King John, ed. E. A. J. Honigmann (London: Arden Shakespeare, 2007).

lacks.[2] In typical Machiavellian fashion, however, Castruccio was able to found a regime through his personal *virtù*, but in the end he failed to maintain his political acquisitions because he did not sufficiently secure his state against internal dissent, external rivals, or the loss of his personal leadership.

In Shakespeare's *KJ*, the memorable Bastard is presented as an intelligent and witty, though somewhat skeptical, observer of political power who remains loyal to a flawed king whose legitimacy is in doubt. Castruccio's life is one of political triumph marred by fortune's caprice—"Fortune… did not grant me sufficient judgment early enough to understand her"[3]—whereas the Bastard's journey and maturation, by contrast, is one of ironic detachment and eventual patriotism, encapsulated in his resigned acceptance of "Commodity" and his final pledge to England. His closing speech—"This England never did, nor never shall, / Lie at the proud foot of a conqueror"—offers a patriotic resolution to the play's political turmoil and intrafamilial conflicts, positioning him as a voice of national resilience rather than personal ambition.[4] While both Castruccio and the Bastard rise from unconventional origins to wield influence through strategic brilliance and loyalty, Castruccio's pragmatic reliance on Machiavellian *virtù* and personal ambition contrasts with the Bastard's eventual patriotism, highlighting Machiavelli's focus on individual power versus Shakespeare's emphasis on national unity and civic virtue.

I

"Fortune, wishing to show the world that she—and not Prudence—makes men great, first shows her forces at a time when

---

[2] Niccolò Machiavelli, *Florentine Histories*, trans. Laura F. Banfield and Harvey C. Mansfield (Princeton, NJ: Princeton University Press, 1988), 65–67; Machiavelli, *Castruccio Castracani*, 533.

[3] Machiavelli, *Castruccio Castracani*, 540.

[4] Shakespeare, *King John*, 5.7.119.

Prudence can have no share in the matter, but rather everything must be recognized as coming from herself."[5]

Machiavelli opens *The Life of Castruccio Castracani* by addressing his friends Zanobi Buondelmonti and Luigi Alamanni, inviting them and the reader to consider the role of chance in human affairs. He marvels at how great men rise from humble origins through Fortune's dominance, asserting, "Fortune, wishing to demonstrate to the world that it is she—and not Prudence—makes men great."[6] He identifies two types of obscure beginnings: those exposed to danger, like infants left to wild beasts, and those with humble fathers who, ashamed, claim divine lineage as "sons of Jove or some other god" through ambition.[7] Thus, Machiavelli begins by discrediting the Renaissance fascination with classical myths (e.g., Romulus and Remus) and divine legitimacy, by highlighting human agency over divine intervention. As his treatment of Castruccio will show, great men overcome *Fortuna* through *virtù* by reshaping their circumstances through their own human effort. Machiavelli's Castruccio's obscure birth and exemplary life make him a fitting subject and test case for how far human effort can test the limits of fortune, which Machiavelli offers to his friends and the reader who admire noble deeds. As we shall see later, while Machiavelli aims to strip politics of exaggerated mythological accounts of politics, Shakespeare will use the Bastard in *KJ* to introduce a new English hero steeped in the tradition of chivalry but recast as a national hero who remains faithful to a questionable King for the sake of English liberty and out of a sense of civic duty.

Machiavelli presents Castruccio as an exemplar of one of those great men who arises from an obscure origin through ruthless cunning, serving as a model for studying how *virtù* interacts with *Fortuna*. Machiavelli introduces Castruccio's family as having once been one of those noble Italian families of the city of Lucca but who have

---

[5] Machiavelli, *Castruccio Castracani*, 533–534.
[6] Machiavelli, *Castruccio Castracani*, 533–534.
[7] Machiavelli, *Castruccio Castracani*, 533.

since disappeared, in an obvious nod to Fortune's capricious mutability. Though not explicitly stated, Lucca's factionalism (Guelfs vs. Ghibellines) and political upheavals, themes Machiavelli explores in *Florentine Histories*, likely contributed to the family's decline. Nevertheless, Machiavelli introduces Castruccio's adoptive father, Antonio, as a respected priest who was also Canon of St. Michael of Lucca, "and as a mark of respect was called Messer Antonio."[8] The formal title "Messer Antonio" lends religious dignity to the father while setting a contrast with Castruccio's martial path. But it also reflects the Church's influence on the noble families in medieval Lucca, which Machiavelli critiques as incompatible with political power and stability in *The Prince* (Chapter 11).

Castruccio's story begins with his humble and mysterious origins. One morning, while walking around gathering herbs, Antonio's sister, Madonna Dianora (whose name is a combination of Christian and pagan, e.g., "Madonna" and "Diana") discovers Castruccio, then only a baby boy, weeping and abandoned in a vineyard. He is adopted by Messer Antonio and his sister, Dianora, in Lucca. As Castruccio matures, he exhibited charm, ability, and prudence. He excelled in Antonio's teachings who intended to prepare Castruccio for the priesthood: "But [Castruccio] had found a subject wholly *alien* to the priestly character, for as soon as Castruccio reached the age of fourteen and began to get a little courage in respect to Messer Antonio and not to fear Madonna Dianora at all, laying churchly books aside."[9]

Castruccio's "alien" interest that prompted him to abandon the priesthood was military affairs. The young Castruccio opted for a love of military activity and war rather than a life devoted to religion and peace. At a young age, Castruccio began to busy himself with weapons. His future greatness and political energy were evident in the delight he took in nothing else than in handling of weapons or, "with his companions, in running, jumping, wrestling and similar

---

[8] Machiavelli, *Castruccio Castracani*, 534.
[9] Machiavelli, *Castruccio Castracani*, 535, emphasis added.

sports, in which he showed the utmost strength and far surpassed all others of his age."[10] He was not inclined to academic pursuits either, but when he did read, he immersed himself in books about war and the exploits of the greatest military heroes. Although Machiavelli establishes Castruccio's mythic origins as akin to figures like Moses or Romulus, abandoned yet destined for greatness, Castruccio's rejection of the Church reflects disdain for ecclesiastical power as antithetical to political ambition. Already at the age of fourteen, Castruccio is a self-determined young man with a natural inclination for martial pursuits.

His talents catch the eye of Francesco Guinigi, a wealthy Ghibelline condottiere, who notices Castruccio's "kingly authority," and soon takes him under his tutelage and trains him as a soldier. Castruccio quickly excels in horsemanship, combat, and leadership, earning respect and admiration in Lucca.[11] Castruccio's "kingly authority" foreshadows his political destiny, while his rejection of the priesthood indicates its irrelevance to political life. Guinigi learns Castruccio's identity and desires to recruit him. Guinigi questions Castruccio about his preference for a military or priestly life. And so, "one day calling the boy, he asked him where he would prefer to live, in the house of a gentleman who would teach him to ride and to handle arms, or in the house of a priest where he would never hear anything other than holy offices and masses."[12] Castruccio, of course, responds that he "could have no greater pleasure than to leave the studies of a priest and take up those of a soldier."[13] The binary choice dramatizes the line often attributed to Machiavelli: "I love my fatherland more than my soul." Disappointed in Castruccio's decision to devote himself to military affairs rather than religious vocations, Messer Antonio acquiesced, recognizing that "Castruccio's nature" is simply not cut for the Church and is more suited for martial

---

[10] Machiavelli, *Castruccio Castracani*, 535.
[11] Machiavelli, *Castruccio Castracani*, 536.
[12] Machiavelli, *Castruccio Castracani*, 536.
[13] Machiavelli, *Castruccio Castracani*, 536.

matters.[14]

Castruccio quickly became an excellent horseman, skillfully riding even the wildest horses. Although he was still quite young, he also surpassed all his peers in jousts and tournaments, military sports were associated, especially in Machiavelli's era, with the Christian tradition of chivalry. Unlike Shakespeare's Bastard, whom we will encounter later, who retains aspects of chivalry combined with national loyalty, Machiavalli's intention is to present something entirely new grounded in secular affairs rather than anything associated with religion, as Castruccio's binary decision makes clear. This is not to suggest, however, that Castruccio lacks civic property, especially when called for, as he practiced "all the methods necessary for gaining men's friendship."[15] In fact, Machiavelli points out that he was "respectful to his elders, modest with his equals, and gracious with his inferiors; these things made him loved not merely by the entire Guinigi family but by all the city of Lucca."[16] So even at a young age, Castruccio's innate qualities embody the necessary social capital necessary for political success.

By the age of eighteen, Castruccio entered public life and distinguished himself in military campaigns, notably in Pavia, gaining fame across Lombardy. After Francesco Guinigi's death, Castruccio becomes guardian to Francesco's young thirteen-year-old son, Pagolo, and his growing influence sparks envy among Lucca's Guelf faction: "hence many slandered him as a man to be feared and of tyrannical spirit. Among these was Messer Giorgio degli Opizi, head of the Guelf party."[17] Although the Guelf-Ghibelline conflict, that is, Italy's factionalism between the Papal and Emperor parties, resurfaces, Machiavelli strips them of their religious and political pretensions and treats them both as mere factions driven by ambition. As Machiavelli explains: "Since [Messer Opizi] hoped that on

---

[14] Machiavelli, *Castruccio Castracani*, 536.
[15] Machiavelli, *Castruccio Castracani*, 537.
[16] Machiavelli, *Castruccio Castracani*, 536–537.
[17] Machiavelli, *Castruccio Castracani*, 537.

Messer Francesco's death he would be left as it were prince of Lucca, he feared that Castruccio, who was in that position through the favor that his qualities gave him, had taken away his own opportunity; therefore he kept spreading gossip that would put Castruccio out of favor."[18] The factionalism within Lucca is a microcosm of Italy's disunity.

To secure his position and thwart Opizi, Castruccio allies with Uguccione della Faggiuola, ruler of Pisa, and orchestrates a coup to oust the Guelfs. Uguccione rose within the military to take control of Pisa. He allied himself with Lucchese exiles of the Ghibelline party, with whom Castruccio "was scheming about bringing…back with" Uguccione's help to seize Lucca.[19] Castruccio exploited the growing frustration with Opizi and secretly fortified the Onesti tower with munitions and food in case he needed to defend himself in it for a few days. On the planned evening, Castruccio gave the signal to Uguccione, who had arrived with a large force, and set fire to the barbican at Saint Peter's Gate. Castruccio rallied his allies and the people, "who could no longer endure the power of Oprizi," secured the gate from within, and let Uguccione's forces in.[20] "Castruccio within the wall raised the alarm, calling the people to arms, and mastered the gate on the inside, so that Uguccione and his men, coming in, occupied the city and killed Messer Giorgio with all the members of his family and with many of his friends and supporters, and drove out the chief magistrate."[21] They reorganize the government and place Uguccione in power. Machiavelli underscores the brutality of the coup, as "more than a hundred families were driven out of Lucca" fleeing to cities ruled by the Guelfs and hostile to Uguccione and to the Lucchese.[22]

---

[18] Machiavelli, *Castruccio Castracani*, 537.
[19] Machiavelli, *Castruccio Castracani*, 538.
[20] Machiavelli, *Castruccio Castracani*, 538.
[21] Machiavelli, *Castruccio Castracani*, 538.
[22] Machiavelli, *Castruccio Castracani*, 538.

Virtù, Fortuna, *and Nation*

The Florentines and the other Guelfs are alarmed by the rapid rise of the Ghibelline party in Tuscany and join forces to restore the exiled Lucchese in an effort to curb their rival's growing power. The Guelfs assemble a large army consisting of Pisans, Lucchese, and German cavalry, and capture Montecatini, and besiege Montecarlo to access Lucca. Minor cavalry skirmishes occur, but, as *Fortuna*'s caprices would have it, Uguccione becomes ill and his illness delays a full battle, as his forces avoid engagement. As Uguccione's condition worsens, he withdraws to Montecarlo and delegates command to Castruccio. As fortune delivers a blow to Uguccione, she provides Castruccio with a golden opportunity. But the Guelfs' fortunes will soon reverse, as their assumption that Uguccione's army was left without a leader "caused the overthrow of the Guelfs, because they took courage, since they supposed the hostile army left without" someone in charge.[23] Castruccio exploits their confidence and growing arrogance by "making a show of being afraid and not letting anybody leave the fortifications of the camp."[24] The Guelfs' overconfidence grows; "so every day, drawn up for battle, they presented themselves before Castruccio's army."[25] Having lulled the Guelfs, Castruccio learns of their military formation and decides to engage. Castruccio rallies his troops with a speech that "gave firmness to the spirit of his soldiers," assuring them of victory through obedience.[26]

Castruccio outsmarted his enemy by having observed their tactic of placing their strongest men in the center of their array and the weaker soldiers on their wings. He reversed this by moving his weaker men at the center, and his strongest soldiers on the outside of their formation. This meant that only the wings engaged in battle initially, allowing Castruccio's superior force to weaken the enemy first while "their strongest were standing still, without being able to

---

[23] Machiavelli, *Castruccio Castracani*, 539.
[24] Machiavelli, *Castruccio Castracani*, 539.
[25] Machiavelli, *Castruccio Castracani*, 539.
[26] Machiavelli, *Castruccio Castracani*, 539.

injure those they had opposite them or to give any aid to their companions."[27] The result was a resounding victory for Castruccio and his military: "Hence, without much difficulty, both wings of the enemy were put to flight, and those in the center—denuded of their flanking forces, without having had a chance to show their valor—fled."[28] Over ten thousand enemy soldiers were slaughtered, including many Guelf leaders and princes, "such as Piero, King Robert's brother, Carlo his nephew, and Filippo lord of Taranto," were killed, while Castruccio lost fewer than three hundred, though Uguccione's son Francesco died in the initial clash.

The victory enhances Castruccio's reputation, but Uguccione, jealous of Castruccio's success, "came to have so much jealousy and fear of Castruccio's position that he meditated on nothing else than how he could destroy him."[29] Uguccione continued to stew, awaiting for the right opportunity to present itself, and it did. It happened that a distinguished nobleman was murdered in Lucca. When Uguccione learned that the murderer sought refuge in Castruccio's house and he protected him, Uguccione saw his chance to punish Castruccio with justification. He ordered his son Neri, ruler of Lucca, to arrest Castruccio at a banquet. Neri detained him but hesitated to execute him without a trial, fearing the people would revolt, as Castruccio was very popular with the Lucchese. Uguccione, frustrated by his son's reticence and cowardice, rode to Lucca with four hundred horsemen to kill Castruccio. *Fortuna's* intervention disrupts Uguccione's plan. Upon his leave, a revolt in Pisa killed his vicar and household before he reached Lucca. The Pisans appoint Gaddo della Gherardesca as ruler. The Lucchese, inspired by Pisa's uprising, demanded Castruccio's release. They escalate from speaking publicly without restraint to armed demands. Castruccio's public support proved too much for Uguccione who, "for fear of worse" freed

---

[27] Machiavelli, *Castruccio Castracani*, 539.
[28] Machiavelli, *Castruccio Castracani*, 539–540.
[29] Machiavelli, *Castruccio Castracani*, 540.

Castruccio.[30] Castruccio rallied his allies and the people drove Uguccione out, forcing him to flee to Lombardy, where he died in poverty.

Castruccio, no longer a prisoner but, as it were, prince of Lucca, managed with the assistance of his friends, "and with the new support of the people," was appointed military leader for a year.[31] To bolster his reputation, he allied with Pisans and sought military glory by recapturing rebellious towns like Sarzana, which he conquered in two months, and by conquering Massa, Carrara, Lavenza. In a short time, he conquered all of Lunigiana and Pontremoli, and drove out Messer Palavisini, who was her ruler, in order to control a key pass. Castruccio returned to Lucca triumphantly and "was welcomed by all the people."[32] While back in Lucca, he bribed key figures "of high reputation" and "made himself ruler, and formally and by the decree of the people was chosen prince."[33]

At this time Frederick of Bavaria, "King of the Romans, came into Italy to take the crown of the Empire. Castruccio allied with him and visited him with 500 cavalry."[34] Castruccio was received by Frederick with honor and was made viceroy in Tuscany. Frederick also appointed Castruccio ruler of Pisa after their revolt, which accepted him out of fear of the Guelfs. After Frederick returned to Germany and left a viceroy in Rome, all the Tuscan and Lombard Ghibellines flocked to Castruccio, promising him control of their cities if "with his aid they themselves could get back into them again."[35] Castruccio ultimately sought to become ruler of all Tuscany, so "Castruccio, to raise his reputation, made an alliance with Messer Matteo Visconti, prince of Milan, organized Lucca's defenses, and armed its districts.[36] When Visconti was attacked by Guelfs in

---

[30] Machiavelli, *Castruccio Castracani*, 541.
[31] Machiavelli, *Castruccio Castracani*, 541.
[32] Machiavelli, *Castruccio Castracani*, 541.
[33] Machiavelli, *Castruccio Castracani*, 541.
[34] Machiavelli, *Castruccio Castracani*, 541.
[35] Machiavelli, *Castruccio Castracani*, 542.
[36] Machiavelli, *Castruccio Castracani*, 542.

Piacenza, Castruccio raided the Valdarno, forcing Florence to recall its troops from Lombardy.

Despite his military triumphs, Castruccio faced internal threats that challenged his authority. "For in that city the Poggio family, powerful because it had made Castruccio not merely great but prince, and thinking it had not been rewarded according to its merits, united with other families in Lucca to make the city revolt and to drive out Castruccio."[37] Although Castruccio was popular with the people, the powerful nobles back in Lucca who helped him to power, feeling underappreciated, conspired to overthrow Castruccio. One morning, the Poggio family attacked and killed Castruccio's deputy, aiming to incite a broader uprising. Stefano di Poggio, an elder uninvolved in the plot, intervened and convinced his family to disarm and offered to mediate with Castruccio. The conspirators complied "with no more prudence than they had shown in taking" up arms against Castruccio.[38] Castruccio returned to Lucca with troops, found the rebellion quelled but seized the opportunity to secure his power. He stationed loyalists strategically and met Stefano, who pleaded for leniency for his family, citing their past support and youth's recklessness. Castruccio responded graciously, assured Stefano he was pleased the unrest had ended, and invited the conspirators to meet him, "saying he thanked God that he had a chance to show his clemency and kindness. Having come, then, on faith of Stefano and of Castruccio, along with Stefano they were imprisoned and put to death."[39]

Meanwhile, the Florentines regained San Miniato from Castruccio. Castruccio decided against going to war against the Florentines until he could solidify his control over Lucca. The Florentines and Castruccio agreed to a two-year truce, as both sides were exhausted from war and wanted to put an end to their costly engagements. During this period, both sides were allowed to keep their

---

[37] Machiavelli, *Castruccio Castracani*, 542–543.
[38] Machiavelli, *Castruccio Castracani*, 543.
[39] Machiavelli, *Castruccio Castracani*, 543.

existing territories. Freed from war, "Castruccio, in order not to run again into dangers that he had run into before," purged Lucca of ambitious rivals, stripped them of property, exiled, or executed them, claiming their disloyalty as pretext for eliminating anyone who aspired to rival him.[40] To further secure his rule, "he built a fortress in Lucca using materials from the towers of those he had driven out or killed."[41]

While maintaining the truce with the Florentines and while fortifying himself in Lucca, Castruccio schemed to capture Pistoia in order to "add to his grandeur," seeing it as a stepping stone to gain Florence.[42] He cultivated allies in the surrounding mountains and exploited Pistoia's division between the White and Black factions. "The head of the Whites was Bastiano di Possente; of the Blacks, Jacopo da Gia."[43] Both leaders, distrusting Florence and valuing Castruccio's military prowess, had secretly met with Castruccio separately, to express how they "wished to drive out the other."[44] Castruccio promised help to both, "telling Jacopo that he would come in person, and Bastiano that he would send Pagolo Guinigi, his foster son," to aid him.[45] At midnight, both entered Pistoia as allies, but Castruccio signaled Pagolo to strike, "after which one killed Jacopo da Gia and the other Bastiano di Possente."[46] They killed both men's supporters, and took the city without resistance. Castruccio ousted the government and "compelled the people to give him allegiance" with debt relief and "many promises."[47] And similarly, he pacified the region by leveraging his reputation to quell unrest, "so that

---

[40] Machiavelli, *Castruccio Castracani*, 543–544.
[41] Machiavelli, *Castruccio Castracani*, 544.
[42] Machiavelli, *Castruccio Castracani*, 544.
[43] Machiavelli, *Castruccio Castracani*, 544.
[44] Machiavelli, *Castruccio Castracani*, 544.
[45] Machiavelli, *Castruccio Castracani*, 544.
[46] Machiavelli, *Castruccio Castracani*, 544.
[47] Machiavelli, *Castruccio Castracani*, 544.

everybody, full of hope and moved in great part by his abilities, became quiet."[48]

During this time, the Roman people rebelled due to economic hardship brought about by the high cost of living. They blamed the Pope's absence in Avignon and German mismanagement. Daily violence ensued, as the Avignon Papacy (1309–1377), a period in Church history when popes resided in France, weakened Roman authority and caused local discontent. The absence of leadership destabilized and finally weakened governance and invited chaos. This episode enables Machiavelli to demonstrate how tensions between the Holy Roman Empire's German representatives and the Romans, a recurring issue during imperial interventions in Italy, highlight the fragility of foreign rule without local legitimacy, fostering internal conflict and inviting foreign intervention and aggression: "Hence every day there were homicides and other troubles, which Henry, the Emperor's deputy, could not deal with. So there came upon Henry a great fear that the Romans would call in King Robert of Naples and drive him out of Rome and give her back to the Pope."[49]

Consequently, due to a lack of local legitimacy, and "not having any nearer friend on whom to call," Emperor Henry's deputy called on Castruccio, his closest ally, for help.[50] Castruccio recognized the urgency of the situation, seeing it as an opportunity to repay his obligations to the Emperor. He also aimed to position himself strategically for command. Castruccio put Pagolo in charge of Lucca and arrived in Rome with six hundred cavalry. His presence bolstered the Emperor's cause and enhanced the imperial faction's prestige: "In a very short time his presence brought such great reputation to the Emperor's party that, without bloodshed or other violence, everything was assuaged."[51] Castruccio then resolved the economic crisis by importing grain from Pisa and thus "removed the cause of the

---

[48] Machiavelli, *Castruccio Castracani*, 544–45.
[49] Machiavelli, *Castruccio Castracani*, 545.
[50] Machiavelli, *Castruccio Castracani*, 545.
[51] Machiavelli, *Castruccio Castracani*, 545.

disorder."[52] Castruccio secured Roman loyalty to Henry's rule through a skillful combination of persuasion and punishment "of the chief men in Rome."[53] The grateful Romans named Castruccio a senator, and he accepted the honor with "the greatest pomp," wearing a brocaded toga inscribed with phrases proclaiming divine will—on the front it said: "That is which God wills"; and behind it said: "That shall be which God shall will."[54]

Angered by Castruccio's seizure of Pistoia during a truce, the Florentines schemed to incite a rebellion in Castruccio's absence. Pistoian exiles in Florence, Baldo Cecchi and Jacopo Baldini, worked with allies in Pistoia and, with Florentine support, entered the city at night, expelled "Castruccio's partisans and officials—part of them they killed—and restored" Pistoia's independence.[55] Furious, Castruccio left Henry in Rome and rushed back to Lucca. The Florentines, however, anticipated Castruccio's move to retake Pistoia, and thus assembled a large Guelf army and occupied the Val di Nievole to block his path. Castruccio, however, informed of the Florentines' location, chooses to fight at Serravalle's pass rather than open plains. He moved twelve thousand troops to Montecarlo where he planned to ambush the Florentines' thirty thousand-strong army at the narrow Serravalle pass, where his smaller force could negate their numerical advantage.

Castruccio's *virtù* shone in his strategic capture of Serravalle, a fortified town above the Val di Nievole pass, which he seized by covertly infiltrating four hundred men to kill its neutral lord, Messer Manfred.[56] To lure the overconfident Florentines into the narrow pass, Castruccio feigned weakness, positioning his army at Montecarlo before silently moving to Serravalle at dawn. His surprise attack exploited the terrain, trapping the Florentine cavalry and

---

[52] Machiavelli, *Castruccio Castracani*, 545.
[53] Machiavelli, *Castruccio Castracani*, 545.
[54] Machiavelli, *Castruccio Castracani*, 545.
[55] Machiavelli, *Castruccio Castracani*, 546.
[56] Machiavelli, *Castruccio Castracani*, 546.

infantry in disarray, unable to maneuver.⁵⁷ By deploying additional forces to flank the enemy, Castruccio secured a decisive victory, capturing leaders like Bandino de' Rossi and Francesco Brunelleschi. This triumph showcased his tactical brilliance and ability to bend *Fortuna* to his will, though his reliance on such bold maneuvers foreshadowed vulnerabilities to chance and internal dissent.

After the Florentine defeat at Serravalle, Pistoia expelled the Guelf faction and surrendered to Castruccio. He then captured Prato and other towns in the Arno plain and encamped at Peretola, two miles from Florence. There, he lingered to distribute plunder, celebrate, and mock the Florentines with staged races and coin minting. He also tried but failed to bribe Florentine nobles to betray the city, as the plot was uncovered and led to the execution of Tommaso Lupacci and Lambertuccio Frescobaldi. The Florentines were desperate and feared for their independence. They offered their city and sovereignty to King Robert of Naples in an effort to regain their freedom. Robert accepted, "not so much because of the honor done him by the Florentines, as because he knew of what importance it was to his position that the Guelf party should retain control of Tuscany."⁵⁸ And so he sent his son Carlo with four thousand cavalry to Florence in exchange for two hundred thousand florins annually.

Castruccio was forced to leave Florentine territory to quell a plot in Pisa led by Benedetto Lanfranchi, one of the chief men of Pisa. Benedetto was unable to endure having his native city enslaved by a Lucchese and thus conspired against Castruccio and aimed to seize the citadel and oust Castruccio's garrison. The conspiracy faltered when a recruit betrayed Lanfranchi to Castruccio. Implicated in the plot were exiled Florentines Bonifacio Cerchi and Giovanni Guidi. Castruccio executed Lanfranchi and exiled his family, and beheaded many other nobles. The ferocity of Castruccio's violence was designed to reinforce his grip on Pisa and Pistoia through force and cunning, "since he knew that Pistoia and Pisa were not very

---

⁵⁷ Machiavelli, *Castruccio Castracani*, 547.
⁵⁸ Machiavelli, *Castruccio Castracani*, 548.

loyal, with sagacity and force he tried to make himself sure of them."⁵⁹

The Pisa conspiracy gave the Florentines time to regroup and await Carlo's, the King of Naples' son, arrival. Upon his arrival they amassed a massive army of over thirty thousand infantry and ten thousand cavalry made up of mostly Guelf allies. They debated attacking Pistoia or Pisa. They settled on Opted due to its recent unrest and strategic value. In May 1328, they swiftly captured Lastra, Signa, Montelupo, and Empoli, and encamped at San Miniato.

Castruccio was undaunted; he saw a chance to dominate Tuscany, as he believed the Florentines would fare no better than at Serravalle. He gathered twenty thousand infantry and four thousand cavalry and positioned himself at Fucecchio, a fortified town between the Usciana and Arno rivers, elevated above the plain. He sent Pagolo Guinigi with five thousand infantry to Pisa. Fucecchio's strategic location made it difficult for the Florentines to cut his supply lines from Lucca or Pisa without splitting their forces, which would expose them to attacks from both Castruccio's army and Pisa's garrison. As he had done previously, Castruccio used cunning to entice the Florentines to cross the Arno by positioning his forces near Fucecchio's walls, leaving space between his army and the river, thus daring them to advance into a trap.

Undeterred by the Florentines' advance, Castruccio saw an opportunity to dominate Tuscany, leveraging his *virtù* at the Arno River.⁶⁰ Positioning his forces at Fucecchio, a fortified town, he enticed the Florentines to cross the Arno by feigning vulnerability, daring them into a trap. As the Florentines struggled through the river, weighed down by water and equipment, Castruccio launched a devastating attack, exploiting their disarray.⁶¹ His strategic deception and timely assault routed the enemy, killing over twenty thousand and capturing leaders like Carlo of Naples. This victory exemplified

---

⁵⁹ Machiavelli, *Castruccio Castracani*, 549.
⁶⁰ Machiavelli, *Castruccio Castracani*, 550.
⁶¹ Machiavelli, *Castruccio Castracani*, 551.

Castruccio's ability to manipulate *Fortuna* through cunning, yet his reliance on personal brilliance left his regime exposed to chance, as his sudden death soon revealed.

Florentine generals tried redirecting troops upstream in order to find more solid ground from which to counterattack. Castruccio's light infantry blocked them from crossing, however, and armed with shields and galley-darts, "wounded horses in the face and in the breast, so that frightened by the wounds and the shouts, not wanting to go ahead, they fell one on top of another."[62] The battle was fierce with heavy casualties on both sides. Castruccio's men pushed to drive the Florentines back into the river, while the Florentines fought to clear space for their troops. "Castruccio reminded his men that these were the same enemies that not long before they had beaten at Serravalle; and the Florentines reproached their men that the many were letting themselves be beaten by the few."[63] Castruccio deployed five thousand fresh infantry to relieve his exhausted soldiers and ordered a feigned retreat to lure the Florentines forward. The fresh troops overwhelmed the tired Florentines and forced them back into the Arno. The cavalry battle was a stalemate, but was deliberately planned to be so by Castruccio, for he knew that "his were inferior, [and] had ordered his officers merely to resist the enemy."[64] Castruccio's weaker cavalry held their own. Castruccio prudently reallocated his resources to prioritize defeating the infantry, "since he hoped to defeat the infantry and, when they were defeated, then more easily to beat the cavalry."[65] Once the Florentine infantry collapsed, his remaining infantry and cavalry attacked their cavalry and routed them. The Florentine leaders attempted to have their infantry cross downstream in order to make a flank attack on Castruccio's soldiers, but they failed since the Arno's banks were high and the tops of the riverbed were held by Castruccio's men. Castruccio's army defeated

---

[62] Machiavelli, *Castruccio Castracani*, 551.
[63] Machiavelli, *Castruccio Castracani*, 551.
[64] Machiavelli, *Castruccio Castracani*, 551.
[65] Machiavelli, *Castruccio Castracani*, 551.

them with devastating results: two-thirds of the Florentine army was lost, with 20,231 killed and leaders including Carlo (King Robert's son), Michelagnolo Falconi, and Taddeo degli Albizzi fled or were captured. Castruccio lost 1,570 men but gained significant booty.

Castruccio's psychological warfare (shouts to frighten the Florentine horses), deception (feigning weakness), and morale-building speeches embodied his *virtù* and his attempt to navigate a world in which chance plays such a role. Fortune, however, had different plans for him and abruptly ended Castruccio's life: "Yet Fortune, hostile to his fame, when it was time to give him life, took it from him and broke off those plans that he for a long time before had been intending to put into effect nor by anything other than death could he have been impeded."[66] Despite the triumph and the many examples of his personal skills, Castruccio ultimately dies from a fever brought about by some random wind blowing from the direction of the Arno. Castruccio Exhausted stood, soaking wet from battle, in Fucecchio's gate to greet his victorious troops who were returning from victory: "hence, standing exposed to a wind that generally midday rises from up the Arno and is almost always unhealthful, he grew cold as ice. This, not being regarded by him, as one who was used to such discomforts, was the cause of his death."[67] By night he caught a severe fever which worsened rapidly. His doctors deemed it fatal, and Castruccio, aware of his impending death, summoned Pagolo Guinigi to share his regrets and gratitude.

Castruccio blamed Fortune for not granting him the wisdom or time to outmaneuver fate: "But Fortune, who is admitted to be arbiter of all human things, did not give me so much judgement that I would early understand her, nor so much time that I could overcome her."[68] He regretted not having established a more secure empire and admitted he should have settled for ruling Lucca and Pisa, and avoided conflict with Pistoia and Florence. This, he believed, would

---

[66] Machiavelli, *Castruccio Castracani*, 552.
[67] Machiavelli, *Castruccio Castracani*, 552.
[68] Machiavelli, *Castruccio Castracani*, 553.

have left Pagolo a smaller but safer state with fewer enemies. His aggressive campaigns against Pistoia and Florence "stirred up the Florentines" and generated powerful enemies and envy, weakening his empire's foundation.[69] The Florentines, weakened but not crushed, were hostile and would rejoice at Castruccio's death more than a Tuscan conquest. Allies like the Milanese princes and the emperor were too distant and were unreliable, too slow to provide timely aid. Pagolo, Castruccio advised, "must not, therefore, trust in anything except your own cleverness and the memory of my ability, and in the reputation brought to you by the present victory."[70] This victory, if used wisely, could secure a peace agreement with the terrified Florentines, who would likely accept terms. Unlike Castruccio, who sought glory through enmity with Florence, Pagolo should pursue their friendship for stability and ease. He expressed gratitude to Pagolo's father, who raised him as a son despite his humble origins. The care and security his adoptive father provided made him capable of great achievements. Out of loyalty, Castruccio raised Pagolo with the same love and expanded his inheritance. He even avoided marriage to focus on enriching Pagolo's family in order to fulfill his debt to them.

Another central lesson Castruccio wished to impart to Pagolo is the importance of self-awareness in leadership. Castruccio urged Pagolo to "know oneself, and to be able to measure the forces of one's spirit and of one's position."[71] Castruccio recognized his own martial nature and thus pursued conquest, but advised Pagolo, whom he saw as unsuited for war, to "endeavor to reign" through "the arts of peace."[72] Although this pragmatic shift reflects *The Prince's* emphasis on adapting to one's circumstances (Chapter 18), it proves to be a failure: "But ability[*virtù*] and Fortune were not so friendly to Pagolo Guinigi as to Castruccio, because not much later he lost

---

[69] Machiavelli, *Castruccio Castracani*, 553.
[70] Machiavelli, *Castruccio Castracani*, 554.
[71] Machiavelli, *Castruccio Castracani*, 554.
[72] Machiavelli, *Castruccio Castracani*, 554.

Pistois and then Pisa, and with difficulty kept sovereignty of Lucca, which remained in his family until the time of Pagolo his great grandson."[73]

Castruccio's fateful end illustrates how *Fortuna* is both an enabler and destroyer. The mundane cause of his illness (a random wind generated from the river Arno) which ultimately led to his death and the focus on *Fortuna* as Castruccio lies in his deathbed together reprise Machiavelli's vivid imagery of the destructive force of *Fortuna* in chapter 25 of *The Prince*. Here as in the *Prince*, *Fortuna* is presented as a capricious force that can overwhelm a state and thwart a ruler's plans. In the *Prince*, however, Machiavelli suggests that not all is lost or futile. A ruler can prepare for her potential devastation by building institutions and defenses like dams and dykes, and not just rely upon personal *virtù* (skill, courage, and initiative) or Christianity to maintain power. This seems to be the moral of the lesson here with Castruccio, especially with respect to his failure to establish a secure government, and Pagolo's inability to maintain his inheritance through the "arts of peace." Although Machiavelli's tragic hero is stripped of the mythology of Christian chivalry, he lacked the wisdom to unify his empire in a manner that would endure.

II

"This England never did, nor never shall, Lie at the proud foot of a conqueror."[74]

The Bastard in *King John* provides an alternative model of leadership to Machiavelli's Castruccio. The Bastard is a patriotic and loyal English citizen. He is clever and a keen observer of human character. He possesses moral integrity, and a vision of national unity. Like Castruccio, the Bastard emerges from low origins as the illegitimate son of Richard I and plays a crucial role in his nation's conflicts,

---

[73] Machiavelli, *Castruccio Castracani*, 554–555.
[74] William Shakespeare, *King John*, ed. E. A. J. Honigmann (London: Ardeen Shakespeare, 2007), 5.7.118–120.

particularly with respect to "Church and State" relations that embroiled King John in crippling entanglements with the Catholic Church and a hostile France with designs on English sovereignty. Castruccio is a founder who embodies many, but not all, of Machiavelli's teachings on politics, the Bastard, however, is concerned more with maintaining the integrity and sovereignty of his nation, which he strongly identifies with throughout the play. Whereas Machiavelli carves out a new and partly mythical hero removed from any tradition of chivalry or Christian virtue, Shakespeare presents the Bastard as a new prototype of a faithful and English hero who is a synthesis of Christian and nationalist ideals. Rather than seeking personal power, the Bastard acts as a loyal advisor and warrior for England. His military contributions, such as beheading Austria, are driven by patriotism: "Saint George, that swinged the dragon.... Teach us some fence!"[75] Unlike Castruccio's authoritarianism, the Bastard's leadership is collaborative, as seen in his defense of Hubert against treacherous nobles. The Bastard's nationalistic political instincts and ability to mollify extremes position him as a unifying figure, contrasting with King John's divisive rule and Castruccio's failure to think of his empire apart from his own personal ambitions. Indeed, the Bastard is a new English hero who prioritizes collective welfare over personal gain.

The play is set during a period in English history where the Catholic Church wielded extraordinary authority over all of Christendom. Like the period in Italy's history in which Castruccio makes his way in the world, England is dealing with an internal and external conflict. Richard I died without an heir and there are doubts about the legitimacy of his brother King John's inheriting the crown. The French side of the family claims the kingship rightfully belongs to King John's young nephew, Arthur. Arthur's family aligns with the French nobility to advance Author's claim to the throne, and thus poses a national threat to England. The Church is upset at King John over his attempt to name the Archbishop in England, which she sees

---

[75] Shakespeare, *King John*, 2.1.297.

as an attempt to usurp the jurisdiction and role of the Church over critical ecclesiastical offices. So, England is caught between an international spiritual authority located in Rome, and a possible invasion of France at its border.

The hero of the play is not King John, as one might be led to believe on the basis of the title of the play. Rather, that honor belongs to Philip Faulconbridge (the Bastard). The Bastard and his younger brother, Robert Faulconbridge, have come from the countryside of England before King John and Queen Eleanor to dispute an inheritance. King John asks Philip and Robert to identify themselves. Philip, the Bastard, responds: "Your faithful subject, I," and claims to be the eldest son of Sir Robert Faulconbridge, a gentleman and soldier knighted by Richard Coeur de Lion, Richard the Lionheart[76] Robert, however, asserts he is the true son and heir of their father. King John, however, notes the contradiction: if Philip is the elder, why does Robert, the younger, claim the inheritance? Robert suggests they might not share the same mother, prompting Philip to confirm they do but to cast doubt on their shared father, deferring the truth to "heaven and my mother." Philip slyly suggests that he may be illegitimate, a response that draws Queen Eleanor's rebuke for shaming his mother: "Out on thee, rude man! Thou dost shame thy mother / And wound her honor with this diffidence."[77] Philip denies intending to shame his mother, stating the illegitimacy claim is Robert's, not his. He notes that if Robert proves he's a bastard, Philip loses an inheritance worth five hundred pounds a year. He humorously wishes "Heaven guard my mother's honor and my land!"[78] The Bastard's response prompts King John to call Philip a "Good blunt fellow."[79] When John asks why Robert claims the estate despite being younger, Philip suggests it is greed and references Robert's past accusation of his bastardy. He boldly leaves his legitimacy

---

[76] Shakespeare, *King John*, 1.1.49.
[77] Shakespeare, *King John*, 1.1.65.
[78] Shakespeare, *King John*, 1.1.70–73.
[79] Shakespeare, *King John*, 1.1.73–74.

to his mother's account and invites King John and his mother, Eleanor, to compare their faces and to judge who resembles Sir Robert. Philip mocks Robert's appearance, thanking heaven he doesn't look like him, earning John's amusement as a "madcap."[80]

Eleanor, in an aside, notes Philip's resemblance to Richard Coeur de Lion in both appearance and speech, and suggests Philip may indeed be Richard's son. King John agrees, privately confirming Philip's likeness to Richard I. Robert explains that their father, Sir Robert, was sent by King Richard (John's brother) on a diplomatic mission to Germany. During his absence, Richard stayed at their home and seduced their mother. On his deathbed, Sir Robert declared Philip was not his son and alleged he was born fourteen weeks premature, and willed his lands to Robert. Robert argues this makes him the rightful heir. Philip interjects and sarcastically notes Robert's story focuses on their father's absence rather than their mother's actions, implying the real issue is Richard's involvement. King John retorts pointing out that according to English law and custom, "your brother is legitimate: / Your father's wife did after wedlock bear him.../ Your father's heir must have your father's land."[81] In other words, King John rules that Philip is legitimate under English law because he was born to Sir Robert's wife after their marriage. Any infidelity is the mother's fault, a risk all husbands face. John argues that even if Richard fathered Philip, Sir Robert raised him as his own, so Philip remains the heir. If Richard had claimed Philip, Sir Robert could have kept him, but since he didn't, Robert has no claim, and Philip inherits as the "mother's son." Robert protests but to no avail.

Eleanor poses a choice to Philip: remain a Faulconbridge with the land, like Robert, or be recognized as Richard Coeur de Lion's son, gaining status but no inheritance. Philip, with sharp wit, rejects Robert's appearance and the Faulconbridge name, describing Robert's thin frame and weak features mockingly. He chooses to be

---

[80] Shakespeare, *King John*, 1.1. 85.
[81] Shakespeare, *King John*, 1.1.117.

Virtù, Fortuna, *and Nation*

Richard's son, valuing a noble identity and lordly presence and relinquishes his inheritance to join Elinor, declaring he would rather have his face than Robert's inheritance. In response to the Bastard's decision, King John renames the Bastard Richard Plantagenet and rewards him with the title of knight. In bringing together royal blood, country manners and wit, and loyalty to England, a new English prototype begins to emerge.

Immediately after being knighted, the Bastard delivers one of his two soliloquies followed by a private conversation between him and his mother. The first soliloquy playfully mocks the manners of a chivalrous knight of the distant past in order to prepare us for the eventual emergence of the Bastard as a new English version of the faithful knight, but one faithful to his nation, rather than to a universal spiritual authority. Alone on stage, the Bastard reflects on his elevated status, noting he's "a foot of honor better" but "many a many foot of land the worse" after renouncing the Faulconbridge estate.[82] His new identity as Richard's son grants him social prestige but no wealth. With mock grandeur, he imagines knighting others and elevating common women ("any Joan") to ladies, reveling in his newfound authority. He humorously describes forgetting names due to his "new-made honor" and mimics a pompous conversation with a worldly traveler at his table, exchanging flattery and discussing geography (Alps, Apennines, Pyrenees, Po River) until supper. Philip embraces this "worshipful society" as fitting his ambitious spirit and declares that one is a "bastard to the time" (out of step with the era) if they do not observe and adapt. He vows to learn the art of flattery ("sweet poison") to navigate deceit without practicing it, seeing it as a tool for his rise within courtly life.[83]

The Bastard's first soliloquy is interrupted when his mother, Lady Faulconbridge, and her servant James Gurney appear. The Bastard noticed a woman in riding robes approaching in haste. He initially wonders why no husband heralds her arrival. As she

---

[82] Shakespeare, *King John*, 1.1.188.
[83] Shakespeare, *King John*, 1.1.190–220.

approaches, however, he recognizes his mother, Lady Faulconbridge, and greets her, asking why she's come to court so urgently. Lady Faulconbridge demands to know where Robert, Philip's brother, is, calling him a "slave" who's tarnishing her honor by spreading rumors of her infidelity: "Where is that slave thy brother? Where is he / That holds in chase mine honor up and down?"[84] Philip sarcastically refers to Robert as "Colbrand the Giant," mocking his brother's claim as Sir Robert's son.[85] When Lady Faulconbridge insists both are Sir Robert's sons, Philip dismisses her servant, James Gurney, with a playful nickname ("Philip Sparrow"), and promises to explain later.[86]

Alone with his mother, Philip bluntly denies being Sir Robert's son. He claims Sir Robert could have "eaten" him on Good Friday without breaking his fast (implying he's not of Robert's flesh). He jests that Sir Robert could not have fathered him, pointing to his own vigor as evidence. He directly asks who his real father is, pressing for a "proper man"—"To whom am I beholding for these limbs? Sir Robert never holp to make this leg."[87] Lady Faulconbridge is outraged and accuses Philip of conspiring with his brother Robert to shame her for personal gain. She calls him an "untoward knave" for his scorn. Philip, however, is undeterred and flaunts his new knighthood ("dubbed" with a mark on his shoulder) and reiterates his rejection of the Faulconbridge name, land, and legitimacy. He demands to know his father's identity, hoping for a worthy figure.[88]

Lady Faulconbridge confesses that King Richard Coeur de Lion was his father, and admits she was seduced by Richard's persistent and forceful courtship while married to Sir Robert. She pleads that heaven not judge her for this "dear offense," which overwhelmed her defenses, since infidelity is a mortal sin.[89] The Bastard enthusiastically embraces the revelation and declares that he would want no

---

[84] Shakespeare, *King John*, 1.1.220–221.
[85] Shakespeare, *King John*, 1.1.220–221.
[86] Shakespeare, *King John*, 1.1.236.
[87] Shakespeare, *King John*, 1.1.245.
[88] Shakespeare, *King John*, 1.1.250.
[89] Shakespeare, *King John*, 1.1.265.

Virtù, Fortuna, *and Nation*

better father than Richard. He absolves his mother and argues her "sin" carries earthly privilege (his noble lineage) and to have refused Richard I would have been a sin:

> And so doth yours. Your fault was not your folly.
> Needs must you lay your heart at his dispose,
> Subjected tribute to commanding love,
> Against whose fury and unmatchèd force
> The aweless lion could not wage the fight
> Nor keep his princely heart from Richard's hand.[90]

He praises his mother for yielding to such a man and invokes "heaven" and "hell" and vows to "send [a detractor's] soul to hell for dishonoring her reputation.[91] The Bastard invites his mother to meet his kin (John's court) and asserts that they will agree her union with Richard was no sin. He claims anyone who says otherwise is a liar, solidifying his loyalty to her and his pride in his royal lineage.

Religious overtones permeate this short but important scene between the Bastard and his mother and help to frame his personal transformation as the play progresses: "Good Friday," "fast," the pun on Mary and Confession, "Marry, to confess," "I deny the devil," "Heaven," "transgression," "sins," and "hell," are but a few examples of how the Bastard begins to emerge as a new English noble.[92] The religious undertones are not merely decorative. A closer examination of this section reveals how the Bastard inverts Christian morality to justify his mother's adultery, thereby legitimizing his noble identity and her honor in society. He adopts the role of a priest when he absolves his mother of sin to protect her reputation. He suggests her infidelity was divinely sanctioned because it produced him, a "privileged" son of Richard. By claiming her refusal of Richard I would have been sinful, he aligns her acquiescence with divine will, thus

---

[90] Shakespeare, *King John*, 1.1.270–275.
[91] Shakespeare, *King John*, 1.1.280.
[92] Shakespeare, *King John*, 1.1.225–283.

absolving her guilt and elevating his birth to a quasi-sacred event. The references to heaven and hell reinforce his loyalty to her and his readiness to defend her honor, like a knight, frames his illegitimacy as a Christian virtue tied to Richard's lion-like strength. This strengthens his bond to his mother and establishes him as a loyal son.

His description of himself as a "Knight, knight, good mother, Basilisco-like. / What, I am dubbed!" is a reference to Basilisco, a pompous knight from a contemporary tragic play (circa 1589–1592), *Soliman and Perseda*.[93] Basilisco is one of several foils to the Bastard. *Soliman and Perseda* is set against a fictionalized backdrop of the Turkish invasion of Rhodes in the early sixteenth century. Unlike the Bastard, who displays courage and is presented as a modern English Guy of Warwick (more on that later) devoted to his nation, Basilisco, while captured during the Turkish assault on Rhodes, agrees to "turn Turk" to save his life, but eventually returns to Rhodes to reclaim his Christian faith. The Bastard's references to catechism, absey-books, and "God-a-mercy" mock the superficial piety of courtly life and scholastic education. Unlike Castruccio, the Bastard knows how to use religion to advance his ambitions. He rejects the Faulconbridge name using Christian imagery (Good Friday, denying the devil), and invokes divine will to vindicate his birth and his mother's choice in order to transform his illegitimacy into a source of honor. His clever rhetoric aligns his ambition within a Christian framework that ostensibly forgives his mother's transgression while providing him respectable cover for navigating issues concerning legitimacy and honor within the play.

Basilisco is not the only foil to the Bastard. Recall when the Bastard's first soliloquy is interrupted by the arrival of his mother, in response to her query about the whereabouts of his brother, the Bastard refers to his brother Robert as "Coldbrand the Giant, that same

---

[93] Shakespeare, *King John*, 1.1.252.

mighty man" whom Guy of Warwick had killed in single combat.[94] By comparing his brother to Coldbrand, the Bastard compares himself to Guy of Warwick, a legendary Anglo-Norman Christian knight popular from the thirteenth to sixteenth century with both English and French audiences. The juxtaposition of his new Richard Plantagenet name and his reference to Guy of Warwick highlights the Bastard's nationalism, a quality Castruccio lacked, contributing to his empire's fragility due to internal dissent and Fortune's caprice. According to legend, Guy of Warwick falls in love with Lady Felice, a woman above his social rank. In order to prove himself worthy of her love, Guy embarks on a series of adventurous acts of chivalry, fighting dragons and monsters and enemies of Christendom, such as Goldbrand whom he beheads in battle. This act of beheading is later replicated in the Bastard's beheading of Austria.

The legend of Guy of Warwick and the Bastard highlight themes of duty, redemption, and patriotism, but with important differences. Guy, a crusader knight, fights for love and personal honor but later withdraws to a hermitage to seek forgiveness for his violent past. He chooses spiritual salvation over public duty. In contrast, the Bastard embodies English nationalism, giving up his inheritance and personal comfort to fight for England against France, believing his actions are justified on earth. He still retains an element of religion, however. As Roy Battenhouse suggests, the Bastard regards his loss of troops in the Lincoln washes as an omen sent from heaven.[95] His

---

[94] Shakespeare, *King John*, 1.1.230. Portions of this section rely on my earlier work on *King John* where I develop the Bastard's character in relation to England's conflict with the Church. See Khalil M. Habib, "The Bastard in *King John*; or On the Need for a Unified English Nation," in *The Soul of Statesmanship: Shakespeare on Nature, Virtue, and Political Wisdom*, ed. Khalil M. Habib and L. Joseph Hebert Jr. (Lanham, MD: Lexington Books, 2018), 128. In this present chapter, I am interested in how the Bastard offers a vision of politics rooted in duty to England and how this moral framework provides the necessary foundation for unity and liberty that Castruccio lacked.

[95] Roy Battenhouse, "Religion in *King John*: Shakespeare's View," *Connotations* 1, no. 2 (1991): 142

Christian beliefs are shaped by fierce loyalty to England, as evident in his prayers to St. George, England's military patron saint, whom the Bastard invokes just before beheading Austria: "Saint George, that swinged the dragon, and e'er since / Sits on his horseback at mine hostess' door, / Teach us some fence!"[96] When the Bastard beheads Austria, a Christian foe of England and the murderer of its former king, he invokes a supernatural "airy devil" causing mischief.[97] This suggests his actions, though violent, are framed by a patriotic reinterpretation of religious virtue. Shakespeare uses the Bastard to depict a devout-like commitment to England, where defending the nation requires a nuanced balance of zeal and strategy, blending religious and political ideals. The contrast underscores a shift from personal, spiritual heroism to patriotic, collective duty. In contrast, Machiavelli's Castruccio, as noted, separates religion from politics entirely, treating them as mutually exclusive, unlike Shakespeare's integrated vision of national devotion.

The Bastard's sense of national duty is the source of compassion, loyalty, and equitable judgment, which elevates him above the other characters and helps him bridge social divides and promote national cohesion. In addition to caring for his family, for example, he defends Hubert, a commoner, against the disloyal nobles Salisbury, Pembroke, and Bigot in Act 4. These nobles, who are secretly plotting to join the Dauphin, deride Hubert's humble origins and character. In contrast, the Bastard champions Hubert and prioritizes his personal integrity over the nobles' empty claims to superiority based on rank. By evaluating people based on their individual worth, not social status, the Bastard builds connections with others, regardless of class, laying the foundation for a unified community and nation. His fair and moderate approach allows him to transcend divisive factions, which Castruccio was never able to achieve accept through fear and force.

Another contrast between Castruccio's interest in his personal

---

[96] Shakespeare, *King John*, 2.1.288–290.
[97] Shakespeare, *King John*, 3.2.2.

Virtù, Fortuna, *and Nation*

gain and the Bastard's growing focus on national unity and interest can be seen in the Bastard's second and last soliloquy. The Bastard's second soliloquy in Act 2 follows King John and King Philip II of France's negotiations to resolve their dispute over the English throne, claimed by both John and Arthur, a young heir supported by France (2.1). They agree to a treaty involving the marriage of John's niece, Blanche of Castile, to the French Dauphin, Louis, with John ceding territories as part of Blanche's dowry. Though John retains the crown, he sacrifices significant English land. King Philip betrays Constance and Arthur's cause for personal gain, despite his initial moral posturing. The marriage treaty may ease Philip's conscience, but it reveals his abandonment of principle for self-interest.

The Bastard is clearly disappointed and sees this peace treaty as a betrayal of honor and principle on the part of the two kings, who have revealed they are both driven by self-interest rather than justice or faith, to say nothing of national interest. Disillusioned by the king's betrayal, the Bastard reflects on the corrupting power of self-interest in his famous "Commodity" soliloquy. He declares: "Mad world, mad kings, mad composition!"[98] His horror and suspicions at the blatant hypocrisy and lack of honor and virtue around him constitute the central theme of this soliloquy. He agonizes that, in order to prevent Arthur from claiming the whole kingdom, King John "hath willingly departed with a part."[99] Meanwhile King Philip of France, "whose armour conscience buckled on / Whom zeal and charity brought to the field / As God's own soldier," has reneged on his oath to protect Arthur and fight for his claim to the throne.[100] The Bastard is indignant by King Philip's pretended chivalry—the charitable tradition that taught those in power to serve and to protect the weak.

His view on "Commodity" may as well be a critique of Machiavellian policy. He blames "Commodity," that "sly devil, that broker

---

[98] Shakespeare, *King John*, 2.1.561.
[99] Shakespeare, *King John*, 2.1.573.
[100] Shakespeare, *King John*, 2.1.590.

that still breaks the pate of faith / That daily break-vow, he that wins of all."[101] For the sake of Commodity, one's obligations are to be performed when one is being observed or can be punished for disobedience, as when "having no external thing to lose." Betrayal, duplicity, and dishonesty are all the work of Commodity, whom the Bastard personifies as a "sly devil." As I have pointed out elsewhere, "we witness a religious dimension in the Bastard's devotion to England and his religious sentiments are in harmony, and not in opposition, to his sense of duty."[102] Commodity, the Bastard observes in disgust, is the rationalization of self-interest. The casuistry of Commodity produces conventional agreements and empty promises that are no more than a temporary restraint on self-interested impulses for fleeting desires. Commodity provides an appearance of a moral cover for duplicity by allowing tyrannical rulers to exploit people under the guise of providing them with the direction which they cannot give themselves. No one, the Bastard tells us, is wholly immune to Commodity's beguiling charms:

> Of kings, of beggars, old men, young men, maids,
> Who having no external thing to lose
> But the word "maid," cheats the poor maid of that,
> that smooth-faced gentleman, tickling commodity
> Commodity, the bias of the world.[103]

The Bastard uses the metaphor of a biased bowling ball weighted to curve to describe Commodity's harmful effect on the world. The world, he thinks, is *naturally* "peisèd well" (balanced) and meant to "run even," but is thrown off course by Commodity's "vile-drawing bias." This disrupts "indifferency" (impartiality), "direction," "purpose," and "intent," leading to moral and political chaos. Commodity is further described as a "bawd" (procurer), "broker"

---

[101] Shakespeare, *King John*, 2.1.567–568.
[102] Habib, "The Bastard in *King John*." 132.
[103] Shakespeare, *King John*, 2.2.580–584.

(middleman), and "all-changing word" in order to emphasize its role as a manipulative, morally corrupt force that sways decisions and undermines prudence and loyalty and the noble. In France's case, Commodity has led King Philip to abandon a "resolved and honorable war" for a "base and vile-concluded peace."[104]

Unlike the other characters in the play, the Bastard is honest with himself and tries to probe his own motivations. He questions why he rails against Commodity. He admits it is because he has not yet been "wooed" by it—his hand has not been tempted by "fair angels" (gold coins, a pun on heavenly beings). Like a "poor beggar" envying the rich, he criticizes Commodity because he has not yet profited from it, so he is at least aware of the source of his own resentment. Once he recognizes that even kings "break faith" for Commodity, the Bastard declares, "Gain, be my lord, for I will worship thee!"[105] He vows to serve self-interest and, for now at least, adopts the same opportunistic mindset he critiques, as he sees it is the path to advancement in a corrupt world.

The Bastard's famous "commodity" speech reflects his growing cynicism about political motives and his resolve to adapt to this reality for personal gain, but that is not the end of the story. By the end of the play, the Bastard learns that Commodity leads to contradictions, unhappiness, and also nearly tears England apart. The invasion of France is narrowly avoided, both Arthur and King John are dead (along with Elinor), and the nobles prove to be unfaithful to England and their sovereign. Under the spell of tickling Commodity, individuals are locked in a warring struggle with others that can never be resolved once they have abandoned their duty toward society.

A sense of dread over the breakdown of society hangs over the Bastard, for example, when he makes the following remark as he watches Hubert lift young Arthur's dead body to carry him off stage:

---

[104] Shakespeare, *King John*, 2.2.589–625.
[105] Shakespeare, *King John*, 2.1.625.

> I am amazed, methinks, and lose my way
> Among the thorns and dangers of this world.
> How easy dost thou take all England up!
> From forth this morsel of dead royalty,
> The life, the right and truth of all this realm
> Is fled to heaven; and England now is left
> To tug and scamble and to part by the teeth
> The unowed interest of proud-swelling state.
> Now for the bare-pick'd bone of majesty
> Doth dogged war bristle his angry crest
> And snarleth in the gentle eyes of peace:
> Now powers from home and discontents at home
> Meet in one line; and vast confusion waits,
> As doth a raven on a sick-fall'n beast,
> The imminent decay of wrested pomp.
> Now happy he whose cloak and cincture can
> Hold out this tempest.[106]

The Bastard's final speech, which closes the play, aligns nationalist pride with virtuous civic duty, and is a direct challenge to Commodity's view of a fundamental disharmony between naked self-interest and his own honest political norms that make it possible for him (or anyone) to live in a community.

For the Bastard, unlike Castruccio, loyalty to one's nation is a moral obligation, and violation of one's moral obligations results in political disorder and misery. Though the nation still seems imperfect and less than ideal, it nevertheless provides most of its members with common ground rooted in a sense of place and affection for one's fellows. The nation is an alternative to Commodity since it enables individuals to live together in peace by repressing their desire to exploit and oppress others, while providing them with a sense of national independence necessary for thwarting foreign and domestic threats.

---

[106] Shakespeare, *King John*, 4.3.147–163.

Virtù, Fortuna, and Nation

III

By the end of the play, the Bastard transform into a leader defined by strategic diplomacy and dedication to England's defense. While Castruccio's pursuit of personal gain left his empire vulnerable to Fortune, the Bastard's collaborative leadership and national loyalty provide a model for enduring stability. The setting of *King John* parallels Machiavelli's *Life of Castruccio*. Both depict the rise of upstarts who achieve significant success, and grapple uniting subjects and rulers, nobles and nation, while reconciling loyalty to a universal church with national interest. Unlike Machiavelli, Shakespeare does not frame politics as a binary choice. Instead, he blends these elements in the Bastard to present a vision for England.

The Bastard begins the play seeking his true identity, which is revealed in Act 1 when he is acknowledged as the son of King Richard I. Unlike his initial pursuit of status, his patriotism develops into a moral framework that prioritizes the common good over personal gain. This transformation is evident in his Commodity soliloquy, where he grows cynical about politics and critiques the self-serving motives of King John and King Philip II, and in his final speech, which closes the play, where he champions England's unity and resilience:

> O, let us pay the time but needful woe,
> Since it hath been beforehand with our griefs.
> This England never did, nor never shall,
> Lie at the proud foot of a conqueror,
> But when it first did help to wound itself.
> Now these her princes are come home again,
> Come the three corners of the world in arms,
> And we shall shock them. Nought shall make us rue,
> If England to itself do rest but true.[107]

---

[107] Shakespeare, *King John*, 5.7.110–118.

His love for England and its people replaces his earlier cynicism with a sense of duty. In contrast to Castruccio, whose ambition to build an empire left it unstable, the Bastard's patriotism, rooted in moral conviction, offers an alternate to Machiavelli's vision, fostering a more enduring legacy. He rejects "Commodity" through his experience and reflections on politics, particularly after witnessing King John's territorial concessions, King Philip's betrayal of Arthur, and England's internal divisions. These events reveal that selfish actions, at the expensive of the love of one's nation and fellow citizens, cause to societal harm rather than liberation. For the Bastard, freedom is tied to a moral duty that prioritizes England's sovereignty. Shakespeare's King John illustrates that a notion of liberty based on seizing power, as exemplified by Castruccio, lacks the moral foundation necessary to maintain a secure and strong nation.

The Theology of *Coriolanus*[1]

Kevin M. Cherry

William Shakespeare's *The Tragedy of Coriolanus* is set at the moment when, as Niccolò Machiavelli says in his *Discourses on Livy*, Rome's mixed regime was perfected by the introduction of the tribunes of the plebs as a way of restraining the insolence of the nobility.[2] Caius Martius Coriolanus, of course, does not see it that way. He thinks that the tribunes will nurture sedition, deprive the senate of its authority, and divide the city (see, for the longest account of his views, 3.1.120–62).[3] The tribunes, for their part, are suspicious of Coriolanus, who has awed the city with his martial deeds and is about to attain the consulship notwithstanding his disdain for the common people. Despite the efforts of his fellow patricians—especially his mother—the tribunes goad Coriolanus into openly mocking the people, who not only withdraw their support for his consulship but also ultimately vote to exile him from Rome, a reprieve from executing him. In Book I of Machiavelli's *Discourses*, the story famously ends here, and all's well that ends well. Shakespeare, though, reveals that Coriolanus joins with the very enemies he had just defeated and leads them in a direct attack on Rome. With the city in his grasp, Coriolanus's mother beseeches him to withdraw. He acquiesces, Rome rejoices, but Coriolanus himself is killed by his new, albeit

---

[1] I am grateful to Charlotte Thomas and Will Jordan for the invitation and to the other participants for their insightful talks. My understanding of Shakespeare as a political thinker was significantly influenced by a series of seminars led by Paul Cantor at the University of Richmond in May of 2010, and even where I have come to disagree with him, I have never failed to learn from him.

[2] Machiavelli, *Discourses on Livy*, I.7, 24–5. References are to the book, chapter, and page number of this edition.

[3] All references to *Coriolanus* will be to act, scene, and line numbers as found in William Shakespeare, *Coriolanus*, ed. Lee Bliss (New York: Cambridge University Press, 2010, rev. ed.).

short-lived, allies.⁴ It is perhaps worth noting that Shakespeare, too, omits part of the story, leaving out Plutarch's report that after Coriolanus's death, the Volsces were ultimately conquered by Rome and forced to accept a peace far less favorable than that which Coriolanus had negotiated.⁵

In this paper, I explore how Shakespeare's particular presentation of Rome's institutions is sufficiently imprecise to call our attention less to those institutions than to the beliefs that support them. In particular, and through some key departures from Plutarch, he highlights the challenges posed to a republican regime by one who sees himself, and is seen by others, as something akin to a god. Such a claim depends upon a view of the highest good, a view that is easily disputed in republics. Shakespeare thus illustrates how such a dispute may be resolved through the careful cultivation of appearances in order to appeal to the people. Although Coriolanus belatedly recognizes this and attempts to do so, he is unable to put aside years of habit and be someone he is not. The play thus ends with "the body of Martius" borne offstage in a way that the body of Mars could never be.⁶ The conclusion of the play thus leads us to reflect briefly on Shakespeare's account of Julius Caesar, who more successfully cultivates popular support at the expense not merely of his own

---

[4] Later in the *Discourses*, Machiavelli acknowledges Coriolanus's betrayal and that Rome was saved "more through piety for his mother than by the strength of the Romans" (III.13, 249).

[5] T. J. B. Spencer, ed., *Shakespeare's Plutarch* (New York: Penguin, 1964), 362. Unless otherwise indicated, all references to Plutarch's *Life of Coriolanus* are to this edition. References to the other parallel lives, as well as to the comparisons that re excluded from Spencer's edition, are to Plutarch, *The Lives of the Noble Grecians and Romans Compared Together*, trans. James Amiot and Sir Thomas North (Cambridge, 1676), https://www.proquest.com/docview/2240869286. This includes the comparison between Alcibiades and Coriolanus, which is, as several commentators note, the source for the exchange between the officers in 2.2. See E. A. J. Honigman, "Shakespeare's Plutarch," *Shakespeare Quarterly* 10, no.1 (1959): 26–9.

[6] Bliss notes that Shakespeare refers to the titular character as "Martius" rather than "Caius" in order to preserve the association with Mars (in Shakespeare, *Coriolanus*, 117).

life—"Caesar" becomes immortal as name and as title—but of Rome's republican character.

Paul Cantor has argued that Shakespeare depicts the various regimes of Rome in his three Roman plays, with *Coriolanus*, given its presentation of the "conflict of the orders" representing the early republic; *Julius Caesar*, the decline of that republic; and *Antony and Cleopatra* representing the dawn of the empire.[7] Although Ben Jonson famously alleged that the Romans in Shakespeare's plays "are merely Elizabethan Englishmen in disguise," Cantor praises "Shakespeare's grasp of the essential nature of the Roman regime."[8] In particular, he praises Shakespeare's understanding of "the functioning of the republican regime in *Coriolanus*," including the "two consuls [who] were chosen every year."[9]

If we look more closely, it is curious that in *Coriolanus* the consulship—so famously divided during the Roman republic, lest one man resemble a king—is presented primarily as an office held by one man, and one man only. To be sure, there is a moment in the play where an officer asks "How many stand for consulships?" implying

---

[7] Paul A. Cantor, *Shakespeare's Rome: Republic and Empire* (Chicago, IL: University of CHiago Press, 2017), 21–7. The contrast, as he acknowledges, is most pronounced between *Coriolanus* and *Antony and Cleopatra*, which were written later in his career than *Julius Caesar*. Although Cantor suggests that Shakespeare was primarily interested in sketching the "different mixtures of heroic virtues and vices" to be found in distinct types of regime, republican Rome may have held more interest for him because it was less familiar to him and his audience than monarchical government (*Roman Trilogy: The Twighlight of the Ancient World* [Chicago, IL: University of Chicago Press, 2017], 13–7, 25).

[8] Cantor, *Republic and Empire*, 7, 10. Similar sentiments are voiced by Spencer, who claims Shakespeare "shows a great deal of care to get things right, to preserve Roman manners and customs and allusions," including "the usual Roman officials, and political and religious customs" ("Shakespeare and the Elizabethan Romans," in *Shakespeare Survey* 10, ed. Allardyce Nicoll [Cambridge: Cambridge University Press, 1957], 34–5).

[9] Cantor, *Roman Trilogy*, 26. Jan H. Blits, however, observes that "the competitive and constant flux of Roman politics" makes it hard to define the boundaries of any particular institution (*Spirit, Soul, and City: Shakespeare's "Coriolanus"* [Lanham, MD: Lexington Books, 2006], 126).

that there is more than one, but the reply is that although there are three candidates, "tis thought…Coriolanus will carry it," in the singular (2.2.1–4).¹⁰ The play thus seems to (mis)represent the nature of the Roman consulship as something closer to a monarchy than the divided office that it was and was consciously intended to be. We moderns, accustomed to a unitary executive, may reject the wisdom of such an institution,¹¹ but what might account for Shakespeare's deviation from the historical reality of the Roman consulship in a play that purportedly articulates the Roman regime?

It is frequently noted that the play follows the life of Coriolanus written by Plutarch rather closely. Peter Holland even suggests "it is impossible" to imagine Shakespeare writing his play without "the weighty tome of North's translation [of Plutarch] open beside him as he wrote," and his use of Plutarch was "remarkably single-minded," with little evidence of other influences.¹² Perhaps, then, we might simply blame Shakespeare for following Plutarch too closely, for he also emphasizes the singular place of Coriolanus in Rome. And yet Shakespeare is perfectly capable of departing from Plutarch when he so chooses. As we shall see, there are several aspects of

---

[10] Michael Platt adduces a second piece of evidence, Coriolanus's own complaint that the tribunes undermine the consuls (3.1.109), but there is no reason to assume that Coriolanus means only the current consuls rather than all of the consuls moving forward. Either way, Platt concedes that overall the play's focus is narrowed "because Coriolanus overshadows all others in excellence" (*Rome and Romans According to Shakespeare* [Lanham, MD: University Press of America, 1982, rev. ed.], 180 n1).

[11] See, however, David Orentlicher, *Two Presidents Are Better than One: The Case for a Bipartisan Executive Branch* (New York: New York University Press, 2013). The obvious counterargument is Alexander Hamilton's *Federalist 70*.

[12] Peter Holland, ed., *Coriolanus* (New York: Bloomsbury, 2013), 33–5. Anne Barton, however, suggests that Shakespeare also drew heavily on Livy, not merely for Menenius's fable in Act I but for the play's depiction of an "evolving" republic in which the plebians were entitled to greater "respect" ("Livy, Machiavelli, and Shakespeare's *Coriolanus*," in *Shakespeare Survey* 38, ed. Stanley Wells [New York: Cambridge Uniersity Press, 1985], 116–7, 121). Bliss contends that although Shakespeare likely "read all of Livy's version" of the story of Coriolanus, he "preferred to follow Plutarch's version of the events" (in Shakespeare, *Coriolanus*, 12).

Plutarch's life which Shakespeare omits, such as Coriolanus's strategy of stoking the division between plebian and patrician in Rome before attacking it with the Volsces; there are also things Shakespeare adds to what is in Plutarch, such as Coriolanus's refusal to show the people his scars, for Plutarch's subject displays no such compunction. It is, perhaps paradoxically, the very care with which Shakespeare read Plutarch that should caution us against assuming he followed him unthinkingly.[13]

In this particular case, Shakespeare seems less to be following Plutarch than going beyond him. Plutarch surely presents Coriolanus as a singular figure, unmatched in Rome for his valor. Yet Shakespeare exaggerates even this depiction. The Coriolanus of Shakespeare's play, for instance, both acts and portrays himself as acting singlehandedly in the sack of Corioles.[14] The play accordingly almost always proceeds as though there is but a single consul to be found in Rome. Michael Platt contends that Shakespeare is simply following Plutarch, who "says nothing of the second consul," but Plutarch in fact frequently refers to consuls in the plural.[15] Indeed, in the passage where the people refuse to elevate Coriolanus, the Greek text indicates that "others" were chosen [ὡς δ᾿ ἀνηγορεύθησαν ἕτεροι]. We should not, however, focus on what Plutarch wrote in Greek but rather what Shakespeare—having before him only North's English translation of Amyot's French—would have read. And that English

---

[13] Spencer suggests that Shakespeare's "deviations from Plutarch are all in the direction of theatrical effectiveness" (*Shakespeare's Plutarch*, 16). This view cannot account for perhaps the most original scene in the play, the discussion between the Volsci Adrian and the spy Nicanor in 4.3, a conversation which includes none of the main characters and does nothing to advance the plot—which is why, as Cathy Shank reports, "it is frequently cut in modern performances" ("Civility and the City in *Coriolanus*," *Shakespeare Quarterly* 54, no. 4 [2003]: 419). Cantor suggests that precisely because he is a spy, and thus truly independent of the political community, Nicanor offers the most objective account of the divisions in Rome (*Republic and Empire*, 119). See also Blits *Spirit, Soul, and City*, 164 ff.

[14] This allows Coriolanus to famously contend "Alone, I did it!" in his fiery, final speech (5.6.119).

[15] Platt, *Rome and Romans*, 180 n1.

translation is even more clear, with North stating that, after rejecting Coriolanus, the people "made *two others* that were suitors Consuls" (emphasis added).[16] The choice to treat the consulship as a unitary office is emphatically Shakespeare's own.

Perhaps the confusion arises because Shakespeare is not interested in politics but rather in the "rich inner lives" of his protagonists.[17] Edwin Honig, for instance, suggests that the play is fundamentally about "the alienation of a 'natural' leader" due to "fissured pride and mother domination," which means that the drama is primarily "psychological and moral" and "only secondarily social."[18] If Shakespeare is primarily interested in psychology, he might simply be indifferent "to questions of constitutional theory" and unable "to understand the ideals of an antique self-governing commonwealth controlled by all its free members."[19]

At least on its surface, *Coriolanus* offers little evidence of extensive self-reflection: The play, as Michael Platt observes, "is remarkable for the comparative absence of soliloquy."[20] Even Honig acknowledges that Coriolanus at the end of the play seems to be precisely who he was at the beginning.[21] It is, however, worth considering whether this absence of self-reflection is a flaw of Coriolanus himself or a flaw in the Roman way of life. The tribunes, too, are accused by Menenius of lacking self-knowledge (2.1.31–3). The limitation, therefore, seems to reflect something about the broader political culture, or regime, of ancient Rome as much as it does a

---

[16] Plutarch, *Lives, Vol. IV*, ed. Bernadette Perrin (Cambridge, MA: Harvard University Press, 1914], 152–3; Spencer, *Shakespeare's Plutarch*, 314–6, 320.

[17] Kay Stockholder, *Thinking About Shakespeare*, ed. Amy Scott (Hoboken, NJ: Wiley-Blackwell, 2018), 67.

[18] Edwin Honig, "Sejanus and Coriolanus: A Study in Alienation," *Modern Language Quarterly* 12, no. 4 (1951): 407.

[19] M. W. MacCallum, *Shakespeare's Roman Plays and their Backgrounds* (New York: Macmillan, 1925), 518.

[20] Platt, *Romans*, 57. See also Cantor, *Roman Trilogy*, 137. To the extent there is a soliloquy in the play (2.3), Cantor suggests that it is deliberately awkward: "wooden verse reveals wooden thought" (*Republic and Empire*, 115).

[21] Honig, "Sejanus and Coriolanus," 411.

personal shortcoming of Coriolanus.

And there is a great deal of evidence that Shakespeare is in fact concerned about the political questions raised by the play. The word "power," for instance, appears more in this play than any other.[22] The very first lines of the play are spoken by Roman citizens, and it is commonly noted that the Roman citizens appear more fully as characters in *Coriolanus* than either of the other two Roman plays.[23] Indeed, the designation of "citizen" is significant within the play itself, for the residents of Antium are, by contrast, identified only as serving-men (4.5) and watchmen (5.2), conspirators and lords (5.6). A clear indication of Shakespeare's awareness of political issues is that he has Sicinius check to be sure that the people have been organized into tribes to vote on Coriolanus's fate (3.3.10–2), which, as Plutarch explains, increased the power of those poor people more likely to oppose him.[24]

Given the play's attention to political questions, it is possible that Shakespeare unified the consulship to make the comparison "to English kingship more pointed" given contemporary political dilemmas. One scholar even suggests that Coriolanus's disdain for the people is more of "a reflection of [King] James's well-known dislike of crowds and commoners" than the hero depicted by Plutarch.[25] The play thus ultimately presents "a rivalry between absolute monarchy and democracy, between rule and misrule, between order and chaos," precisely the divide between King James and Parliament, with

---

[22] Annabel Patterson, *Shakespeare and the Popular Voice* (Cambridge, MA: Basil Blackwell, 1990), 141.

[23] See, for instance, David Lowenthal, *Shakespeare's Thought: Unobserved Details and Unsuspected Depths in Thirteen Plays* (Lanham, MD: Lexington Books, 2017), 293.

[24] Spencer, *Shakespeare's Plutarch*, 331–2.

[25] Clifford Chalmers Huffman, *"Coriolanus" in Context* (Lewisburg, PA: Bucknell University Press, 1972), 188, 193n45.

Shakespeare taking the former's side.[26]

The majority of those who read Shakespeare as reflecting the monarchical debates of his time, however, tend to find him sympathetic to the popular cause. They find in the play an anticipation of King James's invocation of the doctrine of divine right; the tribunes' charge that Coriolanus is a "traitorous innovator" (3.1.176) echoes the accusations made against that assertion.[27] (To be fair, it is strange to think that opposing an institution that was created about 1500 lines earlier amounts to wild innovation.) The Englishmen of Shakespeare's time, perhaps, needed to learn from the Romans how to identify and resist dangerous rulers. This reading is the basis for the recent treatment of *Coriolanus* by Stephen Greenblatt in his book *Tyrant*. Greenblatt praises the tribunes, Sicinius and Brutus, for their manipulation of the people to get them to oppose Coriolanus since they correctly perceive the danger he poses to the city. The lesson for contemporary audiences, as for Shakespeare's own, is that "cynical, conniving, and manipulative…career politicians, bent principally on protecting their own positions" are necessary to protect the people from oppression because the people too often fail to see adequately the dangers of tyranny on their own.[28]

I share Peter Kaufman's suspicion that any approach to the play that endorses the tribunes' behavior is "ill-conceived."[29] Indeed, another way in which Shakespeare departs from Plutarch is in making the tribunes even more objectionable: they are not only responsible for the people's decision to revoke their approval of Coriolanus for

---

[26] Despite emphasizing the popular nature of Shakespeare's theatrical productions, Huffman argues that the play ultimately suggests a preference for monarchy (*"Coriolanus" in Context*, 180, 196).

[27] Barbara L. Parker, *Plato's "Republic" and Shakespeare's Rome* (Newark, DE: University of Deleware Press, 2004), 55–7, 70–2.

[28] Stephen Greenblatt, *Tyrant: Shakespeare on Politics* (New York: W. W. Norton, 2018), 169–77.

[29] Peter I. Kaufman, "Machiavelli's People and Shakespeare's Prophet: The Early Modern Afterlife of Ciaus Martius Coriolanus," *Leadership and the Humanities* 1, no 1 (2013): 13.

the consulship but they also insist that the citizens give them the credit for their initial support and exculpate them for the reversal (2.3.199–240). The tribunes are, in the words of Allan Bloom, "vile self-seekers who mislead an innocent populace."[30] I am, therefore, hesitant to adopt the idea that Shakespeare is simply making the Roman model fit the English situation so as to warn against the perils of tyranny and to elicit support for "calculating and deceptive" popular politicians.[31]

To criticize the tribunes is, of course, not to suggest that Shakespeare is simply a monarchist who unquestioningly admires Coriolanus or, for that matter, King James. It is, rather, to recognize that, as Elizabeth Fraser nicely put it, "Shakespeare 'presses' rather than seeks to solve political problems."[32] We see this in *Coriolanus* insofar as the problem of the unified consulship is not the only difficulty revealed by a close reading of the play. Although there are said to be five tribunes (1.1.198–200), we encounter only two: Sicinius and Brutus—yes, the two named by Plutarch, although his "Life" refers to the others, if not by name.[33] However, the pair of tribunes throughout the play only highlights the absence of a pair of consuls. In fact, there are occasions where the play itself calls attention to the fact that there is a pair of tribunes, rather than a pair of consuls and five tribunes. Menenius, for instance, calls attention to the pair precisely five times in Act 2, Scene 1 (ll. 11, 14, 19, 44, 64). Moreover, the method of choosing these tribunes is unclear, for the revolting

---

[30] Allan Bloom, with Henry V. Jaffa, *Shakespeare's Politics* (Chicago, IL: University of Chicago Press, 1996), 82. Bloom suggests that Shakespeare's criticism of Coriolanus is not that he is wrong about the people but that he "is full of hatred and bitterness" toward them, rather than approaching them—as Shakespeare does—with "a spirit of acceptance" (*Shakespeare's Politics*, 84).

[31] Greenblatt, *Tyrant*, 172.

[32] Elizabeth Fraser, "Shakespeare's Politics," *Review of Politics* 78, no. 4 (2016): 506n11.

[33] In Plutarch, the names of the other tribunes are simply not mentioned; in the play, Coriolanus seems to forget them, just as he did the name of his benefactor in Corioles (1.1.199–200, 1.9.89–90).

plebians were unaware of their existence and so presumably played no role in selecting them (1.1.198–200).

There is also the odd scene in which the citizens of Rome approach Coriolanus so he may ask for their support for the consulship. They are explicitly told to approach him in ones, twos, and threes (2.3.37); the first group of citizens contains three people, but after conversing, Coriolanus dismisses them by saying "There's in all two worthy voices begged. I have your alms. Adieu." As the *third* citizen objects, "But this is something odd!" (2.3.72–4). There are, in other words, oddities about the number of voters, the number of tribunes, and the number of consuls. To the extent that *Coriolanus* is supposed to tell us about the Roman regime, it seems to present a fairly muddied version of it, at least in terms of its institutions.

Of course, a regime is more than merely institutions, though contemporary political science too often takes the narrower view. The classical view is that a regime fundamentally represents a way of life, a conception of what the city holds to be good. Perhaps it is this understanding of regime that Shakespeare seeks to highlight.[34] Coriolanus claims to deserve his consulship on the basis of his deeds on behalf of the city. He is courageous, and this is what Rome values. As Cominius puts it, "it is held that valor is the chiefest virtue" (2.2.78–80). The patricians obviously agree that Coriolanus's deeds merit the consulship, because they believe that there is, in fact, a highest virtue and that it is valor.

The plebians, however, are less certain.[35] They recognize Coriolanus's martial excellence, though they are uncertain whether this virtue is not offset by other vices, which is one reason why they struggle to decide whether he ought to be made consul. It is not simply their inconsistency, as Coriolanus charges (and they themselves concede, referring to their "diversely colored" wits, 2.3.15–20), but

---

[34] Cantor specifically ascribes Shakespeare's understanding of "regime" to his reading of Plutarch's *Lives* (*Roman Trilogy*, 7; cf. ch. 4).

[35] Cf. Lowenthal, who claims there was a single "dominant and unchallenged moral custom" in Coriolanus's Rome (*Shakespeare's Thought*, 111).

perhaps also their perception that valor, even if the "chiefest" good, is not the only good. The play offers some support for this in the character of Cominius himself, whose very phrasing—"It is *held* that valor is the chiefest virtue"—indicates, as Anne Barton puts it, "a slight but significant tremor of doubt."[36] His hesitation is not surprising since he had earlier counseled that Romans should be "neither foolish in our stands nor cowardly in retire" (1.6.1–3) and later insists that "manhood is called foolery when it stands against a falling fabric" (3.1.247–9). Sicinius grounds the opposition between patrician and plebian in what he calls an "ancient malice" that is not easily overcome (2.1.202) and would make it hard to find a common basis for the highest good, be it valor or something else.

Coriolanus, however, seems to accept the view that singles out valor as the highest virtue, even to the extent that he is more concerned with doing courageous deeds than the honor that might accrue to them, refusing, for instance, to hear his deeds recounted (1.9.13, 28–9; 2.2.62–4, 68–70). Commentators on the play have therefore often considered whether Coriolanus might embody Aristotle's magnanimous man.[37] Others have found in it fodder for reflecting about Aristotle's famous observation in his *Politics* that one who is without a political community must be either a beast or a god.[38] For instance, Coriolanus is considered a beast by the tribune

---

[36] Barton, "Livy, Machiavelli," 115. See also Blits, *Spirit, Soul, and City*, 93–6.

[37] Explorations of this theme include Carson Holloway, "Shakespeare's *Coriolanus* and Aristotle's Great-Souled Man," *The Review of Politics* 69, no. 3 (2007), and Lowenthal, *Shakespeare's Thought*, 296–301. Both ultimately conclude Coriolanus lacks this virtue, but one might reflect on whether Coriolanus or Cominius is closer to the genuine kind of courage Aristotle discusses in the *Nicomachean Ethics*.

[38] See, in this volume, the contribution by Vickie Sullivan, as well as Cantor, *Republic and Empire*, ch. 3, and Platt, *Romans*, 165–75. F. N. Lees goes farther, arguing that Shakespeare was familiar enough with Aristotle's *Politics* that the play was intended to treat this question: The playwright was able to grasp "the essential similarity between Aristotle's fairly extreme and obvious monster and Plutarch's great, proud, and humanly incapacitated Roman" ("Coriolanus, Aristotle, and Bacon," *The Review of English Studies* 1, no. 2 [1950]: 122). Although Lees claims the

Sicinius, who calls him a "viper" who seeks to "depopulate the city" (3.1.265–6, 292), as well as by his friend Menenius, who refers to him as a dragon and "a male tiger" (5.4.10, 24). His rival Aufidius refers to him as an "osprey" preying on the birds of Rome (4.7.34), and even Volumnia calls her son "a bear" (1.3.26). The plebians, too, are characterized as beasts not only by Coriolanus—"The beast / With many heads butts me away" (3.4.1–2, cf. 1.4.35 and 4.5.40)—and his mother ("cats," 4.2.36) but also by their own tribunes, who assert that even "nature teaches beasts to know their friends," the tagline for the 2011 film adaptation (2.1.5).[39]

But if several characters in the play are considered bestial, it is Coriolanus alone who is identified as, and self-identifies as, a god. He tells Aufidius, for instance, that Menenius had "godded" him back in Rome (5.3.8–11), and Menenius confirms this, saying that Coriolanus "sits in his state as a thing made for Alexander," wanting "nothing of a god but eternity and a heaven to throne in" (5.4.17–20).[40] Even Cominius—who seems more reflective than the other Romans—agrees when he encounters Coriolanus leading the Volsces: "He is their god; he leads them like a thing / Made by some other deity than Nature / That shapes man better" (4.6.94–6). Such descriptions occur even before Coriolanus departs Rome: As Michael Platt observes, Shakespeare modifies Plutarch by having Cominius try to reward Coriolanus with not ten of each good they

---

contrast between the bestial and divine can be found only in Aristotle, not Plutarch (116–7). such a tension is presented quite clearly in Plutarch's life of Publicola. In describing Brutus's execution of his sons, Plutarch calls it an act that surpasses "the common nature of man, that have in it both Divineness and sometime beastly brutishness" (*Lives*, 84). The most thoughtful consideration of Aristotle's treatment of the tension can be found in Mary P. Nichols, *Aristotle's Discovery of the Human: Piety and Politics in the "Nicomachean Ethics,"* (Notre Dame, IN: University of Notre Dame Press, 2023).

[39] Coriolanus refers to Aufidius as "a lion / That I am proud to hunt" (1.1.219–20), but never anything divine.

[40] This comparison is bracketed by his references to Coriolanus as a dragon and a tiger (5.4.10, 24). Platt suggests that Coriolanus so transcends his fellows that he is incomprehensible to them (*Romans*, 93).

seized in Corioles but rather a tithe: "the traditional portion of crops, spoils, or wealth given to a god who has rendered aid to men."[41] The tribunes are informed that he is being saluted by the nobles as though he were "Jove's statue" (2.1.239–40) and fear that, in his pride, he will "not spare to gird the gods" (1.1.240). Even his sworn enemy Aufidius, upon Coriolanus's arrival in Antium, says that he accepts Coriolanus's promise of loyalty as he would accept Jupiter's own (4.5.100–2) and refers to him as "thou Mars" (4.5.115).

The serving-men of Antium, by contrast, are more restrained: they see him only as "son and heir to Mars," rather than Mars himself (4.5.186–7). This more mortal view of Coriolanus is paralleled by the references to him as Hercules—the son of Zeus or, in the Roman pantheon, Jupiter—in Act 4, one of which is provided by Coriolanus himself (4.1.17) and the other by Menenius (4.6.104).[42] Despite his claims of surpassing ordinary humanity, when Coriolanus departs Rome for that "world elsewhere" (3.3.143), he does not find—much less create— such a world but rather simply goes to another city that is, in many ways, much like Rome. And though he famously promises to stand "as if a man were author of himself" (5.3.35–6)—entirely independent and wholly self-sufficient—he is soon reminded of his dependency upon his mother. The obvious conclusion for most scholars is that Coriolanus, at least initially, misunderstands his nature: He is not a combination of beast and god but rather, as Aristotle might put it, something *between* beast and god.

That Coriolanus considers himself something akin to a god may well account for the way in which Shakespeare emphasizes the singular consulship for which he stands. Coriolanus's self-understanding warrants more consideration, however, for in Rome it is not always consistent and it is presented differently once in Antium. Perhaps Shakespeare's most significant departure from Plutarch's life of Coriolanus is his elimination of nearly all the institutions of

---

[41] Platt, *Rome and Romans*, 94.

[42] Coriolanus's reference is a bit jarring insofar as he addresses not Virgilia but his mother as "the wife of Hercules."

civil religion—temples, sacrifices, auguries, the soothsayers who play a memorable role in *Julius Caesar*—from Plutarch's account. There is, to be sure, an augurer mentioned briefly by Menenius at the beginning of Act II, Scene 1, but it is not clear whether the augurer in fact relies on divine knowledge, for Volumnia, Virgilia, and Valeria soon bring the same news with a decidedly mundane origin: letters from Coriolanus to his mother and wife, the state, and Menenius himself (2.1.89–90). Yet in Plutarch's life, there is a lengthy description of how the Romans feared that the tension within the city after his Coriolanus's departure was prompted by impieties during a sacred procession and how they sought to atone for these.[43] Given how closely Shakespeare generally followed Plutarch, it is worth reflecting on the absence of such a scene.

To be sure, such a digression on impiety and atonement may have been difficult to dramatize, but its place is taken by the previously mentioned conversation between Adrian and Nicanor that—at least on the surface—lacks much dramatic effectiveness. Insofar as the description of processional rites is connected by Plutarch to his "Life of Numa," however, one wonders whether Shakespeare excised this not merely for theatrical purposes but because Numa's reforms were ultimately of minimal effect. Although Numa sought to make Rome less warlike, the city reverted to its martial nature after his death. Valor was once again believed to be the chief virtue by the Romans, even by those descended from Numa—as Coriolanus himself was (cf. 2.3.224–5). Ironically, as Plutarch notes in his comparison of Numa to the Spartan founder Lycurgus, Rome flourishes precisely *because* it overturns his laws, making valor the chiefest virtue. In removing this scene, Shakespeare is perhaps more in accord with Plutarch's analysis than Plutarch himself was in sketching the life of

---

[43] Spencer, *Shakespeare's Plutarch*, 339–41. Plutarch also reports that an embassy composed of "goodly rabble of superstition and priests" was sent to Coriolanus to persuade him not to attack Rome, to no avail (349). Cf. *Julius Caesar*, 1.3.15–32; 2.2.13–26.

Coriolanus.⁴⁴ Moreover, though Shakespeare seeks to show how the divisions in Rome are deep and not caused merely by impieties or even by Coriolanus's attempt to set patrician against plebian, recounted in detail by Plutarch but omitted from Shakespeare's drama.⁴⁵ Rather, the central question on the table seems to be what to do with a figure who stands within the city as Jupiter or Mars.

The answer to this question may be related to the particular regime. Paul Cantor has argued that in *Antony and Cleopatra* Shakespeare shows the connection between hierarchical theology and politics, insofar as the decline of republican government into imperial rule "prepared the way for Christianity in the Roman empire," pointing to details like the reference to King Herod.⁴⁶ Alexis de Tocqueville similarly argues that imperial Rome made possible the acceptance of the radical equality proposed by Christianity:

> At the moment when the Christian religion appeared on earth, Providence, which was undoubtedly preparing the world for its coming, had united a great part of the human species, like an immense flock, under the scepter of the Caesars. The men who composed that multitude differed much from one another, but they nevertheless had this common point: they all obeyed the same laws; and each of them was so weak and small in relation to the greatness of the prince that they all appeared equal when one came to compare them to him.⁴⁷

But these, of course, are not the views of god or politics found in *Coriolanus*.

Just as the institutions of republican Rome are muddy in the

---

⁴⁴ Plutarch, *Lives*, 57–8, 60–1, 65. Cantor suggests that Shakespeare excises the religious rituals "prominent" in Plutarch to emphasize the self-reliance of the Romans (*Roman Trilogy*, 56–7). Coriolanus says the women deserve a temple for saving Rome (5.3.207–8), but unlike in Plutarch, it is not said that this is a temple to Fortune (Spencer, *Shakespeare's Plutarch*, 359).

⁴⁵ Spencer, *Shakespeare's Plutarch*, 339–46.

⁴⁶ Cantor, *Roman Trilogy*, 3–4, 69.

⁴⁷ Alexis de Tocqueville, *Democracy in America*, trans. Harvey C. Mansfield and Delba Winthrop (Chicago, IL: University of Chicago Press, 2000), II.i.5, 420.

play, I wish to suggest that the view of the gods is similarly unclear and that understanding the problems associated with theology in the play can help us understand some of the difficulties with the way political institutions are portrayed. The Romans worshipped gods in the plural, as is clear from the variety of invocations made by a wide range of characters, yet some gods—such as Jupiter—seem to be superior to others. The play thus alternates not only between identifying Coriolanus as a beast and a god but also between treating the gods as a broad group and as particular divinities that seem higher than others. This difference results in some of the tensions that drive the plot forward.

For instance, at the beginning of the play, Coriolanus praises the Senate for maintaining order "under the gods" (1.1.169–70), but almost simultaneously he mocks the popular view that these very gods send food for the poor as well as the rich (1.1.190–1).[48] By contrast, when he himself enters into battle, he invokes Mars (1.4.11). Shortly thereafter, he shouts "Pluto and hell!" when chastising the Romans for retreating in battle, reflecting his perception of the gap between his eagerness for battle and their reluctance (1.4.37). Coriolanus thus appeals to these other nameless "gods" alongside "Supreme Jove," but the former references are sometimes ironic, whereas nearly all of the latter uses are about Coriolanus himself—indicative of his potentially divine character that fits uneasily with the existing popular commitments of Rome. A republic may be under the protection of the gods but it has little place for a Jupiter or Mars within it.

There are two places in the play where this tension is especially pronounced. When the tribunes inform Coriolanus that the people oppose his elevation to consul, he does not merely criticize this particular decision but rather alleges a "plot/To curb the will of the nobility" (3.1.39–40) by encouraging "rebellion, insolence, sedition" among "the mutable rank-scented meinie"—"those measles" of the

---

[48] A similarly ironic invocation of the gods can be found during his trial, when Coriolanus sarcastically hopes that "the honored gods" will keep Rome safe, led by "worthy men" and filled with "love" among the people (3.3.35–7).

body politic (3.1.67, 71, 79). Brutus warns Coriolanus that he speaks "as if he were a god, to punish, not a man of their infirmity" (3.1.81–3), and Coriolanus responds with a lengthy speech in which he twice invokes "Jove himself" (3.1.87, 108) in support of "the honored number" who possess "gentry, title wisdom," against the "general ignorance" of the "multitudinous tongue" (3.1.73, 145–7, 157). Coriolanus thus places the supreme god Jupiter on the side of the patricians, particularly himself, against the people, who have none of the noble qualities that warrant political power.

A similar view is expressed by Coriolanus's mother after he is exiled from Rome. Upon encountering the two tribunes, Volumnia attacks them: "As far as doth the Capitol exceed / The meanest house in Rome, so far my son…whom you have banished does exceed you all" (4.2.41–4). She explicitly advocates a proportion: The Capitol exceeds the meanest house in Rome in the same way that Coriolanus exceeds all the other people of the city.[49] Upon exiting, Volumnia urges Virgilia to join her in lamenting "in anger, Juno-style" (4.2.54–5, cf. 2.1.82, 5.3.46)—that is, in the manner of the wife of the greatest of the gods. We again see here the view of Coriolanus as Jupiter, alone and superior among even the gods.[50]

And yet the play as a whole presents the Capitol not as a dwelling only for the most godlike man but rather for all the citizens of Rome. Indeed, we see a variety of people headed to the Capitol throughout the play: The citizens are about to go to the Capitol when they first encounter Menenius in Act I; when the senators try to send them to their homes, they are directed to go to the Capitol by none other than Caius Martius himself (1.1.232). The senators go to the Capitol to celebrate Coriolanus's conquest in Act II, but also call for the tribunes to meet them there (2.1.178, 234, 242). The

---

[49] As scholars generally acknowledge, Shakespeare misunderstands the Capitol, treating it as "the seat of the Senate," rather than as the temple of Jupiter Capitolinus, near the Senate's meeting place near the Forum (Holland, *Coriolanus*, 236n).

[50] Menenius speaks similarly of Volumnia herself as surpassing the rest of the city after she successfully persuades her son not to destroy Rome (5.4.48–51).

confirmation of Coriolanus's elevation to consul is supposed to take place at the Capitol, amidst all the citizens, nobles and plebians alike (2.3.131–2). When the patricians gather to discuss Coriolanus's invasion, they meet at the Capitol and the tribunes join them (4.6.151, 162). If the Capitol is a home, it seems to be a home for all the citizens, those who excel and those who do not. A disproportion there may be, but it is not as extensive as Volumnia thinks, perhaps because the alleged basis for the disproportion—Coriolanus's deeds in battle—is not a standard accepted by everyone. Although there is little evidence that Coriolanus genuinely sought to re-establish a monarchy in Rome—he opposes sharing power with the plebians, not with other patricians like Cominius—he nevertheless provides a rationale for doing so: one who exceeds others, as the Capitol does the meanest house, in the chiefest virtue ought to have a corresponding amount of political power.[51]

However, Coriolanus is far more circumspect among the Volsces and thus does not encounter the same difficulties he did in Rome until the end of the play. To be sure, one reason is that the people there seem to look forward to war.[52] Whereas Coriolanus assailed his fellow citizens for their reluctance to fight (1.1.151–2, 1.4.35–41, 3.1.121–6), the serving-men of Antium prefer war to peace, not least because it shows men the need they have of one another (4.5.210–22). They are thus more similar to Coriolanus in temperament and may well be open to the idea that valor is the highest virtue. Moreover, Coriolanus genuinely sees Aufidius as an equal (1.1.212–20) and thus at least attempts to treat him as his "partner in this action" (5.3.2), even if the soldiers continue to worship him

---

[51] Both Patrick Ashby ("The Changing Faces of Virtue: Plutarch, Machiavelli, and Shakespeare's *Coriolanus*," *Early Modern Literary Studies* 19, supp. 25 [2016], 12) and Platt (*Rome and Romans*, 158–9) claim Coriolanus is inclined toward monarchical power.

[52] Cantor suggests that Coriolanus is able to be more divine among the Volsces than the Romans because he is less familiar to them (*Roman Trilogy*, 94). I argue that Coriolanus refrains from provoking the same response until charged with betrayal by Aufidius.

(4.7.3–4, cf. 5.6.38). Coriolanus takes steps to avoid any such confusion, splitting the army in two and sharing the command with Aufidius (4.7.14), as did the Romans between Cominius and Titus Lartius when attacking Corioles. Indeed, one of the most notable things about Coriolanus once in Antium is that he avoids denigrating the people or praising himself, acknowledging that he comes to Antium as a "marvellous poor" gentleman (4.5.27) Even when Aufidius invokes Jupiter and Mars in welcoming him, Coriolanus avoids such comparisons and says only "You bless me, gods!" (4.5.132).

But alongside these changed circumstances seems to be a change in Coriolanus himself. As I mentioned earlier, Shakespeare's Coriolanus, as opposed to Plutarch's, refuses to show his scars, his body, to the plebians whose approval he seeks. (Cominius, incidentally, seemed willing to show the people his scars, 3.3.117–8). Coriolanus is, however, reminded of his shared bodily character when he threatens Sicinius: "I shall shake thy bones / out of thy garments" (3.1.180–1). The plebians and aediles rush to the tribune's defense, which is what turns the argument into a brawl. The tribunes did not merely have various political powers but were also "sacrosanct": anyone who laid a hand on a tribune could be killed.[53] It is immediately after Coriolanus violates their sacrosanctity that the tribunes sentence him to death (3.1.209, 213–14).[54] Hence Coriolanus is reminded, at a crucial moment, of the body that he shares with others, but he also is given the opportunity to see that the sacral character of the tribunes arises not from their heroic deeds of valor but from the support of the people.

There is some evidence that Coriolanus takes this lesson to heart. After he accedes to his mother's request to spare Rome, he

---

[53] Andrew Lintott, *The Constitution of the Roman Republic*, (New York: Oxford University Press, 1999), 121–8. Livy reports that the body of one who attacked a tribune was cursed by Jupiter, the very god to whom Coriolanus had appealed, but that may have been a later development.

[54] Prior to this, the tribunes had only asserted that Coriolanus would not be consul (3.1.118–9, 173) and should be charged with treason (163–4, 176–8).

recognizes that doing so may well be "most dangerous," indeed "most mortal," to him (5.3.189–90). One reason is that he responds to their solicitations with some of his earlier hierarchical language, swearing fidelity to his wife by "the jealous queen of heaven" (5.3.46), asking Mars and Jupiter to watch over his son (5.3.70–1), before choosing to frame "convenient peace" rather than war (5.3.191–2). Upon his return to Antium, therefore, Coriolanus touts the benefits of the peace treaty he has signed as a victory, recouping significantly more than the Antiates' cost of the war as well as their honor (5.6.77–80).[55] It is perhaps the spoils he has acquired that matter most in gaining the support of the people. If they are anything like the Romans, the Antiates value victory in war for the material things it brings, rather than the honor it bestows (1.5.4–8), though Coriolanus does not chastise the Volsces as he did the Romans. In bringing the benefits of war without the costs, Coriolanus has apparently won the people over to his side. The stage directions say that Coriolanus enters Antium accompanied by the commoners. As Jan Blits observes, unlike in Rome, he not only seeks to address the people but also plans to depend on them for support.[56] Even Aufidius and the other conspirators recognize that the people must be on their side for success (5.6.15) and fear that Coriolanus—despite his difficulties in Rome—might be successful in acquiring the people's favor (5.6.54–6).

A second departure from Plutarch similarly raises the issue of how ambitious individuals might appeal to the people and what the rewards of successfully doing so might be. In Plutarch's account, the idea for the Roman women to approach Coriolanus was, quite literally, an inspired one. As Coriolanus leads the Volsci army toward Rome, Valeria prays in the temple of Jupiter Capitolinus and receives a vision of the women of Rome begging Coriolanus to spare the

---

[55] There may be a gap between speech and deed here. Parker observes that despite his promise of obedience, Coriolanus has acted "like some deity," framing a peace treaty without the consent of the lords of Antium (*Plato's "Republic"*, 71).

[56] Blits, *Spirit, Soul, and City*, 223.

city—not at the command of the Senate or of the consul but of "our god."[57] Since it was her idea (or at least her presentation of the god's idea) it would therefore be unsurprising if she were to accompany Coriolanus's wife and mother as they seek to save Rome.[58] Shakespeare may have avoided this *deus ex machina* not merely because it would have made for an unsatisfying resolution to the play but also because allowing a divine command from Jupiter to solve the problem would result in a confirmation, at the climax of the play, of the sort of hierarchical worldview that the play questions. And although it makes sense for Shakespeare to include her, her role is so minimal that even attentive scholars simply omit her from their considerations of that scene.[59] Perhaps looking more closely at Shakespeare's depiction of Valeria might account for her presence.

When Volumnia presents Valeria to Coriolanus, he immediately recognizes her as "the noble sister of Publicola" (5.3.64)—that is, Publius Valerius Publicola, former consul and favored pseudonym of Alexander Hamilton.[60] As David Lowenthal observes, this would remind Coriolanus that there is another way, and not a ignoble one, of treating the people that might lead to greater success.[61] When Publicola is suspected of harboring monarchical ambitions, however, he responds very differently than Coriolanus. He tears down his fancy house, removed the axes from the magisterial rod, and, of

---

[57] Spencer, *Shakespeare's Plutarch*, 350–2. Livy makes no mention of Valeria or divine inspiration (II.40).

[58] Although he says that "all the other Roman ladies" accompanied Volumnia and Virgilia, Plutarch does not specifically mention Valeria's presence (Spencer, *Shakespeare's Plutarch*, 352).

[59] Hermann Heuer, "From Plutarch to Shakespeare: A Study of *Coriolanus*," in *Shakespeare Survey* 10, ed. Allardyce Nicoll (Cambridge: Cambridge University Press, 1957), 54; Cantor, *Republic and Empire*, 104, cf. other references at 23, 133, 142. See Blits, *Spirit, Soul, and City*, 207–8.

[60] In addition to the *Federalist* papers, Hamilton also used the identity in attacking Samuel Chase in 1778.

[61] Lowenthal, *Shakespeare's Thought*, 302.

course, sought a consul to rule alongside him.⁶² And, also unlike Coriolanus, he went on to have a long and successful political career. He was elected consul four times and died after living as "honourably and vertuously" as any man. Indeed, the comparison of Publicola to Solon represents a rare exception in which Plutarch suggests that the Roman surpassed the Greek.⁶³

Coriolanus praises Valeria as "chaste as the icicle/That's curdied by the frost from purest snow / And hangs on Dian's temple" (5.3.64–7). Patrick Ashby thus argues that Valeria is included in the embassy because she, like Coriolanus, represents "an archetype…of static, inviolable virtue."⁶⁴ But this description of Valeria—though faithful to Plutarch's account of a woman who behaved "modestly and wisely" and was thus "greatly honored and reverenced"—does not fit easily with the image of Valeria that Shakespeare himself creates earlier in the play.⁶⁵ When she visits Virgilia and Volumnia, she insists that they put away their sewing to "play the idle huswife with me this afternoon" (1.3.62–3). When Virgilia refuses, Valeria tells her she "confine[s]" herself "most unreasonably" and mockingly refers to her as "another Penelope" who did nothing but "fill Ithaca full of moths" and should "turn thy solemnness out o'door" (1.3.69, 75–6, 97–8). As they depart on what is ostensibly a trip to visit a pregnant woman, Volumnia warns that Virgilia would "disease our better mirth" if she accompanied them, and so the older depart (1.3.69–70,

---

⁶² Perhaps unfortunately for Coriolanus, among the laws he passed to increase the authority of the people was one that allowed for the immediate execution of anyone who "did aspire to the kingdom" (Plutarch, *Lives*, 85–7). Although Shakespeare takes the description of Valeria from Plutarch's life of Coriolanus (Spencer, *Shakespeare's Plutarch*, 350–1), in Plutarch's life of Publicola, there is no mention of a sister; a daughter named Valeria, however, is among the hostages who escape from King Porsena (Plutarch, *Lives*, 89–90).

⁶³ Plutarch, *Lives*, 91–4.

⁶⁴ Ashby, "Changing Faces," 20–1.

⁶⁵ Spencer, *Shakespeare's Plutarch*, 351.

94–8).⁶⁶

Shakespeare thus borrows an authentic character from Plutarch's life to provide some valuable background information about Coriolanus and his son (1.3.47–60). However, Shakespeare imbues Valeria with a personality at odds with both that Plutarchan source and the play's later description. The juxtaposition of these scenes shows how appearances can be can be cultivated, so that one may be "honored and reverenced" even if she is in fact out looking for "much mirth" (1.3.99–100). It is possible that Volumnia brought Valeria along precisely to teach Coriolanus this lesson; she sought earlier in the play to persuade him that it would be honorable to dissemble before the people where "My fortunes and my friends at stake required" (3.2.40–65). Moreover, in reminding Coriolanus of her brother's successful and honored cultivation of the people, Valeria provides a warrant for him to adopt a similar strategy. There are also hints that Coriolanus's appeal to the people is a tactical shift rather than a genuine one. First, some of his mannerisms do not change between Act I and Act V. At the beginning of the play, he enters and, after a curt "Thanks" to Menenius, asks the plebs what is the matter (1.1.147). In Act V, he enters the Volsces' camp with the same question, even if he does not berate them (5.2.58). And although he initially apologizes to the Volsci lords for his outburst, he surely goes too far in claiming "tis the first time that ever/I was forced to scold." Ten short lines later, however, he compares himself to "an eagle in a dovecote" in having slaughtered their relatives in Corioles (5.6.107–8, 117–8).

Coriolanus's attempt to secure the people's support forces Aufidius to act quickly. It is unclear whether Coriolanus genuinely wishes to establish a monarchy in Antium any more than he did in Rome or whether Aufidius seeks simply to eliminate a rival who has diminished his reputation—not, perhaps, unlike what motivates

---

⁶⁶ Perhaps Virgilia's decision to sew at home while other women were out should call to mind another Roman noblewoman who did likewise and inspired an earlier poem of Shakespeare's.

some of the opposition to Caesar in the play bearing his name (1.10.12–16; 3.1.15–17; 4.7.56–7; 5.6.48).[67] And yet it may be a wise move: Would the heroic warrior Coriolanus, welcoming rather than rejecting the love of the people, be a threat to the lords of Antium? Aufidius seems to think so, promising to explain to the lords of the city "the great danger" that Coriolanus posed to them (5.6.138–41). Although Aufidius hints at some evidence to be used against Coriolanus (4.7.18–19), he also acknowledges in the wake of Coriolanus's retreat that his "pretext to strike at him admits / A good construction" (5.6.19–20). Aufidius may simply be seeking revenge against someone he acknowledges to be his superior (4.5.178–9), but Shakespeare has made clear what a figure like Coriolanus can do with the support of the people.

Both Coriolanus and Aufidius, in seeking popular support, must confront the fact that "the vulgar eye" will be the judge (4.7.21). As we saw in Rome, the people can be persuaded by appearances: Coriolanus may seek to present himself as a loyal servant of the lords who achieved a significant victory without the loss of life, whereas Aufidius wants him to be seen as a traitor. The problem for Coriolanus is not that, as Menenius once said, his "nature is too noble for this world," (3.1.257), but rather that he simply cannot be other than who he is. As Aufidius observes, Coriolanus's nature is to bear himself "more proudlier" and he cannot change it (4.7.8–12, cf. 5.6.24–5). Thus, when confronted with the charge of treason by Aufidius, Coriolanus responds just as he did in Rome: he invokes Mars, the god of war (5.6.102), and both reminds the Volsces of the slaughter at Corioles and takes sole credit for it: "Alone I did it" (5.6.119). The former offense may not have stirred the people to abandon him but the latter surely does, as the script calls for not only the lords and conspirators but also "all people" to call for his death (5.6.123).[68] For

---

[67] Consider, for instance, 1.2.135–51.

[68] This represents a change from North, in which the people merely did not oppose the conspirators; nevertheless, Plutarch says most of the Volsces did not

all his martial prowess, Coriolanus simply struggles—perhaps even refuses (3.1.15–17, cf. 3.1.47–52)—to maintain a salutary appearance before the people, whereas the tribunes and Aufidius excel at presenting him in a negative light.

Martial prowess may indeed be a reason why Coriolanus struggles to cultivate popular support. He not merely considers himself to resemble the highest gods but is particularly associated with Mars, the god of war. And war is simply not something the plebians tend to value. The plebians do not doubt Coriolanus's valor; they doubt whether this is the most important trait for a consul to possess. Far more important to them is the availability of bread, which Coriolanus seeks to restrict. This simple desire for bread is why Menenius's fable is persuasive (1.1.184). The image of the Senate as the belly is an image that gives the people precisely what they want: nourishment. It is Caesar's willingness to satisfy the people's desires, rather than his insistence on chastising them for those desires, that may account for his success.[69]

Despite his obvious interest in political problems, Shakespeare's *Coriolanus* presents a complicated and somewhat misleading depiction of Roman political institutions, at least as they are traditionally understood. One reason for that is that the titular figure challenged those institutions, claiming a place for himself as something akin to a god. Moreover, though, that divinity was based on a particular conception of the highest good for human beings: "valor is the chiefest virtue." The play shows, however, that this conception was not universally accepted within Rome or even among the patricians. In the

---

approve of the killing and "came out of all parts to honour his body" (Spencer, *Shakespeare's Plutarch*, 362).

[69] Such satisfaction may also be a means of self-defense: It is the "lean and hungry look" of Cassius that worries Caesar (*Julius Caesar*, 1.2.194–5). Bloom (*Shakespeare's Politics*, 80–1), Lowenthal (*Shakespeare's Thought*, 105), and Platt (*Rome and Romans*, 84n3, 188, 199) all contend that the people are more corrupt in *Julius Caesar* than in *Coriolanus*, but Shakespeare rather calls our attention to the changing traits of the leaders: Caesar is willing and able to do what Coriolanus would or could not.

absence of such a consensus about the best way of life among citizens, there will be a lack of consensus about the appropriate ruling offices for the city as well as the kind of people who ought to occupy them.

The ambiguities about the institutions of Rome to be found in the play thus reflect a deeper ambiguity in the Roman regime, an ambiguity that can perhaps be clarified only by basing political power on popular support. This, Shakespeare intimates, is the path taken by Julius Caesar.[70] It is a path of which Coriolanus becomes belatedly aware but could not walk consistently when challenged. After all, it is difficult, as Machiavelli famously observes in Chapter twenty-five of his *Prince*, to change one's behavior. It is unsurprising that Coriolanus fails to abide by his newfound popular egalitarianism when challenged by Aufidius. You can take the "boy of tears" out of Rome, but you cannot take Rome out of the boy.

---

[70] See the arguments of Cantor, *Republic and Empire*, 74–5 and Lowenthal, *Shakespeare's Thought*, 94.

The Power of the Particular: Liberal Education and Cosmopolitanism in *Titus Andronicus*

Bernard J. Dobski

I am more attached to France than ever, and I do not believe that Europe can have any living reality if it does not include France and her Frenchmen, Germany and its Germans, Italy and its Italians, and so forth. Dante, Goethe, Chateaubriand belong to all Europe to the very extent that they were respectively and eminently Italian, German and French. They would not have served Europe very well if they had been stateless, or if they had thought and written in some kind of integrated Esperanto or Volapuk – Charles de Gaulle[1]

Who is the Shakespeare of Esperanto?

In May of 1962, the French statesman Charles de Gaulle was asked during a press conference if he had spoken of post-war European integration in terms of a "Europe des patries." This was another way of asking if de Gaulle thought European "unification" should proceed along confederal, as opposed to supranational, lines. De Gaulle denied ever using that particular locution. But, as Daniel J. Mahoney points out, de Gaulle's robust defense of national political identity, quoted above, indicated his affinity with "the spirit behind that notion" of unification and testified to his "vision of a plural Europe."[2] While de Gaulle may not have spoken of a "Europe des patries," he certainly thought that a unified Europe could only retain its identity if it also preserved the distinctive national characters of its individual political members.

These twentieth-century recollections resonate with us today

---

[1] See Daniel J. Mahoney, *de Gaulle: Statesmanship, Grandeur, and Modern Democracy* (Westport, CT: Praeger Publishers, 1996), 133.

[2] See Mahoney, 1996, 133.

insofar as public opinion in the West is divided over the significance of national borders. Specifically, the debate concerns whether a robust defense of national borders, and the particular and exclusive goods that they preserve, is consistent with the arguments for the rights that belong to all human beings regardless of their place of birth. Advocates of the view that "no human is illegal" tend to support a more relaxed approach to national border control and immigration reform and characterize as racist and illiberal efforts to strengthen territorial integrity and civic identity, efforts that effectively deny many foreign nationals access to the rights they so desperately seek. For those who would urge our political leaders to embrace the borderless world of global humanitarianism, de Gaulle's modest defense of the nation and of national differences as the key to European integration must sound paradoxical, perhaps even downright atavistic. Indeed, to many leaders of popular opinion, de Gaulle's statements reflect the same national chauvinism that he helped destroy. Attitudes like these explain the hostility to those leaders, like Hungary's Viktor Orban or Geert Wilders of the Netherlands, and to those movements, like the populism growing in Europe and America, whose policies and preferences buck the trends of progressive elite opinion.[3]

But de Gaulle was no fascist. And his defense of national character, which is about how particular expressions of national genius *contribute* to the universal goal of human flourishing, is at odds with the spirit of fascism. That spirit, in elevating one nation over others, *identifies* one community with humanity as such, effecting an

---

[3] This chapter was written in the summer of 2024, during the surprise French elections called for by Prime Minister Macron. In an interview with CNN correspondent Christiane Amanpour, Marine Le Pen, the de facto leader of the National Rally (NR), the party many assumed would take control of the government, offered a "Gaullist" defense of national integrity. To Le Pen's claim that such a defense does not make NR "far-right," Amanpour could only respond incredulously: "You're kidding me, right?" See https://www.cnn.com/2024/07/05/world/video/france-elections-marine-le-pen-amanpour-trump-politics. Accessed July 7, 2024.

equation of particular with universal that eliminates the difference between the two. Those who would rescue a humane respect for well-defined political identity from the smears of xenophobia or barbarism will find in de Gaulle's view of European unification a useful antidote. Inspired by his examples, they can even challenge the progressive consensus in Washington and Brussels. For, if it is true that cosmopolitanism provides the more humanizing alternative, as many of its defenders allege, then why is there no Shakespeare of Esperanto?

To compel one to acknowledge that there is none, indeed, that there can be none, is to compel the defender of cosmopolitanism to confront the view that the human wisdom made possible by Shakespeare's plays and poetry depends on a kind of national genius, and a particularly British one at that. It forces "oikophobes"[4] to consider the potential truth of the view that wisdom about mankind is made possible by the emergence of and attachment to particular political identities, that is, to one's home, and that it is through the emergence of those particular identities that elements of human flourishing, common to us all, come into greater focus. To make such a claim is not to degrade other cultures or civilizations or to elevate some ways of life over others. Nor does it legitimize excluding individuals from sharing in the treasures of our common humanity. It is only to say that the genuine contributions to civilization writ large, such as were made by individuals from France, Germany, and Italy, or England, China, and Russia, for example, were made precisely insofar as they reflected the peculiar genius of the French, the Germans, the Italians, the English, the Chinese, or the Russians. In other words, these contributions to humanity were predicated on the existence of distinct communities, themselves given life by particular and—more

---

[4] Coined by the late Roger Scruton as a combination of the Greek words "*oikos*" (home) and "*phobos*" (fear), the term "oikophobes" refers to those who repudiate their "inheritance and home," and thus their nation, often in pursuit of global community. See Scruton, *England and the Need for Nations* (London: Civitas, 2004), 35.

often than not—exclusive views of the human good, views generated by the diverse regimes, philosophies, religions, languages, and economies of such disparate peoples. To erase these differences by erasing the political preconditions that make them possible would be to undermine, and not advance, the cause of humanity and our ability to understand it. There can be no Shakespeare of Esperanto because there can be no particular perspective or identity behind that artificial, stateless, and lifeless language; such a construction reflects no shared expression of the human person, justice, freedom, nature, and God that we can love and interrogate.

That human flourishing should depend crucially on the emergence of discrete political communities is not propaganda by the contemporary alt-right. In fact, up until the last few decades, this was a view shared across the political spectrum.[5] This should come as no surprise. It is, after all, a very old insight, one whose most powerful articulation is located in Aristotle's *Politics* (I.2). There, Aristotle claims that the development of our humanity is possible only within the *polis* because it is only in these small, self-sufficient, and autonomous communities that human beings can develop the

---

[5] One should compare the defenses of the nation by conservatives like Roger Scruton, *England* (2004), Pierre Manent, *A World Beyond Politics? A Defense of the Nation State* (Princeton: Princeton University Press, 2006), and Daniel J. Mahoney, *The Idol of Our Age: How the Religion of Humanity Subverts Christianity* (New York: Encounter Books, 2018) with that of Zbigniew Brzezinski. In "Examining the crisis of democracy," published in *The St. Petersburg Times* August 2, 1974, 22A, the advisor to Presidents Johnson and Carter notes that "the nation state has been a social unit to which man could commit himself in the sense of being willing to sacrifice for something larger than himself. The nation has provided a focus for loyalty, for social sacrifice, and for constancy. Many advanced democracies are today experiencing a decline in the nation state, along with the waning of patriotism and the rise of ethnic, class and group conflicts. These are all symptoms of a profound illness which is only thinly veiled by alleged global humanism to which young people are particularly said to respond…it does seem to me that much of our universal idealism is really a hedonistic escape from the most immediate problems confronting us." See https://news.google.com/newspapers?id=FkBSAAAAIBAJ&sjid=QXkDAAAAIBAJ&pg=7385,1213898&dq=crisis+of+democracy&hl=en. Accessed July 5, 2024.

capacity for reason, that is, the capacity to deliberate about how to live well, and thus reflect on what constitutes the true, the beautiful, and the good.[6] Such a capacity is the hallmark of our natures and agreement upon those ends forms the basis of our shared lives together. What Aristotle defends in his treatise on "the regime," Shakespeare dramatically illustrates in his plays dedicated to the birth, growth, and devolution of the Roman republic. This is especially true of *Titus Andronicus*, the play that marks the chronological conclusion of his Roman tetralogy.

Unfortunately, scholars tend to ignore *Titus* when discussing *Coriolanus*, *Julius Caesar*, and *Antony & Cleopatra*, a neglect largely attributed to the play's grotesque violence. But this is a mistake. Far from being gratuitous, the violence of *Titus* is fundamental to its political wisdom. In portraying the savage inhumanity of a Rome that has exceeded all limitations and seemingly embraced all people, Shakespeare shows what happens when we ignore Aristotle's insight that "the fully flourishing human life is only cultivated" in a discrete and coherent community in which a defined populace participates in a shared view of what constitutes "true freedom, virtue, and excellence."[7] Shakespeare's *Titus* reminds us that we "fulfill our most profound human aspirations by living within, and in accordance with, the limits of a higher law, an encompassing order that does not simply emanate from us or from our choices, but encloses and in a

---

[6] This insight is spelled out with particular power by Leo Strauss in chapter five of *Natural Right and History* (Chicago: University of Chicago Press 1953) where he argues that "the natural articulation of the whole," a view that "makes possible…the study of human things as such" (123), supplies a necessary precondition "within which knowledge is possible" (125).

[7] See the chapter "Shakespeare and the Body Politic" by Bernard J. Dobski and Dustin Gish in *Shakespeare and the Body Politic*, edited by Dobski and Gish (Lanham, MD: Lexington Books, 2013), 3. The present reading of *Titus* represents an expanded and deepened version of the fourth section of that chapter (see 14–16). And it has been improved by the thoughtful comments of my former collaborator as well as by the editor of the present volume. Any errors that remain are, naturally, my own.

certain sense perfects us—or at least ennobles us."[8] But to see how *Titus* illuminates the wisdom that can inform practical political life, we must understand why so many scholars dismiss the conclusion of Shakespeare's Roman drama. And to see that, we must remind ourselves that "the play's the thing"[9] and recall why we are drawn to Shakespeare in the first place.

Titus and the Possibilities of Self-Understanding

One of the great joys in watching and reading and thinking along with Shakespeare's dramas comes from the power of such works to prompt us to reflect on their artistry and thus on the conditions under which Shakespeare's wisdom comes to sight for us. In other words, not just the joy of becoming wiser, a wisdom that comes from seeing our natures staged in all their splendid glory, their riotous absurdity, their devastating tragedy, their awesome promise and power, but the joy that comes from understanding how and why one can become wise about oneself and others constitutes one of the deepest and most abiding pleasures of engaging Shakespeare. One might call this the joy of learning how to learn.

When it comes to those plays of his that help us learn how to learn, that illuminate the conditions under which we can become wise with Shakespeare, we have no shortage of fruitful options. We can look to the educations of rulers like Prospero, Lear, and Henry V, to the Prince of Denmark and the Duke of Dark corners; we can study Shakespeare's great teachers like Portia, Puck, Rosalind, Petruchio (or is it his Kate?); and we can benefit from the fantastic failures of an Othello, a Macbeth, a Coriolanus, a Falstaff, even those lovable laboring losers Berowne, Dumaine, and Longaville. But when we think of learning to learn with Shakespeare, we do not think of *Titus Andronicus*, the play that concludes Shakespeare's Roman story. Indeed, though it is still performed with some regularity, it is one of the least read, least loved, and perhaps least understood,

---

[8] Ibid., 4
[9] *Hamlet*, II.2.633.

of Shakespeare's plays.

This is understandable. For starters, the play is wildly gruesome. Ostensibly set in the age of the late Roman empire, near the end of the third or fourth century, the play opens with the renowned, elderly general Titus returning from his conquest of the Goths, the seemingly last step in Rome's imperial march. In victory, he returns with the remaining 4 of his 25 sons, the rest of whom gave their lives to Roman conquest (I.1.82; 198).[10] And he brings with him many prisoners, including the Gothic Queen Tamora and her three sons: Alarbus, Demetrius, and Chiron (I.1.99–150). But while Rome may have completed its imperial expanse, the city Titus returns to is missing its head; the previous emperor is dead (I.1.187). Rome now faces the crucial political question: who will be the rightful ruler of the eternal city's vast empire? The play presents three candidates, each with a different ground for his claim. The former emperor's eldest son, Saturninus, asserts his right to rule on the basis of heredity (I.1.1–8); his younger brother, Bassianus, asserts his right on the basis of virtue (I.1.9–17); and then there is Titus himself, whom the Roman people, according to their customs, have selected as a candidate and who, if he should ask for the throne, would obtain it (I.1.20–24; 182–189; 204). While the empire appears Titus's for the taking, he defers on account of his advanced age and instead advises the tribunes to elect Saturninus (I.1.227–234) who, in return for such largesse, agrees to marry Lavinia, Titus' only daughter (I.1.242–247).

Unfortunately, that betrothal doesn't last long. There is some ambiguity about what happens here, but the upshot is that almost immediately Lavinia ends up with Bassianus—the brother of Saturninus, to whom she was previously engaged[11]—and Saturninus

---

[10] All textual citations are to the act, scene, and lines of the Third Series of *Titus Andronicus* published by The Arden Shakespeare and edited by Jonathan Bate (London: Routledge, 1995).

[11] For evidence of Bassianus' prior engagement to Lavinia, see I.1.55, 280, 283, 284–85, 289–90, 302–03, and 410–413.

engages the Queen of the Goths.[12] All of this takes place within the first three hundred lines of the play. At this point, Titus has already executed, dismembered, and burned one of Tamora's sons, Alarbus (I.1.145–150). Not long after that, Titus senselessly "silences" his son Mutius (I.1.295–96). Meanwhile, the Gothic sons of Tamora, Chiron and Demetrius, having been freed by decree of the newly empowered Saturninus (I.1.278), and under the instruction of Aaron the Moor (their mother's lover, I.1.544–635), plot and execute the murder of the emperor's brother, Bassianus, and the rape of his new wife, Lavinia (II.2.89–191). To prevent her from identifying them, Chiron and Demetrius cut out Lavinia's tongue and chop off her hands (II.3). This is followed by: the execution of two more of Titus' sons (II.2.302–03; III.1.234), Martius and Quintus, framed by Aaron for the murder of Bassianus; the amputation of one of Titus' hands (III.1.192); the eventual murder of Chiron and Demetrius (V.2.154, 163, 203–05) whose dismembered bodies Titus cooks and then serves to Tamora (V.3.25, 59–62); the beheading of Lavinia by Titus (V.3.47); and the killing in rapid succession of Tamora, Titus, and Saturninus (V.3.63–65). Titus's last remaining son, Lucius, now at the head of an army of Goths, mercifully brings this bloodletting to a close when he is acclaimed emperor (V.3.136–154), putting a new head on a Roman body politic the limbs of whose members

---

[12] The ambiguity here concerns what Saturninus intends when he asks Lavinia "Lavinia, you are not displeased with this?" (I.1.274). Just before, Saturninus swore eternal gratitude to Titus (257–61) for securing him the title of emperor and promised to wed his daughter Lavinia in return. But once he sees the beauty of the captive Tamora, Saturninus, in front of both his new fiancée and father-in-law to be, praises the Gothic queen's beauty and appears to raise the prospect of marriage to *her* (265–273). So, when Lavinia, to the question posed by Saturninus, replies "Not I, my lord, sith true nobility / Warrants these words in princely courtesy" (275–276), one is forced to wonder: was Saturninus apologizing for his tactless remark, which Lavinia here forgives? Or does she understand Saturninus to be cancelling their engagement, to which she consents? Bassianus' seizure (280) of his beloved suggests the latter. Saturninus's anger at such a seizure suggests the former (304–312).

litter the stage.¹³

In addition to the gore, which seems somehow beneath the Bard's artistry, none of his characters here undergo any significant change or development (their dismembered bodies aside). Aaron the Moor remains implacably evil, as does Tamora, Saturninus, Chiron and Demetrius.¹⁴ Lucius, Titus' son, is, as ever, the stout patriot and loyal son. Marcus Andronicus, Titus' brother, plays the feckless tribune. The dim and passive Lavinia never seems to brighten up. And Titus himself, though he recognizes his betrayal at the hands of the man he enthroned and the Goths he conquered, never reflects on how a Rome that valorizes savagery and has grown great through butchery could also be the source of his and his family's destruction. The result is a cast of characters that seems one-dimensional and uninteresting.

Finally, there is the matter of *Titus*'s poetry. It's not bad. But it never rises to the level of Shakespeare's other masterpieces; to wit, one never hears or sees people quoting lines by Tamora, Aaron, or Titus. For these reasons, *Titus* has been dismissed, considered evidence of the immature Shakespeare, the product of another author(s), and unworthy of sustained study.¹⁵ Thankfully, exceptions are

---

¹³ As bad as all of this is, there is even more. The list above makes no mention of infidelities, Titus' madness, the execution of a clown, the murder of two nurses, and the lack of gratitude and mercy shown by Goths and Romans alike.

¹⁴ Aaron represents a possible exception. At the close of the play, having been captured by Lucius' Gothic soldiers, he refuses to repent for "the evils I have done. / Ten thousand worse than ever yet I did / Would I perform if I might have my will. / If one good deed in all my life I did / I do repent it from my very soul" (V.3.185–89). But Aaron has already protected his bastard son, at great risk to his mother no less, sparing him first from the murderous designs of his half-brothers, Demetrius and Chiron (IV.89–182). Then, later, he negotiates with Lucius to spare his son from hanging (V.1.49–86). Surely, he does not repent of the good deeds noted here, revealing an underappreciated complexity in his character. We will explore the significance of this below.

¹⁵ If one accepts the composition date of 1593, as argued for by Bate (1995, 78–9), then *Titus* was written around the same period as the masterpieces of *Rape of Lucrece* and *Richard III*. And yet its poetry never approaches the level of these

to be found in the work of John Alvis and Grace Starry West. In his masterful book *Shakespeare's Understanding of Honor*, published over thirty years ago, Alvis convincingly demonstrates the textual, performative, and thematic basis for reading *Titus Andronicus* as the intended final frame of Shakespeare's Roman story.[16] That story, which begins with the death of Roman kingship in his epic poem *The Rape of Lucrece*, dramatizes the birth of republican liberty in *Coriolanus* and stages its imperial growth and decay in *Julius Caesar* and *Antony & Cleopatra*. *Titus* concludes this "narrative" with an exhausted Rome, one bereft of that concern with honorable service on behalf of the common good which proved the source of the city's power and liberty, a city which is, by play's end, as much Gothic as it is Roman.[17]

---

two works. It thus belongs to those who attribute *Titus's* presumed weakness to Shakespeare's "immaturity" to account for such alleged unevenness. For a list of others who place *Titus's* composition within this same time frame, see the note for Appendix B in *Souls with Longing: Representations of Honor and Love in Shakespeare*, 308. For an account of Shakespeare's "heavy freight of allusiveness" (55) in *Titus*, see John Alvis's *Shakespeare's Understanding of Honor* (Carolina Academic Press, 1990), 55–58.

[16] See especially "From *The Rape of Lucrece* to *Titus Andronicus*: The Genius of the Romans and the Cause of Their Decline" in Alvis (1990), 35–58.

[17] Alvis's arguments on behalf of Shakespeare-as-author-of-*Titus* are bolstered by Jonathan Bate who, in his introduction to the Arden edition, presents additional stylometric evidence in support of this claim (see especially pp. 78–83). Scholars like Alvis, West, and Bate usefully respond to the claim, so characteristic of contemporary scholarship on Shakespeare, that one cannot profitably mine his plays and poetry for human and political wisdom because any consideration of Shakespeare's work must begin with questions about his plays' compositional integrity, their authorship, and the historical conditions in which they were produced and performed. Insofar as this approach prioritizes these questions, it reduces Shakespeare to the reigning opinions and prejudices of *his* time. And a timebound Shakespeare has nothing timeless to teach us. As a result, scholars, unburdened by reflecting on his universal wisdom, are free to read into Shakespeare the opinions and prejudices of *our* time. And even if we agree with those who, like Gary Taylor and Stanley Wells, think that *Titus* is the work of George Peele or some other author (1987, 115), there is still the "problem" posed by the bastard child at the end of *Titus*. While this nameless baby is the biological offspring of

Like Alvis's book, West's essay, "Classical Allusions in Shakespeare's *Titus Andronicus*,"[18] makes the case for taking seriously Shakespeare's use of classical learning in the play and for understanding its role in the moral corruption of its Romans, Goths, and Moors. This is important because the political significance of classic literature and philosophy represents one of the themes tying together Shakespeare's broader Roman story. For instance, the ancient Greek myths embroidered on Lucrece's family's tapestries shape her resolve to reclaim her honor through suicide, a reclamation critical to the formation of republican liberty.[19] On the other hand, the next three plays point to the potential dangers to republican liberty of an excessively lettered people; this is as true of the republic in *Coriolanus*, arguably Shakespeare's most political play, which is practically silent about writing of any kind,[20] as it is of the imperial Rome of Caesar, Antony, and Cleopatra, a Rome where literature, rhetoric, and Greek philosophy (to say nothing of an emerging Christianity) abound, representing and pointing to alternatives to the practice of

---

the work's foreign villains (Aaron and Tamora), he will be raised by Lucius Andronicus, the "savior" of Rome and last remaining son of Titus. Will such a child necessarily reflect the vices of those who created him? Or the virtues of the one who adopted him? Or does common sense not require us to understand the life of such a human being in terms of what *he* does and does not do and what *he* does and does not say? To grant that the diverse conditions of his formation might exercise some influence on this man does not preclude the possibility that his speeches and deeds provide an intelligible meaning and unity to his life. So too then with *Titus Andronicus*. The long life of this play has little to do with its authorship and everything to do with the political wisdom it dramatizes. Regardless, then, of how one resolves questions of "origins" one must still take seriously the possible wisdom that gives meaning to the life of any bastard—be it man or text.

[18] *Studies in Philology*, Vol. 79:1 (Winter, 1982), 62–77.

[19] See *The Rape of Lucrece*, lines 1366–1568.

[20] In the early Roman republic, writing, it seems, was reserved for the practical purpose of personal and diplomatic correspondence. The oblique use of Nicanor in *Coriolanus* (IV.3) would appear to affirm the potential dangers of writing and reading liberated from public use. On the significance of this otherwise insignificant character, see Jan Blits, 2006, *Spirit Soul and City: Shakespeare's "Coriolanus"* (Lanham, MD: Lexington, Books), 163–167.

politics at its peak. At first glance, *Titus Andronicus* would appear to reinforce this lesson; the play is filled, perhaps more than any other work by Shakespeare, with references to books and letters, to reading and writing, to schools and libraries, to the stories and lessons of classical literature (whose allusions alone number well north of 50), that is to say, to the signs of civilized life. And not only are these barbaric Romans and Goth culturally literate, but, as both West and Alvis stress, their literary refinement actually inspires and informs their cruelty against others.

But *Titus Andronicus* doesn't just show us the potential dangers of literature to politics; it shows us the potential dangers that a cosmopolitan politics can pose to the liberal learning which an education in classical literature should effect. To her credit, West, in her essay, hints that the cause of Rome's moral decadence is to be found in Rome's imperial decay.[21] But she does not explain why a seemingly borderless world should impede the humanizing effects of the works by Homer, Virgil, Plutarch, Horace, Livy, Ovid, Seneca, and Cicero that everyone in the Romanized world seems to know or to have read. What accounts for the connection between Rome's imperial expanse and the failure of its liberal learning to limit the savagery that is the play's most famous trait? Why is a particular political context, absent from Titus' cosmopolitan empire, so critical to liberal education?

Cosmopolitan Formlessness in *Titus'* Rome

To answer these questions, we must explore what it means to say that cosmopolitan Rome lacks a particular political context. In the first place, *Titus's* Rome, as an empire with seemingly global dimensions, lacks any discrete physical boundaries or limits. While *Coriolanus* repeatedly demonstrated the small republic's Volscian limits, and while *Caesar* and *Antony and Cleopatra* give us an empire intent on absorbing those beyond its borders, *Titus* opens with a Rome whose

---

[21] West, 1982, especially 65 and 76–77.

lust for expansion appears sated. Having conquered the Goths, Titus and, it seems, the Rome he embodies can retire from their many years of military service (I.1.197). At this point, nothing exists beyond Rome's territorial reach. As such it is home to peoples of varying races and ethnicities: to Romans and to Goths, to Goths named after Greeks, to those who speak French and Latin,[22] and to North Africans with Hebrew names who live among Gallic tribes.

More important, however, is that, in this multicultural Rome, none of these distinctions possess political salience. As Saturninus's emancipation and betrothal of Tamora makes clear, anyone—regardless of birthplace, character, or loyalty—can become a Roman citizen, a soldier, even a queen. And that means that no one is really a citizen because no one is really a foreigner. By contrast, citizenship under the republic was an exclusive matter of great import. To grant one republican citizenship was to acknowledge one's dignity as a free man; to deny one a say in political affairs was to treat one as a slave, risking an uprising from those so deeply offended.[23] For this reason, it was not enough to be born in Rome if one wanted to assume the burdens and privileges of citizenship. As Coriolanus's taunts of the plebs make clear, one must also regularly and publicly display the devotional virtue of the regime if one wanted to share in the benefits of republican self-government. But under the empire of *Titus*, "Roman" virtue has vanished because Romans are no different than Goths in their barbarism. Saturninus' grasping selfishness, Titus's pitiless murders, and Lucius's war on his own city all match or exceed the viciousness of the Goths.

Shakespeare previews this development in the play's opening scene. There Titus prefers the hereditary claim of Saturninus to the "empery" of Rome to that of Bassianus's more modest and decent

---

[22] For examples of French usage, see I.1.498, 499; IV.2.7; for Latin, see I.1.101, 284, 633, 635; IV.1.78, 81–82; IV.2.20–21; and IV.3.4, 54–55.

[23] Act I, sc. 1 of *Coriolanus* offers a perfect illustration of this; there the plebeian revolt against the patricians is allayed only by the decision of the senate to create the office of the tribune to represent the interests of the people.

argument from justice and virtue. (The wishes of the people do not really factor into Titus's deliberations here.) That Titus should prefer Saturninus's tribal claim[24] to Bassianus's virtue or to the will of the people, however, is also beside the point. For, regardless of their respective merits, both brothers are here arguing over *kingship*, an office that was, once upon a time, anathema to a republic born in opposition to the Tarquins, the mere suspected pursuit of which proved lethal to Julius Caesar. The Romans of *Titus* are willing to serve kingly masters because they no longer care about the virtue needed to secure the republican liberty enjoyed by their ancestors, a development crucial to their approach to literature.

The Romans no longer seem to care for their freedom because they are no longer politically sovereign. And they are no longer politically sovereign because "Romanness" no longer represents any kind of political distinction. Put differently, there is no sovereignty in Rome because there is no Roman community, no recognized common good that could unite them over and against other peoples, no shared agreement or voice (it is quite literally "headless") on the most authoritative views about how they might live well or nobly together as a people. This failure to discriminate between those who are Roman and those who are not means they are unable to determine whose voices can legitimately contribute towards the welfare of the community. As a result, there is no lawful way for Rome to maintain the republican order that proved the foundation of its power, glory, and freedom. Without that common law necessary to produce ordered liberty, one cannot find among the "Romans" any public spiritedness, any elevating principle that could honorably inform, guide, and restrain their pursuit of self-interest or direct citizens towards the welfare of others. A cosmopolitan Rome, like we see in *Titus*, lacks any concern for honor or the self-respect indispensable to the formation of noble character. Traditional Roman

---

[24] Saturninus not only expresses a willingness to use violence against his brother's claim to the throne. He also threatens violence if Titus should stand in his way (I.1.207–211).

virtue loses its anchor in a legitimate concern with one's genuine good and the proud self-assertion that it requires and gets reduced to self-abnegation.[25]

This tendency towards self-abnegation gets reinforced by the religious diversity in *Titus*, an aspect of the play that often proves vexing to scholars. On the one hand, the action of the play suggests a classical setting where pagan gods and civil religions rule. But one also finds littered throughout the drama anachronistic references to both Catholic and Protestant Christianity.[26] And, in the figure of Aaron the Moor, one encounters a character who testifies to the presence of Judaism and Islam (though he confesses to atheism). This messy combination of theisms not only suggests a world where the major sources of spiritual and ethical order are as indeterminate as the political and geographic limits of its global empire.[27] It also suggests a world whose temporal space cannot be neatly located. Cosmopolitan Rome exists in a space that is at once classically pagan, early Christian, and post-Reformation, which is to say that it exists in no fixed place and at no fixed time. There is literally nothing in this Rome to allow the embodied individual to orient himself,

---

[25] To see how manly self-assertion and selfless service to the community combine to make up Roman virtue, see Volumnia's effort to join honor with policy at *Coriolanus*, III.2, especially 39–45, 46–51, and 52–68.

[26] For the range of religious anachronisms in this play, see Aaron's identification with "devils" (IV.2.48, 67, V.1.147–48). He also swears by God's wounds (IV.2.71), "never hopes more heaven than rests in [Tamora]" (II.2.40) and refers to Lucius's "conscience" and his "twenty popish tricks and ceremonies" (V.1.76). Titus himself refers to "limbo" (III.1.150), "begging hermits", "holy prayers," and "heaven" (III.2.41–42). The Clown in act IV mentions "heaven" (3.89; prompted by Titus, 88), "grace" (3.99, again, prompted by Titus, 98, 105), and St. Stephen (4.42). Tamora's nurse tells Aaron to "christen" his son with a knife (IV.2.72). And Lucius' Goths discover Aaron in a "ruinous monastery" (V.1.21).

[27] Some scholars account for the anachronistic references to Christianity by arguing that Shakespeare intends his ancient Romans to represent his fellow British (but in togas). Given Shakespeare's multivalent artistry, I would not preclude this reading of the play. But it also doesn't fully address the cosmopolitan aspect of the play. Nor does it account for its incredible butchery.

take his bearings, and lead his life in a morally healthy manner.[28]

It is not surprising that people in a limitless world do not insist on the dignity of their particularity. When Titus secures the crown for Saturninus and resigns his military office, he does so by submitting completely to his new overlord: "And here in sight of Rome to Saturnine, /…do I consecrate / My sword, my chariot, and my prisoners / Presents well worthy Rome's imperious lord: / Receive them then, the tribute that I owe, / Mine honour's ensigns humbled at thy feet" (I.1.250–56). Titus reveals the extent of such slavish submission when, moments later, he kills his son merely for defending the honor of his sister from the dishonorable graspings of the newly enthroned Saturninus (I.1.295). Later, when Titus pleads for the lives of his sons who have been framed for the murder of Bassianus, he does not invoke justice or a concern with legal process or the common good. Instead, he calls upon that least Roman of passions: pity (III.1.1–58), the opposite of manly self-assertion. As if to make such self-abnegation visible, Titus here lops off his hand to give to the emperor so that he might spare his sons (III.1.192). It is only fitting that a man "surnamed Pius" (I.1.23) should call upon others to join him in a weeping that effectively dissolves (or "melts") oneself and promises to wipe away all earthly order.[29] The tear-filled pity to which he

---

[28] This may also help to explain the number of references to Christianity in a play ostensibly set in antiquity. A religion whose universal claims about man and God exceed all earthly places and times will be right at home in the amorphous empire we have just described. Here, as in other Shakespearean dramas, Christianity's universalism threatens to undermine the dignity of political life and thus dilutes the particular political limits that give communities their shape, identity, and vitality.

[29] Titus invokes pity here three times (III.1.2, 8, 35), ultimately confusing stones for the tribunes who could spare his sons. In doing so, he promises an eternal weeping that will confuse the natural seasons (18–21). The association of weeping with "melting" oneself or upsetting the natural order can also be found at III.1.212–214 and 220–234; and see III.2.50–51, V.3.89 and V.3.163. For a contrasting version of "piety" upon which Romans could respectably draw, one should consider the example of Aeneas whose Vergilian epic is invoked numerous times in *Titus*.

beckons his countrymen compels one to put himself in the place of another, to (momentarily) adopt his condition and feel what he feels, surrendering one's individuality in the process of eliminating all distinctions.

One sees this absence of self-respect, and the subsequent failure to preserve one's integrity (both literally and figuratively) in Titus's offspring. When Lavinia witnesses her husband's murder and is about to be raped and butchered, she neither rages against these atrocities nor calls upon justice, virtue, or the city's gods for her protection.[30] Like her father, she, rather foolishly (i.e., self-destructively), appeals to Tamora's pity[31] motivated only by the desire to avoid "a worse-than-killing lust" (II.2.175). The same passivity attends the pathetic demise of the sons, Martius and Quintus, who are killed more like sheep than men.[32] And when Lucius, Titus's last remaining son, gets exiled for trying to "rescue my two brothers from their death" (III.1.49),[33] he does not challenge the injustice of that punishment or appeal to his fellow citizens for aid. Instead, he meekly leaves Rome only to return later at the head of an army of Goths without any thought for what that foreign army might do to him, his fellow citizens, or the Roman body politic as a whole.[34] To

---

[30] Alvis (1990, 41–45) points out that Lucrece, unlike Lavinia, opted to endure her rape so as to preserve her reputation for virtue, a sacrifice that proved foundational to Rome's republican self-government.

[31] In her appeal to Tamora's pity, Lavinia invokes her father's mercy in sparing Tamora's life (II.2.158–59). But it was Titus who earlier rejected Tamora's earlier pitiful pleas to spare her son Alarbus, as Tamora here recalls (II.2.161–167).

[32] In this scene, Shakespeare has his characters physically enact the self-destructive process of pity in *Titus*. While Martius fell into the "pit" where the murdered Bassianus lay, Quintus chooses to share his brother's suffering by jumping into the "pit" with him (II.2.245), the full pit creating a pitiful scene.

[33] Shakespeare supplies no evidence that Lucius did anything more to rescue his brothers than indicate an interest in doing so; it is his father who must urge him to raise a foreign army (III.1.286).

[34] When Emillius announces to Saturninus that Lucius marches on Rome at the head of an army of Goths, he states that Lucius "threats in the course of this revenge to do / As much as ever Coriolanus did" (IV.4.61–67). But Lucius does

citizens who don't seem to care for their community, their family members, or even themselves, what can classic texts of liberal education possibly say?

Cosmopolitanism and Liberal Education

Without a concern for noble character that inspires public spiritedness or animates the pursuit of individual wholeness, *Titus'* Romans lack any impetus, supplied by their regime or its principles, to turn to literature for their own moral and intellectual perfection. To be sure, education abounds in this play, but it is an education that bears none of the traditional markers of a particular people or its genius; thus, the Goths and the Romans share the same literary curriculum. Indeed, throughout the play, Goths draw on the same classic Greek and Roman resources that "inform" the Romans.[35] But as should be clear, this doesn't make them more civilized or humane. This is partly because the purpose of Roman education has changed.

One gets a sense of just how much Roman education has changed in the moments before Lavinia reveals who ravished her. There, the young Lucius (Titus' grandson), chased by his aunt Lavinia, begs for help from his grandfather and great uncle. Marcus replies to his grandnephew that Lavinia, pursuing the young boy who just dropped the books he was carrying, meant no harm. He says to Lucius, "Somewhither would she have thee go with her. / Ah, boy, Cornelia never with more care / Read to her sons than she hath read to thee / Sweet poetry and Tully's *Orator*" (IV.1.11–14). The Cornelia to whom Marcus refers was the mother of Tiberius and Gaius Gracchus, two of Rome's "greatest" political reformers. Famed as much for her ancestors as for her descendants, Cornelia was also

---

much more than Coriolanus did, as Shakespeare well knew. In his presentation of *Coriolanus*, Shakespeare shows that the great general was prevented from sacking Rome with a foreign army by a profound attachment *to his mother*.

[35] See, for instance, the references to Roman literature made by Goths at I.1.139, 500, 516, 589, 608, 633, 634; II.2.22, 30, 43, 61, 63; IV.2.20–23, 24, 95–97; and V.1.139.

renowned for the role she played in the political education of her revolutionary sons. Lavinia, however, plays no political role in her nephew's upbringing.

In the late republic, literature was still understood to serve a decidedly civic function; it was the means by which one could attain the standards upheld by the regime. But in *Titus*'s imperial Rome, literature, even that intended for political ends like Cicero's work on rhetoric, offers nothing more than a source of private and personal pleasure. Thus, Titus, to alleviate his suffering, calls upon his daughter and grandson to join him in reading "Sad stories chanced in times of old. / Come boy, and go with me; thy sight is young, / And thou shalt read when mine begin to dazzle" (III.2.83–86). Later, he urges Lavinia "Come and take choice of all my library, / And so beguile they sorrow till the heavens / Reveal the damned contriver of this deed" (IV.1.34–36). And at the play's end, the elder Lucius bids his son remember that "Thy grandsire loved thee well /...Many a story he hath told to thee, / And bid thee bear his pretty tales in mind / And talk of them when he was dead and gone" (V.3.160; 163–65).[36]

Of course, in the immediate sequel, Lavinia does use her nephew's copy of Ovid's *Metamorphoses*, with its tragic tale about Philomela, Procne, and Tereus, to "explain" to her family what happened. Given the action of the play, we are not surprised that the central literary reference is to the rape of Philomela by her brother-in-law Tereus, the subsequent murder and cannibalism of his son Itys by his mother Procne, and the translation of all of their humanity into birds. But the moral of this story,[37] that we lose our humanity when we give free reign to the unlimited desire of the tyrant and unhinged rage of his wife, lacks traction in a Rome where global imperialism dissolves the power of traditional limits, relationships, and hierarchies.

---

[36] When Marcus refers to Lavinia's lute playing and singing, he does so only in terms of the pleasure they produce (II.3.45–50).

[37] On the question of Ovid's moral intentions in writing the *Metamorphoses*, see West, 1982, 71–72, 76–77.

This paradox, the loss of humanity in a community where cosmopolitanism reigns, is reflected in those moments when particular attachments—to ourselves and to others—should be most in evidence. We thus recall that while the filicide of Mutius was initially deplored by his family, Titus's brother Marcus abruptly and successfully diverts attention from this grievous matter ("My lord—to step out of these dreary dumps—" [I.1.396]) to the question of Tamora's rapid political ascent; Marcus stops the natural grief and anger over the murder of a family member in favor of calmly reflecting on matters of state. Then there is the rape and butchery of Lavinia, arguably the most horrific moment in a play with no shortage of horrifying moments. As noted, Lavinia expresses no grief over the murder of her husband and offers only pathetic resistance to her violators. The aftermath reflects this same kind of abstracted self-concern. Consider when Lavinia meets Marcus in the woods. One might reasonably expect an uncle, encountering his ravished niece, her hands amputated and tongue ripped out, to respond with a kind of inarticulate horror. Instead, Marcus replies:

> Alas, a crimson river of warm blood,
> Like to a bubbling fountain stirred with wind,
> Doth rise and fall between thy rosed lips,
> Coming and going with thy honeyed breath.
> But sure some Tereus hath deflowered thee
> And, lest thou shouldst detect him, cut thy tongue.
> Ah, now thou turn'st away thy face for shame,
> And notwithstanding all this loss of blood,
> As from a conduit issuing spouts,
> Yet do thy cheeks look red as Titan's face,
> Blushing to be encountered with a cloud. (II.3.22–32)

And he goes on bloviating like this for another *thirty* lines! So concerned is Marcus with witty remarks and clever allusions, that he fails to register in any humane way the horror standing before him. Instead of allowing him to identify the suffering of his niece, to offer her compassion, solace, sympathetic rage…*even first aid*, his cultured education distances him from fellow feeling, preempting humane action on her behalf. It's almost as if Lavinia was some lifeless character in Ovid's poetry and not the living, breathing, and bleeding kinswoman standing before him.[38]

This inhuman remove finds its parallel in the lackluster effort to find Lavinia's violators. For while Lavinia has been deprived of her tongue and hands, she, like Philomela, still knows how to read and write and so she, like her tragic predecessor, can still communicate with her family. And yet, despite this, it takes her and her family *about nine months* to identify Chiron and Demetrius as the culprits.[39] And the particular method of communication devised—using her mouth and feet to guide a staff to write in the dirt—is not terribly ingenious and "discovered" almost by chance.[40] How are we to

---

[38] While Marcus alludes to Ovid's account when he first sees the ravished niece, he does not actually think she has been raped since he will later need her to literally spell it out for him (see IV.1). See West (1982, 67) for this point. There, West, in fn. 11, pointing to the chapbook version believed to be Shakespeare's source for this play, also notes that Marcus's speech here and Lavinia's delayed response are *not* located in this pre-Shakespearean text, reinforcing the argument that they are the Bard's inventions. See also Alvis (1990), 45, fn. 11 as well as *Narrative and Dramatic Sources of Shakespeare* by Geoffrey Bullough cited by both scholars.

[39] This timeline is determined in the first place by the fact that no one in the play questions the legitimacy of Tamora's pregnancy. In fact, until we hear from a surprised nurse that Tamora's son is Moorish (IV.2.60) there is no mention of her even being with child. Since the classical world knew well the natural gestation period for women, the lack of scandal can only be explained by a pregnancy that ran its expected legitimate course. That means Tamora's child was conceived around the time of her marriage to Saturninus, and thus right around the time of Lavinia's violations. As for the timing of Lavinia's disclosure of her violators, that news, once revealed, leads Titus to conspire with his grandson (IV.1.113) who begins to carry out that conspiracy at the very beginning of the next scene (IV.2). In sum, Lavinia reveals her ravishers just before the birth of Tamora's child is announced, that is, almost a year after being violated.

[40] Marcus's so-called "innovation" is entirely unnecessary, especially for an audience steeped in Ovid. In Book One of his *Metamorphoses*, Ovid relates the tale of Io who was raped by Jupiter and transformed into a cow to cover up her

understand Lavinia's pathetic indifference to her own plight, her family's neglect of her humiliation and pain, and everyone's lack of concern for the common good (after all, whoever did this is still just walking around Rome)?

The plot to ravish Lavinia, its execution, and its aftermath are littered with references to Roman poetry. But this literature does not serve to moderate its audience or make it more humane or public spirited. This is partly because literature has become a stand-in for reality and not an aid to its apprehension or to the pursuit of human flourishing. Thus, young Lucius can only make sense of his madly grieving aunt because he read about Hecuba in Ovid (IV.1.20), *not* because he lives with a grandfather who spent the last year going crazy. So too with Titus. Even though Lavinia has just scratched her story in the dust, Titus insists: "I will go get a leaf of brass / And with a gad of steel will write these words, / And lay it by. The angry northern wind / Will blow these sands like Sibyl's leaves abroad, / And where's our lesson then? Boy, what say you?" (IV.1.102–106). Later, when Tamora and her sons visit Titus at his home, he asks "Who doth molest my contemplation? / Is it your trick to make me ope the door, / That so my sad decrees may fly away / And all my study be to no effect? / You are deceived, for what I mean to do / See here in bloody lines I have set down, / And what is written shall be executed" (V.2.9–15).[41] Things are only real for Titus, they can only be fixed or stable and hence knowable, if they are written down. The irony for Titus is that while he inhabits one of Shakespeare's most lettered and literate communities, he cannot find real justice

---

violation. But Io promptly informed her father of her plight by using her hooves to write in the dust. That the Andronici draw on the more lurid story of Philomela but forget the less graphic, if more useful, account of Io reflects their propensity to turn to literature for its ability to titillate not educate.

[41] Writing can also be the source of the truth. See Marcus' comments at IV.1.75–76. Of course, the written word can also be the instrument of revenge. See IV.1.113–117; IV.3.50s–60s; IV.3.104–120.

anywhere.[42]

Such abstracted reality is the effect of a cosmopolitan empire that transcends the integrity of particular political bodies and a liberal education that doesn't take seriously the demands made by individual souls for their own wholeness or perfection. Life here takes place at an intellectual remove, one detached from that community of embodied souls where passionate loves, hatreds, and ambitions drive their often-combustible relations with each other. But to expect it to be otherwise is foolish; how could genuine human attachments and the individual flourishing they make possible emerge in a community that dissolved their essential preconditions? With the obliteration of the distinctions between citizen and foreigner, friend and enemy, "thine" and "mine," pagan and Christian, past and present[43]—even human and animal[44]—it becomes all too easy to confuse, as Titus does, "false shadows for true substances" (III.2.80–1).

---

[42] On the absence of "justice" in Rome, see Titus' quotation of Ovid ("*Terras Astrea reliquit*"; IV.3.4), his references to justice at IV.3.9, 15, 24, 50–52, 79, and 103, and Publius's comments at IV.3.38–40. See also what Saturninus says at IV.4.4–25.

[43] In addition to the anachronistic references to Christianity, the opening scene presents a similar problem. Marcus states that Titus "hath returned / Bleeding to Rome, bearing his valiant sons / In coffins from the field and at this day / to the monument of the Andronici / Done sacrifice of expiation, / And slain the noblest prisoner of the Goths" (I.1.33–38). Of course, Alarbus, who *will be* slain shortly, has *yet to be* slain. Bates (1995, 99–100) points out that this apparent slip-up constitutes evidence of a false start by Shakespeare. The broader reading I supply, however, shows how one could read this apparent "nod" consistent with other apparent oddities in the play.

[44] The extent to which Shakespeare uses animal imagery to illustrate human behavior in this play, further blurring the distinctions between them, has been far too under-appreciated. To provide a few examples here, Tamora is likened to a "tiger" (II.2.142; V.3.193) a "lion" (II.2.149 and IV.1.98) and is called a "dam" at least six times. Aaron is an "adder" (II.2.35) and "tiger" (V.3.4) who refers to his son as a "coal-black calf" (V.1.32). Saturninus is called a "stag" (II.3.71). Demetrius and Chiron are "bearwhelps" (IV.1.96) and are served as food for their mother. And Lavinia is referred to as a "doe" (I.1.593 and 617; II.1.26) and "wasp" (II.2.132).

Unable to distinguish appearance from reality, one will also be unable to understand causality. And in the absence of discernible causes, there can be no way to determine or fix, and thereby limit, their effects.[45] Without the ability to determine cause and effect, what is left to the human pursuit of knowledge, whose very intelligibility requires fixity, but to bid, as Lavinia does just before her dismemberment, "confusion fall" (II.2.183)?

"Confusion fall" indeed. Rome's descent into confusion is the theme of the play, as its portrayal of physical, political, and psychological madness indicate. Oddly enough, the foregoing lessons about the need for "limits" appear to find confirmation in the figure of Aaron the Moor. Despite his stated commitment to villainy, Aaron is the one character who successfully defends his offspring against the threats of others and who does so at great risk to both himself and Tamora, the child's mother. This is surprising. This career criminal—a man who will murder innocent women to protect himself—performs arguably the greatest act of humanity in the play. And because this newborn is his first child, his devotional energies cannot be attributed to prior relations with this or any other offspring. Then again, the fact that this is Aaron's only child might explain the intensity of his attachment and thus his willingness to run great risks on its behalf. After all, Titus has *twenty-six* children and we have seen how he can be casually indifferent to their welfare.

To this we could add that Aaron's black skin, African origin, and avowed atheism set him aside from those pious, white Europeans among whom he lives, highlighting his radical particularity. Such heightened awareness of his own "otherness" might explain why he seeks refuge for his son among those Goths still friendly to Tamora; the preservation of a particular demands a community dedicated to

---

[45] Titus attests to this after chopping off his own hand. There he laments to Marcus, "If there were reasons for these miseries,/ Then into limits I could bind my woes" (III.1.220–21). In other words, lacking knowledge of causes prevents Titus from setting limits to his own pains; if *anything* can cause grief, then griefs are potentially limitless.

particulars. But, and more importantly, it might also explain why he is willing to save his son and to do so in the service of the truth. Having been captured by those Goths now serving under Lucius, Aaron agrees to confess his crimes and reveal the conspiracy against the Andronici on the condition that Lucius agrees to raise his son. Of course, the truth doesn't set Aaron free, and he later repents any good deed he might have done (see note 14 above). But the truth he tells *does* set his son free. Aaron's powerful attachment to the good of someone outside of himself, a good that is rooted *in* a love of his own but that is not reducible *to* or understood *in terms of* his own self-interests, supplies the grounds for virtuous action and the disclosure of the truth.[46] When set against the backdrop of all that preceded, Shakespeare's portrayal of this villain suggests that the preconditions of human flourishing, with which virtue and the concern for the truth are so closely associated, demand a narrower radius of human affection, one in which particulars can live alongside—while carefully delineated from—each other, than the cosmopolitanism of Rome can ever hope to provide.

Shakespeare and Cosmopolitanism: Contemporary Applications

When we return to the cosmopolitanism with which this essay began and wonder about its relation to the possibility of self-knowledge, the preceding treatment of *Titus* yields the following insight. A Rome that ceases to exist in a particular political context, defined by a particular set of exclusive goods for a distinct set of

---

[46] One could say the same of Lucius here. As the price for hearing the hard truth about Aaron's villainy, he agrees to accept as part of his own family a child who most definitely stands out as someone else's; that is, as the price for possessing a good for oneself that is itself not identical to a love of one's own, Lucius is willing to accept the manifest particularity at odds with cosmopolitanism. One might say, to paraphrase one of this essay's reviewers, that a combination of both the just defense of one's own and the humane acceptance of the "other" constitutes the necessary grounds for living in the light of the truth.

people, is a Rome where the insights into human nature, which are universal, exist at a considerable remove from those particular concerns that guide and shape our lived reality. Lacking any traction on our individual souls and the passionate attachments that animate them, the classical learning that abounds in this play is unable to guide its subjects and thus unable to restrain the savagery of its audience, to say nothing of civilizing or perfecting it. The absence of discrete political forms thus prepares the way for psychological madness and the assault on the bodily forms of those people whose education knows no higher purpose than entertainment.

Read in the context of Shakespeare's broader Roman drama, *Titus* suggests that a Rome that was more serious about its particular identity, and thus more serious about the political principles that elevate and refine its behavior—which is to say, a Rome that was more republican—is a Rome where those universal insights can take on concrete shapes and forms, which are always particular, and thus guide our lives in morally and intellectually meaningful ways. Respect for republican political limits represents the precondition for our becoming wise about ourselves and others, a precondition necessary if we are to engage fully Shakespeare's universal wisdom.[47] To be sure, Shakespeare does not spell out the intricate operations by which the limits of political life produce these psychological and intellectual effects within human beings. Instead, he provides a dramatic retelling of the birth, life, and death of Rome, illustrating how its expansive foreign policy changed its regime and reshaped its

---

[47] On the broader point here, one should consult again the passage in *Natural Right and History* cited above in note 6, especially 120–127. As for the play *Titus*, thinking about it in this way not only helps us tie together the Roman plays but allows us to link *its* story to Shakespeare's later plays set in Venice (another cosmopolitan republic in Italy): *The Merchant of Venice* and *Othello*. In these works, the more controversial representations of the "other" appear in the form of Shylock, a Jew, and Othello, a Moor, two of the more beautifully developed characters whose fates test the limits of the cosmopolitan thesis. But we find the original embodiment of these two men in the singular villain of *Titus*, a Moor who bears the name of a Jew.

citizens' approach to and use of literature, poetry, and philosophy. In prompting his audience to reflect on the relationship between Rome's foreign policy and its citizen body, Shakespeare calls his audience to reflect on the often-mysterious relationship between part and whole, particulars and universals, a mystery whose unraveling and reweaving stands at the core of human self-understanding.

For Shakespeare's contemporary readers, acknowledging the wisdom of *Titus*, that is, granting the significance of distinct political borders and identities to the possibilities of human flourishing, does not require one to become a member of a particular political party, right or left. But it does have important lessons for those who want to navigate responsibly the debate over immigration in Western countries. For while *Titus Andronicus* seems to valorize distinctive and exclusive particular communities, such valorization is not the exclusive preserve of national chauvinism. On the contrary, it is the precondition for the realization of democratic politics championed by progressive liberals. For without salient political distinctions, one cannot determine what constitutes the sovereign will (i.e., the majority) of a democratic people. After all, one cannot determine the will of the majority without knowing whose voice rightfully counts towards the formation of that will and whose does not. And one cannot make this distinguishing determination without knowing who is "in" and who is "out." This demands boundaries between political bodies. And if one is to avoid the absurdity of infinite regression, then the determination of who is one of "us" cannot be made democratically. That means the criteria or conditions that define a people will often be given, the product of chance or tradition or even force, and not simply chosen or rationally determined.

Those who wish to extend the benefits of democratic politics to their fellow man must embrace the paradox in which the greater humanity of democracy requires greater fidelity to preserving the often arbitrarily given boundaries (demographic, linguistic, religious, economic, etc.) that separate men from one another. In doing so, one preserves the possibility not only of democratic politics, but, as the preceding has tried to show, of human flourishing. Retaining this

Aristotelian insight should highlight the close connection between political boundaries and limits and those other categories, like "citizen" and "foreigner," for example, that arouse the passionate attachments which make possible our liberal education. Of course, there will still be those who think this defense of discrete political bodies legitimizes the violence associated with certain forms of nationalism. Perhaps. But Shakespeare's *Titus* reminds us that an additional, and maybe even greater, threat to humanity resides within the cosmopolitan temptation. For what can be said of a civilization whose abandonment of national identities in the name of global humanitarianism prepares the way for the elimination of those categories fundamental to our humanity except that it, like Titus's Rome, is preparing to perform a "shameful execution on herself" (V.3.75)?

"Law and Form and Due Proportion":
Richard II, Sir Thomas More, and the Challenge of Constitutional Reform

L. Joseph Hebert

Shakespeare's *Tragedy of King Richard the Second* seems calculated to stir the political passions of an Elizabethan audience.[1] Parallels between the 1595 play's titular monarch and the reigning Queen led to its revival on the eve of the 1601 Essex rebellion. Like Richard, Elizabeth was accused of being "susceptible to flattery" and of imposing "burdensome taxes" without popular consent, while asserting a divine right to govern that excluded resistance on the part of subjects. In response, the Queen's most strident critics called for her parliamentary deposition. A year prior to Shakespeare's original dramatization of Richard's uncrowning, Jesuit Robert Parsons published a treatise citing the historical event as legal precedent.[2] After the play's revolutionary restaging, Shakespeare's patron Southampton was convicted of treason and sentenced to life in prison, and the playwright and his company escaped a similar fate only "by a plea of ignorance."[3]

At the level of topical application, *Richard II* manages to avoid charges of smiling at sedition by eliciting sympathy as well as

---

[1] I am deeply grateful to Will Jordan and Charlotte Thomas of the McDonald Center for America's Founding Principles for the opportunity to present and publish this paper, and to Elena Hebert, Nicholas Hebert, Daniel La Corte, Clinton Allen, Carson Holloway, Martina Saltamacchia, and Joseph Alulis for their advice, encouragement, criticisms, and suggestions. All remaining defects are my own.

[2] Charles R. Forker, "Introduction" to *King Richard II*, The Arden Shakespeare, Third Series, London (Bloomsbury, 2002), 5, 203 (note 37–41), 10, 19–21.

[3] Peter Milward, *Shakespeare the Papist*, Ann Arbor, MI (Sapientia Press of Ave Maria University, 2005), 85.

indignation for the imperious Richard, and inspiring suspicion of as well as admiration for his successor Bolingbroke.[4] Yet it is precisely this "detachment" from both kings—old and new, proto-Yorkist and proto-Lancastrian,[5]—that points to a more profoundly "subversive element" in the drama. If, as Allan Bloom contends, Shakespeare shows "the divine right of kings" to be "responsible for [Richard's] tyrannical deeds,"[6] the foundations on which Bolingbroke erects his reign prove similarly defective. Whether Henry IV introduces new tensions into the English regime, or simply fails to quiet ancient quarrels, civil discontent produces periodic civil wars until the accession of Henry VII, and continues to vex Henry VIII's most potent successor. For these reasons, *Richard II* and its companion plays seem to raise "the disquieting possibility that the institution of hereditary monarchy may itself be unviable," so that "there can be no model kings or adequate model conceptions of kingship."[7]

Whether or not Shakespeare finds a model king in English history, the conception of kingship implicit in his evaluation of monarchs is a question of political philosophy. Yet among those who discern a theoretical coherence in the Bard's political thought, opinions differ as to its provenance. For Bloom, Richard's vices and Bolingbroke's real but wavering superiority are to be understood in light of Machiavellian maxims, such as reliance on one's own's arms, the conquest of Fortune, the harmfulness of humility, and the unjust foundations of justice. On this view, only Henry VIII's decisive

---

[4] See Forker, "Introduction," 27.

[5] In England's subsequent dynastic wars, Lancastrians tended to depict Richard II as a "weak, incompetent, and despotic king," while Yorkists defended him as "more victim than villain"; likewise, the former party celebrated Bolingbroke as a "strong and capable leader," while the latter denounced him as "an ambitious, unscrupulous, opportunistic and dissimulating politician." Forker, "Introduction," 24.

[6] Allan Bloom, "Richard II," in *Shakespeare as Political Thinker*, ed. John E. Alvis and Thomas G. West, Wilmington, DE (ISI Books, 2000), 59–60, 69 (note 1).

[7] Forker, "Introduction," 1; Michael Tomlinson, "Shakespeare and the Chronicles Reassessed," *Literature and History*, vol 10, no. 1 (1984), 58; cited in Forker, "Introduction," 49–50.

subordination of ecclesial to political authority enables England to regain control of its own destiny.[8] For Joseph Alulis, the Machiavellian overtones of Bolingbroke's rebellion obscure Shakespeare's subtle endorsement of the Aristotelian notion of "absolute kingship," according to which a man so superior in virtue as to be "like a god among human beings" is gladly to be obeyed without the interference of law. Though Richard falls painfully short of this standard, his claims to divine assistance and insistence on the inalienable right of kings, combined with Bolingbroke's closer approximation of kingly strengths, point to a "practical teaching about politics, that good rule requires virtue in the ruler and makes the ruled virtuous."[9] In a similar vein, Pamela Jensen sees Shakespeare as engaged in "the quest to join a commanding and free nature to a sovereign place," while noting that Richard and Henry fail in this quest for superficially opposite but essentially similar reasons: in his pride, each refuses to accept his limitations as a human being, and therefore falls short of the genuine virtues made possible by self-knowledge and self-discipline.[10]

While these approaches yield valuable insights, more remains to be said about the complex philosophic framework informing the history plays. Though Shakespeare is clearly fascinated by Machiavelli, for example, he is staunchly critical of the only king explicitly following the Florentine's lead: Richard III.[11] And even where he

---

[8] Bloom, "Richard II," 63, 65, 66–68.

[9] "To Make High Majesty Look Like Itself: Shakespeare's *Richard II* and the Nature of the Good Regime," in *The Soul of Statesmanship*, ed. Khalil M. Habib and L. Joseph Hebert, Jr, Lanham, MD (Lexington Books, 2018), 148, 151, 155.

[10] Pamela K. Jensen, "Beggars and Kings: Cowardice and Courage in Shakespeare's *Richard II*," *Interpretation*, 18:1 (1990), 111–124.

[11] See L. Joseph Hebert, "The Reward of a King: Machiavelli, Aquinas, and Shakespeare's *Richard III*," *Perspectives on Political Science*, 44:4, 238–246. As noted there, scholars have rightly observed that Richard is an imperfect Machiavellian, yet I argue that Shakespeare uses Richard to illustrate, and expose the folly of, fundamental premises upon which Machiavelli's teaching stands or falls. For a different reading of Richard's relation to Machiavelli and to morality, see Dana Jalbert Stauffer, "Richard III, Moralist: Shakespeare's Critique of the Politics of Christian Piety," *Interpretation*, 47:3, 483–502.

appears sympathetic to the promised advantages of an amoral "effectual truth," the playwright's keen awareness of its defective premises and disruptive consequences prevents him from finally embracing it.[12] As Jensen aptly observes, Shakespeare's world is one in which the genuine conquest of fortune is achieved not (per impossible) by mastering all external contingencies, but rather by regulating the passions that would enslave our souls to a futile quest to conquer such contingencies.[13] Furthermore, Shakespeare's treatment of the machinations by which Henry VIII abuses the legal rights, public honors, and moral integrity of nobility, clergy, and his own Queen makes that revolutionary figure an unlikely model for monarchs, and gives the Bard's perfunctory, compulsory, and ambiguous affirmations of the Elizabethan settlement an ironic tinge.[14]

As for Aristotle, his account of a true king—like Plato's treatment of the philosopher king—is part of a complex dialectical argument presented in largely hypothetical terms. Though a thorough analysis is beyond our present scope, it is important to stress that the notion of an absolute monarch provides both a measure of political perfection and a caution as to the limits of practical politics. In his

---

[12] See L. Joseph Hebert, "'When Vice Makes Mercy': Classical, Christian, and Modern Humanism in Shakespeare's *Measure for Measure*," in *In Search of Humanity: Essays in Honor of Clifford Orwin*, ed. Andrea Radasanu, Lanham, MD (Lexington Books, 2015), 209–224. For evidence of such ambivalence in the history plays, consider the discussions of Shakespeare's reservations about Henry V in John E. Alvis, "Spectacle Supplanting Ceremony: Shakespeare's Henry Monmouth," in *Shakespeare as Political Thinker*, 107–141; and R. V. Young, *Shakespeare and the Idea of Western Civilization*, Washington, D.C. (The Catholic University of America Press, 2022), 120–131.

[13] "Beggars and Kings," 128–129.

[14] See Gerard Wegemer, "Henry VIII on Trial: Confronting Malice and Conscience in Shakespeare's *All Is True*," *Renascence: Essays on Values in Literature*, Volume 52, Number 2 (2000), 111–130; Nicolas McAffee, *Political Wisdom in Late Shakespeare: A Way Out of the Wreck*, Lanham, MD (Lexington Books, 2024), Chapter 2; and L. Joseph Hebert, *Poetry and Politics in the Play Sir Thomas More*, Washington, DC (Catholic University of America Press, 2025), "Conclusion."

account of conflicting claims to political preeminence, Aristotle makes clear that no single principle is adequate, including virtue (3.13.9).[15] Since the city aims at a life of excellence shared by all citizens, the proper measure of fitness to rule is the ability to secure the "advantage of the city as a whole" (3.13.12). Yet if one person's virtue is so outstanding as to be incommensurable with others', it seems he "can no longer be regarded as part of the city" (3.13.13). In the course of his dialectical treatment of this dilemma, Aristotle considers two simple solutions, neither of which satisfy his own criteria for good government. Though it may seem expedient to expel such a man for the sake of the common good, this is to offend directly against the virtue at which civic life aims (ibid.). On the other hand, to expect "everyone to obey such a person gladly" (3.13.25) is not only naïve—as if the less virtuous were inclined to obey their superiors—but also self-defeating, since political participation is both practically necessary and definitive of the civic virtue at which the polis aims (3.13.6, 3.13.12). For these and related reasons, anyone worthy of staking a claim to unlimited power on Aristotelian terms—anyone who is truly "like a god among human beings" (3.13.13)—would recognize that absolute kingship is a regime type confined by nature to the realm of speech.[16]

Just as genuine virtue includes knowledge of one's human limits, so too the flourishing of political society depends on more than the virtues of individual leaders. Though there can be no foolproof formula for integrating virtue into the polis, Aristotle crucially explores

---

[15] Parenthetical references are to Aristotle, *Politics*, Second Edition, trans. Carnes Lord, Chicago (The University of Chicago Press, 2013), Book III, Chapters 12–13.

[16] In Chapter 17 of Book III, Aristotle returns to the hypothesis of absolute kingship, stating that this mode of rule would be fitting for "a multitude of such a sort that it accords with its nature to support a family that is preeminent in virtue relative to political leadership" (3.17.4). Aside from the problem of how such a regime would cultivate virtue among citizens, one wonders under what historical conditions an entire people would be fit for obedience, while members of one of its families were reliably divine in character.

the hypothesis that the city will do "better if the legislator constitutes the regime from the beginning in such a way that it does not need [the] sort of healing" represented by ostracization (3.13.23).[17] As the phrasing implies, this view holds that the tensions between personal and political perfection are best mitigated by a system in which "the ruler [is] a legislator," law itself is the ultimate authority, and those who govern do so "as law-guardians and servants of the law" (3.15.6, 3.16.4). Though not a recipe for perfection, and daunting enough in its own terms, this approach seems to offer a more realistic chance of approximating the standards of good government. While laws cannot (like the "best man") provide an answer for every circumstance, they guard against several defects of absolute kingship. Not only is a true king incommensurable with the city as such, but there is no guarantee that he will leave a successor equal to himself, and even the most able man will have difficulty surveying the city's affairs without "rulers under him"—a mode of power sharing which is already a step toward the law's "arrangement of ruling and being ruled" (3.16.3, 3.16.9). By asking the best men to function as lawgivers and equitable guardians of the law, rather than autocrats, the city is able to receive, preserve, and transmit their virtue in a form capable of educating other citizens. Furthermore, since "every human soul" is affected by passion, and "spiritedness perverts rulers and the best men" (3.15.5, 3.16.5), it is prudent to mitigate the influence of passion by acknowledging the supremacy of an impartial standard, while enabling officeholders to question and improve upon one another's decisions. Ironically, though such a system inevitably dilutes the wisdom possessed by preeminent men, the most effective way to ask "god and intellect alone to rule" (3.16.5) is not to depend upon the institutionalized supremacy of a race of godlike men, but to embed the wisdom of the wisest citizens in a set of laws under which

---

[17] Parenthetical citations are to Aristotle, *Politics*, Book III, Chapters 13, 15–16.

no one possesses absolute power.[18]

Alulis characterizes Shakespeare's history plays as engaging Englishmen in "a dialogue about the nature and merits of [their] regime."[19] The substance of that dialogue shows its author to be aware of significant flaws in English government and receptive to notions of reform, while remaining resistant to the abandonment of classical ethics and skeptical as to the definitive solution of political problems. Though all of these traits may be traced directly to Aristotle, it is also worth considering more proximate sources from which Shakespeare may have drawn them. As R. V. Young reminds us, one neo-Aristotelian school of thought familiar to Shakespeare is "the humanist Catholicism associated with Desiderius Erasmus and Sir Thomas More." As Young explains, the premise of Erasmus's *Education of a Christian Prince* is that if one cannot choose a ruler who is wise, then one must carefully select "the man who is going to educate the future ruler" in wisdom. Grounding himself in "precepts of classical philosophy and the demands of Christian discipleship," Erasmus attempts to persuade hereditary monarchs to respect principles such as "liberty under a lawful ruler," the equal dignity of men, the need for consensual government, and the avoidance of unjust wars. Doing so requires an ironic exposure of Christendom's failure to live up to its highest standards, and an irenic search for practical means of better approximating them. For Young, it is this brand of Christian classicism that best explains Shakespeare's rejection of the "feckless idealism of Henry VI" as well as the ruthless malice of Richard III, and which motivates his efforts, in scrutinizing rulers who fall between these extremes, to distinguish genuine kingly virtue from its seductive but sterile counterfeits.[20]

---

[18] On a more practical note, Aristotle admits that it is natural for peoples among whom virtue is rare to be ruled by kings "selected on account of their benefactions." Since such kings are chosen by the people, and are merely "good men," it is likewise natural for their authority to diminish as a people becomes "more similar with respect to virtue (3.15.11).

[19] "High Majesty," 141.

[20] *Western Civilization*, 105, 107–108, 124, 110–111, 115, 131.

In a similar vein, scholars such as Stephen W. Smith and John Alvis make a case for exploring Shakespeare's indebtedness to Thomas More. Given that the first tetralogy culminates in a play closely adapted from More's *History of King Richard III*, and that Shakespeare contributed (at minimum) one major scene and a central soliloquy to the collaborative play *Sir Thomas More*, the evidence for this connection is particularly compelling. Noting that "the young Shakespeare would have looked at Sir Thomas More as an excellent example of an English author," and "an excellent model of historical tale telling," Smith wonders whether the Bard's bleak but illuminating portrayal of monarchical politics echoes that of the more forthrightly republican More, and whether Shakespeare, like Brutus in his *Rape of Lucrece*, means to combat "the tyranny of the king" by "acquaint[ing] the people with the doer and the manner" of his iniquities.[21] Likewise, Alvis notes the close congruity between Shakespeare and More in numerous matters of wit and wisdom, and asks whether More's open criticism of hereditary monarchy is reflected, albeit cautiously, in Shakespeare's depiction of few (if any) good kings.[22] In a study of the play *Sir Thomas More*, I note that scenes attributed to Shakespeare probe More's views on the most fundamental questions of authority and conscience, and demonstrate the author's intimate familiarity with the argument of that play as a whole, and with the writings of and about More informing the playwrights' treatment of their subject.[23]

With these considerations in mind, this paper will take a fresh look at Shakespeare's *Richard II*, paying particular attention to themes resonant with the play *Sir Thomas More*, the works and life of More himself, and related sources. In particular, we shall find that the problems depicted in the play center on a defective application

---

[21] "The Politics of Imitation: Exploring Connections between Thomas More and William Shakespeare," *Moreana* Vol. 48 (2011), 109, 111, 115.

[22] "Thomas More and Shakespeare: A Proposal for Furthering an Inquiry," *Moreana* Vol. 48 (2011), 78, 83–84.

[23] *Poetry and Politics*, "Conclusion."

of the Aristotelian idea of the rule of law, whose centrality to the English regime More and others sought to establish. By helping us to appreciate the complexity of the challenges of monarchical governance, and the difficulty of devising institutional or political mitigations of those challenges, More's example can enrich our understanding of Shakespeare's profound wisdom regarding the nature of political things.

Freedom of Speech and the Rule of Law

Richard II begins with the King addressing his uncle, aged son of the legendary Edward III, as "Old John of Gaunt." Thus Shakespeare introduces a contrast between old and new that will culminate with Baron Fitzwater's intention to "thrive" in the "new world" he and others hope to see under Henry IV (1.1.1, 4.1.79).[24] Commentary on the play tends to respond to this theme by associating Richard with medieval superstitions such as trial by combat and the divine right of anointed kings, and linking Bolingbroke with the promise of new and more rational modes of government. While Shakespeare is aware of such associations and willing to evoke them—making legal and even constitutional reform a definite theme of the play—his structuring of the conflicts plaguing English society, and of the contrasting attempts of Richard and Henry to mitigate those conflicts, points to a more complex, ironic, and illuminating account of the faults of the *ancien régime* and what it would take to remedy them.

Richard's glance at Gaunt's age alerts us to the fact that his chief action in the play's opening act is not to preserve old ways, but rather (ostensibly at least) to avert a trial by combat between Henry Bolingbroke, Duke of Hereford, and Thomas Mowbray, Duke of Norfolk. Though we will soon learn of Richard's likely crimes, flagrant vices, and ulterior motives, his conduct in this scene is to all appearances well-intentioned, if ineffectual, inviting us to ponder the

---

[24] All references to *Richard II* are to the Arden edition cited above.

genuine challenges he faces before probing the culpable causes of his failure. Describing Bolingbroke's accusation of Mowbray as "bold" and "boist'rous" or violent in nature, Richard questions Gaunt, Henry's father, as to its motive. A "good subject," he stresses, will only make accusations "on some known"—and hence demonstrable—"ground," whereas disturbing the peace on account of "ancient malice" is (he implies) the mark of a poor subject at best. When Gaunt dubiously responds that the charges involve "some apparent danger...aimed at your highness," Richard resolves to hear "the accuser and the accused freely speak." Though he fears that their mutual "rage" will render them "deaf as the sea, hasty as fire," Richard announces his intention to settle their dispute on the basis of a reasoned examination of available evidence (1.1.1–19).

As Richard's framing of the trial makes clear, good governance requires freedom of speech so that both rulers and subjects may reason well about what is just and advantageous.[25] As he also implies, such freedom encounters obstacles from without, in threats of reprisal by offended superiors, and from within, in the blinding influence of unregulated passions. Officially, Richard sets the stage for a fair trial by promising to remove the first obstacle. When Mowbray complains that "fair reverence of your highness curbs me from giving reins and spurs to my free speech"—alluding in part to Henry's kinship to Richard—the King responds by declaring himself "impartial," and confirming Mowbray's right as a subject to "free speech and fearless." As Richard predicts, however, the order of the proceedings is disrupted by the passions of the contending parties. Before complaining that reverence for the king curbs his speech, Mowbray dismisses arbitration by "the bitter clamor of two eager tongues" as "the trial of a woman's war." Similarly, declaring it a "deep sin" to withdraw his accusations though he cannot prove them, Bolingbroke promises to bite off his own tongue before permitting it to "sound so base a parle." To all appearances, the first trial of *Richard II*—a trial by words and not by arms—is aborted not by Richard's tyranny,

---

[25] Aristotle, *Politics*, 1.2.11, 3.16.5.

but by the unwillingness of his "high-stomached" subjects to submit to the (personal or political) governance of reasoned speech (1.1.47–57, 115–123, 190–195, 17).

Though Richard's England is formally governed by law, and its eminent men are aware that the rule of law implies the rule of reason, the laws of the realm are hindered in achieving this end by a customary disposition to violent arbitrarion. Quite predictably, Bolingbroke and Mowbray insist—against Richard's counsel, pleas, and threats—on settling their dispute by battle. As Bloom points out, this premise of this procedure seems to take for granted that God "will directly indicate where the truth lies by the victory in arms," so that "divine action and brute force preempt entirely the field properly governed by prudence."[26] In gauging the significance of its shortcomings, however, it is crucial to note the pagan origins of this custom, and its stark opposition to Christian doctrine and canon law.[27] Shakespeare hints at these tensions not only in the attempts of Richard and Gaunt to command the would-be combatants to make peace, but also in the terms by which the parties themselves rationalize their "boisterous" conduct. Declaring that "what I speak my body shall make good upon this earth, or my divine soul answer it in heaven," Bolingbroke tacitly admits that physical force cannot prove the veracity of words, and that God has promised to judge souls in the next life, not here below. Mowbray is yet more explicit about the

---

[26] "Richard II," 60.

[27] Ecclesial authorities and saints denounced the "judicial duel" as "no law, but murder," and a form of "tempting God," but its abolition took centuries. In his (perhaps contemptuously) brief treatment of the topic, Thomas Aquinas considers duels a form of "sortilege" or casting of lots, which is generally "superstitious and unlawful," and particularly offensive when presuming to call upon "divine judgment" without the sanction of "divine authority." See Henri Daniel-Rops, *The Church of Cathedral and Crusade*, Volume I, trans. John Warrington, Providence, RI (Cluny, 2023 [1957]), 350–351; and Robert Bartlett, "Trial by Battle," in *Trial by Fire and Water: the Medieval Judicial Ordeal*, Oxford (Clarendon Press, 1986), 103–126; Thomas Aquinas, *Summa Theologiae*, trans. Fr. Laurence Shapcote, O.P., ed. John Mortensen and Enrique Alarcón, Lander, WY (The Aquinas Institute for the Study of Sacred Doctrine, 2012), II–II, 95.8.

evidentiary irrelevance of the contest when he proclaims himself to be a "just and upright gentleman" whose "truth" affords him a "quiet breast," "however God or Fortune cast my lot" on earth (1.1.35–48, 1.3.85–96). The only connection here between Christianity and combat is the assertion by each party that he would not risk death and divine judgment if he were in the wrong. In the case of a man of unimpeachable piety the argument might have some weight,[28] but the impenetrability of the human breast, coupled with the opponent's resort to the same logic, renders such reasoning juridically indeterminate at best.[29] In truth, eagerness to settle a dispute by a method that proves little about its substance is rooted in something other than reason or religion.

Though Mowbray makes what appears to be a credible case for refusing to decline Bolingbroke's challenge, its subtle flaws expose a central problem of English government around which the tragedy of *Richard II* revolves. When Richard attempts to quell the defendant's "rage" by insisting that "lions make leopards tame," Mowbray retorts that even lions cannot "change [the leopard's] spots." Reminding the king that he has no power over nature, the Duke insists upon his right to a "spotless reputation," which is "the purest treasure mortal times afford." If "mine honor is my life," he reasons, the king can no more command him to betray his honor than to kill himself (1.1.173–185). Though illuminating in several respects, this argument fails in application to the circumstances. In a warlike regime,

---

[28] Consider Thomas More's defense against the sworn testimony of Richard Rich: "If I were a man, my lords, that did not regard an oath, I needed not, as it is well known, in this place, at this time, nor in this case, to stand here as an accused person. And if this oath of yours, Master Rich, be true, then pray I that I never see God in the face, which I would not say, were it otherwise, to win the world." William Roper, *The Life of Sir Thomas More*, in *Essential Works*, 1412.

[29] Trial by battle was generally favored in (and sometimes limited to) cases in which "other forms of proof were not available," or when a party was accused of "bad faith," such that his oath could not be trusted (Bartlett, "Trial by Battle," 108–109). As noted above, even as a last resort the evidentiary value of this solution is dubious.

losing one's reputation can be fatal, but Mowbray's willingness to risk his life for honor is inconsistent with its reduction to a means of survival. If he intends to appeal to the intrinsic merits of honor, however, we must reply that honor is good only insofar as it constitutes the recognition by society of virtuous conduct. Because men are imperfect judges of virtue, Aristotle teaches, the worthy man must discriminate between deserved and undeserved honors, accepting the former but disdaining the latter. Since virtue consists in governing one's actions in accordance with reason, honor that is premised on rash, disorderly, or impious conduct is unworthy of a true and upright gentleman.[30] Though Mowbray indeed has cause to fear the social consequences of obeying Richard's call for peace—and though in a better governed polity he would better defended against them—his unwillingness to face those consequences here, though pardonable in light of human frailty, is something closer to cowardice than courage.

Of course, Mowbray's intemperate notions of honor are not peculiar to himself but characteristic of the warrior caste to which he belongs. Though useful when it inspires a willingness to die in a just cause, the spiritedness characteristic of knightly valor can also pose a threat to the regular administration of justice. Richard's attempt to tame the rage of these rivals appears commendable, but his admission of impotence in the face of inveterate custom foreshadows his eventual surrender of the crown. By eliciting Mowbray's appeal to nature, even the crude customs on which he stands might provide an opening for counterargument, thereby furthering the core purpose of law. Yet the King fails to respond with substantive reasoning. In a certain sense, Richard anticipates Bolingbroke by playing the role of a failed reformer. Initially, he bids these "wrath-kindled gentlemen"

---

[30] Aristotle, *Nicomachean Ethics*, trans. Joe Sachs, Newburyport, MA (Focus Publishing, 2002), Book I, Chapter 5; Book IV, Chapter 3. For an insightful analysis of Aristotle's treatment of honor and its reception by Christian Aristotelians, see Carson Holloway, "Christianity, Magnanimity, and Statesmanship," *The Review of Politics* 61:4 (1999), 581–604.

to be "ruled by me," attempting to "purge [their] choler without letting blood." Yet, admitting that he is "no physician," Richard soon gives up on his attempt to prescribe forgiveness, yielding to his nobles' spirited protests and specious arguments. When Mowbray insists that Richard may command his life but not his shame, the king is reduced to hollow threats of force. After Bolingbroke shows a similar defiance, Richard engages in what we shall find to be his characteristic form of vainglorious impotence. Complaining that he is "not born to sue but to command," he abandons all efforts at persuasion and yields to the parties' demands. Behind a smokescreen of superiority Richard admits his inferiority to the herculean but ineluctable task of mastering the unruly passions of his subjects. Comparing himself to Phaëton, son of Apollo, whose attempt to steer the sun ended in disaster, Richard will be forced to hand the crown to a more skillful man, admitting that he is "wanting the manage of unruly jades" (1.1.152–205; 3.3.178–180).

The problem Richard faces here is a variation of that identified by Aristotle as endemic to political life. Barring the absolute rule of a supremely virtuous man, political society is left in the care of parties whose excesses or deficiencies must eventually provoke a contest for power by those similarly unfit. The only hope of escaping this vicious circle is the rule of law. The king who rules not in his own name but as guardian of the law can appeal to the wisdom of the law in addition to his own, as can his subjects, and the latter, disciplined by the impersonal force of law, are less likely to seek vengeance on those correcting them.[31] Yet in Richard's effort to moderate the rage of Bolingbroke and Mowbray, initial references to law and its rational foundations soon give way to ineffectual appeals to authority and to force. His attempt to steer his subjects toward a more reasonable course founders due to his proud refusal to "sue" or make claims within a legal framework, followed by his verbal appeal to a mode of government—absolute monarchy—that his present defeat proves to be unmerited. A better physician would see that the remedy to the

---

[31] Aristotle, *Politics*, Book III, Chapters 9, 15–16.

ills depicted in this scene is the artful use of existing laws, or the pursuit of legal reform, with the aim of binding both unruly subjects and abusive kings to procedures in which freedom of speech gives reason its due. Yet, clever and perceptive as Richard is in his finer moments, we shall see that he is unwilling to turn to that remedy due to selfish and ultimately self-destructive motives. Additionally, though Bolingbroke differs from Richard in many prominent ways, on this crucial point his defects prove essentially the same. While accusing Richard of violating the laws he is sworn to uphold, and even gesturing toward his legal deposition by Parliament, in the end Henry decisively declines to embrace the supremacy of law, paving the way for continued constitutional turmoil.

Morean Lessons on Law and Leadership

Thus far we have noted that Shakespeare portrays Richard's half-hearted attempt to govern by means of reason as hinging on a freedom of speech that, threatened as it is by both passion and force, cannot reliably be achieved without a robust adherence to the rule of law. As it happens, the first (and in Shakespeare's day the only) recorded attempt to establish freedom of speech as a principle of law was made in 1523 by none other than Sir Thomas More. As William Roper relates, More was chosen Speaker of the House of Commons while holding a position on Henry VIII's Council. When the King rejected his request to avoid this conflict of interests, More presented the monarch with "two lowly petitions": first, that prior to More's reporting their decisions, Henry would permit him to confer privately with the Commons for their "prudent instructions" and "substantial advice"; and second, that Henry would relieve members of the House of "all doubt and fear" by granting "license and pardon, freely, without doubt of your dreadful displeasure, every man to discharge his conscience, and boldly in everything incident among us to declare his advice."[32]

---

[32] *Essential Works of Thomas More*, ed. Gerard B. Wegemer and Stephen W. Smith, New Haven, CT (Yale University Press, 2020), 1393–1394.

Though couched in terms of kingly prerogative, the reasoning behind More's petition is clearly aimed at establishing a precedent favoring an Aristotelian rule of law in England. Through the King's "prudent advice," "due diligence" has been used to select "a very substantial assembly of right wise and politic persons" to advise the king. "Since among so many wise men neither is every man wise alike," nor "every man like well spoken," and since "much folly is uttered with painted polished speech," while "many, boisterous and rude in language, see deep indeed," men are likely to hold back their wise counsel for fear of misspeaking or being misunderstood, "to the great hindrance of the common affairs."[33] More's assumption that the realm will suffer without such advice gently reminds the King that he too is fallible, and that legal guarantees are necessary to ensure that wise but contrary views receive a royal hearing. Indeed, in an epigram published several years earlier asking whether "a king or a senate governs better," More observes that "it's easy and more common to find a bad monarch." A senate is preferable because as a body it is often "neither good nor bad but indifferent," because even "a wicked senator is guided more by virtuous advisors," and because senators are more likely to feel obligated to the people.[34] In the course of his career, More twice led Parliament to reject royal bills, and once bested the King in a lawsuit.[35] Clearly he thought that the promise of an England governed by law, embodied in such constitutional features as Parliament, the Magna Carta, and King's Coronation Oath,[36] could be made to stick in practice as well as in theory.

Despite his preference for Parliamentary government, More (like Erasmus) understood that, in the monarchies of his day, "it is from the ruler—as if from some everlasting spring—that there flows

---

[33] *Essential Works*, 1393–1394.

[34] Epigram 198, in *Essential Works*, 249; the translation above is taken from *Utopia & Selected Epigrams*, ed. Gerard Wegemer and Stephen W. Smith, trans. Bradley Ritter, Carl Young, and Erik Ellis, Dallas, TX (CTMS Publishers at the University of Dallas, 2023), 113.

[35] *Essential Works*, 1392–1395.

[36] *Essential Works*, 1363.

a torrent of all goods and evils for the whole nation." Where Erasmus emphasized the education of a future prince, however, More argues in *Utopia* that a man of "noble" and "philosophical mind" is obliged to adapt his "talents and industry to public affairs" by "becoming an advisor to some great ruler, and by persuading him…to do right and honest things." When the fictional Raphael Hythloday objects that kings are too "steeped in perverse opinions from childhood and deeply tainted within" to listen to sound advice, More agrees that wisdom unadorned "will never be accepted" by kings, since "an opposite opinion already holds their minds captive." If the royal advisor is to "make something good, [or] at least make it the least bad [he] can," he must employ "another, more citizen-like philosophy, which knows the stage it plays on, and adapting itself to the play in hand, maintains its own part aptly and with decorum." The drama of politics, More insists, must be treated like "some comedy of Plautus [in which] the household slaves are joking around," rather than "the *Octavia* where Seneca is disputing with Nero," with results both futile and fatal. In an ominous retort, Raphael warns that even the most artful statesman may be put in a position where he must either "approve the worst plans openly," or "be treated like a spy, almost a traitor."[37] As More's life confirms and the play *Sir Thomas More* stresses, even the most skillful political comedian must be prepared to meet a tragic end.

Sir Thomas More provides a dramatic model of the virtues qualifying a man for absolute kingship, which in practice are better directed to shoring up the rule of law in a regime otherwise resistant to wisdom. In a scene revised in Shakespeare's hand, More's "calm breath," "breath of gravity," "little breath," or "gentle breath" achieves what Richard's "breath of kings" cannot: the taming of unruly passions by an appeal to law backed by tactfully reasonable speech. More shines where Richard fails, persuading an unruly mob to submit to

---

[37] *Utopia*, in *Essential Works*, 159, 168, 171–172. The texts quoted above are taken from Gerald Malsbary's translation in *Utopia & Selected Epigrams*, 22–23, 35, 40–41.

the king's laws, despite that king's failure to enforce them impartially, by demonstrating that their own good as well as that of their children, of their country, and of humankind depends on the rule of law.[38] Later, in a soliloquy attributed to Shakespeare, More reflects on the power he wields as Chancellor or chief legal officer of the realm. In a poignant reminder that virtuous governance begins with one's own soul, More warns himself against the corrupting influence of his "sharp state," resolving to play physician to himself first by remembering the transitory nature of earthly prerogatives.[39] In a speech made just before he refuses to sign certain articles sent by the King, exposing himself to the charge of high treason, the play's More advises the Privy Council that they are the physicians of the land, effecting its "health and preservation" by "choice diet" and "letting blood," while the King sleeps peacefully. He then proceeds to steer the Council toward what is "most honorable, most commodious," by opposing Henry's direct engagement in a war against France. Echoing *Utopia*'s critique of kings for thinking more about foreign conquest than domestic governance, and for plundering their own subjects to pay for it, the play's More strives to bring out the best in England's constitutional legal system, to work within that system to secure domestic peace and justice, and to "prevent in French wars England's loss" of lives and livelihoods.[40]

In *Richard II*, More's artful voice is discernable when the Duke of York's gardeners "talk of state," lamenting the King's failure to "keep law and form and due proportion" in the commonwealth, as they do in the "model" of their "firm estate." Though its references to decapitating "too fast-growing sprays" and pulling out "noisome weeds" may be suggestive of the proverbial tyrannical method of

---

[38] *Sir Thomas More*, 2.2.39, 51; 2.3.182 (this scene is revised by Shakespeare); 3.2.104, in *Essential Works*, 1434, 1439, 1450; compare *Richard II*, 1.3.215.

[39] *Sir Thomas More*, 3.1.1–21, in *Essential Works*, 1443.

[40] *Sir Thomas More*, 4.1.14–21, 57–67, in *Essential Works*, 1454–1455; *Utopia*, in *Essential Works*, 168–171.

eliminating rivals,[41] their discourse as a whole details a variety of devices for cultivating "wholesome flowers." After his crew employs a panoply of metaphors, including binding, supporting, pruning, deworming, trimming, and dressing, the head Gardiner sums up their professional wisdom by explaining that wounding the bark of fruit trees protects them from confounding themselves by "being overproud in sap and blood." Had Richard treated the "great and growing men" of the realm likewise, he opines, "they might have lived to bear and he to taste their fruits of duty."[42] Left prudently unstated is the inference that Richard failed to clip the pride of his greatest subjects due to the overgrowth of his own.

If the gardeners' counsel is expressed in "essentially negative" terms, this is because the governance of imperfect men requires correction.[43] Yet these analogies show that the skillful use of authority can assist nature in achieving its wholesome potential. We are reminded that the goal of law, even when it punishes, is not to elevate some at the expense of others, but rather to foster the conditions in which all but the incorrigibly criminal can live to enjoy a state of approximate health. The remedy to England's ills is therefore neither the supremacy nor the surrender of kingly power, but rather the regular and regulated exercise of that power in support of "law and form and due proportion."[44] Lacking the physician's or gardener's arts, or an advisor possessing them, both Richard and his successor fail to heed this Morean lesson.

---

[41] See Forker, *Richard II*, 365, note 33. Aristotle cites this image in his discussion of ostracization, noting that the elimination of disproportionate elements "is something that is advantageous not only to tyrants," but also to regimes "that look to the common good" (*Politics*, Book III, Chapter 13).

[42] *Richard II*, 3.4.29–66

[43] See Jensen, "Beggars and Kings," 142, note 9; Aristotle, *Ethics*, Book X, Chapter 9.

[44] *Richard II*, 3.4.41. Aristotle notes that, in a regime ruled by law, the king's power must be carefully calibrated to enable him to "safeguard the laws," such that the forces he commands render him "superior to individuals" but "inferior to the multitude" (*Politics*, Book III, Chapter 15).

Kingly Corruption, Cowardly Counsel, and the Failure of Constitutional Reform

After witnessing Richard's inability to govern his quarrelsome nobility, we are privy to a conversation in which John of Gaunt complains of his inability to press a related quarrel. Though bound in honor to avenge the murder of his brother, the Duke of Gloucester, he is thwarted by the suspicion that Gloucester's death was caused by "God's substitute, His deputy anointed in His sight"—in other words, the King. While he is not certain of Richard's guilt, Gaunt is sure that he cannot confront God's "minister," and so must leave the correction of this crime to heaven (1.2.1–8, 37–41).[45] Since Richard too will make much of the notion that he is God's untouchable vicar, it may seem that the play's tragic plot does hinge upon a point of medieval superstition. As with trial by combat, however, it turns out that these appeals to divine right are theologically dubious, serving largely as a cloak for more mundane human failings, which must be understood as the underlying causes of England's political dysfunctions.

As Young points out, the divine right of kings "is an understanding of monarchy associated less with the historical John of Gaunt than with the absolutist propaganda of the Tudor establishment," which sought to forestall rebellion while justifying royal supremacy in ecclesial as well as civil affairs.[46] Since medieval kings were anointed by bishops, and the ritual was sometimes spoken of as a sacrament, Richard's imaginative insinuations that his anointing

---

[45] Gaunt specifically insists that he cannot "lift an angry arm against" the King (1.2.41), discounting the possibility of using argument or tact to address the dilemma.

[46] *Western Civilization*, 116. John Figgis associates divine right with four claims: that "monarchy is a divinely ordained institution"; that "hereditary right is indefeasible"; that "kings are accountable to God alone"; and that "non-resistance and passive obedience are enjoined by God." Though it crystalized in the seventeenth century, Figgis finds roots of the doctrine in the ambitions of earlier emperors and kings, including Richard II. *The Divine Right of Kings*, New York (Harper Torchbooks, 1965 [1896]), 5–6, 73–80.

has left an indelible mark on his soul like baptism, or effected an indissoluble bond like matrimony, are not entirely idiosyncratic (3.2.54–55, 5.1.71–73).[47] Yet as a byproduct of the Church's multigenerational effort to Christianize a pagan culture, the anointing of kings never rose to the level of an eighth sacrament.[48] More importantly, nothing in orthodox theology suggested that the ceremony absolved kings from the responsibility to rule justly, or mandated blind obedience to their unjust commands.[49] In fact, Aquinas went so far as to insist that "there is no sedition in disturbing a [tyrannical] government," since the tyrant is himself "guilty of sedition" for encouraging "discord and sedition among his subjects."[50] And since "most (*plures*) tyrants exercise tyranny under the cloak of royal dignity," he added, the title of king cannot shield a ruler from the consequences of this teaching. While the slaying of tyrants by private persons is likely to cause more harm than good, and is therefore reprobated, it is "not unjust" for an abusive king to be deposed by a "multitude," for "even though it had previously subjected itself to him in perpetuity," this was on the understanding that he would "act

---

[47] See Henri Daniel-Rops, *Cathedral and Crusade*, 261–264. According to Figgis, the historical Richard II "regarded himself as king by virtue of unction," which he regarded "as conferring a sacramental grace" (*Divine Right*, 79).

[48] In 1274, the Second Council of Lyons accepted a creedal confession from Emperor Michael Paleologus declaring that the Church "holds and teaches that there are seven sacraments"; in the same era, Aquinas says nothing about the anointing of kings in his discussion of the seven sacraments; and in 1521 Henry VIII, who would later embrace the theory of divine right, had no difficulty in numbering the sacraments at seven. See Heinrich Denzinger, *Compendium of Creeds, Definitions, and Declarations on Matters of Faith and Morals*, eds. Peter Hünermann, Robert Fastiggi, and Anne Englund Nash, Forty-Third Edition, San Francisco, CA (Ignatius Press, 2010), paragraph 860; *Summa*, III, 65.1; Henry VIII, *Assertio Septem Sacramentorum, or, Defence of the Seven Sacraments* (American Theological Library Association, 1908).

[49] Alulis, "High Majesty," 148–150, Daniel-Rops, *Cathedral and Crusade*, 264–265.

[50] *Summa*, II–II, 42.2, ad 2.

faithfully as the office of a king demands."⁵¹ As Thomas More put it, "any man who rules alone over many men owes this to those over whom he rules," and the king will therefore "be safe if he rules his people in such a way that the people believe no man to be more expedient to them."⁵² As we have seen, More holds that the only expedient form of kingship is that limited by law and guided by good counsel.

That Richard has no sincere intention of ruling by law becomes increasingly clear as the story unfolds.⁵³ When Bolingbroke accuses Mowbray of misappropriating the king's funds and of murdering Gloucester, he replies that he had the king's consent to keep a sum in repayment of debt, and though he did neglect his "sworn duty" while guarding Gloucester, he did not slay him. Richard's failure to corroborate the first claim demonstrates that his ostensible interest in fact-finding is severely limited by self-regard. Likewise, Richard's silence on Mowbray's cryptic confession regarding Gloucester makes sense only if the King is indeed responsible for the crime, and willing to allow a (possibly innocent) subordinate to take the blame (1.1.87–134). Immediately prior to the aborted duel, Richard claims to "espy virtue with valor couched in [Mowbray's] eye," all but confessing personal knowledge of his guiltlessness, but proceeds to condemn the loyal Duke, "with some unwillingness," to a life of "hopeless" exile. Then, hearing of Gaunt's mortal illness, Richard callously prays for his death, salivating over the seizure of his estates to fund a military expedition after having drained his coffers with unprecedented luxuries (1.3.97–98, 148–153). When the Duke of York points out that Richard's kingship rests on the same "customary

---

⁵¹ Thomas Aquinas, *On Kingship*, trans. Gerald B. Phalen and Ignatius T. Eschmann, O.P., in *Opuscula I: Treatises*, Green Bay, WI (Aquinas Institute, 2018), Book I, Chapters 4, 6.

⁵² Epigrams 121, 120, in *Essential Works*, 238; text from *Utopia & Selected Epigrams*, 113.

⁵³ According to Figgis, Richard II "desired to found an absolute monarchy, and to relieve the Crown of all limitations, with which custom had fenced it about" (*Divine Right*, 77.)

rights" violated in Gaunt's case, his answer is "think what you will." In his contempt for his subjects and for the laws protecting them, Richard is blinded to his own dependency on those laws and on the common good they are meant to foster. It comes as no surprise when we hear that the King, "basely led by flatterers," has lost the hearts of both commons and nobles "with grievous taxes" and fines, and that their hopes are set on the return of banished Bolingbroke, who they expect will "redeem…the blemished crown" (2.1.186–210, 241–248, 291–295).

Though bad advice cannot excuse Richard's shortcomings, the play's emphasis on his flatterers highlights the Morean theme of the necessity of good counsel for good government. And while his primary corruptors are Bagot, Bushy, and Green, a crucial factor in Richard's failure is the absence of competent correction from those best positioned to check his follies. The King's decision to banish Bolingbroke and Mowbray, for example, is made in Council, and a distraught Gaunt admits to having advised Richard against his genuine wishes, seeking to impress the King with a display of impartiality. Later we will see a more extreme version of this posturing when York begs King Henry to convict his son the Duke of Aumerle for treason (1.3.123–124, 236–246; 5.3.38–98). As Bloom notes, these aging props of the old order exhibit a pronounced artificiality,[54] but the root of that artifice is not religious conviction. On his deathbed, Gaunt speaks freely in condemnation of Richard's vices, demonstrating that it was not reverence for the King's anointing that previously stopped his tongue. Though Gaunt attributes his change to a pious hope that Richard will be receptive to the words of a dying man, it is more likely explained by his equally vain confidence that the King cannot punish the dead. Bolingbroke's disinheritance proves that Gaunt is once again deceived (2.1.1–16, 73–138, 153–162).

Though brave in battle, Gaunt and York are less impressive when it comes to political prudence and the moral courage to act

---

[54] "Richard II," 61.

upon what wisdom they do possess. In his famous encomium of England as "this other Eden," a "demi-paradise" and "fortress built by Nature for herself," Gaunt oversteps the bounds of healthy patriotism by putting a Christian veneer on a vision in manifest tension with both reason and revelation. For him, the martial prowess and geographical isolation of "this sceptered isle" is a sign of its innate goodness, which is threatened only by the "envy of less happier lands," whom it must therefore conquer. Through "Christian service and true chivalry," Gaunt imagines that this warlike spirit does homage to "the world's ransom, blessed Mary's son"—but to the extent that his hyperbolic premises hold, England is less in need than other realms of ransom from an original sin by which it remains comparatively unscathed (2.1.31–68).[55] Of course, as the wiser but unheeded advice of the gardeners stresses, England is and always has been beset by the follies and frailties of its denizens. Like Hythloday in More's *Utopia*, Gaunt dreams of a society inexplicably inoculated against vice, rather than applying himself to the methods necessary for the mitigation of the vices afflicting his society.[56] His brother York, who likewise idolizes a regime characterized by the fierce plundering of enemies and idyllic mildness toward friends, finds himself torn between his duty to the King and his conscience, which bids him right the King's wrongs (2.1.163–185; 2.2.109–116). Yet conscience, as the voice of reason directing one toward the common good,[57] is inseparable from the concept of duty, and York's ultimate duty to a wayward King is to guide him back toward the good by all possible means. When the Duchess of Gloucester accuses her brother-in-law of disguising "despair" as "patience," and the Duchess of York calls her husband's honor "hypocrisy," these aggrieved

---

[55] Note Gaunt's reference to himself as "a prophet new inspired," hinting at the friction between the premises of his vision and those of traditional Christian revelation.

[56] See Gerard Wegemer's analysis of Augustinian elements of More's satire in *Thomas More on Statesmanship*, Washington, D.C. (The Catholic University of America Press, 1998), Chapter 7.

[57] See Aquinas, *Summa*, I, 71.13; I–II, 90.2.

women may exaggerate the point, but they rightly expose the personal limitations at the root of the nobility's failure to offer Richard adequate counsel (1.2.29; 5.3.99–109).[58]

When Richard learns of Bolingbroke's rebellion, he begins to echo Gaunt's rhetoric about the divine prerogatives of anointed kings. Late in the play, in his only soliloquy, Richard explicitly rejects piety as an alternative to his lost kingship, hinting that his appeals to heaven were never a fruit of sincere devotion. Admitting that his pride prevents him from turning to God, the fallen Richard opts to perpetuate his rule by populating his prison with imaginary subjects (5.5.1–17). This suggests that his earlier emphasis on divine right (as Bolingbroke insinuates about his breaking of a mirror) is a theatrical device by which to secure the sympathies of his subjects and thereby abuse power with impunity (4.1.292–293). This is further confirmed when, ignoring the Bishop of Carlisle's pointed correction of his theological error, the King proceeds to take this error to blasphemous extremes, calling upon the soil, an army of angels, and even his kingly title to take up arms on his behalf (3.2.4–62). During his deposition Richard famously compares himself to Christ betrayed (4.1.171–172), but his conduct is consistently contrary to that of his supposed model. As the Incarnation of Divine Logos—literally a "god among men"—Christ was supremely qualified for absolute kingship, but declined a kingdom of worldly dominion in favor of one within the human soul, redirecting fallen men to the source of abundant and eternal life (John 1:1ff; Luke 17:21; John 18:36–37, 10:10, 3:16). Though he established a Church and affirmed the divine commission of civil authorities, Christ granted absolute power to neither, and taught that authority is a form of service (John 20:21, 19:11; Matthew 20:25–28). In heaven, Aquinas argues, the good king will

---

[58] As Shakespeare's audience would know, the rivalry between Richard and his nobles originated almost ten years earlier, when certain lords (including the subsequently murdered Gloucester) used "high-handed tactics in Parliament and council, reducing him to a mere figurehead"; Forker, 186 (note 88–103). Is it surprising that a nobility that once abused Parliamentary power fails to counsel Richard against abuses of kingly power?

be rewarded for his earthly governance with a glory confirming his likeness to God; but a king who seeks glory on earth is likely to go astray, winning the hatred of men and the pains of eternal punishment.[59]

As successive reports inform him of his allies' losses, Richard comically vacillates between baseless confidence and despair, proving that his understanding of kingship is grounded not in the virtue of faith but in the sin of presumption (3.2.63–160).[60] His reference here to kings haunted by ghosts reminds us of Shakespeare's earlier treatment of the later King Richard III, in which the murderous tyrant is plagued nightly by his victims.[61] Though Richard II is a less accomplished villain, the root of his follies is similar: a self-defeating attempt to govern against conscience, and therefore against genuine prudence.[62] As we shall see, Bolingbroke's strategy to win the crown depends upon correctly predicting that Richard will abdicate rather than die fighting (which Carlisle portrays as preferable to despair), showing that his enemy understands the hollowness of his pretensions better than Richard himself. As Forker notes, Richard's surrender contradicts the theory of government to which he intransigently clings, rendering his continued existence insupportable.[63] Through a gradual and grudging admission of his faults, Richard does gain a modicum of humanity, lending the second half of the play a tragic pathos.[64] Yet Richard only begins to know himself after

---

[59] *On Kingship*, Chapters 7–9.

[60] See Aquinas, *Summa*, II–II, 4, 20, 21.

[61] *The Tragedy of Richard III*, ed. Mark Eccles, in Histories: Volume 1, New York (Everyman's Library, 1994), 5.3.119–177. *Richard III* first appeared in 1592–1593.

[62] Like conscience, prudence is the application of right reason to practical questions, inclusive of sound moral judgment. See Aquinas, *Summa*, II–II, 47.

[63] "Introduction," 35.

[64] See Bloom, "Richard II," 62–63; Forker, "Introduction," 31–32. I find Jensen's claim that Richard achieves "real self-mastery" hyperbolic, though she aptly links his critique of music lacking proportion to the gardeners' advice on "law and form and due proportion," and rightly admires his final act of courage; see "Beggars and Kings," 133–139.

reluctantly relinquishing a career of heartless oppression, and his belated undeafening comes too late to contribute to the reform of English government.

Carlisle is the closest Richard comes to a wise counselor, rightly arguing that divine Providence does not absolve men of the duty to exercise prudent self-help.[65] As Alulis observes, the cleric's opposition to Bolingbroke's rebellion and participation in a plot to unseat the newly crowned Henry IV are premised on a perception of the revolution's deleterious effects which proves all too prescient (3.2.27–32, 178–185; 4.1.115–150).[66] Yet Carlisle restricts his otherwise reasonable and disinterested efforts to a defense of Richard's authority, remaining conspicuously silent about Richard's vices and crimes. Though evidently motivated by a genuine concern for the good of the realm, able to see beyond its most glaring prejudices, and quite possibly in possession of the depths of wisdom required to set its government on a safer course, Carlisle appears to lack either the heights of courage necessary to put such wisdom into effect, or the confidence that his advice will be heeded in the kingdom as currently constituted. So far from suggesting that political welfare demands the eradication of ecclesial autonomy,[67] Carlisle's disappointing reticence supports the view of Erasmus and More that a spirited and artful application of classical Christian wisdom is a key to improving the state of a commonwealth. As More argued in his forceful defense of Christendom, if Church and state are composed alike of virtuous and vicious members, the control of one by the other is no guarantee of genuine reform. Only the cooperation of good men in each domain against their corrupt counterparts in both, working through the mediation of revived or revised civil and ecclesial laws, can enhance the influence of virtue over society as a whole.[68]

---

[65] The same point is made more forcefully and fruitfully in the soliloquy Shakespeare writes for *Sir Thomas More*, 3.1, in *Essential Works*, 1443.
[66] "High Majesty," 146.
[67] See Bloom, "Richard II," 65–66.
[68] *Essential Works*, 744–746, 750–751, 754–755.

For his part, Bolingbroke fails to remedy England's ills because, despite the brilliance of his perspicacity and practicality, his primary aim is not the common good. In fact, though he is in many respects Richard's opposite, Henry Hereford manages to replicate his rival's core faults from an alternate angle. If Richard is callous in betraying the loyal Mowbray, Bolingbroke is guilty of accusing an innocent man, forcing Richard to choose between admitting his complicity in Gloucester's death, or provoking the nobility with further crimes. Richard suspects from the outset that Henry is after his crown, and the latter's boastful response to his banishment—"that sun that warms you here shall shine on me"—may constitute a tacit admission of his designs. If Richard intends to prevent Bolingbroke's return after his sentence is served, it is partly because Henry's courting of popular favor seems to signal his revolutionary plans (1.1.109; 1.3.144–147; 1.4.20–36). As soon as Richard and his forces leave for Ireland, Bolingbroke is back on native soil. Though he claims to come in defense of his customary rights, he builds an army by promising his fellow nobles a generous "recompense" when his "treasury" is "more enriched"—that is, when he is king, and imperiously charges and executes the King's favorites without any semblance of a fair trial (2.3.45–50, 59–62; 3.1). Cornering the friendless Richard in Flint Castle, Henry persists in his pretense that he has come merely to petition the King (3.3.185–200), but when Richard formally offers him the crown—whether in despair, or to call his bluff—he instantly accepts, dispelling any doubts about his true motives (4.1.108–114). When Parliament demands a role in this transfer of power, and Carlisle insists that Richard be given the benefit of trial, Henry plays along, but upon Richard's predictable refusal to read the charges against him, his successor swiftly dismisses further formalities (4.1.124–130, 222–272). Like Richard, Henry wishes to wield the scepter in a kingdom ostensibly governed by law, while remaining as free as possible from the constraints law imposes upon rulers.[69]

---

[69] See Forker, "Introduction," 23, 27–28.

Knowing the reliance Richard places on popular belief in his divine right, Bolingbroke maneuvers him into a bind from which the doctrine cannot rescue him. By prompting Richard to surrender, Henry ensures that his succession appears to be the will of God, rather than his own doing. On the surface, his manufacturing of a divine commission contrasts with Richard's passive reliance on heavenly assistance. In truth, both kings manipulate popular perceptions of Providence for their own ends. Though Henry's machinations appear much more effectual, even Machiavelli would warn that it is easier to make friends with promised rewards than to keep them when those rewards inevitably fail to satisfy their insatiable desires.[70] Though Henry puts on a fine act of ushering in a "new world" with prominent acts of clemency, on closer inspection these gestures cost him nothing—Mowbray is dead, Aumerle's inconstancy is on comical display, and Carlisle cannot rally support for a deceased Richard (4.1.87–91; 5.3.130; 5.6.24–29). In his epigram on the best constitution, Thomas More quips that "a king is always most agreeable in his first year," while "over the course of a lifetime, a greedy king will have gnawed away his people."[71] Despite Henry's attempts to appear agreeable, the depths of his greed for power are confirmed by his treatment of Sir Piers Exton, whom he incites to Richard's slaying and then denounces as a murderer. Henry's vow to cleanse himself of Richard's blood by embarking on a Crusade is no sign of contrition, but rather (as he will tell his son) a plot to "busy giddy minds with foreign quarrels," in order to prevent the "friends" by whose power he "was first advanced" from using similar methods to displace him or his heir (5.4; 5.6.34–44).[72]

Like Richard, Henry attempts to settle the controversy over Gloucester's death by inducing his nobles "freely" to "speak [their]

---

[70] *The Prince*, Second Edition, trans. Harvey Mansfield, Chicago (The University of Chicago Press, 1998), Chapter 3.
[71] *Essential Works*, 249; *Utopia & Selected Epigrams*, 114.
[72] *The Second Part of King Henry IV*, ed. Norman N. Holland, in Histories: Volume II, New York (Everyman Library, 1994), 4.5.204–215.

mind[s]." Although at first he succeeds at eliciting some specific testimony, the trial swiftly degenerates into a ludicrous web of thrown gages, chivalrous boasts, and challenges to prove one's honor in a trial of arms (4.1.1–87).[73] In light of the coming civil wars that are here foreshadowed, we know that while Henry's England promises to be a "new world," it will suffer from much the same faults as did the old. And though even the best conceived constitutional reforms can be expected to take time, reading *Richard II* in light of Morean lessons on law and leadership suggests that Henry has no interest in applying his practical genius to the one thing that might actually lift England above the ravages of civil strife: the fulfillment of its aspiration to be a constitutional monarchy governed by law. By grasping instead for personal power, Henry dooms himself and his countrymen to a state of continued turmoil, and serves as a warning to future monarchs tempted to follow the same course.

---

[73] See Forker, "Introduction," 33.

Macbeth and "the milk of human kindness": Nature, Natality, Sex, and Politics in the Scottish Play

Clinton Allen Brand

"How many children had Lady Macbeth?," L. C. Knights famously asked in 1932 by way of a lecture so titled, and would not stay for an answer.[1] Countless other readers, audiences, and critics of Shakespeare's *Macbeth* have nonetheless registered the inevitable force, the compelling curiosity aroused by the question and wrestled for their own answers. But they have done so to no avail, or to mixed results, given Shakespeare's apparently studied determination to leave the matter of Macbeth and Lady Macbeth's actual or possible progeny wrapped in ambiguity, shrouded in silence, and resounding as a thunderous absence at the heart of the tragedy.[2] This absence is as mysterious as the unexplained, inexplicable ambition that motivates Macbeth and his wife to compass the crown and kill an indisputably good and virtuous king. Inducing her husband to murder King Duncan, Lady Macbeth claims the experience of breastfeeding her

---

[1] See L. C. Knights, *How Many Children Had Lady Macbeth?: An Essay in the Theory and Practice of Shakespeare Criticism* (Cambridge: Gordan Fraser, The Minority Press, 1933). For Knights, of course, the question was rhetorical, hardly meriting any sustained discussion, and intended as a rebuke to the kinds of character-based criticism of Shakespeare spinning out of A. C. Bradley's *Shakespearean Tragedy* (1904), including then nascent psychoanalytic approaches. According to Knights, such criticism could give rise to fanciful and unwarranted speculation about the extra-textual existence of Shakespeare's characters, apart from what is specifically divulged in the plays themselves.

[2] See Carol Chillington Rutter, "Remind Me: How Many Children had Lady Macbeth?," *Shakespeare Survey* 57 (2004): 38–53. Rutter sums up the history of this famous Shakespearean "crux" and argues, "the fact of the matter is that Lionel Knights' question refuses to go away—criticism continues to brood upon it, and in the theatre, it cannot be ducked" (40).

child: "I have given suck, and know / How tender 'tis to love the babe that milks me" (1.7.55–56). But she does not hesitate to add, "I would, while it was smiling in my face, / Have plucked my nipple from his boneless gums, / And dashed the brains out, had I so sworn as you / Have done to this" (1.7.57–60).[3] Nevertheless, that the Macbeths, husband and wife, are childless is the fundamental datum of the plot, as we sense from the beginning and as the play amply confirms by its end: "He has no children" (4.3.217), says Macduff learning of Macbeth's slaughter of his own wife and children. The Macbeths' childlessness becomes the negative reality that propels the plot forward to its tragic ending—all the way from the Witches' prophecy that Macbeth "shalt be King hereafter" (1.3.49), even as Banquo will be father to a line of kings in an undetermined future, to Macbeth's despairing conclusion that human life itself, including his own, bereft of meaningful futurity, is no more than "a tale / Told by an idiot, full of sound and fury, signifying nothing" (5.5.26–28).

Although the Macbeths' own children are conspicuous by their absence, other children are emphatically present in the play's language and imagery. We hear about a naked newborn babe, a birth-strangled baby, a bloody child, a child crowned bearing a tree, and another child untimely ripped from his mother's womb. There are dead infants, murdered children, other children threatened with killing, and two fugitive children—Fleance, the little boy who gets away, and Malcolm, the orphaned son who comes of age and assumes Scotland's throne after the tyrannous interregnum of the cursed usurper Macbeth, who called himself king (and was, in fact, validly acclaimed king), but who could only wear a "fruitless crown" and grip a "barren scepter" (3.1.62, 63). Though it has long been tempting to posit or supply the Macbeths' missing child from inferences about their off-stage, extra-literary "lives," by way of the kind of

---

[3] Quotations of Shakespeare are from *The Complete Works of Shakespeare*, ed. David Bevington (New York: HarperCollins, 1992). Act, scene, and line numbers are indicated parenthetically.

psychological speculation Knights sought to rebuke, it is worth remembering that *Macbeth* stages a fundamentally *political* action, engaged as the play is with issues of monarchical inheritance, royal bloodlines, and dynastic succession. To be sure, Shakespeare's handling of the story of Macbeth as gleaned from Holinshed's *Chronicles* elides and suppresses much of what we might call "real" politics, with all the pushing and pulling of competing interests and claims, together with ambiguities of motivation.[4] But he does so, I suggest, to focus and highlight the play's sustained meditation on a different kind of politics, the politics of natality, whereby the presence or absence of children figure forth the contingent future and explore the fragility, the challenges, and the promise of a political life that would aspire to be both generative and generational.

Interestingly, it was Sigmund Freud, the progenitor of the kind of psychoanalytic speculation rejected by Knights, who first saw *Macbeth* as a play centrally concerned with "the theme of childlessness," and it was Freud who readily admitted the limitations of his own psychoanalytic method in accounting for the motivating identities and tragic fates of its protagonists.[5] In an uncharacteristic idiom, strikingly different from subsequent psychoanalytic discourse, Freud wrote, "It would be a perfect example of poetic justice in the manner of the talion if the childlessness of Macbeth and the barrenness of his Lady were the punishment for their crimes against the

---

[4] See the relevant extracts of Holinshed's *Chronicles of England, Scotland, and Ireland* (1587), excerpted in *The Tragedy of Macbeth*, ed. Sylvan Barnett (New York: Signet Classic, 1998), 103–120. Shakespeare's play follows the outline of Holinshed's account, but radically condenses, truncates, and selects among the details of the political story. Shakespeare notably brightens Duncan's and Macduff's characterization, whilst darkening Macbeth's, and turning King Macbeth's ten-year, checkered reign into a dizzying crescendo of tyrannous cruelty. From the most meager evidence in Holinshed, Shakespeare notably seizes upon and amplifies issues of natality and creates Macbeth's war on children.

[5] Sigmund Freud, "Some Character-Types Met with in Psycho-analytic Work" (1916), in *Writings on Art and Literature* (Stanford, California: Stanford University Press, 1997), 159–166.

sanctity of generation."[6] Freud may have picked up from the play more than he realized, even though he here seems to reverse an ordinary calculus of cause and effect. It would be just as plausible to argue that the Macbeths' experience of the privation of fertility, as much as the words of the Witches, catalyzes with their attendant anxiety and compensatory ambition to help motivate their war on children. In either case, I suggest argue that it is not just *poetic* justice, but *political* justice, that is at stake in assessing Macbeth's own "crimes against the sanctity of generation." Acknowledgment of and respect for that "sanctity" serve not only as the bedrock of, but as the precondition for any meaningful concept of political society.

Shakespeare's drama of childlessness is also a profound exploration of radical evil, both psychic and political, as well as an anatomy of tyranny, commencing in regicide.[7] The connections linking these concerns prompt my proposal to offer a fresh exploration of some familiar themes in a new key and in a more focused register than I have encountered in the play's criticism. Arthur Bradley is one among a handful of contemporary critics to argue that "*Macbeth* is—all too literally—a play about natality," concerned as the play is with issues surrounding childbirth and the fates of children.[8] With the

---

[6] Ibid., 163.

[7] Among studies of the play as an exploration of radical evil and of tyranny, see Catherine Gimelli Martin, "The 'Reason' of Radical Evil: Shakespeare, Milton, and the Ethical Philosophers," *Studies in Philology* 113:1 (2016): 163–197; Carson Holloway, "Macbeth: The Spiritual Drama of the Tyrannical Soul," in *The Soul of Statesmanship: Shakespeare on Nature, Virtue, and Political Wisdom*, ed. Khalil M. Habib and L. Joseph Hebert, Jr. (Lanham, Maryland: Lexington Books, 2018), 23–36; Rebecca Bushnell, *Tragedies of Tyrants: Political Thought and Theater in the English Renaissance* (Ithaca: Cornell University Press, 1990); and Stephen Greenblatt, *Tyrant: Shakespeare on Politics* (New York: W. W. Norton, 2018).

[8] Arthur Bradley, "'Untimely Ripp'd': On Natality, Sovereignty and Unbearable Life," *English Studies* 94:7 (2013), 791. Among other recent studies exploring the political implications of the play's themes of children and childlessness, see Sarah Wintle and Rene Weis, "Macbeth and the Barren Sceptre," *Essays in Criticism* 41:2 (1991): 128–146; Luke Wilson, "*Macbeth* and the Contingency of Future Persons," *Shakespeare Studies* 40 (2012): 53–62; Joseph Campana, "The Child's

word *natality* Bradley evokes without really engaging a key concept of the political philosopher Hannah Arendt, who famously but elusively suggested that *natality*, the condition of being born, "may be the central category of political thought" and of fundamental importance for understanding the character of political life.[9] Bradley approaches *Macbeth* as "a tragedy of regicide" that dramatizes "the rule of this Early Modern biopolitical order negatively."[10] Just so, but I would like to take a different approach, by way of a reverse dialectic—flipping the script, so to speak. While *Macbeth* certainly depicts infanticide, literal and figurative, together with regicide, leading to tyranny, *negatively*, the play also and importantly offers evidence for construing natality and legitimate kingship more *positively*, in relation to which child-killing and king-killing assume the character of evil, precisely insofar as they are privations or denials of normative goods.

It makes a difference whether we read *Macbeth* (and Arendt) through the interpretive lens of something like Michel Foucault's postmodern "biopolitics" (naming disciplinary regimes of power for regulating birth and controlling life) or through the different heuristic of St. Augustine's reflections on the nexus between the intrinsic goodness of divine creation and human natality. It was Augustine, of course, who shaped the Christian humanist tradition with his insight that evil is a *privatio boni*, a privation of the good, and hence evil as such has no positive, independent, substantial reality; it has only a negative existence as an absence, a void, actually "no-thing,"

Two Bodies: Shakespeare, Sovereignty, and the End of Succession," *ELH* 82:2 (2014): 811–839; Bryan Lawrence, "'Modern Ecstasy': *Macbeth* and the Meaning of the Political," *ELH* 79:4 (2012): 823–849; and James J. Marino, "All Macbeth's Sons," in *Childhood, Education, and the Stage in Early Modern England*, ed. Richard Preiss and Deanne Williams (Cambridge: Cambridge University Press, 2017), 225-244.

[9] Hannah Arendt, *The Human Condition* (Chicago: University of Chicago Press, 1958), 9.

[10] Bradley, "Untimely Ripp'd': On Natality, Sovereignty and Unbearable Life," 791.

nothing.[11] And it was Augustine who inspired Arendt's notion of a politics of natality as a way of understanding the possibilities for the fruitful renewal of freedom in a meaningful future, as over and against the modern politics of totalitarianism with its "being-toward-death" and its extermination of "life unworthy of life."[12] Arendt was fond of quoting Augustine's statement, "that a beginning be made man was created" (*initium ut esset homo creatus est*).[13] Arendt's interpretation of this phrase, associating creation and childbirth with the possibility of new beginnings and renewal, taken together with the biblical injunction "Be fruitful and multiply," may shed light on Shakespeare's own politics of natality as implied in *Macbeth*. Arguably, this is a vision of political meaning that was still vital in the early seventeenth-century metaphysical, social, and political imaginary, as we shall see in the writings of James Stuart, England's first Scottish king, Shakespeare's patron, and whose dynasty *Macbeth* equivocally and richly commemorates. James VI of Scotland became

---

[11] See Peter King, "Augustine on Evil," in *Evil: A History*, ed. Andrew P. Chignell (New York: Oxford University Press, 2019), 155–193. See also, "Arendt, Augustine and Evil," *Heythrop Journal* 41 (2000): 154–169; and Antonio Calagno, "Hannah Arendt and Augustine of Hippo: On the Pleasure of and Desire for Evil," *Laval théologique et philosophique* 66:2 (2010): 371–385. See also Paul Ricoeur, *The Symbolism of Evil*, trans. Emerson Buchanan (Boston: Beacon Press, 1967).

[12] Arendt's politics of natality and its relation to Augustine are famously complex and multifaceted and have occasioned diverse interpretations. Here I generally follow Wolfhart Totsching, "Arendt's Notion of Natality: An Attempt at Clarification," *Ideas y Valores* 66:165 (2017): 327–346; and John Kiess, *Hannah Arendt and Theology* (London: T&T Clark, 2016), 139–188. See also the chapter "Arendt's Augustine" in Peter Iver Kaufman, *On Agamben, Arendt, Christianity, and the Dark Arts of Civilization* (London: Bloomsbury, 2019), 99–147; and Patricia Bowen-Moore, *Hannah Arendt's Philosophy of Natality* (New York: St. Martin's Press, 1989).

[13] See Arendt, *The Human Condition*, 177, quoting Augustine, *De civitate Dei* XII.20. See also Arendt's *The Origins of Totalitarianism* (New York: Meridian Books, 1958), 479; and Arendt, "What is Freedom?" in *Between Past and Future* (New York: Viking Press, 1961), 167.

James I of England with two apparently healthy sons (Henry and Charles) and did so acceding to the throne after a sequence of three childless monarchs (Edward VI, Mary, and Elizabeth) and after a protracted period of political tumult and anxiety over problems of monarchical succession, which are dramatized in Shakespeare's own history plays. Issues of natality, of childbirth and childrearing, in their political significance were of immediate and topical interest at the time, and such concerns continue to challenge critics of the play.

About a decade after Knights's lecture, another critic, Cleanth Brooks, also like Knights intent on reading Shakespeare's play as a dramatic poem, contained and complete within itself, took up the challenge of grappling with the play's thematics of children and childlessness to more productive results. In a brilliant essay ("The Naked Babe and the Cloak of Manliness"), Brooks also refused to speculate about the offstage reproductive lives of the Macbeths and similarly abjured psychoanalytic approaches to focus on the play's poetic imagery of babies.[14] Brooks's essay is too rich and subtle to summarize here, but a few points may be relevant to the issues at hand, centering on the speech that is central to understanding Macbeth's motivating identity—"If it were done when 'tis done, then 'twere well / It were done quickly..." (1.7).

At the end of Act I, just before Macbeth gives his assent to the killing of King Duncan, and just before he acknowledges the inscrutably compelling force of his ambition, he endeavors to talk himself out of murder. He wonders in the conditional mood, on the cusp of the contingent moment, *if* the act of regicide

> Could trammel up the consequence, and catch
> With his surcease success; that but this blow
> Might be the be-all and the end-all here,
> But here, upon this bank and shoal of time,

---

[14] Cleanth Brooks, "The Naked Babe and the Cloak of Manliness," in *The Well Wrought Urn: Studies in the Structure of Poetry* (New York: Harcourt Brace Jovanovich, 1947), 22–49.

We'd jump the life to come. (1.7.3–7)

Doubtfully, Macbeth ponders whether the killing of Duncan really could gather, as in a net, the "catch" or achievement of all his desires, assuring an inchoate "success" (largely devoid of positive content). *If* this deed could be "the be-all and the end-all," the ultimately decisive act to arrest the uncertainties of time, to end the anxieties of contingency and dependency, *then*, he says, he would "jump" or risk "the life to come," he would risk, that is, the afterlife and the possibility of damnation but also close out any other kind of contingent future life, including that of progeny. Macbeth goes on in the speech to give himself all sorts of good and compelling arguments *against* killing Duncan, *against* violating the presumptive goods of loyalty, kinship, hospitality, and what those goods entail, namely acceptance of one's place in a web of dependency. He further imagines a consequence different from the desired "success" he previously posits. He pictures an image of "Pity" for the murdered Duncan, personified as "a naked newborn babe," seemingly weak and fragile, contingent and dependent, yet morphing into the strong and imperious figure of an avenging angel (1.7.21–25). The image is powerful and powerfully convincing, but even yet Macbeth's moral resolution against killing collapses with his admission that he is powerless in the face of his "vaulting ambition"—something which would be strong but which "o'erleaps itself" and sets him up for a pathetic and inevitable fall (1.7.25–28). Interestingly, though Macbeth *reasons* against killing Duncan, he never ventures to rationalize, justify, or excuse his ambition. It is as if his *libido dominandi* were itself an irresistible compulsion.

At just this point, as he confesses this compulsion, without which he cannot conceive purposeful action—"I have no spur / To prick the sides of my intent" (1.7.25–26)—before Macbeth can even finish his sentence, Lady Macbeth walks in, as if *she* were the completion of her husband's utterance and precisely the embodiment of

Macbeth's own "vaulting ambition."[15] The moment is a masterstroke of dramatic irony. Lady Macbeth is also the one who, reading Macbeth's letter about the Witches' prophecy, readily vaulted from "This ignorant present"—the contingency of time—to claim "The future in the instant" (1.5.56–58). And this is the Lady Macbeth who shortly thereafter invoked the demons of hell to "unsex" her (1.5.41), and thereby to dispossess her womanliness and capacity for maternity, all for the sake of that imaginary future and the "greatness" promised her (1.5.13). In a similar fashion, Macbeth disclaims or foregoes the possibility of paternity ("life to come") for the sake of that "be-all and…end-all" of the likewise imagined "success" of killing Duncan and claiming the crown for his own. But, as we shall see, Macbeth's "success" is undone in the very dynamics of doing which foreclose any possibility of lineal "succession."

Collocating the image of the "naked newborn babe" with the play's other images of children and infants, Brooks argues that "the babe signifies the future which Macbeth would control and cannot control. It is the unpredictable thing itself."[16] Brooks further observes that Macbeth's bargain, exchanging a possible human child for the imagined issue of his ambition, "thus, forces him to make war on children, a war which in itself reflects his desperation and is a confession of weakness."[17] If the image of the missing child—the absent child, or the possible child traded away to become the impossible child, displaced on to the blank slate, the empty cipher of ambition—works thus in a negative valence, Brooks also notes that the

---

[15] That Macbeth and Lady Macbeth, "dearest partner[s] in greatness" (1.5.11), interact here and elsewhere in the play as if they were two sides of a single, split, composite personality is a commonplace of the play's criticism. The insight goes back at least to Freud, "Some Character-Types," 165–166. At the beginning of the play, Macbeth exhibits what Lady Macbeth seems to lack—a sensitive and acute moral conscience; after the murder of Duncan, they trade places as Macbeth becomes more and more coldly ruthless and as his wife descends into guilty, conscience-stricken madness.

[16] Brooks, "The Naked Babe and the Cloak of Manliness," 217.

[17] Ibid., 217.

image signifies as well, at least potentially, in a more positive register:

> The babe signifies not only the future; it symbolizes all those enlarging purposes which make life meaningful, and it symbolizes, furthermore, all those emotional and—to Lady Macbeth—irrational ties which make man more than a machine—which render him human.[18]

Though Brooks does not specify these humane and enlarging purposes that give life positive meaning, the play itself—Macbeth himself—articulates such an affirmative register in the clearest possible terms. Two such utterances, framing the regicide, substantiate the alternative to Macbeth's own negation of normative goods. When Macbeth, newly named Thane of Cawdor, meets Duncan on stage for the first time, just before the king names Malcolm Prince of Cumberland and his presumptive heir, he says,

> The service and the loyalty I owe,
> In doing it, pays itself. Your highness' part
> Is to receive our duties; and our duties
> Are to your throne and state children and servants,
> Which do but what they should, by doing every thing
> Safe toward your love and honor.(1.4.22–27)

Virtue is its own reward, its own good, says Macbeth, particularly in relation to that medieval, monarchical, and feudal economy of reciprocal duties, presuming a beneficent sociality, which is ideally an enlargement or extension of family bonds. It might be tempting to dismiss Macbeth's words here as rank hypocrisy; after all, he has already entertained in his imagination the possibility of becoming king himself. But, more plausibly, Macbeth says these words as much to himself as to his king, as though to resist or push back against his own "horrible imaginings" (1.3.139). After the regicide, however, once he has waded into blood, become a tyrant, and alienated the

---

[18] Ibid., 218.

affection of the very nobles who helped put him on the throne, Macbeth muses on what he has lost or traded away: "that which should accompany old age, / As honor, love, obedience, troops of friends, I must not look to have" (5.3.24–26). Similarly, in the long scene in England during which Malcolm and Macduff warily test each other, while anatomizing Macbeth's tyranny, Malcolm confesses Scotland's (and his own) lack of

> ...the king-becoming graces,
> As justice, verity, temperance, stableness,
> Bounty, perseverance, mercy, lowliness,
> Devotion, patience, courage, fortitude,...(4.3.92–95)

That such "king-becoming graces" are more than pious boilerplate, that they derive ultimately from the "sanctity of generation," and that such virtues, in their very absence, relate back to Macbeth's privation of generative fertility and the drama of his missing child constitute the play's dramatic and moral coherence.

Even yet, many readers and critics, and especially directors and actors, are seldom content to locate the absent child in the penumbra of the play's ethical ideals and poetic imagery. Many are they who seek to supply the lack more palpably or to medicalize the Macbeths' apparent infertility as a presumed function of Macbeth's possible impotence or Lady Macbeth's possible barrenness. Hence we have the temptation of some critics to locate or explain away the Macbeths' missing child or the motives of directors, like Justin Kurzel in his 2015 film, to supply a dead child to explain the Macbeths' motivation in relation to a supposed trauma of grief, a kind of psychic PTSD.[19] However, the absent child figures in the play not as a

---

[19] See the informative review of the play's modern performance history, on stage and film, in Rutter's "Remind Me: How Many Children had Lady Macbeth?," 40–52. See also Paul J. C. M. Franssen, "Flipping Macbeth: PTSD, Gender, and Generation in Adaptations by Wolfert, Kurzel, and De Man," *Cahiers élisabéthains*, 104:1 (2021): 81–94; and Hanh Bui, "Effigies of Childhood in

biological entity, nor as a lack to be accounted for medically or circumstantially. It is rather a psychic and spiritual pathology inhering in the Macbeths' marriage, as manifest in their shared anxieties over what it means to be a man and a woman, a husband and a wife, and at least potentially a father and a mother, and in their seemingly inscrutable, but not unrelated, ambition to greatness. It is, I suggest, something that can only be understood in relation to the wider conspectus of the play's historical resonance in the early seventeenth century and the dramatic inflection of that resonance.

The imaginative and intellectual world of *Macbeth* is poised at the transition Douglas Bush characterized as the tipping point between a world "still more than half medieval" and a world "more than half modern."[20] In its setting and enveloping action, *Macbeth* is among Shakespeare's most patently "medieval" plays, yet it reaches from that atmosphere right through early seventeenth-century topical concerns out into the full blaze of "modernity." And it does so not least in its unflinching articulation of nihilism—the view that *nothing* enduring, stable, or permanent, aside from the "sound and fury" of human will and desire, gives human life value, meaning, or purpose. Yet the world of *Macbeth* is still very much an enchanted world, to be sure, teeming with witches, ghosts, and the preternatural, all of which were still very much part of the belief system of many of Shakespeare's contemporaries, including King James (as testified in his 1597 book *Daemonologie*). This world also had an intellectual climate still enchanted by a metaphysical sense of nature disclosing the moral architecture of degrees and relations of analogical correspondence, constituting a rich fabric weaving together psychic, social, political, and cosmic realities into a coherent order of meaning (as also vigorously asserted in King James's

---

Kurzel's *Macbeth*," *Literature/Film Quarterly* 48:1 (2020): https://lfq.salisbury.edu/_issues/48_1/effigies_of_childhood_in%20kurzels_macbeth.html.

[20] Douglas Bush, *English Literature in the Earlier Seventeenth Century* (Oxford: Oxford University Press, 1945), 1.

speeches and his *Basilikon Doron*). First performed around 1606, in the aftermath of the Gunpowder Plot and a few years after James's accession to the English throne, *Macbeth* was written out of a moment that saw the simultaneous reassertion of this fabric of analogical correspondences and increasing anxiety that this fabric was becoming weaker and frayed. As John Donne expressed this fear only a few years later, it was not only the threat of political instability but also the "new philosophy," including the nascent empirical sciences, that was beginning to call "all in doubt" and unravel the putatively given weaving of personal and political relationships:

> 'Tis all in pieces, all coherence gone,
> All just supply, and all relation:
> Prince, subject, father, son, are things forgot,
> For every man alone thinks he hath got
> To be a phoenix... [21]

The period's ambivalence, as manifest in both the reassertion of a web of normative goods and anxieties about the dissolution or deprivation of that network in pathological forgetfulness or hubristic self-assertion, finds voice in *Macbeth*'s finely calibrated linguistic and dramatic ironies, as well as the play's thematics of equivocation.

As many critics have noted, equivocation that "lies like the truth" (5.5.44) is particularly prominent in *Macbeth* and was an issue of immediate topical concern in the aftermath of the Gunpowder Plot and amid the ensuing persecution of Catholics.[22] In the play, the Witches, of course, speak and act out "the equivocation of the fiend" (5.5.43) and "palter" with words "in a double sense" (5.8.20).

---

[21] John Donne, "The First Anniversary: An Anatomy of the World", lines 213–217, in *John Donne: The Complete English Poems*, ed. A. J. Smith (London: Penguin, 1976), 276.

[22] Among studies of equivocation in *Macbeth*, see Steven Mullaney, "Lying Like the Truth: Riddle, Representation and Treason in Renaissance England," *ELH* 47:1 (1980): 32–47; and William O. Scott, "Macbeth's—And Our—Self Equivocations," *Shakespeare Quarterly* 37:2 (1986): 160–174.

The three Weird Sisters confound categories of meaning and crumble contrarious utterances that might be paradoxical into oxymoronic contradiction: "Fair is foul, and foul is fair" (1.1.11). But they go on to offer Macbeth seemingly categorical reassurances that unexpectedly emerge as paradoxes which come back to bite him—for Birnam Wood marching against Dunsinane, convenient tree branches serve to camouflage soldiers on the move; and for a man not born of woman, Macbeth's nemesis Macduff reveals he was delivered by Caesarian section. But against the equivocations of the Witches, we might recognize also the differently calibrated equivocations of Shakespeare, the dramatic poet. Words, of course, are equivocal things, polysemous and multivalent, particularly in relation to their speakers, actions, and contexts. The equivocity of words can tear down, subvert, and destroy stable meanings, but equally well such words can build up, disclose, and open out richer, more compelling meanings.

One of the striking dimensions of what I'm calling the "equivocation of the poet" inheres in the way that Macbeth and Lady Macbeth inhabit and speak from the very moral and metaphysical register of meaning they go on to deny, cancel, and empty out. Their words so spoken catalyze with the play's enveloping action to enhance the play's moral clarity and to characterize something important about the tragedy's engagement with the politics of natality. In particular, the language of the Macbeths rings the changes on multiple inter-related senses of two clusters of words, words that assume a special prominence in the play and help map the conceptual structure of its action. The first cluster consists in the exchange between the word *nature* and the word *nothing*. The second cluster enriches the first by playing on linked meanings of the words *kin*, *kind*, and *king*—common English words whose deep etymological and conceptual connections we have largely forgotten and often neglect to hear. The associations that circulate among these words do not exhume the lost child of the Macbeths, buried as that child is in what Stanley Cavell calls the intimate and "massive unspokenness" of their hidden secret,[23] but they do help account for the character of the child's absence and may help make sense of the play's action and the motivating identities of its protagonists.

Few words in the English language are more complexly equivocal than the word *nature* in the multiple and often contested contexts of its uses and meanings.[24] In *Macbeth*, and more broadly in Shakespeare's dramatic vocabulary informed by a rich Christian humanist tradition, the word *nature* can denote *the intrinsic character or disposition of a thing or person*. It also refers to the *givenness of things*, opening out to a sense of the *ordered goodness of creation*, even the *moral architecture of the universe*, and the prescriptive character of the *natural law* in its various iterations and inflections. But significantly for *Macbeth*, the English word *nature*, deriving from the Latin *natura*, cognate with *natus* (past participle of *nasci*), connotes the condition of being born, *nativity* or *natality*. In the English language, the word *nature*, as it comes down from Middle English into Early Modern English, reverberates with a sense of *the instinct, disposition, and order of generative fertility* and *generational vitality* (a meaning that is particularly manifest in Chaucer's use of the word, for example).[25] For classical and medieval tradition, still resonant in Spenser and Shakespeare, Dame Nature, among her many roles, is always the great *mater generationis*.[26] In *Macbeth*, repeated

---

[23] Stanley Cavell, *Disowning Knowledge in Seven Plays of Shakespeare* (New York: Cambridge University Press, 2003, updated edition), 239.

[24] Among sundry histories of the word *nature* in its various uses and applications, see C. S. Lewis, *Studies in Words* (Cambridge: Cambridge University Press, 1960), 24–74. See also the lengthy entry for *nature* in the OED with its wealth of historical citations of different senses and inflections of the word.

[25] See the entries for "nature" and "Nature" in *The Oxford Companion to Chaucer*, ed. Douglas Gray (Oxford: Oxford University Press, 2003):
https://wwwoxfordreferencecom.proxy.library.nd.edu/display/10.1093/acref/9780198117650.001.0001/acref-9780198117650-e-1232?rskey=A9SvX8&result=1213.

[26] See Ernst Robert Curtius, *European Literature and the Latin Middle Ages*, trans. Willard R. Trask (Princeton: Princeton University Press, 1953), 106–127.

and prominent references to what is *natural,* and its inversion or cancellation in what is *unnatural,* punctuate the action and measure the course of the Macbeths' descent into evil and Scotland's descent into tyranny. This process of *de-naturing* occurs by way of Macbeth and Lady Macbeth's incremental alienation and estrangement from their own generative fruitfulness, from the fabric of natural human relationships, and from any sense of a politics that could be both generational and regenerative.

Once Macbeth has attained the throne, knowing full well that he cannot pass it on to any son of his, he complains of Banquo's "royalty of nature" (3.1.51)—a curious phrase connected to Banquo's paternity, naming what Banquo has and he can never possess: Banquo has a *son,* and Banquo will be a *father* to a line of future kings. Macbeth curses the Witches for tempting him to a "*fruitless* crown" and a "*barren* scepter," as if a crown not fruitful and a scepter not fertile were no crown and no scepter at all (3.1.62–63; emphasis added). Toward the end of the play, the doctor attending to Lady Macbeth in her madness suggestively sums up in a metaphysical register the whole saga of the Macbeths' revolt against their own human nature, their denial of parental fecundity, their ensuing criminality, and the resultant civil dissension and tyranny afflicting the kingdom: "Unnatural deeds / Do breed unnatural troubles" (5.1.71–72).

Likewise punctuating the drama, the word *nothing* and its cognates delineate Macbeth's estrangement from nature, his alienation from time, his gradual descent into full-blown nihilism, together with the remarkable capacity of his vivid imagination both to summon up an acute sense of metaphysical presence and to feel the devastation of its absence. Just after hearing the Witches greet him as Thane of Cawdor and as king hereafter, and upon hearing the confirmation of the first prophecy when he learns the news of having in fact been made Thane of Cawdor, Macbeth falls into a trance, an intellectual and imaginative reverie. He weighs the tempting effects of the Witches' "supernatural soliciting" and feels both attraction and revulsion, before picturing in his mind's eye an "horrid image" that unsettles him "against the use of nature" (1.3.131–138). But these "horrible imaginings"—which are just that, merely "fantastical" (1.3.140), devoid of actual being—nonetheless so consume him that "function / Is smothered in surmise, and nothing is / But what is not" (1.3.142–143). *And nothing is but what is not*—this densely difficult phrase captures the psychic experience of that eclipse of reality, non-being smothering being, and the goodness of *what is* emptied out into the nothingness of *what is not*. The phrase precisely and richly expresses the Augustinian metaphysics of evil as a *privatio boni*. Even yet, at least for a time, Macbeth endeavors to cling to the presumptive goodness of the real against the phantoms of unreality. When he sees the air-drawn dagger summoning him to murder Duncan and notes on the blade drops of blood, he recoils, saying, "There's no such thing" (2.1.48), but still he follows what is not there, what is preter- or contranatural, into the abyss of nothingness. Even once he once he has attained the throne, when Macbeth and Lady Macbeth claim as their own what she calls "the ornament of life" (1.7.43), they do not enjoy the "renown" and "grace" that died with Duncan (2.3.96), but rather find no satisfaction, no fulfillment: "There's nothing serious in mortality" (2.3.95), *nothing meaningful in human life*, Macbeth notes after the death of Duncan. Lady Macbeth says, "Nought's had, all's spent" (3.2.4)—*we've emptied ourselves out, for nothing*. From thence, for both husband and wife, in different registers, as they become estranged even from each other, the chasm of nothingness widens, evacuating nature of meaningful purpose, of any hopeful futurity, until Macbeth despairs that human existence is but "a tale / Told by an idiot, full of sound and fury, signifying nothing" (5.5.26–28).

Shakespeare's drama, which pits generative nature against the psychic privations of consuming nothingness, finds further explication in a second cluster of inter-related words: *kin, kind,* and *king*. As he does in *Hamlet* and *King Lear* most conspicuously, Shakespeare also in *Macbeth* plays on the homophonic and etymological associations of these three common English words. Interestingly, all three words derive from a shared Anglo-Saxon (and Indo-European) root, meaning "to beget" (*gen-*, *cyn-*), which yields *cynn* (kin), *cynde* (kind), and *cyning* (king), all referring back to nature itself (*gecynde*) as the power of begetting and the fecund network of organic, given relationships.²⁷ The connections linking the three words imply the rudiments of a social and political anthropology, at least one that held a certain sway before the development of "social contract" theory and differently inflected notions of the "state of nature." According to the older view, those linked by consanguinity, *kinfolk*, gather into a tribe of extended *kindred*, all well disposed to one another in presumptive *kindness* for their mutual welfare and flourishing, and thus come to acknowledge a chief or *king* as their ruler and the guarantor of sorting each out according to order, degree, and *kind*. In just such terms, King James in his *Basilikon Doron* (published in England at his accession in 1603) addressed his son Prince Henry on the differences between beneficent kingship and unnatural tyranny, the one a normative ideal, the other a pathological privation of the good, thereby contrasting a "natural father and kindly maister" with a "step-father and uncouth hireling."²⁸ And in similar language, James in his address to Parliament in 1604 outlined his schematic vision of "natural" human society and of "natural" monarchy begotten of the principle of generative fertility:

---

²⁷ That Shakespeare plays with the words *kin* and *kind*, often in relation to the word *king* (as in *Hamlet*, *Lear*, and *Richard II*) is well known, but has surprisingly received little focused treatment. An exception is Arthur Brown, "*Gen-*, Shakespeare, Heidegger, and the Nature of Mortal Being," *Philosophy and Literature* 37:1 (2013): 36–52. Brown notes the same pattern in *Macbeth* that I have here; he offers some suggestive probing, but no firm conclusions about the significance of the word play. See also the entry for "gene-, gen-" in *The American Heritage Dictionary of Indo-European Roots*, ed. Calvert Watkins (Boston: Houghton Mifflin, 1985), 19.

²⁸ *Basilikon dōron; or, His majestys Instructions to his dearest sonne, Henry the Prince. Written by King James I* (London: Wertheimer, Lea & Co., 1887), 28–32.

Order, the Lustre of Nature, guided by a First Essence, put all Government into Form: First, in Two, who, by Procreation, according to the Rule of Power (increase and multiply) made a Family, with One Head; by Propagation, a Tribe, or Kindred, with One Elder, or Chief; by Multiplication, a Society, a Province, a Country, a Kingdom, with One or more Guides or Leaders, of Spirit, aptest, or, of Choice, fittest, to govern.[29]

Moreover, the words *kind* and *kindly* (meaning "natural") are of special interest in linking the words *kin* and *king* in two different but related senses. The word *kind*, as in *kindliness*, signifies a broadly ethical disposition of favor, sympathy, and consideration; *kindness* thus understood is not an insipid virtue, but the binding glue of all human relationships ordered toward trust and shared regard. *Kindness* constitutes what C. S. Lewis called a key principle of the natural law, one he named "the law of special beneficence," which can open out to an ethic of "general beneficence."[30] Yet the word *kind* also has reference to the rational ordering or organizing of things according to categories, classifications, and types by genus and species, as the very capacity for making distinctions and making sense of things in their variety, multiplicity, and relatedness.

From the opening line of *Macbeth* through the suggestive atmospherics of its short first scene, the Witches prefigure the action to come in confounding rational categories and distinctions of *kind*: "When shall we three meet again? / In thunder, lightning, *or* in rain?" (1.1.1–2; emphasis added). The word *or* contradicts or negates the *kindred* relation of three things that go and occur together in nature—thunder, lightning, *and* rain—posing oxymoronic or nonsensical alternatives for an unanswerable question, or a question which doesn't really ask anything—*we will meet in the disturbance of the weather, disturbance of sense, of vision, and of meaning itself*:

---

[29] "House of Commons Journal Volume 1: 19 March 1604," *Journal of the House of Commons: Volume 1: 1547–1629* (1802), 139–140 (quoted in Campana, "The Child's Two Bodies: Shakespeare, Sovereignty, and the End of Successsion," 815):http://www.britishhistory.ac.uk/report.aspx?compid=8419.

[30] C. S. Lewis, *The Abolition of Man* (New York: Macmillan, 1947), 101–103.

"Fair is foul, and foul is fair. / Hover through the fog and filthy air" (1.1.11–12). *Macbeth* dramatizes the mental, moral, and spiritual "fog" that hinders ordered vision, confounding the elementary distinctions between *right* and *wrong, just* and *unjust, beautiful* and *ugly, clean* and *dirty, bright* and *dingy*, the whole range of the interrelated, opposed meanings of "fair" and "foul." Among the dimensions of *kind* confounded, at least in appearance, by the Witches is the very principle of sexual differentiation, the natural precondition for what James called "Procreation" and "Propagation": "You should be women," says Banquo to the Witches, "And yet your beards forbid me to interpret / That you are so" (1.3.45–47).

Articulating something of the comprehensive, composite medieval conception of "nature," Chaucer wrote, "every kindely thing that is / Hath a kindely stede."[31] In *Macbeth*, it is not just the appearances that mark sexual differentiation that are confounded, but more importantly the "kindely stedes" (places or roles) that traditionally distinguish and constrain men and women. After categorically disowning her "womanliness" and renouncing her maternal femininity (1.5), Lady Macbeth chastises her husband's hesitation to go through with the killing of Duncan by attacking his "manliness" and accusing him of cowardice. Macbeth fires back, "I dare do all that may become a man; / Who dares do more is none" (1.7.47–48)—*he who transgresses given limits becomes the negation or privation of a man.* He here associates manliness with the strength of self-control and a principle of moral restraint. With imperious confusion but also, in context, devastating precision, Lady Macbeth retorts, "When you durst do it, then you were the man; / And, to be more than what you were, you would / Be so much more the man" (1.7.50–52). She thus at once unleashes or "liberates" Macbeth's ambition from any sense of restraint and also reduces his manhood to insatiable will and desire and to the unbridling of what Augustine characterized as the *libido dominandi, habendi, et nocendi,* the twisting of human nature

---

[31] Geoffrey Chaucer, *The House of Fame*, lines 730–731, in *The Norton Chaucer*, ed. David Lawton (New York: W. W. Norton, 2019), 1021.

against itself.[32] Won over by his wife's specious reasoning, Macbeth responds: "Bring forth men-children only! / For thy undaunted mettle should compose / Nothing but males" (1.7.73–75). The irony is devastating: the "man-child" she has here "brought forth" is Macbeth himself, delivering him from the womb of his own moral intelligence into the clutches of a patently regressive sense of what it means to be a "man."

The forms of privation that make for evil in *Macbeth* are various and multifaceted. But in the play's language, imagery, and action all these privations arguably issue from and refer back to the Macbeths' mysterious childlessness, their denial or refusal of generative fertility, and the attendant war on children, as evidenced by the attempted murder of Fleance, the slaughter of Macduff's children, and the killing of Young Siward, as though defying and defiling anyone "born of woman" (5.7.12). And yet for all that, the play also depicts the principle of generative fecundity as a normative, natural, and beautiful good. When Duncan arrives at Inverness to make his "fatal entrance" under the Macbeths' battlements (1.5.39), in a bravura moment of dramatic irony, the king commends the attractiveness of the place: "This castle hath a pleasant seat" (1.6.1). Banquo then singles out and remarks upon the striking sight by which "heaven's breath / Smells wooingly here" (1.6.5–6): it is the "temple-haunting martlet," nesting in the eaves where "this bird / Hath made his pendent bed and procreant cradle" (1.6.3–8). The contrast is unmistakable in emphasizing the disparity between the beauty of the breeding birds outside, doing what comes *naturally*, and the hidden impotence or barrenness within the castle, which becomes, for Duncan certainly, a house of death.

As the play continues, as Macbeth takes the crown to become a tyrant, fear and desperation follow him and chase him back to the

---

[32] See Augustine, *Confessions*, trans. Henry Chadwick (Oxford: Oxford University Press, 1992), III.8.16, 47–48. See also Calagno, "Hannah Arendt and Augustine of Hippo: On the Pleasure of and Desire for Evil," 372–374.

Witches. They warn him about Macduff and provide equivocal reassurances, whilst also confirming in a *"show of eight Kings,"* the dynastic issue of Banquo stretching forth over time to the accession of James Stuart. The sight is hateful to Macbeth; the figure of the *fruitful* crown, he says, "does sear mine eyeballs" (4.1.113), whereupon, Macduff out of reach, he resolves to kill Macduff's "wife, babes, and all unfortunate souls / That trace him in his line" (4.1.152–153): "The very firstlings of my heart shall be / The firstlings of my hand" (4.1.147–148). The word *firstling* designates *firstborn progeny*, and Macbeth can now only "crown" his "thoughts with acts" in certifying himself as the father of death (4.1.149).

In this conspectus of meaning, the words *kin*, *kind*, and *king* reverberate in *Macbeth* and interact with the words *nature* and *nothing* to inscribe the normative goods in relation to which we can fathom his and Scotland's tragedy. As this reading has endeavored to show, Macbeth violates and vitiates such an order of meaning to become pathologically *unnatural*. He does so precisely as he disowns the order of generative fertility that is the foundation of human society, as he murders his rightful *king* and honored *kinsman*, as he denies the rational and ethical norms of *kindness*, and as he claims for himself the emptied-out name, but not the relational meaning, of *kingship*. That Macbeth himself is particularly sensitive to this dimension of significance and both feels and knows its normative claims so acutely gives the play its particular power and *frisson*.

He is, after all, the man Lady Macbeth characterizes as having a "nature" "too full o' the milk of human kindness" (1.5.16–17). The play contains three rich and suggestive mentions of *milk*, which might help round out this analysis. Just after this first reference to milk, the second occurs when Lady Macbeth voices anxieties about her womanliness, disowns prospects of maternity, and asks to be "unsexed." She does so, rather specifically, by willing the cessation her menstrual cycle: "Make thick my blood; / Stop up th' access and passage to remorse, / That no compunctious visitings of nature / Shake my fell purpose" (1.5.43–45).[33] The implication is clear: Lady Macbeth wants to be free from any periodic reminder of her capacity to conceive and bear a child, sensing as she does that such a capacity would be incompatible with the steely cruelty she craves and the inhuman, monstrous resolve with which she seeks to infect her husband. She then asks to have the white, nutritious, life-sustaining milk in her breasts replaced with black, bitter, poisonous "gall" (1.5.41–48). As the product of lactation and something cognate with (*akin* to) the biological process of menstruation, conception, pregnancy, and childbirth, *milk*, she suggests, has a natural power in the order of generative fertility to block "the nearest way" (1.5.18) and rebuke the direct, ruthless path to seize the object of ambition. She says of her husband, "Yet I do fear thy nature; / It is too full o' the milk of human kindness / To catch the nearest way." Though spoken contemptibly by his wife and often glossed as a derisive, infantilizing, or effeminizing judgment, this image nonetheless evokes the primal experience of breastfeeding, that elemental bonding of mother and child. The image points to what might be called the primeval ethical, social, and political act—the true "state of nature." Drinking her mother's milk, nursing at her mother's breasts, each infant undergoes a foundational rite of passage from which nature prompts nurture in organic "kindliness" and initiates fragile and dependent babies into those socializing bonds and dispositions of trust, affection, and beneficence that help to generate and regenerate, weave and reweave the social fabric of families and human communities.

The play's third reference to milk occurs in the context of Malcolm's discussion with Macduff about Macbeth's tyranny and about his own lack (and Scotland's need) of "the king-becoming graces" by which a sense of linked *kinship* and *kindliness* can endow a notion of *kingship* with the character of "natural" and beneficent authority.

---

[33] That these lines specifically ask for the cessation of Lady Macbeth's menstruation is seldom noted but fairly clear and certainly important in context. For one study that does address the issue, see Jenijoy La Belle, "'A Strange Infirmity': Lady Macbeth's Amenorrhea," *Shakespeare Quarterly* 31:3 (1980): 381–386.

Malcolm refers to "the sweet milk of concord" (4.3.99), almost as if the expression named a comprehensive personal and political virtue. This image, albeit ironic and equivocal in a world where milk has been unnaturally replaced by gall, nonetheless resonates the abiding ideal and perduring promise of a personal and political order aligned with the presumptive goodness of "nature." The image also helps measure what Malcolm and play's audience could have learned from the negative exemplum of Macbeth's tyranny and from the more positive embodiment of Macduff, that "Child of integrity" (4.3.116). It is Macduff who becomes something of a surrogate father and certainly a role model to the orphaned Malcolm and who bears his own grief to "feel it as a man" (4.3.223). This "sweet milk of concord," cognate with Macbeth's own initial "milk of human kindness," further chimes with Malcolm's concluding speech, which offers a chastened alternative to Macbeth's terminal nihilism with the hope for a politics renewed and dedicated to restoring justice, reckoning with love, and invoking "the grace of Grace" in amity and gratitude (5.8.61–77).

With respect to a residual or nascent politics of natality explored in this essay, *Macbeth*'s references to breastfeeding and evocative images of milk engage an intriguing trope of the early seventeenth-century political imaginary, namely the revival and redeployment of the paradoxical biblical image of the "nursing father": "And kings shall be thy nursing fathers" (Isaiah 49:23).[34] James Stuart seized on this image in his *Basilikon Doron* and characterized himself as just such a "nursing father," one who succors his subjects with "nurish-milke."[35] James suggested thereby a notion of kingly rule wherein patriarchal potency gets softened or re-contextualized in relation to maternal solicitude and tenderness. Whether this curious image

---

[34] Cf. the other important biblical example of the "nursing father," in Numbers 11:12, where Moses characterizes his leadership: "Have I conceived all this people? have I begotten them, that thou shouldest say unto me, Carry them in thy bosom, as a nursing father beareth the sucking child, unto the land which thou swarest unto their fathers?"

[35] *Basilikon dōron*, 51, 53.

should be understood as a bit of mystifying propaganda, or as evidence of an uneasy conscience in early modern political theology, or as a genuine ideal acknowledging the fundamental link between generative nature and nurture in political society is difficult to assess.[36] But in any event the image and its particular resonance in the early seventeenth century share with Shakespeare's *Macbeth* a concern for fathoming the abiding relevance of childbirth and childrearing for any complete account of social and political life. Despite his absolutist pretensions, his authoritarian tendencies, and what would become his overly brittle and defensive notion of the divine right of kings, Shakespeare's own patron and king, James Stuart was not (yet) a tyrant in 1606, when *Macbeth* was first performed. But he was, after a stretch of three childless sovereigns, a father, "nursing" or not, putatively of his subjects and actually of his two sons, Henry and Charles (both to be ill fated, as it turned out).

Shakespeare's *Macbeth* as a negative exemplum of nihilistic tyranny and of natality denied, thwarted, turned against itself, presupposes a countervailing, more normative good, of which the negative exemplum is a privation, and without which the exemplum is unintelligible. We see the tragedy of a tyrant's rise and fall (played out on the stage of nations in history). But we also engage a deeply personal, psychic drama of a man and his wife, their marriage, fraught with the anxieties of childlessness (performed intimately, often shrouded in the privacy of the unspoken). It is drama wherein public and private concerns intersect and converge over issues of monarchical succession, political filiation, and presumptions about inherited bloodlines for continuing and renewing dynastic rule. As this reading has attempted to show, Shakespeare's play limns the differences between what becomes the totalitarian politics inscribed in Martin

---

[36] For an interesting study of the image of the "nursing father" in seventeenth-century literature and political theology, see Rachel Trubowitz, *Nation and Nurture in Seventeenth-Century English Literature* (Oxford: Oxford University Press, 2012), Chp. 3: "Nursing Fathers and National Identity: James I, Charles I, Cromwell and Milton," 94–145.

Heidegger's "being-toward-death" and his student Hannah Arendt's tentative reach for a more auspicious politics of natality, one founded upon "being-toward-life" and stretching out to her other key concept of the conditioned, always conditional "web of human relationships."[37] This is the difference between a vital politics that could be generative and generational, subsisting in regimes that carry on and develop organically over time, giving time itself meaning in purposeful futurity, on one hand, and, on the other, a deprived, contracted, or tyrannical politics that arrests time, ends time, or closes history by thwarting, denying, or destroying the possibilities of generational, generative renewal. Meaning itself, both personal and political, Shakespeare's tragedy suggests, consists not in power over time, but in the acknowledgment of contingency and the acceptance of dependency in a "web of human relationships" and in the many threaded, sometimes raveled fabric of nature which despite its raveling can always be rethreaded and rewoven with the birth of a child.[38]

---

[37] See Arendt, *The Human Condition*, 183–184. See also Totsching, "Arendt's Notion of Natality: An Attempt at Clarification," 341–344.

[38] See Arendt, *The Human Condition*, 246–247.

Banning Shylock

Carol McNamara

"One would have to be blind, deaf, and dumb not to recognize that Shakespeare's grand, equivocal comedy, *The Merchant of Venice*, is a profoundly anti-Semitic work."[1] This is the pronouncement with which Shakespeare scholar, Harold Bloom begins his account of the play. Harold Bloom is not alone. More recently, parental concerns about antisemitic themes in the play led to the cancelation of a New York City school presentation of *The Merchant of Venice*.[2] And not long ago, another production in Australia transformed *The Merchant of Venice* from an uncomfortable comedy to a tragedy, in order to make the play more palatable to our contemporary sensibilities.[3]

The Australian production of *The Merchant of Venice* altered Shakespeare's conclusion to incorporate a final scene with a weeping Jessica, suddenly repentant of her role in the humiliation of her father, Shylock. And yet, readers of *The Merchant of Venice* know that Jessica had recently absconded from her home and her Jewish faith with family jewels and Shylock's money, apparently unrepentantly, to join her lover and conventional Venetian society by converting to Christianity. Allan Bloom argues in his essay: "On Christian and Jew: The Merchant of Venice," that "Jessica, without the slightest trace of filial piety, remorselessly leaves her father and robs him."[4]

---

[1] Harold Bloom, *Shakespeare: The Invention of the Human* (New York: Riverhead Books, 1998), 171.

[2] Jerusalem Post Staff, "NYC School cancels Shakespeare play after parental concerns of antisemitism," https://www.jpost.com/diaspora/antisemitism/article-695668, February 6, 2022.

[3] Betsy Reed, "If Shakespeare is a racist or antisemitic, is it OK to change the Ending? Guardian US, https://www.theguardian.com/culture/2017/nov/03/if-a-shakespeare-play-is-racist-or-antisemitic-is-it-ok-to-change-the-ending.

[4] Allan Bloom also remarks that she "is one of the very few figures in Shakespeare who do not pay the penalty for their crimes: and disobedience to one's

Does our uneasiness with Shakespeare's willingness to test the limits of Venetian civil society justify such a distortion of Shakespeare's script? Many have read *The Merchant of Venice* as an antisemitic play. In the Germany of the thirties, the Nazis delighted in the play's performance as evidence of its antisemitism.[5] Sir Jonathan Bate tells us that Shylock was represented on stage with "a wig of red hair and a long bottle-like nose, making him a stereotypical Jew" during the Restoration of the British Monarchy in 1660.[6] The fact that Bate warns us that there is no indication of such mockery during Shakespeare's time only reinforces the fact that it is impossible to provide commentary on *The Merchant of Venice* without noting the problem of Shylock.

But *The Merchant of Venice* is not simply a pro-Christian, anti-Jewish play. Shakespeare's portrayal of Shylock, the Jewish money lender in Shakespeare's Venice, is often harsh, but it is also complex, reflecting as much on the Christian treatment of Jews in Venice as on Shylock's own behavior. And Shakespeare's depiction of Antonio, the eponymous Christian merchant in the play, is not significantly more flattering. My contention is that *The Merchant of Venice* is neither antisemitic, nor pro-Christian. To the contrary, Shakespeare's portrayal of Shylock is painfully and intentionally paradoxically sympathetic, and his rendering of the relationship between Shylock and Antonio is a searing indictment of the medieval Christian caricature of Judaism, which corrupts Venetian Christianity and produces the injustice that distorts Shylock's soul and incites his undeniably cruel desire for vengeance.[7]

---

parents." "On Christian and Jew: The Merchant of Venice," in *Giants and Dwarfs* (New York: Simon and Schuster, 1990), 81.

[5] Marjorie Garber notes that the Nazis produced *The Merchant of Venice* "with a Villainous Shylock…in 1944," *Shakespeare After All* (New York: Anchor Books, Random House, 2004), 296.

[6] Sir Jonathan Bate, Introduction to *The Merchant of Venice* (New York: The Modern Library Royal Shakespeare Company, 2010), 6.

[7] This is the intriguing and persuasive argument of Hermann Sinsheimer's *Shylock: The History of a Character* (New York: The Citadel Press, 1947, 1964).

Shakespeare's decision to situate Shylock's story in the republic of Venice is not random. In fact, the two plays he situates in Venice, *Othello* and *The Merchant of Venice,* contain perhaps his two most controversial characters, Othello and Shylock.[8] Why was Venice, an aristocratic, commercial republic, of such great interest to him, and why did he choose that city to explore characters whose status as racial and ethnic minorities are essential to their stories? Certainly, the Venetian regime was of a very different shape than the hereditary monarchy that reigned in Shakespeare's England under Queen Elizabeth and King James I. Shakespeare's presentation of the British monarchy in his history plays explores his concern with the inherent instability of one-person rule. His interest in Venice seems to reflect his curiosity about the availability of an alternative regime form that might answer more fully the human longing for freedom and good government. Shakespeare portrays Venice as an outwardly open society, governed not by men but by law, enforced impartially among citizens and non-citizens, who conduct business together. Allan Bloom argues that the enduring success of the Venetian republic represented for many Renaissance thinkers and statesmen the possible revival of the human capacity for public-spirited, republican self-government.[9]

Bloom further contends that republicanism gained in popularity among these Renaissance and modern thinkers who contended that by channeling ambition and self-interest to commerce and the love of gain, the political realm could divert attention away from and moderate divisive religious passion. They hoped to reduce human

---

[8] *The Merchant of Venice* was likely written between 1596–1598, and first published in 1600, and republished in the First Folio in 1623, but first performed later in February, 1605. (https://www.oxfordreference.com/display/10.1093/oi/authority.20110803100151116). *Othello* was likely written just a few years later in 1603, as it was first performed at court in November 1604, and published in quarto in 1622 (https://www.oxfordreference.com/display/10.1093/acref/9780191740763.001.0001/acref-9780191740763-e-494#:~:text=The%20play%20was%20given%20at,was%20played%20without%20major%20revisions).

[9] Bloom, "On Christian and Jew: The Merchant of Venice," 65.

attachment to the divine in favor of material comfort and pleasure.[10] Could a government created as a commercial republic balance the needs and beliefs of its citizens with the business interests of merchants and traders from near and far justly under the impartial rule of law? Shakespeare tests this claim by placing Othello, a Christian moor, and Shylock, a Jew, very different, non-citizens in the midst of Venetian commercial life and society. According to Bloom, the Venetian republic had the repulation as "the most tolerant city of its time," and "the place where the various sorts of men could freely mingle" and "share a common way of life" existing together in harmony."[11] If *The Merchant of Venice* is a study of the Venetian commercial republic, as Bloom contends, then, Venice itself would be the true focus of the play. Shakespeare's story of the tense relationship between the Christian merchant, Antonio, the play's namesake, and his rival and enemy, the Jewish money lender, Shylock, would be a vehicle for that investigation. For Bloom, Shakespeare is testing the hypothesis that the commercial republic has the capacity to adjudicate serious religious belief and practice, and, in the case of Othello, racial difference, under the impartial rule of law, without favoring one over the other. Shakespeare is compelling us to deliberate on the important political question the Venetian example of republicanism poses: is moral neutrality under the rule of law in the service of successful commerce and wealth acquisition possible? To pursue this question fully, we must understand the characters of Antonio and Shylock and their relationship to Venice.

In the absence of Antonio and Shylock, *The Merchant of Venice*, would be a standard romantic play, according to Paul Cantor.[12] In

---

[10] Bloom cites Machiavelli as the most notable of modern thinkers who called for a renewed focus on the republican spirit as a means to restore political virtues and manly self-government to the center of political life. And he names "Harrington and Spinoza" as illustrious advocates of the Venetian model of commercial republicanism, 66.

[11] Ibid., 65.

[12] Paul Cantor, "Religion and the Limits of Community in *The Merchant of Venice*," 239.

romantic plays, the impediment to the happy marriage of the thwarted young lovers is most often the old order. *In A Midsummer Night's Dream*, Hermia escapes from Shakespeare's Athens to marry Lysander and to avoid the marriage arranged by her father to Demetrius. Because *A Midsummer Night's Dream* is a comedy, the lovers are sorted practically at the end of the play avoiding the tragic potential of the opening scenes. In *Romeo and Juliet*, the ancient feuds of the young lovers' families pose a seemingly insurmountable barrier to their union, and although they manage to marry, their escape ends in tragdy. The lovers in *The Merchant of Venice* also confront challenges from the old order. Jessica resorts to disguise and subterfuge, and converts to Christianity, to escape her father's traditional Jewish world in order to marry Lorenzo. Lord Bassanio and Portia contend with the challenge of the gold, silver, and lead caskets the will of Portia's prudent father establishes to test the moral fiber of her suitors after his death.

In *The Merchant of Venice*, Shakespeare complicates the comedy and the romance still further by imposing additional and greater obstacles on the lovers' path to happiness. The first of these additional difficulties is Bassanio's extravagance, which keeps him indebted to his wealthy, pious friend, Antonio. The second challenge and related to the first, is the quarrel between Antonio and Shylock from whom Antonio must briefly borrow money to fund Bassanio's initially mercenary courtship of Portia. Portia is "a lady richly left,"[13] whose beauty and wealth Bassanio believes are the answer to the financial shortfall his prodigality has caused (1.1.168).[14]

---

[13] Garber suggests an intriguing historical allegorical frame, which proposes Portia as a literary Queen Elizabeth, also a lady richly left, pursued by suitors for her wealth and title. Elizabeth refuses to marry, but Portia risks her happiness by agreeing to marry and make Bassanio lord of her estate, *Shakespeare After All*, 288.

[14] Bassanio seeks an additional loan from Antonio to pursue Portia, "a lady richly left" in Belmont, of whose affections he has some suspicion because she has shared "fair speechless messages" with him "sometimes from her eyes" (1.1.168—179). As Michael Zuckert suggests, Bassanio speaks of Portia's fair qualities and virtues, but not of his love for her, "The New Medea," in *Shakespeare's Political*

Cantor helps us see that in *The Merchant of Venice*, Shakespeare is pushing the limits of comedy. He argues that for *The Merchant of Venice* to remain a comedy, both Shylock and Antonio must experience defeat. Shylock's defeat comes in the trial in Act 4, and Antonio's in Act 5 both of which are the consequence of Portia's prudent management of the conflict between the two men. And yet, this observation raises more questions than it answers. Why it is appropriate for the play to achieve a comic rather than a fully tragic ending. Why do Shylock and Antonio, both tragic characters in the midst of a Shakespearean romantic comedy, escape the awful fate of Othello, Shakespeare's other outsider in Venice?

In fact, neither Antonio nor Shylock is in harmony with the contemporary ethos of Shakespeare's Venice. Venice is known for its dedication to commercial venture, the pursuit of wealth, and an atmosphere of feasting and pleasure seeking. Antonio and Shylock are anomalies. They are both unsmiling men and solemn believers. Their religious principles have absolute primacy in the way they conduct their lives, which excludes them from the festive spirit wealth makes possible that typifies Shakespeare's Venetians. Paul Cantor describes them simply as killjoys.[15]

Antonio himself admits early on to one of his friends, Gratiano, a member of the group of aristocratic playboys with whom—paradoxically—he spends time, that he "hold[s] the world but as the world…/ A stage, where every man must play a part, / And mine a sad one" (I.1.81–83). Like Antonio, Shylock is entirely joyless and "anti-comic," a hater of music, masques, and pleasure of all kinds, at least at this point in his life.[16] Certainly, Shylock is a serious man. He disapproves of the masques, Venetian masked street parties, which he dismisses as the "shallow fopp'ry" of "Christian fools with

---

Pageant: Essays in Politics & Literature (Lanham, Maryland: Rowman & Littlefield Publishers, 1996), 6.

[15] Paul Cantor, "Religion and the Limits of Community in *The Merchant of Venice*," *Soundings: An Interdisciplinary Journal*, Spring/Summer 1987, Vol.70, No.1/2, Penn State University Press, 40.

[16] Marjorie Garber, "The Merchant of Venice," *Shakespeare After All*, 308.

varnished faces," warning Jessica to lock up his "sober house" against the night's revels (2.5.30–37).[17]

Shakespeare gives us some indication, however, that Shylock was not always so dour. We learn from Shylock's compatriot, Tubal, sent to find and bring Jessica home, that she has cruelly traded a turquoise ring for a monkey in Genoa. Shylock's lament reveals that it was the "turquoise," he gave to "Leah," his wife, when he was a bachelor, and with which he would not have parted "for a wilderness of monkeys" (3.1.120–21). Shakespeare discloses with this brief scene that although Shylock was always an observant Jew, there was a time when he was young and in love, and that he still prizes that love for Leah above the price of the jewels with which he courted her. In this way, Shakespeare pushes us to ask what experiences have produced such bitterness in Shylock's soul to provoke the desire for vengeance he exhibits in the play?

Antonio is distinguished in Venice for his commercial success as a royal merchant, and the manner in which he conducts his business is presented in vivid contrast to Shylock's orderly adherence to the laws of commercial exchange. Antonio's generosity is informed by his high Christian principles and manifests chiefly in his refusal to charge interest on his loans to friends and fellow Christian citizens. His open disapproval of usury, which Christianity forbids, is an extension of his principled position.

Shylock's ways of doing business are not just presented in contrast to Antonio's. Antonio's business directly and intentionally undercuts Shylock. Apparently, he has rescued many "forfeitures" to Shylock, and he believes Shylock hates him implacably for it (3.3.20–26). Despite his Christian charity, or perhaps paradoxically, because of it, Antonio treats Shylock with venomous disdain because his business, among the only means of commercial activity Venice allows him as a Jew to support his family and his life, is to charge

---

[17] All references to the play are to the Folger Shakespeare Library edition, William Shakespeare, *The Merchant of Venice* (New York: Simon & Schuster Paperbacks, 1992).

interest on the money he lends to Venetians, merchants and ordinary citizens alike. But, when Antonio finds it necessary to borrow money to assist Bassanio, he encounters a situation that drives him to compromise his principles and which brings him into direct and potentially dangerous conflict with Shylock. In his quest to win the lovely Portia and her fortune, Bassanio finds that only Shylock can provide the short term loan of 3,000 ducats they require..

For Shylock, Antonio's exigency becomes an opportunity. Approached first by Bassanio, Shylock reflects silently on his chance for vengeance against Antonio, whom he hates because he is "a Christian," who lends out "money gratis," which brings down the lending rate. But, Shylock's antagonism extends beyond the disruption of his business affairs to Antonio's hatred of the Jewish people, and Shylock as the foremost representative of it in Venice. Shylock observes that Antoinio "hates our sacred nation, and he rails, / Even there where merchants most do congregate, On me, my bargains, and my well-won thrift, / Which he calls 'interest.' Cursed be my tribe / If I forgive him" (1.3.42–51). Shylock reveals that Antonio has singled out Shylock for particular abuse among his colleagues and persecuted him for his livelihood as a usurer.

In fact, Jewish law argues that it is not acceptable for a Jew to exact interest from a fellow Jew, which is parallel to Antonio's practice of refraining from charging interest within the Christian community.[18] Antonio and Shylock live each within his own community and give a place of privilege to members of his own tribe.

Once Antonio grants Shylock a moment of his time, Shakespeare affords Shylock the opportunity to confront Antonio about this mistreatment. This time, he speaks openly: Antonio has berated him about his "money" and his "usances," called him "misbeliever, cutthroat dog, / and spet upon [his] Jewish gaberdine." Shylock remarks that he has borne this abuse "with a patient shrug / (For

---

[18] Leviticus 25.35 and Deuteronomy 23.19–20, *The Hebrew Bible, Volume I, Translation with Commentary*, Robert Alter (New York: W. W. Norton & Company, 2019).

suffrance is the badge of all our tribe)" (1.3.116–122). And yet now, Shylock wonders at Antonio asking him to "bend low" humbly for the honor of lending him money: "Hath a dog money?" Shylock asks (1.3.131). Interestingly, Antonio is unyielding. He responds that Shylock should lend him money, not as a friend, but as an enemy, because this business transaction will not transform him. He is likely to spit on Shylock and spurn him again (1.3.140–147). Antonio shows himself to be a relentless enemy of Shylock, and even Shylock's assistance in his time of need will not change his heart. Antonio's unwillingness to soften his opinion of Shylock, even at this point of necessity, suggests that his disdain for Shylock extends beyond the usury to his Judaism, the fact that he is a "misbeliever" (1.3.121). Usury is an exemplar of the solemn religious differences between the two men.

It is worth pausing to consider more fully this exchange, because it is antecedent to the bond agreement with Antonio and the great controversy over which Portia will contend with Shylock at the trial that decides the fate of Shylock and Antonio.

Shakespeare makes clear to us that Antonio has for many years identified Shylock as his adversary and abused him for his money lending with interest and his Jewish faith. He also demonstrates that Antonio is held in high esteem among Venetians, who emulate his opinion and mockery of Shylock and the Jews in Venice. In evidence is the scene in which Solanio and Salarino recount Shylock's anguish after discovery of Jessica's flight from his house. Yet, while Solanio and Salarino ridicule Shylock's desperation at losing his beloved daughter, who has taken his ducats and "Fled with a Christian," their description of Shylock's tormented panic leaves us with a profound sense of Shylock's obvious pain and loss. In this way, Shakespeare implies his disapproval of their cruelty.

Shakespeare immediately contrasts the pair's lack empathy for Shylock with their concern for how Shylock's suffering might express itself in vengeance against Antonio ("A kinder gentleman treads not the earth," they observe), should he default on his bond (2.8.12–25, 26–37). Through Shakespeare's juxtaposition in this scene of the mockery of Shylock with the concern for Antony, his tormenter, he demonstrates that the "anti-Judaic feeling," which he makes a feature of Antonio's character, a man honored for his virtue and wealthy status in Venice, is widely shared, and even honored.[19]

The terms of the bond between Shylock and Antonio are, then, clearly related to their opposition. Shylock, who previously suffered Antonio's ill-treatment patiently, refuses to take interest from him. Instead, he asks for a pitiless price to which he must not expect Antonio to agree, a pound of Antonio's "fair flesh, to be cut off and taken / In what part of [his] body pleaseth" Shylock, if Antonio cannot repay him (1.3.162–63). Antonio's need is Shylock's opportunity for what could amount to a terrible vengeance for Antonio's incivility and cruelty.

To tell the story of the conflict between Shylock and Antonio, Shakespeare draws upon the ancient "fable of the pound of flesh," which begins in the Far East and finds its way to medieval Europe. There are multiple versions of the story from the far East, and the Jewish Talmud, many of which do not involve Jews at all. After the thirteenth century, these stories are mostly variations on the account of the bond agreement Shakespeare constructs between Shylock and Antonio. The typical formula has the Jew and his debtor pleading their case in court, often resolved with similar legal sleight of hand or the judgment of a ruler at the last minute to prevent a bloody conclusion to the controversy. Sinsheimer explains to us that the bond involving a pound of flesh was understood initially as a sign of legal enlightenment and progress, that the creditor could no longer do whatever he wished with the debtor but could only act within the limits stipulated. In fact, it is important to note that the debtor actually agrees to the terms of the bond, as Antonio does, as security in exchange for the loan. The debtor is not obligated to borrow the

---

[19] Marjorie Garber helpfully warns us that the term "anti-Semitism" "is anachronistic for Shakespeare's time (it was coined at the end of the nineteenth century; before that one might speak of anti-Judaic feeling), but the prejudice to which it gives a name is not," *Shakespeare After All*, 296.

money, but when he does, the bond is a legal document.[20]

We are left to wonder why Antonio accepts the bloody conditions of the bond. In response to Bassanio's strong objection to Shylock's proposed terms, Antonio asserts confidence in the return of his many merchant ships with sufficient profit to pay his debt to Shylock. Is it the confidence of a capitalist that influences Antonio to agree to these dangerous terms for the bond? After all, he is a merchant-adventurer, accustomed to risking money to earn money. Michael Zuckert argues that Antonio agrees to the loan (apparently, one in a long series of loans) Bassanio needs as a means to continue his utility to Bassanio, for whom he has a deep affection, finding "anew in the very moment and in the very deed by which Bassanio attempts to discharge (some of) the bond already in place," a means of prolonging the entanglement of their friendship.[21]

Antonio's self-sacrifice also seems related to a certain Christian otherworldliness that suffuses his demeanor. He begins the play with a discernable but inexplicable sadness, born of what he attributes to a lack of self-knowledge. Zuckert observes that Antonio only revives from his enigmatic sadness when Bassanio describes his pursuit of Portia as a financial quest, to settle his economic need and pay his debts, rather than the pursuit of love and marriage. Garber is skeptical of the notion proposed by Zuckert that Antonio's love for Bassanio is romantic, and instead ascribes it to the high ideal of noble manly friendship common in the Renaissance, an argument with which Cantor agrees.[22]

Whether Antonio's love for Bassanio is romantic or a ardent form of friendship, his affection is confirmed by an observation of Solanio, that he believes Antonio "only loves the world" for Bassanio (2.8.52). By agreeing to Bassanio's request, Antonio creates a love

---

[20] Hermann Sinsheimer, *Shylock: The History of a Character*, 75–82.

[21] Michael Zuckert, "The New Medea," in *Shakespeare's Political Pageant: Essays in Politics & Literature* (Lanham, Maryland: Rowman & Littlefield Publishers, 1996), 8.

[22] Marjorie Garber, *Shakespeare After All*, 293; Paul Cantor, "Religion and the Limits of Community in *The Merchant of Venice*," 240.

triangle, setting himself up as a rival with Portia for Bassanio's love, a drama heightened by the terms of the bond. Certainly, it is only of Bassanio that Antonio thinks when the bond is forfeit and he must face his "bloody creditor" on the next day. Having written to his friend about his plight, Antonio has only one hope before he martyrs himself: "Pray God Bassanio come / To see me pay his debt, and then I care not" (3.4.36–38). He desires an audience of one. Antonio's letter announcing his forfeit and likely demise, arrives just as Bassanio has wed Portia. As Cantor remarks, Antonio "has a way of interrupting other people's moments of happiness and ruining their enjoyment."[23]

Antonio's world weariness would also explain his apparent penchant for martyrdom. His affection for Bassanio seems to be the only thing in his life that gives him some degree of happiness. Shakespeare makes clear that instead of fighting for his life, Antonio accepts his fate in a narcissistic way that appears to welcome death. In response to Bassanio's efforts to keep his spirits up, Antonio laments, he is a

> tainted wether of the flock,
> Meetest for death. The weakest kind of fruit
> Drops earliest to the ground, and so let me.
> You cannot better be employed, Bassanio,
> Than to live still and write mine epitaph (4.1.114–120).

It is clear that Antonio seeks to indebt Bassanio eternally to his memory by dying for the sacrifice he made to bring about his happiness. But Antonio's self-pitying self-description as a neutered ram also suggests that because he has no hope of progeny, he has no expectation of a meaningful future, and hence no reason to live on.[24]

---

[23] Paul Cantor, "Religion and the Limits of Community in *The Merchant of Venice*," 247.

[24] Marjorie Garber suggests that Shakespeare is playing with gender in this scene. While Portia suits herself up as a man to command the attention of the court and defend Antonio (and save Bassanio and their marriage from his eternal,

Antonio insists he seeks "To suffer with a quietness of spirit" Shylock's "tyranny and rage" (4.1.13–14). And this apparent longing for death strikes us as a desire for an escape from this world to the next, that Antonio's beliefs and high moral status and confidence must lead him to believe he will achieve.

Antonio has material wealth and comfort of the kind apparently valued in Venice, but he seems unconcerned with it. Instead, he contends that his money is only of use to him to benefit others. Yet, Antonio's near universal human sympathy cannot extend to Shylock, or by extension, any Jewish businessman, who "denies the fundamental principle of charity," as Antonio understands it.[25] As a result, Shakespeare suggests that although Antonio's practice of Christianity makes a claim to a universal humility and humanity, is it truly universal if it cannot extend the exercise of these virtues towards the Jewish people who do not accept Christianity?

Allan Bloom argues that "Shakespeare does not understand Judaism, for he saw it from the outside."[26] It is indeed the case that England expelled the Jews in 1290, and they were not permitted to return until the mid-seventeenth century, so Judaism would not have been practiced openly in Shakespeare's England, if at all. That said, Shakespeare often depicted characters about whom he could only learn through literary and historical sources.[27] It is also true that there was an insular quality to Jewish life in the Middle Ages, born simultaneously of self-protection and ostracism. But Shakespeare

---

guilty subjugation to his memory), at the same time, Antonio compares himself to a castrated ram, in other words, hardly a man at all anymore. Perhaps it his engagement in commerce, with his livelihood dependent on ships that come and go out of his control on the high seas, or his Christian longing for an end to his life. Either way, Antonio does not present a manly demeanor. Garber notes that it is not "that there is no difference between women and men, but rather that, throughout the play, each character is constantly threatening, or promising, to turn into the other sex," *Shakespeare After All*, 284.

[25] Allan Bloom, "On Christian and Jew: The Merchant of Venice," 69.

[26] Ibid., 80–82.

[27] We do not know, for example, with how many Moors Shakespeare was acquainted, but he depicts two in his Venetian plays.

was clearly aware of the history and medieval caricature of the Jews in England and in Europe at large. In his study *Shylock: The History of a Character*, Herman Sinsheimer carefully traces the development of the Medieval stereotype of the "Wandering Jew," of which he argues Shakespeare's Shylock is a satirical archetype.

The Middle Ages were a period of the Christianization of Europe, Sinsheimer explains. In the effort to convert nonbelievers to Christianity, the Church interpreted Jewish unwillingness to convert to "the true faith" as a "crime against the Christian saviour," for which the Jews were falsely accused, maligned and persecuted, exiled and scattered across Europe and the world. Shakespeare endows Antonio, in particular, with the characteristics of the "medieval man, dominated by the stern doctrines and dogmas of the Church." Antonio understands his own striving as completely good, and hence, resistance to it as evil. And it is Shylock who represents that recalcitrant heresy for Antonio most of all. Shylock is the Jew who is both a stranger in Venice, and who clings to his strange faith.[28] It is from this set of circumstances, inspired by the suspicion of their character incited by the refusal to submit to conversion, that false accusations of crime and ritual murder arise, and the Jews found themselves relegated to the money lending business as a result of exclusion from regular commercial activity..

Judaism is a religion guided by 613 laws that govern every aspect of Jewish life. It is not, then, surprising that Shylock, a non-citizen in Venice, puts his faith in the established laws of Venice to inform and protect his business and his family. Antonio, by contrast, is a "royal merchant," a successful businessman, who trades and sells goods for a profit, who has the respect and sympathy of his fellow Venetians. We might ask, however, in what way is money lending with interest for a profit so very different than selling rather than donating merchandise to others? The fact that even Antonio must borrow money from Shylock, contrary to his own principles, is evidence of the need a commercial republic like Venice has for

---

[28] Hermann Sinsheimer, *Shylock: The History of a Character*, 31–32.

impersonal (non-familial) sources of revenue to conduct its business. By highlighting this financial need, Shakespeare points to a further hypocrisy or purposeful blindness in Antonio and at the heart of Venice that encourages commercial activity and privileges Christianity but relies on the banking of "alien" residents like Shylock it refuses to grant full membership to its society.

In the end, however, Shakespeare indicates that neither Shylock, nor Antonio can prevail in Venice. In Shakespeare's careful look at the commercial republic, the moral seriousness of Shylock and Antonio, which make them both outsiders to the merrymaking ethos in Venice, paradoxically drives their demand for adherence to principle and eventually vengeance for its perceived abrogation. Shakespeare shows us that Shylock prefers to remain separate from other Venetians (1.3.31–36). When Bassanio, who treats Shylock with civility, invites him to dinner, Shylock initially declines: "I will buy with you, sell with you, talk with you, walk with you, and so following: but I will not eat with you, nor pray with you" (1.3.35–38). And yet, we find that he has ultimately agreed to the dinner. He says he will "go in hate, to feed upon / The prodigal Christian," but this explanation seems to fall short. We don't know that Shylock will eat the Christian's non-Kosher food, but even going is a surprising social interaction, perhaps revealing a desire for social inclusion, for Shylock (2.5.15–16).

Perhaps Shylock's reason for joining the dinner becomes clearer in his most well-known appeal for recognition of his equal dignity. Shylock expresses this plea when he demands his "vengeance" under Venetian law. Antonio "hath disgraced" him, hindered his gain, laughed at his losses, scorned his "nation," cooled his friends and heated his enemies, and, Shylock asks: "what's his reason?" Because Shylock is "a Jew." He asks us to acknowledge the justice of his claim.

> Hath not a Jew eyes? Hath not a Jew hands, organs, dimensions, senses, affections, passions? Fed with the same food, hurt with the same weapons, subject to the same diseases, healed by the same means, warmed and cooled by the same winter and summer as a Christian is? If you prick us, do we not bleed? If you

tickle us, do we not laugh? If you poison us, do we not die? And if you wrong us, shall we not revenge? (3.1.63).

Shylock is driven to his awful vengeance by the injustice, disrespect, and social ostracism he endures by his Christian rival and by the hatred for Shylock Antonio inspires among his friends. It is worth noting, however, that Shylock emphasizes in his plea for recognition of his humanity the equal physical condition a Jew shares with every other human being—Jews have the same physical needs as Christians, eat the same food, suffer the same discomfort in the heat and the cold and bleed when pricked. It is striking, however, that, as Timothy Burns remarks, "Shylock abstracts from the distinctively human, the virtues upon which worth or dignity rests."[29]

Burns argues that the Venetian commercial republic must move away from the pre-modern cultivation of the intellectual and moral virtues valued as the highest end of political life for the sake of peaceful coexistence among its assorted subjects and factions. The corollary to this argument is that Shylock's appeal aims to reach the Venetians on their own terms. While Shylock has benefited from the limited Venetian tolerance of his financial activity in Venice, an activity on which its commerce depends, he has kept himself apart, living in a parallel world under Jewish law. This tension, which Shylock tries to bridge in his appeal to the common humanity of Jews and Christians, is natural, and yet it is clear Venice cannot resolve it without suffering. The proof is in the pudding: Bassanio's dinner invitation to Shylock may be an outreached hand of inclusion, but it is ultimately a disastrous decision for Shylock to leave his own community to join the party because his daughter Jessica takes the opportunity of his absence to escape from him and the Jewish way of life with his ducats. It turns out, then, that Shylock is very much alone in Venice. If Shylock is enraged at his treatment, we must ask to what extent Venice must take some of the blame for his fury and his desire for vengeance.

---

[29] Timothy W. Burns, *Shakespeare's Political Wisdom* (New York: Palgrave MacMillan, 2013), 115.

Shylock is an outsider in Venetian society, but Shakespeare reminds us that Antonio, who is a moral and commercial leader of his Venetian peers, somehow does not quite belong in Venice either. In a Christian commercial republic, Antonio is *the* merchant of Venice, but he seems indifferent to, if not even uncomfortable with the success of his worldly commercial pursuits. He is a serious Christian man living among aristocratic pleasure seekers. We focus on the drama of Shylock's quest for vengeance because it demands an apparently inescapable terrible and mortal penalty when Antonio's ships and wealth all seem to be lost at sea. It also gives rise to the dramatic trial scene, which requires Portia's intervention to resolve. Yet, Antonio does little to avert the controversy; in fact, he practically embraces it as a means to exit this tainted world for the next and to embed his love in Bassanio's memory for eternity.

It is also Antonio who grasps the tension between his higher morality and Venetian law when he explains to Solanio that the Duke must allow Shylock to have his pound of flesh to pay the bond of 3,000 ducats Antonio owes him:

The Duke cannot deny the course of law;
For the commodity that strangers have
With us in Venice, if it be denied,
Will much impeach the justice of the state,
Since that the trade and profit of the city
Consisteth of all nations (3.3.26–31).

Antonio understands that the higher law in Venice—at least on paper—is not Christian but commercial. He is also aware, but does not regret, that his deliberate effort to challenge Shylock's usury by delivering "from his forfeitures/Many that have at times made moan to me," has led to this moment (3.3.21–26). Antonio contends here that it is Shylock's business of charging interest for the money he lends that divides them, which is true. But elsewhere, it is apparent that the usury is only an outward manifestation of the deepest reason for Antonio's hatred of Shylock identified. As Shylock tells Salarino, he seeks revenge against Antonio because he laughs at his losses and mocks his gains because he is a "Jew" (3.3.54–57). The difference between Antonio and Shylock is a matter of religious belief and principle. Antonio cannot accept Shylock's rejection of Christianity and his determination to remain a Jew.

In the end, if we read carefully, it is Antonio's vengeance Shakespeare privileges at the conclusion of the play. It is Venice, though, not Shakespeare, that reveals its own preferences. Venice, as it is manifest in its laws, privileges Christianity over Judaism. It would like to think it promotes toleration over discrimination for the sake of neutral commercial activity, but the legal gymnastics necessary to avoid tragedy at the trial raise questions about the genuine impartiality of Venetian law. Portia's interpretation of the Venetian law skillfully averts Antonio's death, by splitting hairs. She argues artfully that the Venetian law allows Shylock his pound of flesh but not a drop of Christian blood on pain of death, an impossible undertaking from which Shylock finally retreats. This legal scenario results because Portia, disguised as the attorney Balthazar, could not persuade Shylock to be merciful or accept the money of others to satisfy his thirst for vengeance. The participants in the trial, Bassanio in particular, are relieved by Portia's final Solomon-like, "manly" capacity to resolve the legal impasse that eludes the men of Venice, and it stands in interesting stark contrast to Antonio's gelded perspective on life.

At this moment in the play, Portia and the Duke of Venice give Antonio the chance to offer a merciful escape from the death penatly and impose his own punishment in reprisal for Shylock's thirst for vengeance. Gratiano insists on the most severe of penalties, "a halter gratis, nothing else, for God's sake!" the hangman's rope free of charge (4.1.395). Not satisfied with the preservation of his own life, perhaps even disappointed by it, Antonio requires the transfer of Shylock's wealth to his now Christian daughter upon his death. And because Shylock's Judaism is itself an affront to his beliefs, he also compels Shylock's conversion to Christianity. We should consider that as a Christian, Antonio must believe that his requirement that Shylock subject himself to conversion from Judaism to Christianity is an eternal act of mercy. But from the perspective of the toleration Venetian law espouses, Antonio seems to forsake mercy when he imposes this final act of cruelty on Shylock.

The Merchant of Venice concludes as a comedy only by denying Shylock his seething vengeance, averting Antonio's death, and allowing the happy young couples to marry in Belmont, which exists beyond the reach of Venetian law. To accomplish this comedic conclusion and avoid tragedy, Portia prevents the straightforward application of Venetian law as Antonio understood it. Shakespeare thus demonstrates that the commercial republic cannot maintain the tolerant legal neutrality it espouses publicly, but must choose a side to prevent Antonio's death. Shylock sadly abets his own defeat through his implacable desire for retribution, but the blame for his terrible pursuit of Antonio's life and his ultimate defeat and subjection is multi-faceted. Antonio's Christian principles do tolerate the practice of Judaism and as a result he abrogates daily the neutrality Venetian law seeks to champion for the sake of the peaceful conduct of commerce. The moral of Shakespeare's story is that the commercial republic has not ascertained how to tolerate or navigate serious moral difference under the neutral rule of commercial and maritime law.

Venice tolerates Shylock and Tubal as long as they serve the needs of the commercial republic without controversy and remain on the sidelines of Venetian economic and social life. Money lending is necessary for the conduct of the public commerce on which Venice depends as a commercial port. The conclusion of *The Merchant of Venice* reminds us that there is no easy or light way to adjudicate the sort of serious human differences Shylock and Antonio represent about the good life. Portia's Belmont avoids human difference by excluding it.[30] Perhaps Venice does too. Shylock is compelled to join

---

[30] Portia applauds the failure of every foreign prince who seeks her hand in marriage but fails her deceased father's "casket" test. Instead, she desires a husband with whom she has everything in common, a Venetian husband, "a scholar and a soldier," Bassanio, who "was the best deserving a fair lady." And she rejects every foreign prince who seeks her hand (I.2.110–118).

the Venetians in their Christian worship, following his daughter, in order to avoid tragedy in the play. Even Antonio, the cause of the controversy, ends the play alone, unpartnered, isolated, and unclear about his place in the world.

Allan Bloom argues that it is not entirely relevant that Shakespeare "does not understand Judaism." He claims that Shakespeare is less interested in Shylock as a Jew, than he is interested in Shylock as a human being dedicated to a set of opinions "about the highest things" that are "invested in doctrine and law and bound up with established interests." Bloom's point is that Shylock's high principles inevitably clash with the similarly invested opinions of others, like the Christian principles of Antonio, even in a city like Venice dedicated to uniting men around the politically and economically beneficial on which they might all be able to agree. Bloom concludes that Shakespeare ends *The Merchant of Venice* in Belmont as a comedy to escape the unpleasant divisions, "ugly passions and unfulfilled hopes" that even Venice cannot escape. In Belmont, the daughters find a happy end to their rebellion against their intractable fathers. Portia can orchestrate "a human harmony for a few" with happy marriages, especially her own, among "men and women in love," without the complications of law, convention, or religion. Even Jessica escapes censure in utopian Belmont, which is why the effort to add a repentant Jessica to the end of *The Merchant of Venice* is untrue to Shakespeare's play.[31] There is no empathy for Shylock, or Antonio, in Belmont; their Venetian anguish is entirely forgotten, as it must be to arrive at a happy ending.

Paul Cantor agrees that Shakespeare's happy, comic conclusion of *The Merchant of Venice* requires the subjugation of religious principles, but he is less concerned than Allan Bloom with where we find ourselves after Shylock and Antonio's high religious beliefs are subdued. For Cantor, instead of the tragedy of death and dissention, the moral of *The Merchant of Venice* comes to us through Portia's clever, politically savvy interpretation of the bond. The rule of law and the

---

[31] Ibid., 80–82.

power of interpretation rescues Venice from its predicament and leaves Venetian law intact, allowing the world of nature and vitality to resume. Cantor believes Shakespeare privileges the comic perspective, which accepts compromise for the sake of living together without the civil war and tragedy to which religious difference tends, if not in perfect harmony. There is a practical place for such comedic moderation, but Bloom would argue that Shakespeare does not allow us to rest entirely satisfied with the sacrifice of "all that is noble and true" it requires.[32] In *The Merchant of Venice*, Shakespeare makes us aware of the benefits of moderation, while also making us keenly aware of what we forgo with regard to the highest things when we content ourselves with comfort and pleasure.

---

[32] Allan Bloom, "On Christian and Jew: The Merchant of Venice," 82.

A Place in the Story: Autobiographical Shakespeare

Sheila T. Cavanagh

Over the past several years, there have been a number of successful and noteworthy one-person plays interweaving autobiography and Shakespeare. These include, among others, Shakespeare Behind Bars' Sammie Byron's presentation of *Othello's Tribunal,* military veteran Stephan Wolfert's *Cry Havoc,* Mohegan theater-maker Madeline Sayet's *Where We Belong,* Harlem Shakespeare Festival Founder Debra Ann Byrd's *Becoming Othello: A Black Girl's Journey,* Founding Artistic Director of the *Los Angeles Women's Shakespeare Company* Lisa Wolpe's *Shakespeare and the Alchemy of Gender,* and musical and theatre performer Conrad Murray's *DenMarked.* [1] For the purposes of this discussion, I am also including actor Keith Hamilton Cobb's *American Moor* in this category, although Cobb's play presents both autobiographical and composite elements from other people's experiences in this play he both wrote and performs. These dramas have each been presented widely, although Wolfert is no longer presenting live performances of *Cry Havoc* and Sayet recently completed her most recent tour of *Where We Belong,* a play that is now often presented by another actor.

While the comparative cost-savings from offering one-performer shows presumably has helped these productions thrive, the talented writers and performers at the heart of these plays tell

---

[1] With the exception of Conrad Murray, I have spoken with each of these writers and performers and have seen their plays, sometimes repeatedly. I appreciate their contributions to my understanding of their works. I am also grateful to Sammie Byron and Lisa Wolpe for providing unpublished scripts of their plays and to Keith Hamilton Cobb for sharing a copy of a talk he gave at the American Shakespeare Center.

compelling stories that raise important questions about biographical insights that can be derived from Shakespeare as well as about widespread educational and societal presumptions and practices. Shakespeare consistently intersects with these narratives, providing a lens that facilitates significant engagement with both the individual and broader issues that emerge in these performances. Some of these writers and performers openly resist Shakespeare's influence across global culture, while appreciating his talent. Others incorporate his writings into their presentations without openly addressing what Sayet terms the "Shakespeare System."[2] These texts include a variety of perspectives about Shakespeare's role in culture, education, and on stage, while highlighting this canon's place within the creator/performer's own personal history. Shakespeare contributes powerfully to each of their narratives, although contestations associated with his cultural position repeatedly loom large. Social justice remains at the forefront of all of these dramatic conversations.

Where We Belong has been presented at numerous locations, including Shakespeare's Globe Theatre in London, New York's Public Theater, Baltimore's Center Stage and the Oregon Shakespeare Festival. During the pandemic, it was streamed by D.C.'s Wooly Mammoth Theatre, in conjunction with the Folger Shakespeare Theatre. It then toured before returning in early 2024 to the Folger. Sayet is an accomplished writer, producer and performer. Currently, a clinical assistant professor in the Department of English at Arizona State University and a member of the Arizona Center for Medieval and Renaissance Studies, Sayet previously served as the Executive Director for Yale's Indigenous Performing Arts Program. Her innumerable accolades include inclusion in *Forbes* 30 Under 30 in Hollywood & Entertainment, as well as serving as a TED Fellow, MIT Media Lab Fellow, National Directing Fellow, Drama League Director-In-Residence, and receiving The White House Champion of Change

---

[2] 21 August 2020. Madeline Sayet, "Interrogating the Shakespeare System." Howlaround. Theatre Commons. https://howlround.com/interrogating-shakespeare-system.

Award from President Obama.³ According to Sayet, in an article she co-wrote about what she and her co-authors term "The Shakespeare Problem": "*Where We Belong* chronicles my struggle with the role of Shakespeare and my wish that my Mohegan culture and language were equally valued. It was performed at Shakespeare's Globe, making it the first work by a Native American playwright to be performed in that space."⁴

The play details Sayet's decision to leave her doctoral studies at the Shakespeare Institute in Stratford-upon-Avon. She talks about her long-term enthusiasm for Shakespeare, but she also relates her mother's ongoing concern about the physical and emotional distance from the Mohegan community in Connecticut this educational pursuit required. Sayet remarks, for example that

> I spend *a lot* of time with Shakespeare. A language that I don't have to worry about losing. I find my voice in Shakespeare, my friends in Shakespeare, even my love in Shakespeare. I come back to it again and again. Inside it, I can transform. Whatever it is, I have to say, when I speak Shakespeare, people listen.⁵

Her mother, however, demands to know "Why are you running across the ocean to study a white man?"⁶ Throughout the play, Sayet wrestles with these often-conflicting commitments to advanced literary and dramatic studies and her tribal roots. She also investigates

---

³ Credentials are included for some of these authors in order to emphasize their professional roles within various realms of Shakespearean drama. While these writers consistently emphasize their individual experiences of being "inside" or "outside" various groupings in society, education, and employment, it seems relevant to identify their placements within a range of Shakespearean-related enterprises. As many of these dramas make clear, educational, theatrical, and broader societal situations all contribute to the so-called "Shakespeare System."

⁴ Sarah Enloe, Madeline Sayet, Mei Ann Teo, and Dawn Monique Williams. "The Shakespeare Problem: A Conversation" 2021. Lindsey Mantoan, Matthew Moore, Angela Schiller, eds. *Troubling Traditions: Canonicity, Theatre, and Performance in the US*. London: Routledge. 36–48, 36.

⁵ Madeline Sayet, 2022. *Where We Belong*. London: Methuen Drama, 16.

⁶ *Where We Belong*, 24.

ways that her tribal identity influences how her professors and members of the public expect her to behave, recounting, for example, feedback she receives on her PhD work at the Shakespeare Institute: "While the *passion* behind this writing is evident, we would appreciate a *cooler* rewrite."[7] She also remembers presentations where audience members demand that she focus on "her love of Shakespeare," rather than upon colonialist aspects of Shakespearean literature and its educational history."[8] According to the play, these experiences led to what she terms her "breaking point"[9] where she decides that "I don't want to be the Native American in front of the word Shakespeare."[10] After this realization, she leaves the Shakespeare Institute with a Master's degree (she also holds an MA from NYU in in Arts, Politics, & Post-Colonial Study) and continues her successful professional career.

Sayet's experience with what she elsewhere titles "the Shakespeare System" imbues *Where We Belong* and her other writing. Sayet identifies the "Shakespeare System" as not only being "Shakespeare's written work, but the complex and oppressive role his work, legacy, and positionality hold in our contemporary society."[11] In the play, she talks about the way that Shakespeare was used oppressively in many American educational environments:

> One way we know Shakespeare was taught at Carlisle Indian School, one of the residential schools that children were stolen from their homes and taken to, is that one student—when forced to give up his name for a new English name—took the name Will Shakespeare.[12]

---

[7] *Where We Belong*, 45.
[8] *Where We Belong*, 38.
[9] *Where We Belong*, 45.
[10] *Where We Belong*, 44.
[11] "Interrogating the Shakespeare System."
[12] *Where We Belong*, 37–38. Roman Catholic Bishops recently released a statement about the Church's role in these abusive environments, although it seems to be illustrative of the axiom "too little, too late."

In "Interrogating the Shakespeare System," she maintains that the harm associated with Shakespeare runs throughout much modern education and theatrical practice: "I'm not saying that if you love Shakespeare you shouldn't…but [when] everything is compared to one white man's legacy [that] is inherently destructive."[13] Instead, she argues that "if Shakespeare is to be done at all, it should be done in ways that encourage each student, performer, and artist to interpret it for themselves."[14] Pushing against Shakespeare as a measure for intelligence, Sayet and one of her Routledge co-authors, Sarah Enloe (formerly President of the Shakespeare Theatre Association and Director of Education for the American Shakespeare Center in Staunton, Virginia), push strongly against a common premise regarding Shakespeare. In Enloe's words: "I think we have been conditioned to use Shakespeare as a ruler against which we measure intellect and culture."[15] While both Sayet (and Enloe) possess strong intellectual attachments to Shakespeare, they each resist the "Shakespeare system" and encourage significant reform to what is often called "Bardolatry," a belief structure that offers seemingly deific status to this writer and his works. *Where We Belong*, in contrast, situates respect for Shakespeare's canon within a broader context of neglect for other voices, including Native American writers. The conversation around such topics is likely to continue for some time. Sayet's contribution to these discussions is timely and nuanced. She provides a valuable perspective on a subject of important contemporary significance, as many confront a range of issues involved with social justice and related topics.

Debra Ann Byrd's *Becoming Othello: A Black Girl's Journey* is a similarly powerful and impressive piece of theatre that details this theatre-maker's life journey through poverty and abuse before

---

https://www.washingtonpost.com/investigations/2024/06/14/catholic-church-indian-boarding-schools/.

[13] "Interrogating the Shakespeare System."
[14] "Interrogating the Shakespeare System."
[15] "The Shakespeare Problem," 37.

recognizing and achieving her place as an artist. The play continues to be performed widely in the US and abroad. It was also streamed by the Elm Shakespeare Company during the pandemic. To my knowledge, it does not yet appear in print, but I am hopeful that will be forthcoming. A recording of the performance can currently be rented on Vimeo.[16] Byrd's play was directed by Tina Packer, Founding Artistic Director of Shakespeare & Company in Lenox, Massachusetts. Byrd and Packer constitute a formidable creative team, whose combined skills fashion a personal and professional story that points attention at a number of societal issues that both differ from and complement those addressed by Sayet. Byrd's life journey has been complex and often painful and she tells her story unflinchingly. Through music and adept storytelling, *Becoming Othello* demonstrates, one hopes, what Annie Brewster and Rachel Zimmerman designate as "The Healing Power of Storytelling," in their book of that name, which is subtitled "Using Personal Narrative to Navigate Illness, Trauma, and Loss." Byrd's story is often difficult to hear, but the craft demonstrated through this carefully conceived performance illustrates the power that Brewster and Zimmerman locate in such endeavors. In their words:

> It is true that the events of our lives play an important role in shaping who we are, but it turns out that *how we make sense of those events* matters even more. We make meaning out of what happens to us, reflected in the stories we tell about ourselves, and in doing so, we choose how we move forward. While life is full of events we do not expect and cannot control, we play an active role in determining how the story unfolds by the moments we choose to remember and how we remember them.[17]

---

[16] https://vimeo.com/ondemand/becomingothello.
[17] Annie Brewster and Rachel Zimmerman, *The Healing Power of Storytelling: Using Personal Narrative to Navigate Illnesses, Trauma and Loss.* (Berkeley, CA: North Atlantic Books), 2022. 43. Brewster is a medical doctor contending with serious medical issues herself. Zimmerman is a journalist, who recently published a narrative focused on her husband's suicide and its effect on herself and their

Byrd's ability to recount harsh truths, interspersed with haunting musical segments, and recreations of herself at various ages, makes this a memorable immersion into a life filled with upheaval that leads to the initially unimaginable enactment of Byrd's artistic goal of playing *Othello* on stage.

Her ambition cannot be achieved, however, before she confronts and challenges impediments resembling the "Shakespeare System" described by Sayet. While the financially unstable single mother of a severely medically fragile child, Byrd bravely determines to gain a college degree as a way to forge a career in the theatre. She tells of seeing an advertisement on public transportation for the drama program at Marymount Manhattan College shortly before the start of the academic year.[18] Applying substantial determination and talent, she successfully enrolls in the program and wins multiple accolades over the next several years for her dramatic achievement. As she approaches graduation and prepares to begin her career formally, however, all too common presumptions about classical theatre threaten to undermine her progress. Although she speaks highly of the faculty she encountered during most of her degree program, the people she met as she approached graduation refused to admit that she could make a career in classical theatre, even though she had won great acclaim for her portrayal of Lady Bracknell in a student production of *The Importance of Being Earnest*. She was told she should turn her professional attention to August Wilson and other black playwrights, something she had already undertaken for several years. It was made clear to her that choosing Shakespearean and other classical drama would be career suicide. At the point of abandoning her major in theatre, however, Byrd went in tears to her cherished Shakespeare professor, who successfully encouraged her not to let

---

children. Rachel Zimmerman 2024. *Us, After: A Memoir of Love and Suicide*. Santa Fe Writer's Project.

[18] Marymount Manhattan recently announced its merger with Northeastern University. https://www.nytimes.com/2024/05/29/nyregion/marymount-manhattan-northeastern-merger.html.

others dislodge her from her goals. Much success as an actor, director, and artistic director has ensued, although her administrative prowess briefly also threatened to undo her goal of playing Othello, since her Harlem Shakespeare Board of Directors temporarily lost sight of her equally impressive acting ability. Fortunately for all of us, Debra Ann Byrd had the talent and drive to dismiss the challenges consistently offered by the "Shakespeare system" and other sceptics. While I have never seen Byrd's *Othello* in toto, the reimagining of this character that she brings into *Becoming Othello* suggests that this production was remarkable. Working with Lisa Wolpe, the writer and performer of *Shakespeare and The Alchemy of Gender*, who is renowned, in part, for playing male roles in Shakespeare, Byrd had the opportunity to create a important Shakespearean production that her background could easily have made impossible.

Related challenges also appear in *American Moor* and *Den-Marked*. Cobb, for example, as "the Actor" in *American Moor* describes his realization as a young man that he "*was* an actor, you know, like somebody is gay, I am an actor."[19] He further explains:

> I had learned that I wanted to act Shakespeare. Now, no one had taught me that, but I had learned it…I had been presumptuous enough to buy into the preposterous notion that I, my intellect, my instrument, and my crazy-ass African American emotionality would serve the words well, *and* be served well by them.[20]

This play is permeated, however, by racialized and other conflicting expectations while "the Actor" is auditioning in front of a young, white director for the role of Othello. Thus, the Actor struggles to stay cool while receiving instructions about how to interpret and perform this part. Accordingly, he responds:

> Put on your poker face, Brotha…You think that he needs me to do…"a number" for these guys [Venetian Senators] in order to

---

[19] Keith Hamilton Cobb. 2020. *American Moor*. London: Methuen Drama 6–7.

[20] *American Moor* 7.

> succeed in getting from them the thing that *you* think he wants…And so, in order to get this gig, ah no wait! In order to succeed in getting from *you* the thing *you* think *I* want, you're implying that *I* need to do "a number" for *you*…It's brilliant. You're sittin' there, lookin' expectantly at me, thinkin' we're speaking the same language. But you wouldn't understand a single word of all that's *not* being said…if I said it…if Othello said it.[21]

"The Actor" further explains that:

> in matters of race, throughout my American life, whenever some white person, well-meaning or otherwise, has asked me to "be open" they have invariably meant, "See it my way." And in this instance, in *this* play, that is unacceptable. You think I want to be *your* Othello.[22]

This interior conversation then dissolves as the Actor remembers that he is there in order to audition for a job, not to engage in spoken or silent dialogue with the Director.

The play ends with no indication of whether "the Actor" has auditioned successfully. In a series of appendices, Cobb offers material that has been excised from the published play. In one, he recounts his experience as an NYU undergraduate, studying Shakespeare for English majors: "Of my professor, proud, elder, learned, and white I thought the world."[23] Despite Cobb's deep engagement with the course material, however, he notes that he received a "C," which he interprets as a grade denoting "Mind your place."[24] Once again, it seems, "the Shakespeare System" highlights deeper cultural divides.

Cobb elaborates on his perspective upon such issues in a 2023 keynote address he offered at the Blackfriars Conference at the American Shakespeare Center. Entitled 'Untitling Shakespeare: A

---

[21] *American Moor*, 19.
[22] *American Moor*, 19.
[23] *American Moor*, 46.
[24] *American Moor*, 47.

Brief Biography of an Evolving Practice." He talks about his current "Untitled *Othello*" project (working in collaboration with Sacred Heart University and other institutions of higher education) as well as the cultural conditions in education and theatre that spurred his creation of this endeavor.[25] This undertaking seeks to dismantle conventional responses to Shakespeare's drama on stage, but also in classrooms:

> For students and educators, either of Shakespeare or of Theater, or Philosophy, or History, or of Poli-Sci, or any discipline that begins with the science of people, accompanying the actor on the deep dive into Shakespeare's anthropological abyss uncovers insights into the intricacies of the human condition that *underlie* the texts. These insights cannot be excavated by curriculum confined by the semester system. For all engaged—and *all* with open minds and hearts and minds interested in what it means to be human are invited—it inspires by instilling a sense of intrinsic inclusion in a process of social change. Not a product. It is a process.[26]

Similar to Sayet and others, Cobb finds great meaning in Shakespeare, coupled by significant toxicity, a perspective that warrants quoting at length:

> [Understanding the complexity of the plays] requires that you interrogate, mercilessly but with care, the human hearts of the human beings endeavoring to portray the human beings that people the play. The depth of exploration required to expose and understand the ancient toxicity inherent in the play—in all of Shakespeare as emblematic of white, Euro-centric excellence—and put it to any transcendent theatrical or educational use is an arduous and often uncomfortable exercise in introspection.[27]

---

[25] https://untitledothello.com/.

[26] Keith Hamilton Cobb. 2024. "Untitling Shakespeare: A Brief Biography of an Evolving Practice." Unpublished Keynote Address, Blackfriars Conference, American Shakespeare Center, Staunton, Virginia.

[27] "Untitling Shakespeare," 6.

Cobb speaks persuasively about his love for Shakespeare's language[28] as well as his contempt for "the American capitalist ecosystem including theater, education, and Him."[29] In both his play and his keynote, Cobb presents arguments that support the distinctive kinds of autobiographical Shakespeares included in this essay. He finds intensive value, as noted, in the personal and collective introspection that engaging with Shakespeare can support, while simultaneously rejecting innumerable aspects of the "Shakespeare System" in both theatres and educational establishments.

Conrad Murray's *DenMarked* details the experiences of an Anglo-Indian musical and theatre creator and performer rather than an American, but the parallels between Murray's story and those presented earlier are striking, as the abstract accompanying Bloomsbury's online description of the text indicates:

> This solo performance is an autobiographical story that weaves hip hop with Shakespeare's *Hamlet*. It narrates Conrad's account of growing up in a violent family in South London, as an abused mixed-race child in the social care system, trying to make his way in the world and seek reconciliation with his absent father. [*DenMarked*] uses hip hop to highlight the inequalities produced by the UK's class system, and weaves lyricism, musicality and dialogue to offer authentic accounts of inner-city life written by working- class Londoners.[30]

Like the other writers considered here, Murray combines his interactions with Shakespeare with his autobiographical account of a difficult journey through life. Similar to Cobb, he situates his play within a job interview, as he endeavors to be hired as a drama teacher, something he fears he will fail to achieve:

---

[28] "Untitling Shakespeare," 10.

[29] "Untitling Shakespeare," 8. Cobb may be deliberately circumspect here about whether "Him" means Shakespeare or a deity in this context.

[30] https://www.bloomsbury.com/uk/beats-and-elements-a-hip-hop-theatre-trilogy-9781350270602/.

I start convincing myself that I'm not going to get this job because of this coffee cup. They are going to know exactly what kind of lowlife I am all because of this cardboard coffee cup. I don't deserve to be here. I'm a piece of shit. How can the agency not have seen this? How? Why am I here? What the fuck am I thinking? I can't talk properly, I have bad handwriting, I haven't read *King Lear*, and I call myself a drama teacher?!

What have you, my good friends, deserved at the hands of fortune that she sends you to prison hither?
Is that *Hamlet* or *Lear*? Fuck, I can't remember!
Prison my lord... We think not so.
To me it is a prison.

And what happens when they see this cardboard cup of coffee? I'm going to look like a fraud! They are going to know that I am a blagger! I grew up on a council estate and I'm here in this school.[31]

Scenes involving this job interview bookend *DenMarked*. In between, he details the journey he took to reach this employment possibility, encountering Shakespeare at a key moment in his development, similar to several of the writers considered here:

Miss Nelson pulled out a copy of Hamlet and said, "This is for you. Keep it." I hated Shakespeare, but it was kind of cool to have something brand new. And mine. The one book I owned. Confusing, long and dark. The Prince of Denmark. Who thought the world was a prison, as long as he saw it that way. She told me to take my drama and acting serious, and to read it. The whole thing. The whole thing?!This was shocking to me. My teacher seemed to really give a shit. She didn't have to. She said I was special. That I had potential. Still, I didn't get any GCSEs, but it did, for a time, calm me down. Even if she was lying.[32]

---

[31] Conrad Murray. *DenMarked*. In Katie Beswick and Conrad Murray, eds. *Beats and Elements: A Hip Hop Theatre Trilogy*. London Methuen Drama. 2022. 48.

[32] *DenMarked*, 69–70.

There is not time here to repeat all of Murray's story, other than to note that he wryly reports that he successfully passed his job interview and was hired as a drama teacher:

> Then after she asked me some questions, she asked me if I wanted the job. Just like that. Just asked me. She didn't even mention the coffee cup. And I almost left an uncomfortable silence thinking about all the reasons why it was totally implausible for me to get the job before saying, "Yes. Yes, I think this is right for me." She told me I should fit right in and she'd see me on Monday. Then she asked if I had read King Lear. FUCK! Then she said, "No, no…it's Hamlet they are doing." And I said, "Yeah, Yeah I know that one."[33]

When it comes to Shakespeare, each of the authors discussed above "know that one" and many others. They also know how complicated classical drama can be in contemporary racialized, socioeconomic realms of education and employment. We are fortunate to have their stories as we continue to examine how and whether to integrate so-called "great works of literature" into our curricula and how best to meet the varied needs of forthcoming generations. These writers raise a series of important questions to be tackled by theatres, schools, and others valuing the role of arts in our society.

Sammie Byron. Stephan Wolfert, and Lisa Wolpe also created and present plays that interweave important facets of their own lives with Shakespearean drama, but the "systems" they challenge largely exist outside of that canon. Byron, a mixed-race man, who was released about ten years ago after several decades in prison, recounts a story involving sexual and child abuse that helped create feelings of worthlessness and anger: "Fearing I'd be reduced to the worthless nothing I felt I was, my rage, which I'd buried deep inside me for my abusive childhood exploded like a volcano."[34] Throughout *Othello's Tribunal*, Byron talks about his life trajectory that led into

---

[33] *DenMarked*, 77.
[34] *Othello's Tribunal*. 2024 version. Co-written by Sammie Byron and Curt L. Tofteland. Unpublished mss. 16.

incarceration, then back into society, over thirty years later. While doing so, he presents scenes from *Othello*, a play he performed inside with Shakespeare Behind Bars (SBB). While SBB presented numerous Shakespearean dramas while Byron was incarcerated, this narrative offers a story redolent with the most serious crime Byron committed. As he acknowledges during his performance, the murder of his victim (Carol) through strangulation mirrors Othello's fatal attack on Desdemona. This close parallel to his own experience led another SBB member to take the role of Desdemona, even though he had vowed repeatedly never to play a woman on stage. His regard and concern for Sammie, however, caused him to undertake this part so that he could support his friend who would be confronted with a recreation of his worst moments:

> Such was the case with SBB circle member, Mike, who was white and grew up privileged.
>
> Mike had vowed never to play a female's role in an SBB production.
>
> Yet Mike was quick to volunteer to play Desdemona when he heard I had chosen to play Othello.
>
> Mike chose to go beyond his fears to help me because he knew the struggle it would be for me since the role resembled the murder I committed.
>
> Mike's choice was perhaps the first time he thought beyond his own self.
>
> Also, playing Desdemona allowed Mike to experience what it was like being a victim.
>
> As a result, I saw Mike develop more compassion and empathy for his own victims.

Playing Othello was pivotal in teaching me that empathy can be learned by holding the mirror up to my face and to see the dreams that might come before I "shuffle off this mortal coil."[35]

Like the other writers of autobiographical Shakespeare's, Byron finds continual interaction between the elements contributing to his life pathway and the composition and performance of Shakespearean drama.

Byron continues to revise his narrative as he performs this play in numerous settings, including one at the Atlanta Shakespeare Tavern where he also engaged in conversation with actor Harry Lennix, who played Aaron in Julie Taymor's film *Titus*.[36] He confronts the actions responsible for his lengthy incarceration without hesitation, just as he details the abuse he encountered at home, school, and in his wider environment. In his words, these verbal, physical, and sexual assaults contributed to the repressed anger that exploded in ways that brought him into the criminal justice system:

> I strangled Carol because I was too afraid of facing myself, taking responsibility, and just telling the whole truth.
> This time, I couldn't blame my troubles on a gun or the bad people I hung out with.
> This time the problem…the problem…I was the problem.[37]

In *Othello's Tribunal*, he focuses on the lessons available to him through this play about an African man at odds with many of those he encounters in an alien environment. Byron often remarks, however, that Shakespeare serves as a touchstone throughout his life and that all the plays he encountered through his years with SBB continually provide avenues through which he can interpret his life journeys and determine ongoing appropriate modes of behavior. He makes no broad claims for Shakespeare in this regard, but he

---

[35] *Othello's Tribunal*. 19.
[36] https://www.imdb.com/title/tt0120866/.
[37] *Othello's Tribunal*, 16.

consistently finds Shakespeare's characters, words, and situations valuable as he navigates the "process" of his life: "Even today, I consider myself to be a work-in-progress."[38] Unlike the writers discussed above, Byron finds Shakespearean drama and its environs more revelatory than oppressive, but he is not currently working predominantly in theater and responds, understandably, from his own life experience. Shakespeare Behind Bars has been a key factor in his ability to redirect his life and these canonical texts remain central in his onward journey. He incorporates Shakespeare regularly into his professional involvement with at-risk youth in sessions he offers at Goodwill Industries in Kentucky. He has played numerous Shakespearean roles and can readily recite those lines. In his case, Shakespeare offers ongoing guidance rather than the conflicted welcome some others perceive.

Stephan Wolfert also credits Shakespeare with key contributions to the positive reconfiguration of his life that disruptively included battles with post-traumatic stress and alcohol abuse after his tenure in the military. *Cry Havoc* details his challenging upbringing which included an abusive home environment, a debilitating injury, and continual obstacles impeding his ability to craft his life according to his personal vision. In Wolfert's case, he engaged with Shakespeare unexpectedly, while AWOL from the army. Finding himself at a production of *Richard III* while on the run, he tells the story of his recognition of the protagonist's experiences with the military, physical differences, and toxic family relationships. While he presumably had earlier encountered Shakespeare during his formal education, *Cry Havoc* suggests that this production of *Richard III* changed Wolfert's life, however counterintuitive it may be to have this conniving ruler serve as a conduit for personal reformation. Wolfert subsequently completed a graduate degree in drama and

---

[38] *Othello's Tribunal*, 2. Byron and his wife Barbara regularly visit my classroom at Emory. We also often talk via phone or Zoom. This information comes from our conversations taking place over many years.

established DE-CRUIT,[39] a program designed to help veterans address the range of problems they encounter after leaving the military. Shakespeare looms large in the workshops DE-CRUIT offers, but Wolfert remains open to people bringing other writers into the healing exercises they undertake through this organization.[40] He has identified a number of Shakespearean monologues with particular resonance for military veterans, but endeavors to find the most appropriate texts for the challenges each individual faces.

Cry Havoc presents Wolfert's path toward recovery from similar challenges confronting the veterans he now serves.[41] Throughout the play, he includes Shakespearean passages, often associated with veteran characters in their respective dramas, to present the painful issues and events that he now seeks to overcome. The performance offers compelling insights into the bumpy passage often experienced by veterans like Wolfert, providing language from the similar, though far distant, struggles of Shakespeare's fictive, early modern veterans. *Cry Havoc* is a gripping piece of theater that invites its audiences to reconsider the trauma experienced by some characters, such as Richard III, while expanding their understanding of the toll created by military service for those without the skills needed to achieve successful "de-cruitment." In Wolfert's practice, Shakespeare remains central in such undertakings. Not surprisingly, he has also created a play focused on Richard III's trauma called *The Head of Richard*, designed to further awareness of the mental health crises often facing veterans:

> *The Head of Richard* is a two-actor, 50-minute adaptation using only Shakespeare's text from Richard III. This retelling of

---

[39] https://www.decruit.org/. Wolfert maintains that the military needs to put as much thought and energy into "de-cruitment" as it does in "recruitment," and titles his veterans program accordingly.

[40] I discuss this program at length in Sheila T. Cavanagh, *Multisensory Shakespeare and Specialized Communities*. 2024. London: Arden Shakespeare. 107–33.

[41] One of the reasons Wolfert no longer performs this play is that he recently undertook graduate work in Social Work at Simmons College, completing his degree in 2024.

Richard III from a military veteran's perspective looks at the havoc created by emotional deformity from chronic abuse and humiliation. On the eve of battle, Richard faces his mother, his life of violence, his shame, and himself.

The Head of Richard was created by Army veteran, Stephan Wolfert, awarded the 2019 Max Gabriel Award from National Alliance for Mental Illness (NAMI) presented in grateful recognition of his outstanding ability to artistically and powerfully share his story in order to broaden the understanding of PTSD and other mental health challenges faced by our veterans.[42]

Wolfert's recent completion of an MSW is indicative of his ongoing commitment to furthering the reach of this work for the benefit of as many veterans as possible.

Like Wolfert and Byron, Lisa Wolpe presents her autobiographical drama, *Shakespeare and the Alchemy of Gender,* by using Shakespeare's plays to help contextualize her life journey rather than displaying the kind of conflicted relationship with the playwright and his legacy demonstrated by Byrd, Cobb, and Murray. Wolpe offers her jarring narrative by providing striking details of her personal history, then turning to Shakespeare as a means to reflect upon her experiences and facilitate future integration of the lessons drawn these events into her ongoing endeavors. Losing each of her parents suddenly, under tragic circumstances, Wolpe had been in recovery mode from the various upheavals of her family life when she was approached unexpectedly by a previously unknown relative. This encounter led to additional unanticipated information, including her Jewish heritage and her father's fraught experiences during the holocaust. Wolpe's previous life challenges had already encouraged her to experiment with diverse gender presentations. These new revelations offered a host of information about her family and their history that furthered the gap between her self-knowledge and the significant parts of her background that had previously been hidden. Shakespearean theatre offers multiple conduits for the kind of

---

[42] https://www.decruit.org/the-head-of-richard-program/.

introspection espoused by Cobb and others. Having lost her father at a young age, Wolpe had no prior access to information about his Jewish identity, his militancy against the Germans in World War Two, or many other key aspects of his life. She also knew nothing about the many family members whose stories emerged once a host of relatives came into the lives of herself and her brother.

Before and after creating this drama, Wolpe has performed many Shakespearean roles designed for characters designated as male. She has also directed many productions and has taken on leadership roles for efforts supporting gender parity and broad inclusion for organizations such as the Shakespeare Theatre Association. *Alchemy of Gender*, therefore, integrates many aspects of her professional life in addition to her personal narrative into a compelling theatrical exploration of various modes of identity. Offered within a Shakespearean framework, this play offers further evidence of the power and versatility available through this kind of narrative when it is done well.

Wolpe imbeds Shakespeare throughout her play. Many of these excerpts are well-known, but she also identifies lines and speeches so her audience need not get distracted trying to ascertain which play she is incorporating into her story at any given time. She notes that she was first drawn to Shakespeare during her teens:

> I fell in love with Shakespeare when I was just 19 years old. It was a time when I needed that bigger conversation, in order to express what my own family was not willing to discuss. Lots of tragedies. I look to Shakespeare to explore the theme.[43]

This play demonstrates her adept ability to draw from Shakespeare as she explores her traumatic personal history in search of a modern mode of alchemy that can transmute sorrowful facets of the past into a better future. In Wolpe's terms, "Alchemy is not merely a metaphor, there is a practical magic involved. It's the transformation of something heavy into something lighter. Fear into Compassion.

---

[43] *Alchemy of Gender*, unpublished mss. 2.

Anger into Love."[44] As she relates the complex details of her often-tumultuous life story, she draws connections between the issues and personalities presented and a range of Shakespearean writings, from the Sonnets to *Hamlet*, *Romeo and Juliet*, *Henry V*, and others. As she recounts her past, present, and hopes for the future, it remains clear that Shakespeare plays a critical role in the personal transformation she undergoes. This alchemy works through more than gender, just as Shakespeare's plays offer perspectives on innumerable topics. Congruent with the other works discussed above, Wolpe's autobiographical drama keeps Shakespeare at the heart of her narrative. She does not fight against the "Shakespeare system," however. There are many other structures detailed here that demand such a response, but Shakespeare contributes towards her ability to reconceptualize multiple facets of her life and her background.

Each of these plays incorporate Shakespeare into their narratives with skill and finesse, even though some of them praise this early modern drama while others resist the cultural attitudes that have accompanied Shakespeare's lengthy era of literary dominance. The Shakespearean canon clearly carries cultural as well as dramatic and poetic resonance that has been used for the benefit—and detriment—of many. Some of the plays referenced—*Othello* and *Merchant of Venice*, for instance—carry lengthy histories of contentious interpretation or performances. Others bear marks of outdated perspectives, such as language choices or characterizations of those who do not fit what are considered to be normative white male standards. Most, if not all, of them have been used in the cultural practices descried by those indicting the "Shakespeare System" or the "Shakespeare Problem." The deification of Shakespeare's writing includes all of his works, even though various plays and sonnets go in and out of fashion. The specifics imbuing the lives of this group of writers and performers imbricating Shakespearean lines, plots, and themes into their dramatic narratives vary, but they have each experienced traumas and challenges that reverberate through many of the issues

---

[44] *Alchemy of Gender*, 3.

confronting modern societies. Their stories, accordingly, raise topical questions. Claims of universality associated with Shakespearean drama have rightly been questioned repeatedly. None of these plays seek to reinstate such generalizations. Nevertheless, they investigate ways that Shakespeare operates in our contemporary moment and typically confirm his achievements, while simultaneously leaving room for other voices to gain their own spaces. Dawn Monique Williams, one of the conversants in "The Shakespeare Problem" maintains that such interrogations can only make Shakespeare stronger:

> Shakespeare will have more meaning, more value, if we stop treating him like the supreme. We should let him live among all the other authors of equal, sometimes greater significance. In hip hop, you're the baddest when you're capable of beating the baddest. So if Shakespeare is a baddie he can hold his own. Shakespeare will not be tarnished.[45]

All of these dramas reinforce the notion that Shakespeare will not be tarnished or otherwise harmed by continual study, performance, and interrogation. This canon is resilient and offers contemporary society many additional lessons, particularly in realms of social justice, even if some of them may be challenging to encounter.

---

[45] "The Shakespeare Problem," 47.

Shakespeare and Political History: Bastards, Nepo-babies, Oligarchs

Gary Taylor

"I like nepotism."
—Donald Trump[1]

Why should we continue to read or perform Shakespeare's history plays? Do his long-ago dramatizations of politics have anything to teach us now?

Thanks to the British Empire, which created the Anglophone empire and laid the foundations for the American empire, Shakespeare has retrospectively become a global literary icon. But unlike the two other most canonical pre-modern English poets, Chaucer and Milton, there is no evidence that Shakespeare ever left the island where he was born, or even left the part of that island called England. Indeed, the English scholar Jonathan Bate, contrasting Shakespeare with other poets and playwrights who focused on the cosmopolitan court or the global port city of London, celebrated "the Bard" for his unique attention to "deep England," its rural counties and provincial small towns.[2] Shakespeare was more insular than most of his literary contemporaries: Samuel Daniel, John Donne, Ben Jonson, Thomas Lodge, Christopher Marlowe, Philip Sidney, Edmund Spenser, and Thomas Watson all traveled abroad, but Shakespeare did not.[3] In his

---

[1] Interview on "Larry King Live" on CNN (October 9, 2006): https://www.youtube.com/watch?v=NZ_KPrK0r28&lc=UgieDQ0SYTb2lHgCoAEC

[2] Bate, *Soul of the Age: A Biography of the Mind of William Shakespeare* (New York: Random House, 2009), 19–29.

[3] For the travels of these writers, see their entries in The Oxford Dictionary of National Biography, online; for Shakespeare's insularity, see Gary Taylor,

own lifetime Shakespeare wrote only for the few inhabitants of England, about four million people. That's comparable to the current population of Los Angeles. Shakespeare's England was less than 40% of today's population of Georgia.

Because Shakespeare wrote for English audiences, it is entirely understandable that, during the Second World War, the quintessentially conservative academic Englishman E. W. M. Tillyard wrote an influential patriotic book celebrating *Shakespeare's History Plays*.[4] Tillyard himself was born in Cambridge, was an undergraduate at Jesus College Cambridge, fought in the British army in the First World War and received for his military service the Order of the British Empire, and then spent his entire academic career in the English School at the University of Cambridge.[5] Very few Shakespeare scholars in 2024 would agree with Tillyard's interpretations, but at least it makes obvious sense for an Englishman of Tillyard's time and type to have read, taught, and written about the ten Shakespeare plays about English monarchs that were posthumously collected and printed together in London in 1623 in *Mr. William Shakespeare's Comedies, Histories, and Tragedies*.

I got my own graduate degree in Cambridge and my first academic job in Oxford. I still visit England regularly, I admire many things about the country's culture, and I have recently learned from genealogical records that during Shakespeare's lifetime most of my direct ancestors were living in England. But despite being a Shakespeare scholar and a descendant of English immigrants, I feel no political or emotional allegiance to any of the kings or queens of England, or to the institutions of English governance, medieval or modern. I am not a British subject, and in fact I find the whole idea of being a "subject" rather than a "citizen" offensive. I have spent

---

"Transeditions: Shakespeare's two French English lessons," *Letras*, v. 33, n. 67 (2024), 3–36.

[4] Tillyard, *The Elizabethan World Picture* (London: Chatto and Windus, 1943), and *Shakespeare's History Plays* (London: Chatto and Windus, 1944).

[5] "E. M. W. Tillyard," *Wikipedia, The Free Encyclopedia*, accessed 8 April 2024.

much of my own career editing and writing about Shakespeare's history plays, but I have no nostalgia for "ye olde" Tudor England or the "sun-never-sets-on-the" British Empire. I don't believe in monarchy or Christian Nationalism or Brexit. In fact, the theatrical representation of an English king that best reflects my own attitude toward the monarchy is the cameo of King George the Third in the American hip hop musical *Hamilton*. Dressed in full royal regalia, the King responds to the American war of independence (what the English monarchy still refers to as "the American rebellion") by singing "You'll be back," Lin-Manuel Miranda's lilting parodic adaptation of a break-up song, sung by an abusive boyfriend: "I will…kill your friends and family to remind you of my love." Miranda's *Hamilton* is, of course, a history play, written in verse, dramatizing a period of American history as chaotic as the medieval English Wars of the Roses. It does not pretend to accurately represent the bodies of the historical people it dramatizes. George III is the only role played by a white male actor.

My initial questions address the past's relationship to the present, or rather to the presents, plural, the many presences of the many linguistic and geographical communities that coinhabit our shared planet in our shared time. But before we can address those transglobal and transhistorical political questions, we have to ask another preliminary question: how do we know, and how did Shakespeare know, what happened in the past?

That's a big question, so it's best to begin with a manageably small and unambiguous example, which I can personally confirm. My birth certificate is an official government document which has been preserved in an official government archive controlled by the State of Kansas. In the unlikely event that any future scholar wants to write my biography, they would naturally consult that historical document for reliable information about the beginning of my life, just as biographers of Shakespeare consult the list of baptisms in the official parish records of Holy Trinity Church in Stratford-upon-Avon. In my case, the birth certificate records correctly my name, gender, date of birth, the town and hospital where I was born, and my mother's legal name. It also records the legal name of my father, my mother's husband, Donald Lee Taylor.

Thirty-five years after the birth recorded in that document, my mother tearfully confessed to me that Donald Lee Taylor did not in fact contribute to my conception. The biological role of male parent was performed by John Devere Brownell, who like Donald Lee Taylor was stationed in the fall of 1952 at Forbes Air Force base, just outside Topeka, Kansas. Brownell was married, but he promised to divorce his wife and marry my mother, and in fact he did file for divorce. But when my mother discovered she was pregnant, Brownell had already left Kansas to fight in the Korean War. He would not be back until after her pregnancy came to term, and in December 1952 she had no way of knowing that, as it actually turned out, (a) "Johnny" would survive his posting to Korea, and (b) his divorce would be finalized, and (c) he would still want to marry her when he returned to the United States. So, in the immediate crisis precipitated by her discovery that she was pregnant, she turned to Donald Lee Taylor, who legally married her and consummated their union shortly before he too flew off to Korea. Fifteen years later, the internet helped me track down John Devere Brownell, a retired re-married Air Force veteran, and I called him up. Over the phone, he immediately confirmed my mother's story, and soon afterwards I flew to Utah and spent two days with him. He was happy to meet me, and I was happy to meet him. In contrast, my two step-siblings and stepmother were cold and suspicious; I was an unexpected, unwanted, and unpredictable intruder. Not surprisingly, the obituary prepared by his family fourteen years later did not mention my shameful existence, and I was not informed of his death or invited to his funeral.[6]

What is the lesson of this story for anyone interested in Shakespeare, history, and politics? First lesson: official records are not

---

[6] "Master Sergeant John D. Brownell, 1929–2018," https://www.legacy.com/us/obituaries/saltlaketribune/name/john-brownell-obituary?id=1641950.

always reliable. The posthumous edition of Shakespeare's *Comedies, Histories, and Tragedies* is one of our best witnesses to Shakespeare's plays, but it includes some scenes and passages written by other playwrights, and omits some material Shakespeare indisputably wrote.[7] In the Introduction to an excellent recent book on Shakespeare's portrayal of "how leaders rise, rule, and fall," Eliot A. Cohen recounts that he was inspired to write it by a production of *Henry VIII*, followed by a graduate seminar in which he and his students analyzed an emotionally powerful scene in that play, Cardinal Wolsey's response to his fall from power; Cohen returns to the same scene in the eighth chapter and in the afterword.[8] But since the middle of the nineteenth century scholars have demonstrated, in dozens of independent peer-reviewed empirical tests, that the material Cohen quotes was written by Shakespeare's young collaborator, John Fletcher. Cohen has decades of experience in government service and in strategic and international studies; what he says about the accuracy and wisdom of the scene is compelling. But the passages he quotes cannot tell us anything about *Shakespeare's* political thought, because Shakespeare did not write them.

Second lesson: some witnesses are more reliable than others. My birth certificate is absolutely accurate about all the other facts of my birth. But in 1953 there was no DNA testing for paternity. The identification of the baby's father was at the time entirely a matter of hearsay, and the only reliable witness to the father's identity was the mother. But mothers, like publishers, sometimes lie about paternity. Half of Shakespeare's plays were published in his lifetime, and the texts of those plays sometimes differ significantly from the 1623 edition; for centuries the legitimacy of some or all of those earlier texts

---

[7] For overviews of attribution issues see Gary Taylor and Rory Loughnane, "The Canon and Chronology of Shakespeare's Works," in *The New Oxford Shakespeare: Authorship Companion*, ed. Gabriel Egan and Gary Taylor (Oxford: Oxford University Press, 2017), 417–602, and Will Sharpe, *Shakespeare and Collaborative Writing* (Oxford: Oxford University Press, 2023).

[8] Cohen, *The Hollow Crown: Shakespeare on How Leaders Rise, Rule, and Fall* (New York: Basic Books, 2023), 2–4, 182, 253.

has been denigrated by critics and scholars. But since the 1980s editors and textual scholars have increasingly concluded that the early printings represent Shakespeare's own first versions of the plays. For instance, the canonical texts of *Hamlet* call the senior minister in the Danish court "Polonius". But in the first edition that time-serving, arrogant character is given the unique, fictitious name "Corambis" (Latin for "double heart"), which can hardly be a misreading or mishearing of "Polonius." However, the long-serving senior minister in the court of Elizabeth I was William Cecil, Lord Burghley, whose self-congratulatory personal motto was "Cor Unus" (Latin for "one heart"), referring to his constancy and loyalty in defending the Queen and the Protestant faith. This apparent satirical allusion to Burghley would have been particularly obvious and relevant if the first edition represents Shakespeare's earlier version of *Hamlet*, written and performed in the late 1580s or early 1590s.[9] The familiar "Polonius" might be the result of political censorship, or Shakespeare might have changed the name when revising the play after Burghley's death in 1598. Either way, the variant names tell us something about the politics of Shakespeare's time and of Shakespeare himself.

Third lesson: conspiracy theories are sometimes correct. My mother and grandmother successfully conspired to conceal the real identity of my biological father for more than three decades. A conspiracy by a woman (my grandmother) and her only child (my mother), more deeply committed to each other than to anyone else, is more likely than, for instance, an alleged conspiracy by thousands of people scattered across the entire United States to conceal who really won the 2020 Presidential election, or a conspiracy theory that all Shakespeare's plays and poems were actually written by the Earl of Oxford.[10]

---

[9] For the first edition as an early version of the play, see Terri Bourus, *Young Shakespeare's Young Hamlet: Print, Piracy, and Performance* (London: Palgrave, 2014), and Bourus, ed., *Shakespeare and the First Hamlet* (Oxford and New York: Berghahn, 2022). For "Corambis" see Bourus, *Young Hamlet*, 169–70.

[10] For the relationship between conspiracy theories and authorship controversies (including the anti-Stratfordian claims about Shakespeare) see Gary

Fourth lesson: politics affects the historical record, and politics affects how we interpret the historical record. In 1953 in Kansas, abortion was illegal. In 1953 in Kansas, unwed mothers and their children were punished socially and economically—and often physically. My mother's father was a big, hard-drinking man with a violent temper, who had physically beaten his wife and his daughter (something else I only learned after his death). If my young unmarried mother had become visibly pregnant while still living at home, it is highly likely that he would have beaten her, possibly causing a miscarriage or even her death, and he would certainly have kicked her out of the house. My mother's decision to lie about my paternity was good for her and good for me. Although Don Taylor was not my biological progenitor, he was economically, socially and psychologically my dad and the dad of my four siblings. The act of impregnation takes minutes; the act of fathering takes decades. The lie was also probably good for Don Taylor, who was a socially awkward nerd all his life, not as good-looking or charismatic as my mother or as John Devere Brownell; my mom's lie gave Taylor a smart, beautiful, hardworking wife and, eventually, five healthy children and ten grandchildren.

Shakespeare would not have been surprised by any of this. He may have had an illegitimate daughter himself.[11] More certainly, he repeatedly dramatized the unreliability of documents, the politics of historical memory, and the uncertainties of paternity. Real bastards, or accusations that a woman's husband was not the actual father of her children, play a major role in seven of his plays: *Titus Andronicus* (1589), *Richard III* (1592), *King John* (1596), *Much Ado about Nothing* (1598), *Troilus and Cressida* (1602), *King Lear* (1605), and *The*

Taylor, "The Politics of Attribution," in *The Oxford Handbook of Shakespeare and Early Modern Authorship*, ed. Rory Loughnane and Will Sharpe (Oxford: Oxford University Press, 2025), chapter 52.

[11] For the story that he had a third daughter (not recorded in Stratford-upon-Avon records), see Gary Taylor, "Shakespeare's Illegitimate Daughter," *Memoria di Shakespeare*, 2 (2015), 177–94.

Winter's Tale (1609).¹²

Bastardy mattered to Shakespeare and his audiences, because England's entire political system, and most of its economic system, depended on inheritance. The current king of England, Wales, Scotland, and Northern Ireland, King Charles III, is king only because his mother was queen; his mother, Elizabeth II, was herself queen only because her father was king and had no sons; Elizabeth II's father, George VI, was himself king only because his father (George V, Elizabeth II's grandfather) had been king, and his older brother (the pro-Nazi Edward VIII, Elizabeth II's uncle) had unexpectedly abdicated. In contrast, in my case, both my legal father and my biological father were young airmen; they would eventually retire as master sergeants, but they were never officers, and my legitimacy or illegitimacy made no difference to the wider world, militarily or financially or politically. And they certainly did nothing to enable or advance my academic career.

But bastardy made a difference, militarily and financially and politically, in Shakespeare's England, because Shakespeare's England was, like Putin's Russia, an autocracy supported by oligarchs. However, unlike Putin's Russia, in Shakespeare's England both the autocracy and the oligarchy, the ruling family and the aristocratic families, depended on the mythology of patrilineal inheritance. Political "legitimacy" was directly related to "legitimacy" of birth. Even today, one-third of one percent of the British population owns 66% of the country, and those 160,000 families who own two-thirds of Great Britain descend from William the Bastard, Duke of Normandy (better-known now as "William the Conqueror") and his army, who invaded and brutally colonized Anglo-Saxon England in 1066.¹³ William's first act, as King William, was to declare that every acre of

---

¹² Although *Titus Andronicus* was written in collaboration with George Peele, the bastardy material is all Shakespeare's.

¹³ Kevin M. Cahill, *Who Owns Britain?* (Edinburgh: Canongate Books, 2001); Guy Shrubsole, *Who Owns England: How We Lost Our Land and How to Take it Back* (Glasgow: William Collins, 2019).

land in the country belonged to the King. Five hundred years after the Norman Conquest, Queen Elizabeth I ruled England for the first thirty-nine years of Shakespeare's life because she was the only surviving descendant of Henry VIII; King James VI of Scotland ruled England (as King James I) for the rest of Shakespeare's life because Elizabeth I had no children, and consequently after Elizabeth's death her kingdom was inherited by the grandson of Henry VIII's sister (Margaret Tudor, Elizabeth I's aunt). Both Elizabeth and James are lineal descendants of Henry VII, who ascends to the throne at the end of Shakespeare's *Richard III*.[14] Shakespeare's English history plays are dominated by descendants of a foreign invader: nepo-babies competing with other nepo-babies.

In his book on leadership Cohen answers the question "Why Shakespeare?" by noting (correctly) that Shakespeare focuses on "court politics," and then claiming (correctly) that "courts run almost all human organizations": "there is someone at the top who rules or reigns...and surrounding all these are the artful behaviors of those who wish access, privilege, or power...Courts can be found in executive suites of any business, university, or charity."[15] But this argument, used in other recent attempts to make Shakespeare relevant to management and leadership studies, overlooks the centrality of nepo-babies to the political systems that Shakespeare dramatizes. In the histories that Shakespeare represents, political legitimacy depends on inheritance, and therefore the most intense struggles for power occur *within and between families*. Richard III orders the murders of his brother, his nephews, and his brothers-in-law; Henry IV orders the murder of his cousin Richard II; King Claudius personally

---

[14] Shakespeare never wrote a play about William the Conqueror, but a contemporary anecdote claims that he jokingly identified with him: "William the Conqueror" [William Shakespeare] "came before Richard the third" [Richard Burbage, who played the role]. And the rousing speech at the end of *King John* (spoken by the Bastard) clearly alludes to him: "This England never did nor never shall / Lie at the proud foot of a conqueror, / But when it first did help to wound itself."

[15] Cohen, *Hollow Crown*, 22–3.

poisons his brother, and then commissions others to murder his nephew Hamlet; Goneril poisons her sister Regan, and Edgar kills his half-brother Edmond in hand-to-hand combat; to revenge the battlefield death of his father, Young Clifford murders the Duke of York's schoolboy son, and then joins others to murder the Duke of York himself; Macbeth attempts to murder Banquo's son (unsuccessfully), and then (successfully) has Macduff's wife and all Macduff's children slaughtered. In the Roman triumvirate's purge of opponents, Lepidus consents to the murder of his brother, and Antony does the same with his sister's son: "Look, with a spot I damn him."[16] Titus Andronicus kills two of his own children, and all three sons of Tamora. Statistically few of us murder our own family members; but we all understand how intense, and often intensely hostile, those relationships can be.

Likewise, because familial systems of governance depend on biological reproduction, Shakespeare's dramatizations of politics also often dramatize sexual politics. Although Shakespeare presents it as though it were a wooing scene in one of his famous rom-coms, the political marriage of the English King Henry V to the French Princess Catherine Valois is negotiated as part of a peace treaty, and their union quickly produces a male heir for the conquering king. Shortly after (or possibly before) Hamlet's father is murdered by his brother, Hamlet's mother hurries to his "incestuous sheets" (2.157). The Emperor Saturninus sexually prefers the Goth Queen Tamora over a political marriage to the daughter of Titus Andronicus; but Tamora prefers the sexual attentions of the Moor Aaron, and gives birth to a baby that is clearly his, not her husband's. Lear's married older daughters, Goneril and Regan, both compete for the sexual attentions of the Bastard Edmund. Antony's two successive political marriages, to Fulvia and then Octavia, cannot stop him from committing

---

[16] *Julius Caesar* 4.1.5–6. Quotations of Shakespeare cite the text and line-numbering of *The New Oxford Shakespeare: Complete Works: Modern Critical Edition*, ed. Terri Bourus, Gabriel Egan, John Jowett, and Gary Taylor (Oxford: Oxford University Press, 2016).

adultery with Cleopatra, with disastrous political and military consequences. Cymbeline annuls the marriage of his only child, his daughter Innogen, to Posthumus because he wants to marry her instead to Cloten, the only son of his new Queen; Cloten, insulted by Innogen's preference for Posthumus, plans to kill Posthumus, rape Innogen, and drag her back to court as his forced bride. In Shakespeare's first English history plays, the collaborative *Henry VI* trilogy, the ahistorical emphasis on a romantic and probably sexual relationship between Queen Margaret and the Earl of Somerset raises suspicions about the legitimacy of Henry VI's only son. Shakespeare's last English history play, *Henry the Eighth*, makes it pretty obvious that the King is committing adultery with Anne Boleyn before he divorces Queen Katherine, and the play culminates in a scene (written by John Fletcher) celebrating the baptism of the child who would become Queen Elizabeth I. But probably everyone in the original audiences in 1613 knew that Henry VIII would, soon after that baptismal celebration, execute his brilliant wife Anne Boleyn, falsely claiming that she had committed adultery and that the baby Elizabeth was a bastard—just as Leontes, in *The Winter's Tale*, falsely accuses his wife Hermione of adultery, claiming that her new-born daughter Perdita is a bastard.

These struggles between and within families, these assertions of sexual independence, define politics in terms that readers and spectators can immediately understand without any knowledge of English or European history, and without any attention to boring subjects like fiscal policy, legislation, taxation, international trade, economic theory, military strategy, institutional and legal norms, political platforms or national governance. This leads Shakespeare apologists to claim that his plays capture "universal" aspects of politics. But his vivid, intelligible, emotionally powerful representations of politics are less sophisticated than Aristotle's, Machiavelli's, or Nietzsche's. *King John* does not mention Magna Carta. In *Henry V*, Llewellyn assures us that "the King most worthily hath caused every soldier to cut his prisoner's throat" (4.7.6–8)—though "one of the oldest and most persistent" laws of war "is that those who have surrendered...should be spared."[17] Henry's order violated the laws of war in his time as well as our own. Unlike Timothy Snyder, Shakespeare does not teach us how to protect ourselves from fascism and autocracy: "Defend institutions," respect "the immensity of factuality," be guided by "Professional ethics...precisely when we are told that the situation is exceptional."[18] Shakespeare's plays take for granted the autocratic nepo-baby monarchs, aristocrats, and royal courts of his own time and place, which licensed, rewarded, and routinely censored performances of his plays—and punished playwrights, like Christopher Marlowe and Thomas Middleton, who challenged or critiqued that system.

Coincidentally or not, Shakespeare's most important collaborator, the actor Richard Burbage, was also a nepo-baby, as are many modern actors; Richard's father was an actor, and (unlike William Shakespeare) Richard Burbage came from a family of theatrical producers and theatre-owners. What we now call "Shakespeare's Globe" should more properly be called "Burbage's Globe," because the Burbage family was the primary investor and owner, and Burbage played the leading role in many plays not written by Shakespeare. But "Shakespeare's Globe" is much better for marketing, because Shakespeare's brand has become much better known than Burbage's. The relationship between theatrical nepo-babies and political nepo-babies is not entirely coincidental; as many critics have noticed, Shakespeare consistently associates political leaders with actors. In the first performances of Shakespeare's plays, many of his nepo-baby kings were played by nepo-baby Burbage.

"Now, gods, stand up for bastards!" says the Bastard Edmund in *King Lear* (2.22). Few people nowadays think of *King Lear* as one of Shakespeare's history plays. It has long been routinely taught in courses on Shakespeare's tragedies and discussed in books and

---

[17] Margaret MacMillan, *War: How Conflict Shaped Us* (New York: Random House, 2020), 148.

[18] Snyder, *On Tyranny: Twenty Lessons from the Twentieth Century* (London: Bodley Head, 2017), 22, 74, 41.

articles about Shakespeare's tragedies; it is included, along with *Hamlet* and *Othello* and *Macbeth*, as one of the "big four" tragedies in the most famous and influential book of literary criticism ever written about Shakespeare.[19] Like Tillyard at Cambridge, A. C. Bradley (Oxford Professor of Poetry) was a quintessentially English critic, born in the nineteenth century but not famous until the twentieth.[20] But unlike Tillyard, Bradley paid little attention to Shakespeare's history plays. Why did Bradley think of *King Lear* as a tragedy? Because it was included among the tragedies in the most important of all documents about Shakespeare, the 1623 Folio edition of *Mr. William Shakespeare's Comedies, Histories, & Tragedies.*

But Shakespeare had been dead for more than seven years before those pages were printed. The first document containing a text of *King Lear* was published in 1608, with the title "HIS True Chronicle Historie of the life and death of King LEAR and his three Daughters." That title makes sense: King Lear was included among the other monarchs in Raphael Holinshed's *Chronicles*, the primary source of all Shakespeare's plays about English history.

Of the thirty-six plays in the Folio, only six had been described in print as "Histories" in Shakespeare's lifetime. But, out of the ten plays included in the Folio's section of "Histories," only a single play, *Henry the Fourth* [Part One], includes the word "history" in its printed title both in Shakespeare's lifetime and in the Folio Catalogue. By contrast, three of the ten Folio histories were identified, on title-pages published in his lifetime, as tragedies: the 1595 edition of *The True Tragedy of Richard Duke of York* (a.k.a. *Henry VI Part Three*), the 1597 edition of *The Tragedy of King Richard the Second*, and the 1597 edition of *The Tragedy of King Richard the Third*. In 1598, Francis Meres famously declared that Shakespeare was "the best" of

---

[19] Bradley, *Shakespearean Tragedy: Lectures on Hamlet, Othello, King Lear, Macbeth* (London: Macmillan, 1904).

[20] G. K. Hunter, "Bradley, Andrew Cecil," *The Oxford Dictionary of National Bibliography* (2004, rev. 2022), https://doi.org/10.1093/ref:odnb/32027 (accessed 15 April 2024).

English writers for both comedy and tragedy, and as proof of that claim listed six examples of each: his six tragedies were *Richard II, Richard III, Henry the Fourth, King John, Titus Andronicus,* and *Romeo and Juliet*.[21] Four of those six "tragedies" were categorized by the 1623 Folio as histories.

The Folio treatment of the Histories has for centuries been regarded as self-evident and transparent, but it is in fact chaotic. The Histories section of the Folio is the most clearly and conspicuously organized section of the book: all ten titles name English kings, all ten are presented in the chronological order of those kings' reigns, and five are identified as a "part" of a numbered chronological sequence within a single king's reign. But the surviving evidence from Shakespeare's lifetime bears no discernible relationship to this tidy Folio box. The majority of early title-pages that specify "History" belong to plays that are not identified as histories in the Folio; none of the Folio histories exactly reproduce the title in an early edition of the same play; plays earlier called tragedies become Folio histories, and vice versa. We also know that the final play in the Histories section had a completely different title when it was first performed: what centuries of readers since 1623 have read as "The Famous History of Henry the Eighth" was originally, in 1613, called "All is True."[22] That title can be read as a guarantee of authenticity ("everything in this play is an accurate account of the past") or a shrug of indeterminacy ("this play represents all the conflicting and incompatible opinions about these past events and people"). Everything is true = nothing is true. The clarity and tidiness of the "Histories" section of the Folio is, like much of the history that Americans believe, artificial and unreliable.[23]

---

[21] Francis Meres, *Palladis Tamia* (London, 1598), 282.

[22] For photographs of all four original documents that name the play "All Is True" (variously spelled), see Gary Taylor, "General Introduction," in Stanley Wells, Gary Taylor, et al., *William Shakespeare: A Textual Companion* (Oxford: Clarendon, 1987), 1–68 (esp. 29–30).

[23] For more on the confusions and unreliability of the Folio's editorial treatment of the "Histories," see Amy Lidster, *Publishing the History Play in the*

How do we know what happened in the past? Rather than basing our understanding of Shakespeare, or of literary and theatrical and cultural history, on a single posthumous document, it makes more sense to rely, whenever we can, on surviving documents from the years when Shakespeare was alive. And if we want to understand Shakespeare's relationship to history and politics, then it is best to begin with books that we know, with absolute certainty, that Shakespeare read. For the history of England and Scotland, he indisputably relied most heavily on the 1587 edition of Holinshed's *Chronicles*; he dramatized material from Holinshed not only in the ten plays that the 1623 Folio includes among the History plays, but also for *King Lear*, *Cymbeline*, and *Macbeth*. For his plays dramatizing the medieval Wars of the Roses, he sometimes supplemented Holinshed with an earlier chronicle by Edward Hall. For classical history, his most important source was Thomas North's English translation of Plutarch's parallel lives of the Greeks and Romans, which provided him with material for *Julius Caesar*, *Antony and Cleopatra*, *Coriolanus*, and *Timon of Athens*. For *Hamlet* and the history of medieval Denmark Shakespeare depended on a French translation of a Latin history by Saxo Grammaticus. For *Troilus and Cressida*, he depended primarily on sixteenth-century editions of Chaucer, rather than Homer. Most editors now agree that Shakespeare collaborated with George Peele on *Titus Andronicus*; Peele, unlike Shakespeare, had a university degree, and was almost certainly responsible for reading the now-obscure medieval sources for the play's account of the chaotic late Roman empire. The classical writer that Shakespeare knew best, and who influenced him most, throughout his career, was not Plato, Aristotle, Thucydides, or Tacitus; it was Ovid—who, of course, was not a historian, political scientist, or philosopher. But in the pursuit of sex, and a universe where metamorphosis is much more pervasive than stability, Ovid—infamously exiled by the Emperor

---

Time of Shakespeare (Oxford: Oxford University Press, 2022), and Gary Taylor, "Shakespeare's Christian Nationalist History Plays," *Shakespeare Review* 60.4 (2024): 785-809. DOI: 10.17009/shakes.2024.60.4.007.

Augustus—was Shakespeare's favorite guide.

Shakespeare was interested in both history and politics, but he was not himself a documentary historian. He freely adapted his historical and literary sources to create a better story, a more stageable story, and to reflect his own understanding of politics. And Shakespeare's understanding of history includes the political production of fake documents. In *King Lear* the Bastard Edmund discredits his brother, whom he mockingly calls "the legitimate Edgar" (2.16), by forging an incriminating fake document, allegedly in Edgar's own handwriting. Their gullible father, Gloucester, believes the fake, and as a result his legitimate son has to go into hiding, roaming the countryside as a homeless, penniless, mentally-ill vagrant, Poor Tom. Likewise, in *Richard III*, Shakespeare gives an entire scene (3.6; sc. 14) to a nameless "Scrivener," somebody who makes a living preparing official documents. The Scrivener enters, alone, carrying a document, and addresses the audience directly:

> Here is the indictment of the good Lord Hastings,
> Which in a fair hand fairly is engrossed,
> That it may be today read o'er in Paul's.
> And mark how well the sequel hangs together:
> Eleven hours I have spent to write it over,
> For yesternight by Catesby was it sent me;
> The precedent was full as long a-doing;
> And yet within these five hours Hastings lived,
> Untainted, unexamined, free, at liberty.
> Here's a good world the while! Who is so gross
> That cannot see this palpable device?
> Yet who's so bold that says he sees it not?

Speaking through this invented Scrivener, Shakespeare recognizes, and asks his audiences to recognize, that official documents may be politically-motivated fictions, excuses for the illegitimate violence of an autocratic regime that routinely manufactures "Fake News." Shakespeare, his family, and his Stratford-upon-Avon neighbors had experienced the use of fabricated official documents to justify the quick execution of an innocent but politically inconvenient man: Edward Arden, head of "the most ancient and worthy family" in Warwickshire, was beheaded in 1583 on the basis of false evidence manufactured by Lord Burghley (whose motto Shakespeare mocked in the first edition of *Hamlet*). The falsehood of the charges and the retrospective forgery of documents to support it were demonstrated in a series of lawsuits brought by Robert Arden from 1586 onward; the lawsuits discredited the charges by strategically using boxes of documents that the falsely accused Edward Arden had hidden away from his accusers; modern specialist historians have painstakingly recovered the truth by scouring uncatalogued and barely legible legal records scattered in multiple public and private collections.[24] Archival research, like investigative journalism, is "hard work that requires time and money"; although contemporary demagogues want to defund such research, and President Trump early in his second term fired the director of the National Archives, "the individual who investigates is also the citizen who builds.[25]

Richard III, through his campaign manager and press secretary Buckingham, tries unsuccessfully to persuade a London crowd that the recently deceased king, Edward IV, was a bastard. Why? Because, if Edward IV was a bastard, his two living sons have no legitimate claim to the throne, and they can be displaced by their uncle, Edward IV's only surviving brother, Richard Duke of Gloucester (soon to become Richard III), whose biological legitimacy is not in doubt. The crowd is not convinced. So Buckingham and Richard plan a public performance of Richard's piety: Richard exits, the Mayor and citizens enter, and Buckingham tells them that Richard

---

[24] Glyn Parry and Cathryn Enis, *Shakespeare before Shakespeare: Stratford-upon-Avon, Warwickshire, and the Elizabethan State* (Oxford: Oxford University Press, 2020), 174–86. They do not link the Arden execution and Burghley scandal to "Corambis."

[25] Snyder, *Tyranny*, 76, 73.

> Is within, with two right reverend fathers,
> Divinely bent to meditation,
> And in no worldly suits would he be moved
> To draw him from his holy exercise. (3.7.60–6)

Soon after, Richard appears "above," on the balcony, "between two bishops," pretending to be annoyed by the political interruption of his piety, and Buckingham vehemently, lengthily, and publicly urges him to accept the crown, not for any selfish reason but for the public welfare of his country. This was, until recently, the most brilliant satire on the supposedly "Christian" motivations of greedy, egotistical English-speaking politicians. It is surpassed only by recent efforts to sell patriotic Bibles to finance the political campaign of the most irreligious Presidential candidate in American history. Like Donald Trump, Richard III tries to persuade his gullible audience that his narcisstic pursuit of supreme power is "for their sake," not his own. Shakespeare's English audience was less gullible than Trump's American one.

Shakespeare's successful petition for a coat of arms, which made him a "gentleman," depended on the claim that his great-great-grandfather had been rewarded "for his faitheful" (or "valiant") "service" to "King Henry 7," the first Tudor king.[26] So Shakespeare might have been proud that his own family had helped Henry VII to depose Richard III. But how did Shakespeare get away with his transparent critique of the cynical autocracy of the English political system? It is worth remembering that playwrighting was, in the late sixteenth and early seventeenth century, a dangerous business. Christopher Marlowe was murdered, probably by a government assassin; Thomas Kyd was certainly tortured by Elizabeth's government, so brutally that he could no longer hold a pen and write, and died not long after. Ben Jonson was imprisoned on two occasions,

---

[26] S. Schoenbaum, *William Shakespeare: A Compact Documentary Life* (Oxford: Oxford University Press, 1977), 228; Heather Wolfe, "Grant of arms to John Shakespeare," drafts 1 and 2 (October 20, 1596), *Shakespeare Documented*, Folger Shakespeare Library, https://shakespearedocumented.folger.edu.

once in the reign of Elizabeth I and once in the reign of James I. Thomas Middleton was imprisoned by James I, and apparently released along with many other prisoners by James's successor, Charles I; but a condition of his release seems to have been that he could no longer write plays, and he died soon after in extreme poverty. Shakespeare's acting company was interrogated in connection with a performance of *Richard II*, requested by conspirators associated with the Essex Rebellion. But Shakespeare, so far as we know, was never imprisoned, and certainly not executed for political resistance.

All plays, including Shakespeare's, including *Richard III*, had to be licensed, for performance, by a censor appointed by the Crown, and in the case of *Richard III* that censor was a bishop. How could Shakespeare write, perform, and publish such a satire of an English king and two bishops? He got away with it because the Tudor dynasty's legitimacy, including the political legitimacy of Elizabeth I and her Protestant regime, depended on its representation of Richard III as an unparalleled tyrant and a violent, illegitimate king, supported by corrupt Roman Catholic bishops. For similar reasons, in 1606 Shakespeare could dramatize the tyranny of *Macbeth* because Elizabeth's successor, James VI of Scotland (a.k.a. James I of England), was directly descended from one of Macbeth's victims, Banquo. Shakespeare dramatically exposed the structural tyranny of the traditional English Christian nationalist nepocracy by dramatizing kings who were allegedly illegitimate exceptions to the rules and norms of Christian royal governance.

As an antidote to tyranny, Timothy Snyder urges us to "Read books"; he recommends writers like Ray Bradbury, George Orwell, Hannah Arendt, Albert Camus, Vaclav Havel—and Shakespeare's *Hamlet*.[27] Shakespeare himself certainly read books, including Tudor histories that included Thomas More's damning critique of the tyranny of Richard III (written to please More's patron, Henry VIII). As readers, we can compare Shakespeare's play to Shakespeare's source, in which, at the decisive Battle of Bosworth, the Earl of

---

[27] Snyder, *Tyranny*, 59, 61, 63, 117.

Richmond "gladly proferred to encounter with [King Richard] body to body and man to man."[28] Shakespeare turns this into a simple stage direction: *"Enter Richard and Richmond. They fight. Richard is slain"* (5.6.13.1). Immediately afterward, Richmond is crowned king, becoming Henry VII. But if we read, instead, the archaeological evidence published after the discovery and identification of Richard's skeleton in Leicester in 2012, we discover that Richard sustained multiple injuries to his head by different weapons from different directions (suggesting multiple assailants), and was probably killed by "one massive fatal blow to the base of the skull," which "could have been caused by a weapon such as a halberd."[29] The halberd was "a curious mix of spear, axe and hook. Wielded in battle, the halberd's point rammed into knights and their horses, the axe could smash heads in and the hooks dragged riders from their horses to make finishing them off on the ground easier."[30] Aristocrats in armor, like William the Conqueror and his army of Norman knights on horseback in 1066, or the Earl of Richmond in 1585, did not use halberds; common infantry soldiers did. The late medieval halberd helped destroy the battlefield dominance of armored knights. Shakespeare's play, in contrast, perpetuates the myth of aristocratic chivalry.

But what makes Shakespeare's political analysis unique is the fact that—unlike Aristotle, Plato, Sir Thomas More, Machiavelli, or any of the modern writers that Snyder recommends—he gives us political stories in two different media: books-to-be-read-in-private and performances-to-be-witnessed-in-public. We can read in Shakespeare's sources that some of the people who heard the public proclamation of "the indictment of the good Lord Hastings" (3.6.1) suspected that it had been written in advance of his arrest.[31] But Shakespeare brings on to the stage, alone, to speak directly and

---

[28] Geoffrey Bullough, ed., *Narrative and Dramatic Sources of Shakespeare, Volume III* (London: Routledge and Kegan Paul, 1960), 297.

[29] University of Leicester, "Richard III," https://le.ac.uk/richard-iii/identification/osteology/injuries/how-richard-iii-died, accessed July 31, 2024.

[30] MacMillan, *War*, 71.

[31] Bullough, *Sources*, 268.

confidentially to the audience, the professional Scrivener who had actually written out the official public text of the indictment. The conventions of the theatrical soliloquy give his speech, by an eyewitness holding the document, an authority that Shakespeare's source text could not match. Historical hearsay becomes, in performance, an incontroverible witness holding incontrovertible documentary evidence that a tyrant has subverted the legal system to remove (and murder) an opponent.

As Francis Bacon observed, "the minds of men in company are more open to affections and impressions than when alone."[32] In live performance, the charisma of the actor playing Richard III, like the charisma of Hitler or Trump in front of their rallies, is hypnotic. To understand the power of a great political performer, you need to see and feel that present-tense performance, to be surrounded by an audience who are being swept away by it. But to analyze the operation of political power, including tyranny, you need to read the historical document, the printed play, the transcripts of Trump's telephone calls and speeches, the financial records, the testimony of first-hand witnesses. Shakespeare, uniquely among political theorists in the English language, gives us both the hot present-tense charisma and the cold past-tense documents. The singularly charismatic Coriolanus fears a political situation "when two authorities are up, neither supreme" (3.1.110–11). But, of course, the American constitution is designed to prevent autocracy by a separation of authorities between the legislative, executive, and judicial branches of government. To understand Shakespeare's understanding of politics, we need both the charismatic authority of performances and the documentary authority of texts.

---

[32] Bacon, *The Proficience and Advancement of Learning, Divine and Human* (London, 1605), 2:13.

Index

Aeneas, 170n29
Aeschylus, 34
Africa, 70, 178, 274; Northern, 70, 167
Agincourt, Battle of, 12-13
Alamanni, Luigi, 94, 96
Alcibiades, 130n5
Alexander the Great, 68, 140
Alighieri, Dante, 155
All's Well That Ends Well, 32
Alps, 117
Alulis, Joseph, 183n1, 185, 189, 209
Alvis, John, 164, 164n17, 165-6, 171n30, 190
Amanpour, Christiane, 156n3
American Shakespeare Center, 260n1, 264, 268
Amyot, Jacques, 133
Anderson, Ethan, 26-7
Andronicus family, 176n40, 177n43, 179; Lucius, 162-3, 163n14, 165n17, 167, 169n26, 171, 171n33, 171n34, 172-3, 176, 179, 179n46; Marcus, 163, 172, 173n36, 174, 174n38, 175n40, 176n41, 177n43, 178n45; Martius, 162, 171, 171n32; Mutius, 162, 174; Publius, 177n42; Quintus, 162, 171, 171n32; Titus, 4, 161-2, 162n12, 163, 163n13, 165n17, 166, 167-8, 168n24, 169n26, 171, 171n31, 172-4, 175n39, 176-7, 177n42, 177n43, 178, 178n45, 290
Antigone, 45
Antium, 135, 141, 146-8, 148n55, 151-2
Antony and Cleopatra, 67, 131, 131n7, 143, 159, 164, 166, 295; Antony, 17-19, 28, 88-90, 92, 165, 248, 290; Cleopatra, 165, 291; Fulvia, 290; Octavia, 290
Apennines, 117
Apollo, 41-2, 45-6, 50, 79, 196
Aquinas, Saint Thomas, 193n27, 203, 203n48, 207
Arden, Edward, 297, 297n24
Arden, Robert, 297
Arendt, Hannah, 217-18, 218n12, 238, 299
Aristotle, 61, 139, 139n37-8, 140n38, 141, 158-9, 182, 185-7, 187n16, 189, 189n18, 191, 195, 195n30, 196, 198, 201n41, 201n44, 291, 295, 300; *Nicomachean Ethics*, 139n37; *Politics*, 139, 139n38, 158
Arizona Center for Medieval and Renaissance Studies, 261
Arizona State University, 261
Arnold, Matthew, 1
Ashby, Patrick, 146n51, 150
As You Like It, 12; Rosalind, 160; Senior, Duke, 12
Athens (Greece), 67, 243

Atlanta Shakespeare Tavern, 274
Augustine, Saint, 69, 206n56, 217-18, 218n12, 229, 232
Augustus, Emperor, 295-6
Austen, Jane, 10-11
Australia, 239
Avignon (France), 106; Avignon Papacy, 106

Bacon, Francis, 301
Baldwin, James, 10
Barton, Anne, 132n12, 139
Bate, Sir Jonathan, 163n15, 164n17, 177n43, 240, 281
Battenhouse, Roy, 121
Berger, John, 35
Berkeley, George, 36
Bertrum, Edward, 11
the Bible, 298; New Testament, 88
Birmingham (England), 8, 24-5
Blackfriars Conference, 268
Bliss, Lee, 130n6, 132n12
Blits, Jan H., 71n6, 91n24, 131n9, 148
Bloom, Allan, 71n6, 137, 137n30, 153n69, 184, 193, 205, 239, 239n4, 241-2, 242n10, 251, 258-9
Bloom, Harold, 5, 239
Boethius, Anicius Manlius Severinus, 58, 60
Boleyn, Anne, 291
Bonaparte, Napoleon, 68
Booth, John Wilkes, 28
Bosworth, Battle of, 299
Bradbury, Ray, 299
Bradley, A. C., 213n1, 293
Bradley, Arthur, 216-17
Brewster, Annie, 265, 265n17

Brooks, Cleanth, 219, 221-2
Brown, Arthur, 230n27
Brownell, John Devere, 284, 287
Brussels, Belgium, 157
Brutus, 17-19, 28, 75, 87, 90-91, 136-7, 140n38, 145, 190
Buondelmonti, Zanobi, 94, 96
Burbage, Richard, 289n14, 292
Burghley, Lord, <u>See</u> Cecil, William
Burke, Edmund, 53, 53n6
Burns, Timothy, 254
Bush, Douglas, 224
Byrd, Debra Ann, 260, 264-7, 277
Byron, Sammie, 260, 260n1, 272-5, 275n38, 277

Cambridge (England), 282
Cambridge, University of, 282, 293
Camillus, Marcus Furius, 45n10, 78-9, 80n18, 82
Camus, Albert, 299
Cantor, Paul, 71n6, 72n6, 75n12, 129n1, 131, 131n7, 133n13, 134n20, 138n34, 143, 143n44, 146n52, 242, 244, 249-50, 258, 259
Capell, Edward, 53, 53n7
Capitolinus, Marcus Manlius, 78, 81-2
Carlisle Indian School, 263
Carter, Jimmy, 158n5
Catholicism, 82, 86, 97-8, 106, 114-15, 121n94, 169, 189, 203, 203n48, 207, 209, 225, 252, 263n12, 299; Jesuism, 183; Roman Catholicism, 263n12, 299; Second Council of Lyon, 203n48

Index

Cavell, Stanley, 226
Cecil, William, 286, 297, 297n24
Charles I of England, 219, 237, 299
Charles III of the United Kingdom, 288
Chase, Samuel, 149n60
Chateaubriand, François-René de, 155
Chaucer, Geoffrey, 58, 227, 232, 281, 295
China, 157
Christensen, Phillip, 23
Christianity, 2-3, 5, 45, 47, 49, 61, 67, 69-71, 71n6, 72-3, 82, 85-90, 97, 99, 113-14, 119, 120-22, 143, 165, 169, 169n27, 170n28, 177, 177n43, 189, 193-4, 195n30, 203, 206, 206n55, 209, 217, 227, 239-40, 242-7, 249, 251, 251n24, 252-8, 283, 298, 299 ;Christian nationalism, 283, 299; Christ, Jesus, 58, 69-72, 83-91, 91n24, 92, 207; Mary, mother of Jesus, 119, 206; Moses, 98, 236n34. See also the Bible; Catholicism; Protestantism
Cicero, Marcus Tullius (Tully), 19, 36, 166, 172-3
Cobb, Keith Hamilton, 260, 260n1, 267-70, 270n29, 277-8
Cohen, Eliot A., 285, 289
Colbrand the Giant, 118, 121
Collmer, Francis, 33n64
Cooper, James Fenimore, 23
Condell, Henry, 21-3
Coriolanus, 12, 16-17, 19, 67, 69, 74, 129, 131, 131n7, 134-8, 143, 153, 153n69, 159, 164-5, 165n20, 166, 167n23, 172n34, 295; Adrian, 133n13, 142; Agrippa, Menenius, 132n12, 134, 137, 140-42, 145, 145n50, 151-3; Aufidius, Tullus, 73, 140, 140n39, 141, 146, 146n52, 147-148, 151-4; Brutus, Junius, 75, 136-7, 140n38, 145; Cominius, 138-9, 139n37, 140, 146-7; Coriolanus, Caius Marcius, 2-3, 16-17, 67, 69-70, 71n6, 72-4, 74n11, 75-6, 76n14, 77, 77n15, 78-80, 80n18, 81-2, 90-91, 91n23, 92, 129-30, 130n4-6, 132, 132n10, 132n12, 133, 133n14, 134-7, 137n30, 137n33, 138, 138n35, 139, 139n37, 140, 140n39-40, 141, 141n42, 142, 142n43, 143, 143n44, 144, 144n48, 145-6, 146n51-2, 147, 147n53-4, 148, 148n55, 149-50, 150n62, 151-3, 153n69, 154, 160, 167, 171n34, 172n34, 301; Corioles, 69, 73-4, 133, 137n33, 141, 147, 151-2; Nicanor, 133n13, 142, 165n20; Superbus, Lucius Tarquinius (Tarquin), 72; Valeria, 142, 148-9, 149n57-58, 150, 150n62, 151; Velutus, Lucius Sicinius, 75, 135-7, 139-40, 147; Virgilia, 141n42, 142, 145, 149n58, 150, 151n66; Volumnia, 76, 140, 142, 145, 145n50, 146, 149, 149n58, 150-1, 169n25
Crawford, Henry, 11
Crispus, Gaius Sallustius, 43

305

Crito of Alopece, 36
Cymbeline, 65, 295; Cloten, 291; Cymbeline, 291; Innogen, 291; Posthumus, 65, 291; Queen, 291

Damocles, 15
Daniel, Samuel, 281
Davenant, William, 29
Dawson, George, 24-5
Denmark, 7, 58, 160, 271, 286, 295
Donn, Alphonse, 30n56
Donne, John, 225, 281

Early Modernism, 12, 20, 54, 61, 65, 217, 237, 276, 279
Edward III of England, 191. See also *Richard II*
Edward IV of England, 297
Edward VI of England, 219
Edward VIII of the United Kingdom, 288
Egypt, 67
Elizabeth I of England, 4, 53n5, 58, 131, 183, 186, 219, 241, 243n13, 286, 289, 291, 298-9
Elizabeth II of the United Kingdom, 288
Elm Shakespeare Company, 265
Emory University, 275n38
England, 8, 11, 23-4, 51, 52n2, 53n5, 53n7, 57-60, 67, 92, 95-6, 113-21, 121n94, 122-8, 131, 133, 135-7, 157, 184, 184n5, 185, 189-91, 193-4, 198, 200-202, 206, 209-10, 212, 218-19, 223, 225-7, 229-30, 241, 251-2, 261, 263, 268, 281-3, 288-9, 289n14, 290-91, 293-5, 298-9, 301; Anglo-Indian, 270; Anglo-Irish, 53n6; Anglo-Norman, 12; Anglophone empire, 281; Anglo-Saxon, 230, 288; English Civil War, 60, 184, 212; House of Commons, 197; *Magna Carta*, 198, 291; Parliament, 135, 183, 197-8, 207n58, 210, 230; Wars of the Roses, 283, 295
Enloe, Sarah, 264
Erasmus, Desiderius, 189, 198-9, 209
Esperanto language, 155, 157-8
Essex Rebellion, 4, 183, 299
Europe, 69-70, 155-7, 178, 248, 252, 269, 291; Indo-European, 230

Fagin-Davis, Lisa, 9
Faulconbridge family, 116-18, 120; Lady, 117-18; Philip, 3, 94-6, 99, 113-21, 121n94, 122-8, 289n14; Robert, 115-18, 120; Sir Robert, 115-16, 118
Felice, Lady, 121
Fielding, Henry, 52, 52n2
Figgis, John, 202n46, 203n47, 204n53
First Folio, 21-4, 241n8, 293-4, 294n23, 295
Flaccus, Quintus Horatius, 53, 53n5, 166
Fletcher, John, 285, 291
Folger Shakespeare Theatre, 261
Ford Theatre, 28
Ford's Theatre National Historic Site, 30n56
Forker, Charles R., 208

Index

Foucault, Michael, 217
France, 10, 106, 114-15, 121, 123, 125, 133, 155, 156n3, 157, 167, 167n22, 200, 290, 295
Fraser, Elizabeth, 137
Frederick of Wales, Henry, 219, 230, 237
Freud, Sigmund, 215-16, 221n15
Frey, Charles, 23

Gage, Jill, 23
Garber, Marjorie, 240n5, 243n13, 248n19, 249, 250n24, 251n24
Gaulle, Charles de, 155-6, 156n3, 157
Gauls, 79, 81, 167
George III of Great Britain and Ireland, 283
George V of the United Kingdom, 288
George VI of the United Kingdom, 288
Germany, 101, 103, 106, 116, 155, 157, 240, 278
Globe Theatre, 261-2, 292
God, 34, 58, 62, 84, 104, 107, 120, 123, 158, 169n26, 170n28, 193, 193n27, 194, 194n28, 202, 202n46, 207-8, 211, 250, 256
Goethe, Johann Wolfgang von, 155
Goths, 161-2, 162n12, 163, 163n13-14, 164-7, 169n26, 171, 171n34, 172, 172n35, 177n43, 178-9, 290
Gracchus, Gaius Sempronius, 82, 172
Gracchus, Tiberius Sempronius, 82

Grammaticus, Saxo, 295
Great Britain, 4, 52n3, 59n22, 67, 157, 169n27, 240-41, 281-3, 288; Brexit, 283; British Crown, 204n53, 299; British Empire, 281-3; Restoration of the British Monarchy, 52, 240
Greece, 45, 54, 73, 133, 150, 157n4, 165, 167, 172, 295
Greenblatt, Stephen, 136
Guy of Warwick, 120-21

Hackett, James H., 27
Hall, Edward, 295
Hamilton, Alexander, 149, 149n60; *Federalist Papers*, 149n60
Hamlet, 8, 11-13, 16, 18, 20, 27, 229, 230n27, 270-72, 279, 286, 293, 295, 297, 299; Claudius of Denmark, 7, 13, 27, 289; Corambis, 286, 286n9, 297n24; Elsinore, 21; Gertrude, 18; Hamlet of Denmark, 7, 10, 13, 21, 27, 32, 160, 271, 290; Horatio, 21; Marcellus, 7, 13; Ophelia, 8, 32; Polonius, 11, 286
Harlem Shakespeare Festival, 260, 267
Harrington, James, 242n10
Haughey, Joseph, 23
Havel, Vaclav, 299
Hector, 73
Hecuba, 21, 73, 176
Heidegger, Martin, 5, 237-8
Helen of Troy, 40
Heminges, John, 21-3
Hemmingsen, Niels, 58-9

Henry IV of England, 184-5, 191-2, 197, 205, 209, 289. See also *Henry IV, Part 1*; *Richard II*
Henry IV, Part 1, 293-4; Falstaff, Sir John, 160. See also Henry IV of England
Henry V of England, 13-14, 160, 186n12, 290-92. See also *Henry V*
Henry V, 12-13, 15, 35, 279, 291; Llewellyn, Captain, 291; Hal, 13; Williams, Michael, 13-14. See also Henry V of England
Henry VI of England, 189, 291. See also *Henry VI* trilogy
Henry VI trilogy, 291, 293; Clifford, Young Lord, 290; *Henry VI Part 3*, 293; Margaret of Anjou, 291; Somerset, Earl of, 291; York, Duke of, 290. See also Henry VI of England; Richard III of England
Henry VII of England, 184, 289, 298, 300
Henry VIII of England, 184, 186, 197-8, 200, 203n48, 289, 291, 299. See also *Henry VIII*
Henry VIII, 11, 285, 291; Katherine of Aragon, 291; Wolsey, Cardinal Thomas, 285. See also Henry VIII of England
Hercules, 141, 141n42
Herod the Great, 143
Hitler, Adolf, 301
Hobbes, Thomas, 14
Holinshed, Raphael, 215, 215n4, 293, 295
Holland, Peter, 132

Holy Roman Empire, 106
Homer, 166, 295
Home, Henry, 53, 53n6, 56-7
Honig, Edwin, 134
Horace, See Flaccus, Quintus Horatius
Hume, David, 52, 52n2
Hungary, 156

The Importance of Being Earnest, 266
Io, 175n40, 176n40
Iraq War, 35
Ireland, 210; Northern, 288
Islam, 169
Italy, 45n10, 46, 76, 78n17, 79, 96, 99-100, 103, 106, 114, 155, 157, 180n47; Arno River, 108-11, 113; Carrara, 103; Emperor party, 99; Empoli, 109; Florence, 83-4, 94, 101, 104-5, 107, 108-12, 185; Fucecchio, 109, 111; Genoa, 245; Lastra, 109; Lavenza, 103; Leontini, 45n10; Lombardy, 99, 103-4; Lucca, 96-109, 111, 113; Lunigiana, 103; Massa, 103; Milan, 103, 112; Montecarlo, 101, 107; Montecatini, 101; Montelupo, 109; Northern, 67; Opted, 109; Papal party, 99; Pavia, 99; Peretola, 108; Piacenza, 104; Pisa, 100-103, 106, 108-9, 111, 113; Pistoia, 105, 107-9, 111-13; Pontremoli, 103; Prato, 108; San Miniato, 104, 109; Sarzana, 103; Serravalle, 107-10; Signa, 109; Tiber River, 89; Tuscany, 101, 103, 108-9, 112; Usciana

Index

River, 109; Valdarno valley, 104; Val di Nievole, 107; Veii, 79; Venice, 5, 180n47, 239-42, 242n10, 244-8, 251, 251n27, 252-7, 257n30, 258-9, 246, 258, 267

James I of England and Ireland, 135-7, 218-19, 224-5, 230, 232, 234, 236-7, 241, 289, 299; *Basilikon Doron*, 225, 230, 236; *Daemonologie*, 224
James VI of Scotland, See James I of England and Ireland
Jefferson, Thomas, 1-2, 51-7, 61, 66; *The Declaration of Independence*, 2, 55, 57, 66; *Jefferson Encyclopedia*, 55
Jensen, Pamela, 185-6, 208n64
Johnson, Lyndon B., 158n5
Johnson, Samuel, 52
John XXII, 106
John of England, 96, 114, 115, 116, 117, 119, 123, 125, 127, 128. See also *King John*
Jonson, Ben, 131, 281, 298
Jove, 96, 141, 144-5
Judaism, 5, 169, 180n47, 239-40, 242-3, 245, 246-8, 251-4, 256-8, 277-8; anti-Judaism, 248, 248n19; anti-Semitism, 5, 239, 240, 248n19
Jugurthine War, 43
Julius Caesar, 3, 12, 16-17, 19, 26, 28, 30, 67, 69-70, 71n6, 90, 131, 131n7, 142, 153n69, 159, 164, 166, 295; Brutus, Decius, 85-7; Brutus, Marcus Junius,17-19, 28, 87, 90-91; Caesar, Julius, 3, 17-19, 22, 28, 68- 71, 71n6, 72, 78-9, 81-90, 90n22, 91, 91n23-4, 92-3, 130-31, 152-3, 153n69, 154, 165, 168; Casca, 87; Cinna, 87; Constantine the Great, 86; Lepidus, 290; Longinus, Gaius Cassius, 28, 87, 91, 153n69; Octavius, 91
Juno, 145
Jupiter, 141, 143-5, 145n49, 147, 147n53, 148-9, 175n40; Jupiter Capitolinus, Temple of, 145n49, 148

Kames, Lord, See Home, Henry
Kant, Immanuel, 53n6
Kaufman, Peter, 136
Kennedy, Robert F., 34
Killigrew, Thomas, 60
King John, 3, 94-6, 113, 121n94, 127, 287, 289n14, 291, 294; Arthur I, Duke of Brittany, 114, 123, 125, 128; Austria, Duke of, 114, 121-2; Bigot, Lord, 122; Blanche of Castile, 123; Burgh, Hubert de, 114, 122, 125; Constance, 123; Eleanor of England, 115-17, 125; George of Lydda, Saint, 114, 122; Gurney, James, 117-18; Lincoln, Battle of, 121; Louis, the Dauphin, 12-3; Pembroke, Earl of, 122; Salisbury, Earl of, 122. See also Faulconbridge family; John of England; Phillip II of France; Richard I of England
King Lear, 1, 51-2, 52n3, 65-6, 229, 230n27, 271-2, 287, 292-3, 295-6; Bastard Edmund,

52n3, 65, 290, 292, 296; Cordelia, 52, 52n3; Edgar (Poor Tom), 52n3, 290, 296; Gloucester, Earl of, 52n3, 296; Goneril, 290; Lear of Britain, 51, 52n3, 53, 160, 290, 293; Regan, 290
King Jr., Martin Luther, 34
Knights, Lionel C., 213, 213n1-2, 215, 219
Korea, 284
Korean War, 284
Kurzel, Justin, 223
Kyd, Thomas, 298; *Soliman and Perseda*, 120

Laam, Kevin, 58
Lamb, Charles, 53
Lancaster (England), 184, 184n5
Lecky, Katarzyna, 61
Lees, F. N., 139n38
Leicester (England), 300
Lennix, Harry, 274
Le Pen, Marine, 156n3
Lewis, C. S., 231
Library of Congress, 30
The Life of Castruccio Castracani of Lucca, 3, 94, 96, 127; Albizzi, Taddeo degli, 111; Antonio, Messer, 97; Baldini, Jacopo, 107; Brunelleschi, Francesco, 108; Carlo of Naples, 101, 108-9, 111; Castracani, Castruccio, 3, 94-114, 120-21, 121n94, 122, 126-8; Cecci, Baldo, 107; Cerchi, Bonifacio, 108; Dianora, Madonna, 97; Faggiuola, Uguccione della, 100-103; Falconi, Michelagnolo, 111; Filippo of Taranto, 102; Frederick of Bavaria, 103; Frescobaldi, Lambertuccio, 108; Gherardesca, Gaddo della, 102; Ghibelline faction, 97-101, 103; Gia, Jacopo da, 105; Guelf faction, 97, 99-103, 107-9; Guidi, Giovanni, 108; Guinigi, Francesco, 98-100; Guinigi, Pagolo, 99, 105-6, 109, 111-13; Henry VII of the Holy Roman Empire, 106-7; Lanfranchi, Benedetto, 108; Lupacci, Tommaso, 108; Manfred, Messer, 107; Neri of Lucca, 102; Onesti tower, 100; Opizi, Messer Giorgio de, 99-100; Palavisini, Messer, 103; Piero, 102; Poggio family, 104; Poggio, Stefano di, 104; Possente, Bastiano di, 105; Robert of Naples, 102, 106, 108-9, 111; Rossi, Bandino de', 108; Visconti, Messer Matteo, 103
Lincoln, Abraham, 1, 9, 26-30, 30n56, 31-3, 68, 69
Livius, Titus, 132n12, 147n53, 149n57, 166
Livy, See "Livius Titus".
Locke, John, 52, 52n2, 55-6
Lodge, Thomas, 281
London (England), 33n64, 261, 270, 281-2, 297; Gunpowder Plot, 225
Los Angeles Women's Shakespeare Company, 260
Lowenthal, David, 138n35, 149, 153n69
Lycurgus of Sparta, 142

Macbeth, 27-8, 30-31, 213, 216-18, 224-5, 225n22, 227, 229, 230n27, 231-4, 236-7, 293, 295, 299; Banquo, 29, 214, 228, 232-4, 290, 299; Birnam Wood, 226; Duncan, 29, 213, 215n4, 219-21, 221n15, 222, 229, 232-3; Fleance, 214, 233; Macduff, 214, 215n4, 223, 226, 233-6, 290; Malcolm of Cumberland, 29, 214, 222-3, 235-6; Siward, Young, 233; Weird Sisters (Witches), 214, 216, 221, 225-6, 228, 231-2, 234. See also Macbeth family

Macbeth family, 214, 216, 219, 223-4, 226, 228, 233; Lady, 4, 213, 220-21, 221n15, 222-3, 226, 228-9, 232, 234-5, 235n33; Lord, 4-5, 29, 160, 213-15, 215n4, 216, 219-21, 221n15, 222-4, 226, 228-9, 232-6, 290, 299

Machiavelli, Niccolò, 2-3, 71, 71n6, 72, 78, 78n17, 79-80, 80n18, 81-85, 91, 91n24, 92, 94-100, 106, 113-14, 122-3, 127-9, 130n4, 154, 184-5, 185n11, 211, 242n10, 291, 300; *Discourses on Livy*, 71, 78-80, 80n18, 81, 83, 85, 91-2, 94, 129, 130n4; *Florentine Histories (FH)*, 94, 97; *The Prince*, 94, 97, 112-13, 154. See also *The Life of Castruccio Castracani of Lucca*

Macron, Emmanuel, 156n3
Maelius, Spurius, 78, 81-2
Mahoney, Daniel J., 155
Mamilius, Gaius, 43

Marius, Gaius, 82
Marlowe, Christopher, 281, 292, 298
Mars, 130, 130n6, 141, 143-4, 147-8, 152-3
Marvell, Andrew, 9
Mary I of England and Ireland, 219
Mary II of England, Scotland, and Ireland, 60
Marymount Manhattan College, 266, 266n18
Mason, George, 55, 57; *Virginia Declaration of Rights*, 55-7
Massachusetts Institute of Technology (MIT), 261
Measure for Measure, 12, 14-15, 19; Angelo, 14-15, 19; Barnadine, 15; Isabella, 15; Vienna, Duke of, 14-15, 19, 160
Medici, Cosimo de, 83-4
Menelaus, 40
The Merchant of Venice, 5, 180n47, 239-40, 240n5, 241, 241n8, 242-4, 257-9, 279; Antonio, 5, 240, 242-3, 243n14, 244-50, 250n24, 251, 251n24, 252-8; Balthazar, 256; Bassanio, Lord, 243, 243n13-14, 246, 249-50, 250n24, 253-6, 257n30; Belmont, 243n14, 257-8; Gratiano, 244, 256; Jessica, 239, 243, 245, 247, 254, 258; Leah, 245; Lorenzo, 243; Portia, 5, 160, 243, 243n13-14, 244, 246-7, 249-50, 250n24, 255-7, 257n30, 258; Salarino, 247, 255; Shylock, 5, 180n47, 239-40, 240n5, 241-9, 251-8; Solanio,

247, 249, 255; Tubal, 245, 257;
  Venice, Duke of– 255-6
Meres, Francis, 293
The Merry Wives of Windsor, 72
Middleton, Thomas, 292, 299
A Midsummer Night's Dream, 243;
  Demetrius, 243; Hermia, 243;
  Lysander, 243; Puck, 160
Milton, John, 281
Miranda, Lin-Manuel, 283
Mohegan people, 260, 262
Montesquieu, 69, 93
Moorish people, 165, 175n39,
  180n47, 242, 251n27
More, Sir Thomas, 4, 183, 189-91,
  194n28, 197- 201, 205-6,
  206n56, 209, 211-12, 299-
  300; *History of King Richard
  III*, 190; *Sir Thomas More*, 190,
  199, 209n65; *Utopia*, 199, 200,
  206
*Mr. William Shakespeare's Come-
  dies, Histories, and Tragedies*,
  282, 285, 293
Much Ado About Nothing, 2, 55,
  61, 65, 287; Beatrice, 62-5;
  Benedick, 62-5; Claudio, 15,
  62-3; Dogberry - 62, 64; Don
  John, 61-2, 65; Don Pedro,
  61-4; Friar, 62; Hero, 61-4;
  Leonato, 62
Murray, Conrad, 260, 260n1, 270,
  272, 277; *DenMarked*, 260,
  267, 270, 271

National Alliance for Mental Ill-
  ness (NAMI), 277
National Archives, 297
National Rally, 156n3
Nazism, 240, 240n5, 288

Nero of Rome, 199
Netherlands, 156
New York University (NYU), 263,
  268
Nietzsche, Friedrich, 69, 71n6, 72,
  291
Nin, Anaïs, 33
Normandy, 300; Norman Con-
  quest, 289. See also William
  the Conqueror
Normandy, Duke of, See William
  the Conqueror
North, Thomas, 132-4, 152n68,
  295
Northeastern University, 266n18
Nussbaum, Martha, 56

Obama, Barack, 262
Orban, Viktor, 156
Oregon Shakespeare Festival, 261
Orwell, George, 299
Othello, 64-5, 180n47, 241, 241n8,
  266-7, 273, 279, 293; Desde-
  mona, 273; Othello, 65, 160,
  180n47, 241-2, 244, 267-8,
  273-4
Otway, Thomas, 52, 52n2
Ovid, 45, 45n10, 47, 166, 173,
  173n37, 175, 175n38, 175n40,
  176, 177n42, 295; *Fasti*, 45;
  Metamorphoses, 45, 45n10, 47,
  173, 173n37, 175n40
Oxford, Earl of, See Vere, Edward
  de
Oxford, University of, 282, 293

Packer, Tina, 265
Paleologus, Emperor Michael,
  203n48
Palfrey, Simon, 20

Index

Parker, Barbara, 148, 148n55
Parsons, Robert, 183
Peele, George, 164n17, 288n12, 295
Peloponnesian War, 67
Penelope, 150
Phaëton, Son of Apollo, 196
Philip II of France, 123, 125, 127-8. See also *King John*
Philippi, Battle of, 91
Philip the Bastard, See Faulconbridge family, Philip
Plantagenet, Richard, See Faulconbridge family, Philip
Plato, 77n15, 186, 295, 300; *Symposium*, 77n15
Platt, Michael, 132n10, 133-4, 140, 140n40, 146n51, 153n69
Plautus, Titus Maccius, 199
Plutarch, 74, 74n11, 75, 75n12, 91, 91n24, 130, 132, 132n12, 133, 133n13, 135-7, 137n33, 138n34, 139n38, 140, 140n38, 141-2, 142n43, 143, 143n44, 147-8, 149n58, 150, 150n62, 151, 152n68, 166, 295; *The Life of Coriolanus*, 130n5; *Lives*, 138n34
Pluto, 144
Pompey, 17, 90n22
Pompilius, Numa, 142
Po River, 117
Porsena of Clusium, 150n62
Protestantism, 54, 58, 169, 286, 299; Calvinism, 59; Protestant Reformation, 169
Publicola, Publius Valerius, 140n38, 149-50, 150n62
Putin, Vladimir, 288
Pyrenees Moutains– 117

The Rape of Lucrece, 67, 163n15, 164, 190; Brutus, Lucius Junius, 190; Lucrece, 165, 171n30
Redpath, James, 24
Renaissance, 61, 96, 241, 249
Rhodes (Greece), 120
Richard I of England, 113-20, 127. See also *King John*
Richard II of England, 4, 183-4, 184n5, 185, 185n11, 191-7, 199, 201-2, 202n45-46, 203n47, 204, 204n53, 205-7, 207n58, 208, 208n64, 209-11. See also *Richard II*
Richard II, 4, 183-4, 190-92, 194, 200, 212, 230n27, 293-4, 299Aumerle, Duke of, 205, 211; Bagot, 205; Bolingbroke, Henry (Duke of Hereford) 184-5, 191-7, 204-5, 207-12; Bushy, 205; Carlisle, Bishop of, 207-11; Exton, Sir Piers, 211; Fitzwater, Baron, 191; Gardiner, 201; Gaunt, John of, 191-3, 202, 202n45, 204-6, 206n55, 207; Gloucester, Duchess of, 206; Gloucester, Duke of, 202, 204, 207n58, 210; Green, 205; Mowbray, Thomas (Duke of Norfolk), 191, 192, 193, 194, 195, 196, 204, 205, 210, 211; York, Duchess of, 206; York, Duke of, 200, 204, 205, 206. See also Edward III of England; Henry IV of England; Richard II of England
Richard III of England, 72, 185, 189, 208, 276-7, 289, 289n14,

313

297-301. See also *Henry VI* trilogy; *Richard III*
Richard III, 163n15, 275, 287, 289, 293-4, 296, 299; Buckingham, Duke of, 297-8; Catesby, William, 296; Hastings, William, 296, 300; Mayor of London, 297; Scrivener, 296, 30. See also Richard III of England
Richmond, Earl of, 299, 300
Richmond, University of, 129n1
Robeyns, Ingrid, 56
Rogers, Thomas, 59
Romano, Giulio, 46
Romanticism, 53
Rome, 3, 16-18, 43, 45, 53n5, 67, 67n1, 68-71, 71n6, 72, 72n6, 73-92, 103, 106-7, 115, 129, 130-31, 131n7-9, 132-3, 133n13, 134-8, 138n35, 139, 139n38, 140-42, 142n43, 143, 143n44, 144, 144n48, 145, 145n50, 146, 146n52, 147-9, 149n58, 150, 151n66, 152-4, 159-63, 163n13, 164-5, 165n17, 165n20, 166-9, 169n25, 169n27, 170, 170n29, 171, 171n30, 171n34, 172, 172n34-35, 173, 176, 177n42-3, 178-82, 290, 295; Ides of March, 87; *Lex Mamilia* - 43; Roman Empire, 69; Eastern Empire, 92; Senate, 81, 85, 144, 145n49, 149, 153, 167n23
Romeo and Juliet, 243, 279, 294
Roper, William, 197
Rosen, Jeffrey, 61
Russia, 157
Rutter, Carol Chillington, 213n2

Sacred Heart University, 269
Sallust, See Crispus, Gaius Sallustius
Savonarola, Fra, 84
Saint Peter's Gate, 100
Sayet, Madeline, 260-66, 269; "Shakespeare System", 261, 262n3, 263, 266-8, 270, 279
Scotland, 53n6, 67, 213-14, 218, 223, 228, 234-5, 288-9, 295, 299
Scott, William, 23, 26-7
Scruton, Roger, 157n4
Sen, Amartya, 56
Seneca, Lucius Annaeus, 166, 199
Shakespeare & Company, 265
Shakespeare Behind Bars (SBB), 260, 273-5
The Shakespeare Hut, 33
Shakespeare Institute, 262-3
Shakespeare Memorial Library, 8, 24-5
Shakespeare Theatre Association, 264, 278
Shank, Cathy, 133n13
Sidney, Sir Philip, 53, 53n5, 281
Simmons College, 276n41
Sinsheimer, Herman, 248, 252
Skipwith, Robert, 1
Smith, Stephen W., 190
Snyder, Timothy, 292, 299-300
Solon of Athens, 150
Southampton (England), 4, 183
Sparrow, Philip, 118
Sparta (Greece), 142
Spencer, T. J. B., 131n8, 133n13
Spenser, Edmund, 227, 281
Spinoza, Baruch, 242n10
Stern, Tiffany, 20

Index

Stillingfleet, Edward, 60
Stoicism, 58, 60
Stratford-upon-Avon, 262, 283, 287n11, 296; anti-Stratfordian, 286n10; Holy Trinity Church, 283
Strauss, Leo, 159n6; *Natural Right and History*, 159n6, 180n47

Tacitus, Publius Cornelius, 295
the Talmud, 248
Tarquin family, 168
Tate, Nahum, 60
Taylor, Donald Lee, 284, 287
Taylor, Gary, 35, 164n17
Taymor, Julie, 274
The Tempest, 31, 34; Ariel, 34; Prospero, 160
Theseus, 67
Thucydides, 295
Tiberius, Emperor, 172
Tillyard, E. W. M., 282, 293
Timon of Athens, 295
Titus Andronicus, 4, 155, 159, 159n7, 160, 163, 163n15, 164, 164n15, 164n17, 165, 165n17, 166-70, 170n29, 170n29, 171n32, 172-3, 179-80, 180n47, 181-2, 287, 288n12, 294-5; Aaron the Moor, 162-3, 163n14, 165n17, 169, 169n26, 177n44, 178=9, 179n46, 290; Alarbus, 161-2, 171n31, 177n43; Bassianus, 161-2, 162n12, 167-8, 170, 171n32; Chiron, 161-3, 163n14, 175, 177n44; Cornelia, 172; Clown, 169n26; Demetrius, 161-3, 163n14, 175, 177n44; Emillius, 171n34; Lavinia, 161-2, 162n12, 163, 171, 171n30, 171n31, 172-3, 173n36, 174-5, 174n38, 175n39, 176, 177n44, 178; Saturninus, 161-2, 162n12, 163, 167-8, 168n24, 170, 171n34, 175n39, 177n42, 177n44, 290; Stephen, Saint, 169n26; Tamora, Queen of the Goths, 161-2, 162n12, 163, 165n17, 167, 169n26, 171, 171n31, 174, 175n39, 176, 177n44, 178, 290. See also Andronicus family
Tocqueville, Alexis de, 143
Troilus and Cressida, 287, 295
Troy, 73
Trojan War, 67
Trump, Donald, 281, 297-8, 301
Tudor family, 202, 283, 298, 299; Margaret, 289
Tully, See Cicero, Marcus Tullius

United Kingdom, 270
United States of America, 1, 23-4, 27, 30, 33, 54, 57, 66, 156, 263, 265, 268, 270, 281, 283-4, 286, 294, 298, 301; Baltimore, Maryland, 261; Boston, Massachusetts, 26n51; Connecticut, 262; *Constitution of the United States of America*, 183; Founders, 1, 57, 61; Georgia, 282; Indianapolis, Indiana, 34; Ithaca, New York, 150; Kansas, 283n 284, 287; Kentucky, 275; Lenox, Massachusetts. 265; Los Angeles, California,

315

282; Massachusetts, 265; New York City, New York, 26, 239, 261; Philadelphia, Pennsylvania, 26; Reconstruction, 30; Staunton, Virginia, 264; U.S. Congress, 31, 68; U.S. Senate, 30, 31; Utah, 284; Virginia, 264; Washington, D.C., 157, 261

Valois, Princess Catherine, 290
Vecellinus, Spurius Cassius, 78
Vendler, Helen, 33
Venus, 47
Vere, Edward de, 286
Vienna, Austria, 14, 19
Virgil, 166, 170n29
Volapuk language, 155
Volsci people, 17, 76, 130, 133, 133n13, 140, 146, 146n52, 148, 151-2, 152n68, 166

Wales, 288
Warner, Benjamin, 36
Warwickshire, 297
Webster, Daniel, 30-31
Wells, Stanley, 164n17
West, Grace Starry, 164, 164n17, 165-6, 174n38
Whitehall, Palace of, 60
White House Champion of Change Award, 261-2
Whitman, Walt, 8, 26-7, 32-4
Wilders, Geert, 156
Williams, Dawn Monique, 280
William the Conqueror, 288-9, 289n14, 300
Wills, Gary, 55-6
Wilson, August, 266
Winter Garden Theater, 28

The Winter's Tale, 2, 36, 36n1, 42, 48, 50, 65, 288, 291; Antigonus, 40, 44-5, 45n10, 47; Archidamus, 37, 45, 49; Autolycus, 44-5; Bohemia, 37, 44-5, 49; Camillo, 37, 40-1, 45, 47, 48, 49; Cleomenes, 41, 45-6; Dion, 41, 45-6; Emilia, 41; Florizel, 44, 47, 49; Hermione, 2, 36-49, 291; Leontes, 36-49, 65, 291; Mamillius, 2, 37, 40-49; Oracle at Delphos, 41-2, 46, 48; Paulina, 41, 45-9; Perdita, 2, 41-2, 44, 47-9, 291; Polixenes, 36-41, 45-6, 49; Sicilia, 36-8, 43, 45, 49; Sir Smile, 39; Time, 37, 44-5, 50
Wither, George, 60
Wolfert, Stephan, 260, 272, 275n 276, 276n39, 276n41, 277
Wolpe, Lisa, 260, 260n1, 267, 272, 277-9
Woolf, Virginia, 9-10
World War I, 33, 282
World War II, 278, 282

Yale University, 261; Indigenous Performing Arts Program, 261
York (England), 184, 184n5
Young, R. V., 189, 202

Zeus, 141
Zimmerman, Rachel, 265, 265n17
Zuckert, Michael, 243n14, 249